MOORE

For this book **Paul Levy**, Phd, FRSL, an
American who lives in England, had
complete and exclusive access to G. E.
Moore's papers and diaries, and, in the
course of researching the background to
Moore's life and thought, he talked to
nearly all the surviving Apostles of
Moore's era and the remaining members
of the Bloomsbury group. Paul Levy was
educated at the University of Chicago,
University College London, and at
Harvard and Oxford. He is the editor of
one volume of Lytton Strachey's writings,
and, with Michael Holroyd, co-editor of
another. He is one of the Strachey
Trustees. Paul Levy is also the author of
several books on food and wine, and on
the staff of the *Observer*.

To Penelope
and
to the memory of Dorothy Moore

Epitaph

For my father, G. E. Moore, OM,
the Cambridge philosopher

Here lies the great philosopher
Who did not like the world to err,
Who did not err himself, but died
Forever not quite satisfied
That he was not a silly, though
His wise friends never thought him so.

Nicholas Moore

Contents

Illustrations

Acknowledgements

Grateful acknowledgement is made to the copyright holders and publishers of the following material : writings by Bertrand Russell in which McMaster University holds the copyright © Res-Lib Ltd., 1979. Open Court Publishing Co. Inc. and the Literary Estate of G. E. Moore for *The Philosophy of G. E. Moore*, ed. P. A. Schilpp.

All other quoted published material is used in accordance with the 'fair dealing' provision of the Copyright Act, 1956, Ch. 74, Part I, 6 (2). Grateful acknowledgement is made to :

Edward Arnold for E. M. Forster, *Goldsworthy Lowes Dickinson*.

Rupert Hart-Davis/Granada Publishing Ltd. for J. M. Keynes, *Two Memoirs*.

Macdonald and Janes Publishers Ltd. for Compton Mackenzie, *Sinister Street*, published by Macdonald and Janes and Penguin Books.

Oxford University Press for Norman Malcolm, *Ludwig Wittgenstein: A Memoir* © O.U.P. (1958) and G. J. Warnock, *English Philosophy Since 1900* © O.U.P. (2nd ed. 1969).

Longman Group Ltd. for G. M. Trevelyan, *British History in the 19th Century and After, 1892–1919*.

Cambridge University Press for G. Lowes Dickinson, *J. McT. E. McTaggart: A Memoir* and Richard Braithwaite, 'Keynes as a Philosopher', in *Essays on John Maynard Keynes*, ed. Milo Keynes.

Martin Secker and Warburg and Harcourt Brace Jovanovich Inc. for P. N. Furbank, *E. M. Forster: A Life*.

George Allen and Unwin (Publishers) Ltd. and the Humanities Press Inc. for Norman Malcolm, 'G. E. Moore', in *G. E. Moore: Essays in Retrospect*, ed. Ambrose and Lazerowitz; and Allen and Unwin and Atlantic – Little, Brown for Bertrand Russell, *Autobiography*, volumes I and II.

Collins Publishers and Patrick Seale Books for A. J. Ayer, *Part of My Life*.

The Hogarth Press, Harcourt Brace Jovanovich Inc. and the Literary Estates of Leonard and Virginia Woolf for Leonard Woolf, *Sowing, Beginning Again* and *The Journey Not the Arrival Matters* and Virginia Woolf, *Roger*

Acknowledgements

Fry; *Diary*, Volumes I and II, ed. Anne Olivier Bell; and *The Letters of Virginia Woolf*, Volumes I and II, ed. Nigel Nicolson.

Chatto and Windus Ltd., Random House Inc. and Mrs Pamela Diamand for *Letters of Roger Fry*, ed. Denys Sutton.

Preface

Most of the narrative of this book has been constructed from primary source material. Because the cast of characters in addition to the hero is so large, and because the number of documents, mostly uncatalogued, was huge, the research for this book was an unusually difficult task. The archives I have used – even the Moore papers – did not always yield their secrets gracefully. I was puzzled for a long time about the 'manifesto' project, and did not discover Moore's views on the First World War until this book was nearly finished. Finding these answers required detective work that was fascinating to do; but more often my difficulties proceeded from my own obtuseness: ignoring Moore's own maxim and practice, I had put the question wrongly or failed to ask the correct question of the appropriate person.

In the course of the ten years it took to complete this book I had an enormous amount of help, support and encouragement from a large number of people and institutions. Three Universities have helped with funds and research facilities; the editors of several papers have sustained me through the leanest years; and many people in the following list have nourished the body as well as the intellect. I am grateful to them all.

Miss Edith Ainsworth, for taking the trouble to write to me and for permission to reproduce passages in the letters of her brother, A. R. Ainsworth, of which she owns the copyright; Peter Allen; Christopher and Marian Allsopp; Cis Amaral; Lord Annan, to whom my intellectual debt is large, for every sort of kindness, and for permission to quote from his articles and broadcasts; The Arts Council of Great Britain; Neal Ascherson; Sir Alfred Ayer; Barbara Bagenal; Ann Barr; Professor John Bayley; Olivier and Quentin Bell for material help, hospitality and friendship, and Quentin Bell for reading the ms and several earlier versions of it; the Henry W. and Albert A. Berg Collection of English and American Literature in the New York Public Library (Astor, Lenox and Tilden Foundations) for passages from letters, from G. E. Moore to Sir Edward Marsh, in their collection; Sir Isaiah Berlin, OM; Hilary Bird; Kenneth Blackwell; Neville Blech;

Professor Morton Bloomfield, who first suggested that I write this book; Professor Richard Braithwaite; Professor Andrew Brink; Robert H. Bruce-Gardner; Benjamin Buchan; Myles Burnyeat; Noël and Catherine Carrington; Professor Stanley Cavell; Lady David Cecil, for permission to quote from unpublished material by her father, Sir Desmond MacCarthy; to her, to Lord David Cecil and to Hugh Cecil, I owe gratitude and affection for too many things to list here; Lynn Chadwick; Eva Chadwick; Marianne Charles, who ably assisted me in organizing my research and my filing system; John Churcher; L. Jonathan Cohen; Professor Marshall Cohen; the late Cyril Connolly; Andrew Cornford; Coutts and Co., the Trustees of Lady Pollock's Will Trust, for permission to use copyright matter by the late Sir Frederick Pollock Bt; the late Rupert Crawshay-Williams; Roy Davids; Anthony D'Offay; Professor Ronald Dworkin; Sarah Eckersley; Sally Emerson; Edward J. Epstein; Joel Fadem; Christopher Farley; Betty Ann Farmer; Mrs Jean Floud; Jerry and Janet Dean Fodor; the late E. M. Forster, OM; Anne Freedgood; Richard Fries; P. N. Furbank, Forster's biographer, who has supplied both information and encouragement.

Professor John A. Gallaher; Angelica Garnett; David Garnett; Philip Gaskell, the Librarian of Trinity College Cambridge, and his staff, especially Rosemary Graham; Nancy Gayer; Mme Winifred Gérin; the late Tony Godwin; Annie Gottlieb; Bob Gottlieb; Susanna Graham-Jones, who organized the information-retrieval program that made it possible to use the vast number of documents involved in this study; the late Duncan Grant; Malcolm and Jenny Green; John Gross; Professor Frank Hahn; Barbara Strachey Halpern, who gave me the letters that supplied the keys that unlocked the mysteries of Moore's and Russell's feelings for each other; Elizabeth Hardwick, who read an earlier version of this book in ms. and who kept up my morale in difficult times; Angela and Tony Harris; the late Sir Roy Harrod; the President and the Corporation of Harvard University, for financial support and the award of a Harvard Travelling Fellowship; the Harvard University Libraries; Professor Francis Haskell; the late Sir Ralph Hawtrey; Lady Jane Heaton; Howard Hodgkin; Michael Holroyd, my colleague on the Strachey Trust, who encouraged me from the first, taught me by precept and example that a book determines its own period of gestation, and read various versions of this book in ms; Angus Hone; Hazel Horrobin; Julian Jebb; Rebecca Sharkey-John; Heather Joshi; Vijay Joshi; Martha Kaplan; Sir Geoffrey Keynes, for permission to quote unpublished letters of John Maynard Keynes, and with the other Trustees of the Brooke Trust, for permission to quote from an unpublished paper of Rupert Brooke; Milo Keynes; Terence Kilmartin; the Provost and Fellows of King's College Cambridge, for permission to quote an unpublished letter by Nathaniel Wedd; the staff of the Library of King's

College Cambridge; Susan Kippax; Marvin Kraus; the late Professor Craig LaDrière, who read several earlier versions of this book with enthusiasm, and gave me constant encouragement and unfailing help; Dee Pak Lal; Margaret Legg, for permission to quote unpublished matter by Sir Maurice Amos; Professor Harry Levin, who has been involved in this book since its inception, and has read every stage of it with meticulous care – I have profited from his scholarship and friendship alike; H. S. Levy and S. E. Levy, for their patient support; Casimir Lewy, who gave me every aid and assistance I required; Professor and Mrs I. M. D. Little; Lord Llewelyn Davies, for permission to quote unpublished material by his father, Crompton Llewelyn Davies; G. E. R. Lloyd; Philip Lloyd-Bostock; the Librarian and staff of the London Library.

Chloë MacCarthy; Dr Dermod MacCarthy, for permission to quote from an unpublished paper by Sir Desmond MacCarthy; the late Michael Mac-Carthy; Brian McGuinness, Wittgenstein's biographer, to whose friendship and constant help this book owes much; David Machin; Denis Mack Smith; Philippa MacLiesh, who has done me many good turns; David and Sandra Margolies; Pauline Matthews; Gabriel Merle; Shirley Meyers; Jonathan Miller; Professor James Mirlees; the late Dorothy Moore, without whose approbation this book could never have been undertaken. She gave me the loan of Moore's papers, on which this book is based, encouraged me in the use I was making of them, and showed her approval of the result whenever possible. There are parts of this book of which, I fear, she would not approve; but I have attempted, when writing it, to benefit from her good judgement of character and the acuity of her criticism of my early chapters. It was my good fortune to get to know Mrs Moore well enough to be able to record here our mutual affection; the memory of that is the greatest profit of my ten years' labour. Other members of her family to whom I owe gratitude are Juliet Moore; Nicholas Moore, for permission to quote a poem by him; and Timothy Moore, by whose permission all unpublished matter by G. E. Moore is used in this book. He shared his mother's decision to help me with this work, and he has never failed to be kind, encouraging and helpfully critical. I also wish to thank K. O. Morgan; Richard Morphet; Raymond Mortimer; Lord Moyne; the late A. N. L. Munby, who as Librarian of King's College, gave me a great deal of material assistance, as well as help in building up my own library, and whose friendship made the many days I spent at King's an unalloyed pleasure; Iris Murdoch, whose affection and conversation have meant much to me; Cathleen Nesbitt; Nigel Nicolson, who helped me when I was stuck, and from whose criticism the book has benefited; Lucy Norton, the Chairman of the Strachey Trust, a steadfast friend; the Warden and Fellows of Nuffield College, who gave me a place among them for two years, with material support and intellectual stimulation; the Librarian and staff of the College and the research services of the College also helped me greatly; Stanley Olson; Professor G. E. L. Owen; Marie O'Shaughnessy; Derek Parfitt; Frances Partridge, who read a very early draft of some chapters; Henrietta Partridge; Margaret Paul; Bud Pauling; Clive Payne, whose help in constructing a mechanical retrieval system for the Moore papers I hope to acknowledge more fully elsewhere; David Pears, who read the final ms, and called to my attention errors in Greek, Latin and philosophy – some of the errors he corrected were made by Moore, though, of course, most were my own – and he is certainly not responsible for the mistakes, or bad arguments, that remain; Sir George Pollock Bt; Venetia Pollock, to whose judicious editing the final ms owes much of whatever art it possesses; Sir Dennis Proctor, for copyright permission for an unpublished letter of G. Lowes Dickinson; Philippa Pullar; Professor Hilary Putnam; Professor W. V. O. Quine; Alice Quinn; Mr and Mrs Anthony Quinton.

Robert Reedman; Professor Joan Robinson, for permission to quote unpublished material by Sir Edward Marsh; D. C. Rose, who early on gave me the benefit of his wide interests and reading in the organization of my research; S. P. Rosenbaum; Lillian Rosenberg; William Rothman; Lady Rothschild; Hilary Rubinstein, whose efforts on behalf of this book have been great; John Paul Russo, the biographer of I. A. Richards; George Rylands; the Duchess of St Albans; Martin Salter, for permission to quote an unpublished letter by A. W. Verrall; Daphne Sanger, for permission to quote unpublished material by C. P. Sanger; Connie Seifert; Michael Seifert, for unflagging support and for reading the final ms; the late Sigmund Seifert; Professor A. K. Sen; the late Ezra Shine; Richard Shone; Professor Robert Skidelsky; the staff of the Society of Authors; George Spater; Professor Jon Stallworthy; the late Professor W. J. H. Sprott; Nicholas Stern; Tom Stoppard, for permission to quote an published letter; Professor Alan Stout, for permission to quote from an unpublished letter by G. F. Stout; the late Alix Strachey, who made all the Strachey papers available to me; the Strachey Trust, Paul Levy and Michael Holroyd, for permission to quote unpublished matter by James and Lytton Strachey; Riette Sturge-Moore, for a good deal of help with Moore's family background; Lola Szladits and her staff at the Berg Collection, New York Public Library; Frank Thompson; Baillie and Christopher Tolkien; George Trevelyan and Dr Thomas Trevelyan, for permission to quote unpublished material by G. M. Trevelyan; William Trinder; John Troyer, who rescued me when I was stuck fast, and by supererogatory acts made me resume writing, ultimately to finish this book; the Provost and Fellows and the Philosophy Department of University College London, for making me an Hon. Research Associate in 1968–9; Dorothea Vaughan (Mrs Magnus Pyke); Ursula Vaughan Williams; the Director and staff of Villa I Tatti; Professor G. H. von Wright; Daniel Waley; Professor John Waterlow, for permission to quote unpublished letters of Sir Sydney Waterlow; Richard Waterlow; Gay Weber; Iris, Lady Wedgwood; Dame Veronica Wedgwood, OM, for permission to quote unpublished material by Sir Ralph Wedgwood; Professor Morton White; Professor David Wiggins; Professor Bernard Williams; Philip Williams; Ann Wilson, who has given me much material assistance; the late David Wilson; Sir Duncan Wilson; Professor Richard Wollheim; the late Leonard Woolf; David Wootton.

Preface to the Papermac Edition

Few books, certainly none that I have written, have had such a curious gestation, difficult birth or unorthodox but long life. Following an unusually short stay as a graduate student in the English department of Harvard University, I was advised by the Chairman, the eminent Chaucerian scholar Morton Bloomfield, to choose a thesis topic that would necessitate my returning both to England and to philosophy. It was he who reminded me that there was no general work on Moore, and no biography; and I suspect that it was he, Harry Levin, and my other supervisor, the late Craig LaDrière, who saw to it that I sailed back to England in August 1968, with a generous grant from Harvard in my pocket.

I was already in touch with Dorothy Moore, G.E. Moore's doughty, pipe-smoking widow. The big task of detection that awaited me was to track down the Cambridge Apostles. From their own autobiographies or Michael Holroyd's newly published life of Strachey, I had learnt the identities of three living members: Leonard Woolf, E.M. Forster and Bertrand Russell. The third of these adamantly refused to see me or even to answer questions in writing, despite the fact that I came highly recommended to him, both through the usual philosophy channels, and by people of the activist Left, with whom he was so entangled in the Sixties. As the reader will discover, he had something to hide. The first two were as helpful as their advanced ages and limited energies allowed. Woolf was all for the Apostles helping me. As things turned out, I did not need to ask for Forster's support.

Chance was on my side. As I sat sipping instant coffee at the kitchen table of the London flat I had arranged to share with friends, one of my new flat-mates said he thought he'd tell me now, as I was certain to find out anyway: he was a Cambridge Apostle. Yes, they still existed, and he would put me in touch with an official spokesman. This interesting, kind and agreeable person reported to me that the policy was not to make the records of the Society available to outsiders; but he gave me useful introductions to many people at King's and Trinity. Some of them lobbied in my favour, and I understand that someone half-seriously proposed me for membership – an honour for which I had absolutely no qualifications, not even a connection with Cambridge. The rest of the story of my dealings with the Apostles is that a very accomplished and famous historian, who did not see why my research should be hampered by this by no means unanimously agreed policy, gave me his own lightly annotated membership list of the Apostles from their beginnings in 1820 until 1916. He also gave me his friendship and encouragement.

That, unfortunately, was still not sufficient for the construction of a narrative. This was made possible by the disaffection of a very young Apostle, who disapproved so strongly of his colleagues' closed shop that he undertook to let me see the entire contents of the 'Ark'. This was made relatively easy by the fact that, at that time, almost nobody knew where the Apostles' archive was actually meant to be kept.

Mrs Moore was a different story. She and I liked each other the moment we met at the house on Chesterton Road in Cambridge, where she had lived with Moore. She was in her seventies; she still wore her silver hair in an Eton crop; her thumb was black from tamping her pipe, and many of the best pieces of furniture in the front room where we sat bore paper luggage tags saying who was to have them after her death. I met her son Timothy, the composer and music master at Dartington; I liked him too. I left for London that afternoon with a shoebox full of letters to Moore, and several concertina files of papers Mrs Moore considered relevant to my work. I had no idea then that I had not been the first suitor for these papers, and I don't know why Dorothy Moore decided to entrust them to me rather than to one of the many others who had come before.

The papers were kept in a cupboard in her bedroom. There were thousands of bits of paper in that small piece of furniture (and tens of thousands more, all relevant, among the Strachey papers, the Keynes hoard, the Russell archive, and so on, all of which I read and very often copied). It was not until Mrs Moore's death, about ten years after I had begun my work, that I got to the bottom of that cupboard, and found the last pieces of the jigsaw puzzle. It was not that anything had been concealed from me intentionally, just that Mrs Moore could not have imagined that the yellowing back numbers of the *Cambridge Magazine* contained crucial information about Moore's attitude to the War, and that that was why he had preserved them in the first place.

One of the reasons the book took me ten years to write was the sheer mass of the primary sources with which I had to deal. In the end this was overcome by indexing them with the aid of a computer. This was before the days of the word processor, and it was a very laborious process, involving a good deal of assistance from ingenious but penurious Oxford undergraduates, who were willing to work for the pocket money left over from my grants. Clive Payne, the computer boffin at Nuffield College (who had taken me in after the Harvard money gave out) devised a programme by which the computer could shuffle bits of information about, and give me a list of the documents in chronological order, or grouped under key word headings. The heuristic uses of this were breathtaking. The plans for the 'Manifesto' project, for instance, did not emerge from a reading (or even several readings) of the half dozen correspondences, because the letters of most of them referred to it only obliquely; the computer, however, detected a pattern that I had not seen before.

My benefactors at Harvard were naturally pleased at my success in assembling such a mighty collection of research material; and they understood and approved my decision to stay on in England to work with it. But it was then 1969, and the Vietnam war was starving the American universities of research funds; it was out of the question for me to receive any more money from Harvard. Nuffield's generosity kept the publishers from the door for a couple of years; but then Harvard kindly and imaginatively waived the dissertation requirement, and agreed to award me a PhD for a published book – quite an unusual concession in those days. This had two advantages: it meant I could finance my research with the two surprisingly large publisher's advances I received in Britain (from the late Tony Godwin, who sadly never got to read the book) and the US, and it meant that I could write a real book rather than an academic thesis. That I took so long to accomplish the task was explained partly by my need for the papers I only acquired on Dorothy Moore's death, partly by sloth and demoralisation, and partly by the fact that literary journalism (I had become a freelance contributor to the book pages of the *Observer* in 1974, and several other papers subsequently gave me work) was more fun and more profitable.

Finally the book was published for the first time (this is, in fact, its fourth or fifth edition, depending on how you count these things) in 1979. It has been consulted by dozens of other writers, some of whom, such as Keynes' biographer Robert Skidelsky, have corrected a point or two; and some of whom have studied it to try to identify others of the Cambridge spies. One author was successful in this, though he seemed to me not to have understood much of what he read in these pages. Others have plundered it wholesale, sometimes with insufficient or no acknowledgement, to write books on similar subjects. I don't really mind. So long as this book continues to have a life of its own, it would be churlish to complain about the use others make of it. It is for others still to assess the worth of this book, as a contribution to the history of ideas and as a part of the business of the Bloomsbury industry. But it is very gratifying to see in print again a work that took its author so long to complete and that cost so much in energy and spirit.

April 1988

Introduction

G. E. Moore was a great and a lovable man. Lovableness is an elusive quality, more difficult to pin down than greatness. Moore's originality as a philosopher is well known and well documented; he and Wittgenstein and Russell, his friends and colleagues, are the three giants of philosophy of the first half of this century. But Moore was an exceptional man in another respect, not as a philosopher, but as a human being, and his lovableness was a part of this.

When Beatrice Webb said to Leonard Woolf that though she knew most of the distinguished men of her time, she had never met a great man, Woolf replied that he supposed Mrs Webb did not know G. E. Moore. 'George Moore', Woolf commented in his autobiography, 'was a great man, the only great man whom I have ever met or known in the world of ordinary, real life.' Leonard and Virginia Woolf's circle of acquaintances was large, perhaps as large as that of Sidney and Beatrice Webb, but Woolf went on to say of Moore that

> There was in him an element which can, I think, be accurately called greatness, a combination of mind and character and behaviour, of thought and feeling which made him qualitatively different from anyone else I have ever known. I recognize it in only one or two of the many famous dead men whom Ecclesiasticus and others enjoin us to praise for one reason or another.[1]

Woolf compared G. E. Moore's own circle to that of Socrates, for 'like Socrates, he attracted a number of friends and followers as different from one another as Plato and Aristophanes were from Alcibiades and Xenophon'. Woolf lists, for examples, the names of Lytton Strachey, Desmond MacCarthy, Sir Ralph Wedgwood, Lord Keynes and Sir Edward Marsh.[2]

How did Leonard Woolf compile this list of people who were influenced by Moore? It contains no philosophers, but includes the man who changed the writing of biography, the leading literary journalist in

England between the wars, the Chief General Manager of the London and North Eastern Railway, the greatest economist of our age, and Churchill's private secretary. They have in common that they, and G. E. Moore, were members of a secret society at Cambridge, generally known as the 'Apostles' or just 'the Society'. The members of this group have included not only most of the great Cambridge names of the nineteenth century, but also: Russell, Wittgenstein and Frank Ramsey; Rupert Brooke; Guy Burgess; Lord Rothschild; Michael Whitney Straight, the American publisher; Professors Sir Alan Hodgkin, Eric Hobsbawm and Arnold Kettle; Peter Shore, a cabinet minister in the Labour governments of Wilson and Callaghan; recent and present editors of the *Listener* and of *The Times Literary Supplement*; and Jonathan Miller.

Woolf was right to illustrate G. E. Moore's circle by a set of names that were unrelated except for their having been Apostles, for it was largely through that group that Moore's influence was transmitted, and a good deal of his early philosophical work began as papers contributed to the Apostles' Saturday night meetings. The history of this discussion society is important on three counts: as a subject of intrinsic interest; as the background to G. E. Moore's life and work; and as the chief source from which the Bloomsbury Group sprang. Most importantly though, it is only by examining the history and traditions of the Apostles that we can hope to solve the central mystery that surrounds G. E. Moore: how did a man who came to be thought of as a philosopher's philosopher have such a wide and influential impact on English intellectual life?

While this is not another book on the Bloomsbury Group, it would not be unfair to regard it as telling the story of the pre-history of Bloomsbury. Certainly there is much in it without which the Bloomsbury Group (and the set of cultural attitudes for which this expression has practically become a shorthand code) cannot be understood.

That G. E. Moore had such an influence is widely accepted. His influence on philosophers is so well documented that the reader can learn about it from any good book on the history of philosophy in this century. It is, by contrast, his 'popular' influence that I hope to describe and explain in this book: I hope to show the breadth of his influence on a wide variety of people. For Moore exercised power over the ideas and behaviour of men and women in several walks of life both in his own generation and in the two succeeding ones.

Allusions to G. E. Moore can be found in places other than histories of philosophy and books on members of the Bloomsbury Group. The first such published reference was in Virginia Woolf's first novel, *The*

Voyage Out, which appeared in 1915, and sixty years later writers, and even comedians, are still attempting to conjure with Moore's name.

Jonathan Miller gave everyone – including G. E. Moore – a good deal of pleasure with his 1954 Footlights sketch, 'Out of the Blue', in which 'Russell' fails to elicit an answer to a question about apples and a basket because 'Moore' is too great a stickler for precision to reply to an everyday question in ordinary language. And Tom Stoppard in his successful (though perhaps *over*-intellectual?) play *Jumpers* called his philosopher protagonist George E. Moore, and gave to the philosopher's stage wife the name of Moore's widow, Dorothy. Although here G. E. Moore is not impersonated – his name is merely borrowed* – Stoppard hopes his name will set up, in the minds of his audience, reverberations that can be used for dramatic purposes.

In a recent essay on 'Conversations'[3] V. S. Pritchett discussed the salutary effect of the Bloomsbury Group on the art of conversation, and paid an oblique tribute to G. E. Moore. Though he does not mention Moore by name, Sir Victor pinpoints Moore's supposed contribution to Bloomsbury talk, 'the precious Bloomsbury question: "What exactly do you mean?"' 'Whatever we may think of what is loosely called Bloomsbury, it gave conversation a new edge'. And Sir Victor ends his piece by praising Virginia Woolf's essay on Sickert as 'one of the few believable accounts of how a real conversation can enlarge as it circulates,' because in it Mrs Woolf shows the uses to which an artist can put 'the central Bloomsbury question. What exactly do we mean by red?' Virginia Woolf's formulation of the central Mooreist question shows, Pritchett feels, how a good 'conversation goes on, winding its way from one speculation to the next but round a central point'.

T. E. Hulme (1883–1917), the critic and poet, had little – as little as possible – to do with Bloomsbury. His anti-humanism and anti-liberalism were as repugnant to Bloomsbury as his militarism (which resulted

---

* The playwright wrote to Dorothy Moore on 20 February 1972:
'I wonder whether it was clear from the reviews that my own George makes a great fuss about not being the *real* George Moore, a fact which he finds painful; and I'm afraid I deliberately married him to a "Dorothy" to rub salt in the wound. In other words the play is very self-aware about the coincidence of names, and continually distances my hero from his famous namesake; so that in the same way that there is no danger of it appearing that your late husband bears any resemblance to my George, there is no danger of anyone in the audience assuming that the real Dorothy Moore cavorts around in the outrageous manner of Diana Rigg.
'. . . I admire your late husband enormously, and I believe he would not have been unsympathetic to the dilemma of "George Moore".'

in his being killed in action in France). He did not have much use for the university, and was sent down from St John's College, Cambridge. He was interested in modern abstract art, but had only scorn for the painting of Vanessa Bell and Duncan Grant and the criticism of Roger Fry and Clive Bell. His heroes and associates were Epstein, Wyndham Lewis and Pound (the last to some extent his follower in the 'Imagist' movement in poetry). His political philosophy is derived from Georges Sorel's *Réflexions sur la Violence*. The two great influences on Hulme's thought were Henri Bergson and G. E. Moore. 'Bergson's anti-intellectualism', says Hulme's biographer, 'seems to have appealed to his fundamentally religious mind; ... He was very ready to accompany Bergson into a world of metaphysical speculation which depended in the end on a "leap of faith" for its acceptance. At the same time, he was convinced that philosophy could, and ought, to become a purely scientific study. He was caught between the speculative, non-moral world of *Evolution Créatrice* and the rational ethics of *Principia Ethica*.'[4] T. E. Hulme's literary remains were gathered by Herbert Read, who gave them the title *Speculations*, and published them simultaneously in New York and London in 1924. The essay called 'Neo-Realism' on page 39 begins:

'Having lived at Cambridge at various times during the last ten years, I have naturally always known that the only philosophical movement of any importance in England, is that which is derived from the writings of Mr G. E. Moore.'

Another poet and critic, I. A. Richards, was for many years Moore's student. With C. K. Ogden he wrote *The Meaning of Meaning* and collaborated on the scheme that became basic English. Richards happily acknowledged to his biographer that Moore was the single greatest influence upon his own thought.[5]

Finally there is a lamentation rather than a testimony to Moore's influence from an unexpected quarter – from Beatrice Webb, who according to Leonard Woolf (see p. 1) could not have known Moore. Writing to Lady Courtney on 18 September 1911 about Alys and Bertrand Russell's marital difficulties, Beatrice Webb comments:

'I am sorry now that Bertie went to Cambridge – there is a pernicious set presided over by Lowes Dickinson, which makes a sort of ideal of anarchic ways in sexual questions – we have, for a long time, been aware of its bad influence on our young Fabians. The intellectual star is the metaphysical George Moore with his *Principia Ethica* – a book they all talk of as "The Truth"! I never can see anything in it, except a metaphysical justification for doing what you like and what other people disapprove of! So far as I can understand the philosophy it is a denial of the scientific method and of religion – as a rule, that is the net result on the minds of young men – it seems to disintegrate their intellects and their characters.'[6]

Grotesque as Mrs Webb's misunderstanding of Moore's book was, it cannot be said that she missed the point altogether, for what she disapproved of does bear some relationship to what some of Moore's followers – and later, Bloomsbury – made of *Principia Ethica*.

These small examples are not the only times that the 'cult' of Moore reached beyond the confines of Bloomsbury and academic philosophy. In 1904 and 1905 a group of Cambridge men joined together to attempt to produce a book that would propound views inspired by Moore's philosophy in language accessible to the educated layman. This was a year after the publication of Moore's *Principia Ethica*, and the group consisted of G. M. Trevelyan, Sydney Waterlow, Goldsworthy Lowes Dickinson, Bertrand Russell and (possibly) Ralph Hawtrey. These men were mostly older than Moore; they were not especially involved with the people who were later to make up the Bloomsbury Group; and their leader, Sydney Waterlow, was not even an Apostle. The most remarkable fact about this project is that the philosopher whose views the group wished to make 'popular' was then only thirty-three years old. This project will be discussed in detail in Chapter 9.

A less documentable claim I have heard made about the breadth of Moore's influence – on the world outside that of Bloomsbury and of philosophy – is that the effect of the propagation of the 'Ideal Utilitarian' position of *Principia Ethica* was to restore the prominence of utilitarianism in political discussion and in parliamentary debate. Through their articles in the *Independent Review*, the *New Quarterly*, *Life and Letters* and later in the *Nation* and *New Statesman*, Moore's followers and their associates were thought to have had a good effect on the prevailing tone of political discussion, bringing it back from the rival attractions of the 'Absolute Idealism' of T. H. Green's followers to the natural utilitarian calculation of the consequences of actions and policies.

But perhaps the most forceful compliment paid to Moore's influence from someone outside Bloomsbury comes from J. B. Priestley in *The Edwardians*:

'It was in 1903 that G. E. Moore, of Cambridge, published his *Principia Ethica*, at the early age of thirty. But who, outside philosophy, cares about Moore and his attacks upon metaphysical idealism, his neo-realistic theory of epistemological monism? Well, I do, for one; and I do because Moore's heightened commonsense, scepticism, and the supreme value he attached to aesthetic enjoyments and personal relationships powerfully influenced a whole remarkable group, based on Cambridge, that included among others Maynard Keynes, E. M. Forster, Lytton Strachey, and Leonard and Virginia Woolf. This group in turn strongly influenced thousands of other intellectuals, who may never have been near Trinity College, Cambridge, nor even read anything by Moore himself. I believe the intellectual climate of Britain and America between the two World Wars would have been quite different if G. E. Moore had not published *Principia Ethica* back in 1903.'⁷

The conventional view of G. E. Moore's 'popular' influence was first put by Keynes in his memoir, 'My Early Beliefs'. Briefly stated, this is that Moore's influence was *doctrinal*, like the influence a teacher has upon his pupils, a master upon his disciples, or a guru upon his cult. Its chief idea is that what Moore offered was a set of '*truths*' – and, of course, the arguments that validated them. And the complement of this view is that Moore's followers, Leonard and Virginia Woolf, Lytton Strachey, Clive Bell and Keynes himself (to name only a few of them) *believed* these 'truths' and accepted Moore's arguments for them.

In his memoir Keynes suggested that these 'truths' can be found in Moore's best-known book, *Principia Ethica*. Thus there is a handy source in which to find the contents of the doctrines, and this view of Moore's influence becomes tidy and very plausible. So plausible was it, that when Sir Roy Harrod wrote his biography of Keynes and presented in it a refined version of the 'doctrinal' view, it was found highly accept-able – even irresistible – by the survivors of the Bloomsbury Group. Nearly all of them, I think, felt that this account reflected their own sentiments and explained their own experiences. Many of these people told Michael Holroyd the same story when, years later, he was writing his life of Strachey. And, naturally, they gave me an identical version of the influence upon them of my own subject when, only a few years after Michael Holroyd, I interviewed many of them. There was no dissent at all, for intelligent people were giving me an account that they genuinely and sincerely believed to be true. The view first pro-pounded by Keynes had been repeated – in print and in conversation – so often that repetition had hardened it, and turned what was originally the view of one man into an orthodoxy.

I disagree with this view. I think it is fundamentally false, though I can see its attractions and how it came to be the accepted wisdom. Its chief inadequacy is that it fails to explain the point Keynes himself made against it, when he said in his memoir that he and his friends accepted Moore's 'religion' but discarded his 'morals'. He meant by that remark that they selected certain parts of *Principia Ethica* – the last chapter on 'the Ideal' – for special attention, while almost ignoring some parts of the book – the sections on duty and moral obligations.

It can hardly be denied that Moore's Bloomsbury followers, when they read *Principia Ethica*, took from it only that which interested them, which was by no means all that it had to offer. They emphasized what Moore and present-day philosophers regard as philosophically the least important and interesting part of the book and, as Keynes himself saw, by overlooking all but the last section gave the (quite false) impression that they were 'immoralists'. They did not do this because they could not understand the book : several of Moore's self-proclaimed followers were quite competent philosophers in their own right, and all of them were clever. If, as seems likely, they were aware that their reading of *Principia Ethica* was highly selective, why did they give the opposite impression when they greeted the book on its publication, and later when they spoke first to Harrod, then to Holroyd and finally to me?

I think this came about because Moore's influence upon them was not importantly doctrinal at all, but *personal*. I think the doctrinal view came to be the orthodox account of Moore's effect upon people because those influenced by him were aware of how much they owed to Moore and wished to show their allegiance to him as a *person* by acknowledging the importance and even the grandeur of his ideas. And when one is of a mind to pay tribute, it may not seem important to make the nice distinction between a man and his work. Each of them had so much in common with Moore intellectually that it was all too easy to overlook any differences there may have been. Virginia Woolf, Lytton Strachey and Maynard Keynes, for example, could hardly have been aware of how much of their ingrained patterns of thinking were the result of a shared intellectual upbringing, of the remains of a legacy of utilitarianism (especially what Richard Braithwaite has called the 'consequentialist' aspect of utilitarianism)[8] which they had in common with Moore. No one, after all, can be so self-conscious and self-analytical as to say which of his ideas – or even of his prejudices – can be traced back to the nursery, and which are the result of what he has read and whom he has met.

In this book I have been forced to adopt a radical stance towards the orthodox explanation of Moore's influence on people other than professional philosophers. I hope the reader will agree, on finishing this book, that I have shown that the chief aspect of G. E. Moore's influence was not doctrinal, not even the result of reading *Principia Ethica*, but was based upon love and admiration for his character – for the striking traits of character that he continued to demonstrate all life long: integrity, incorruptibility, thoroughness and shining innocence. To do this necessarily involves biographical considerations – I have to explain the man himself and his character through the story of his life and through his education and intellectual background. This latter is of great importance, for my scepticism about the orthodox, doctrinal account of Moore makes it incumbent upon me to explore the genesis of Moore's ideas, to see what tradition he drew upon himself; to see how much of this tradition was shared, and perhaps taken for granted by his contemporaries; and to see whether and how Moore himself altered this tradition.

As an old man Moore read Keynes's memoir and Harrod's life of Keynes. He knew then, as he must have known long before, that many of his ideas had been misunderstood – or at least neglected – by those who called themselves his disciples. Why then did he continue to keep his silence? Why did he not speak out about the misinterpretations of points in *Principia Ethica*? Why did he not correct the silly construction placed on some of the conclusions of his last chapter, a construction that led some people to praise it and others to condemn it as homosexual propaganda, and that caused Bertrand Russell to thunder that 'those who considered themselves his disciples' ignored certain aspects of *Principia Ethica* and thus 'degraded his ethics into advocacy of a stuffy girls'-school sentimentalizing'?[9]

I think an examination of Moore's life shows that he was much too honest a man to inveigh against this use of his work, and to anticipate Russell's above blast against (chiefly) Strachey and Keynes. He was too honest a man to deny to the world and to himself that he had not discouraged this attitude to his work, because he had in the past looked with favour upon some of the 'sentimental' conclusions others drew from his arguments. These conclusions are not explicitly to be found in *Principia Ethica* and are not even necessary inferences to be drawn from it. They are not fundamental to Moore's philosophy – they are not even importantly connected with it. But Moore had himself experienced homosexual feelings when he was young, and he was too honest about himself to deny the past or to repudiate attitudes and opinions that he had earlier entertained – even though he never thought that they were correctly derived from his arguments in *Principia Ethica*.

Those who proclaimed themselves his disciples were devoted not so much to his ideas as to certain aspects of his character. Everyone agrees his character was remarkable, and some agree with Leonard Woolf that it was unique. My claim is that what Moore's followers had in common was admiration – even reverence – for his personal qualities; but that as their hero happened to be a philosopher, the appropriate gesture of allegiance to him meant saying that one believed his propositions and accepted the arguments for them. Had the great man been a poet, they would no doubt have showed their fealty (as others have) by reciting his verses; if a composer, by singing or playing his music. This is a radical view to espouse, for one does not often encounter the 'cult of the personality' in the history of philosophy. (But may not some of Wittgenstein's followers have been affected by just this?) It is tantamount to saying that in professing belief in Moore's 'philosophy' his Bloomsbury disciples were, for the most part, gesturing in order to demonstrate their loyalty.* However, this does not make the profession of belief in his philosophy a trivial thing: the gesture of allegiance in no way *excludes* the possibility that the belief is sincerely and genuinely held, or even well grounded.

I think this perspective greatly helps to explain the selectivity of the Apostles and of Bloomsbury in taking only as much from *Principia Ethica* as suited their needs, discarding – but not denying – the bulk of the book which deals with the traditional ethical topics of duties and obligations, and which is chiefly concerned with explicating the meaning of the concept 'good'. Without adumbrating the personal qualities that made Moore so admirable, it has already been implied that Moore's followers regarded him as a sort of intellectual saint. There is a good deal of evidence that they did just that. But in taking this view one is impaled on the sharp horns of an obvious but particularly awkward dilemma: how is one to construct a book that tries to describe and explain the *popular* influence of a man who came to be thought of as 'a philosopher's philosopher'? If I appear to discount the importance of his ideas *as ideas*, and to claim the greatest importance for his character, an explanation of Moore's influence must be sought in his biography. But Moore spent almost his entire adult life as a don in the gentle and seldom exciting environs of Cambridge and other universities; there

---

* E. M. Forster said he was only interested in arguments when they were by way of *being* gestures – clues to somebody's personality.[10]

are few dramatic events or incidents in his life that serve to delineate the character which I am claiming was so remarkable.

G. E. Moore slew no dragons and rescued no maidens; he did not even have the adventures life allotted to other philosophers like Russell, who went to jail, or Wittgenstein, who went to war. An orthodox biography of a man like Moore, it is only a small exaggeration to say, would be a biography without a life. One would be hard put to describe Moore's character by allowing it to emerge, without forcing the issue, from the narrative of the events of his whole life; and one is consequently placed in the unsatisfactory position of having to say : what Moore had that excited his disciples to their well-documented pitch of enthusiasm was a kind of magic. Fortunately many of the very intelligent and articulate people with whom Moore came into contact have recorded their views of him in one way or another – either at the time, in letters or diaries, or later in autobiographies or memoirs – and he himself kept a diary (some of which survives) as well as writing his brief autobiography, so that it is not impossible to sketch a convincing portrait of the man himself and to get some idea of the magical effect he had on other people.

What strikes one again and again is the strong and positive impression that G. E. Moore made on so many different people. Here, for example, is a masterly picture of him from Sir Roy Harrod :

'His devotion to truth was indeed palpable. In argument his whole frame was gripped by a passion to confute error and expose confusion. To watch him at work was an enthralling experience. Yet, when the heat of argument died down, he was the mildest and simplest of men, almost naïve in unphilosophical matters. He was friendly to the young, approaching them on natural and equal terms. Despite his *naïveté*, he seemed to have understanding. In human questions he had none of that intolerance or crabbedness which so often marks the academic man of thought. He was happy and at ease in discussions beyond his proper range. There was no question of his being shocked, and the young had no inhibitions in his presence. When Strachey made one of his subtle, perhaps cynical, perhaps shocking, utterances, the flavour of which even his clever undergraduate friends did not at first appreciate at its full value, Moore was seen to be shaking with laughter. If the veneration which his young admirers accorded him almost matched that due to a saint, we need not think that they were mistaken. It does not follow that the doctrines set forth in *Principia Ethica* are infallible.'[11]

Many have said (and written) that the most striking aspect of Moore's character was his childlike nature. The *'naïveté'* remarked by Sir Roy struck many of Moore's acquaintances, especially other philosophers, as a trait more usually found in children. For example, Norman Malcolm, the American philosopher who was a pupil and friend of Moore's, wrote:

'Moore was himself a childlike person. One thing that contributed to this quality in him was an extreme modesty. It was as if the thought had never occurred to Moore that he was an eminent philosopher. I recall that once when lecturing before a small class he had occasion to refer to an article that he had published some years before, and he went on to remark, without embarrassment, that it was a *good* article. I was much struck by this. Most men would be prevented by false modesty from saying a thing of this sort in public. Moore's modesty was so genuine that he could say it without any implication of self-satisfaction.'[12]

Malcolm thought Moore's childlike nature had three components: modesty, freshness and simplicity. But 'as a philosopher', Malcolm said, Moore

'was not very imaginative. He was not fertile in ideas, as was Russell. He was not a profound thinker, as was Wittgenstein. I believe that what gave Moore stature as a philosopher was his *integrity*, an attribute of character rather than of intellect. He had the depth of seriousness. When he addressed himself to a philosophical difficulty what he said about it had to be *exactly right*. . . .

'The address that Moore delivered to the British Academy, entitled "Proof of an External World", caused him a great deal of torment in its preparation. He worked hard at it, but the concluding portion displeased him, and he could not get it right as the time approached for his appearance before the Academy. On the day of the lecture he was still distressed about the ending of the paper. As he was about to leave the house to take the train to London Mrs Moore said, in order to comfort him, "Cheer up! I'm sure they will like it". To which Moore made this emphatic reply: "If they *do*, they'll be *wrong*".'[13]

Sir Alfred (A. J.) Ayer is another philosopher who was much impressed by Moore's character. He was 'converted' to Moore's ethical views by reading Clive Bell's *Art*,[14] but did not actually meet Moore until much later, when he was 'very much taken with his puckish charm'.[15] Ayer, too, came to see something of the childlike aspect of Moore's character:

> 'He was then in his sixties but had lost none of the enthusiasm for philosophy or the passion for argument for which he had been celebrated in his youth. He resembled Einstein in his simplicity, his single-mindedness, and his ability to make his juniors feel that they were engaging with him on equal terms. He could become angry when someone persisted in what seemed to him a fallacious course of argument or failed to appreciate an obvious point, and the display of literally open-mouthed astonishment with which he greeted a stupid or pretentious remark could make its perpetrator feel and look like a fool: but these were natural reactions, not forensic tricks, and they were directed against the intellectual sin, without animosity towards the sinner. Bertrand Russell, who had a great respect for Moore as a person, but came to disapprove of his philosophical influence, once said to me, "The trouble with Moore is that he believes everything that his nurse told him." Though Russell here fell into the prevalent mistake of exaggerating Moore's attachment to common sense, his comment, if unkindly, was not altogether unjust. For all his subtlety and sophistication in argument, Moore always kept some hold of nurse. But though in one way a weakness, this was also part of his strength. His chief service to philosophy was that of the child in Hans Andersen's story: he saw and was not afraid to say that the Emperor had no clothes.'[16]

In contrast, the reader must not be surprised to find in these pages a picture of Moore that sometimes differs from the foregoing sketches: not a charming, good-natured man, but occasionally a man in a thoroughly bad state of mind, in fact, in a temper. The objects of Moore's bad temper – which it must be admitted sometimes amounted to rage – were, in a single notable instance, Graham Wallas, and, almost regularly, Bertrand Russell. Moore loathed Wallas, and, on balance, disliked Russell. His disapprobation of Wallas and Russell was not the anger, interesting though that phenomenon itself is, described by Professor Ayer in the passage quoted above. It was something altogether more intense. It was a special kind of anger, and could only have been felt by a special kind of man. To most of us it is (perhaps happily) not given to feel the emotion Moore experienced, for it was the rage that is the complement of pure innocence.

Outraged innocence – the genuine article, at least – is seldom encountered in real life, and can never have been common. It is familiar enough from fiction, and perhaps the best fictional analogue for Moore is Dostoevsky's Idiot, Prince Myshkin. I am not the first to make this comparison, but did Leonard Woolf think of Moore's rages when he drew this parallel?[17] I think he did not, and intended the analogy only to illustrate Moore's simplicity and innocence; Woolf would not, I feel sure, have cared to dwell upon Moore's thundery moods. Indeed very few people ever saw Moore angry in this particular way. But it is nevertheless one of the keys to understanding the uniqueness of Moore's character. And the fact that it *was* possible to outrage his innocence rendered him the more lovable – frightening in his wrath, certainly, but vulnerable as only the pure in spirit can be.

Moore's wrath was titanic, the anger of a giant. But there was an aspect of his character that was distinctly unheroic. It would be wrong to omit any mention of it, not merely on the warts-and-all principle (in this case, it is not a case of portraying warts, but something more like a tic), but because it may have some bearing on the way Moore 'did' philosophy. From those diaries that he did not destroy, it is apparent that Moore was obsessive: in them he records each time he cleaned his pipe; he itemizes every walk he ever took, and those walks he habitually took alone he characterized not geographically or topographically, but geometrically. He would write that he had walked 'the parallelogram' or 'the rectangle', where someone else might have said he had walked, for example, to Granchester or around Parker's Piece. (I cannot identify the locations of Moore's regular walks.) He was also meticulous in recording having the piano tuned, and making a note whenever he had anything mended. It will also become evident in the course of my narration that Moore was a compulsive maker of lists – of books he read, of dates when he first encountered people who later became friends, of holidays he took and in whose company, of work done, and of dates he considered significant in his life.

Whether or not this was a neurotic trait I am not competent to say and do not much care. Though Moore was said by his wife to have been opposed to having a biography of him written, these lists, and the choice of which diaries to withhold from consigning to the flames, seem to me suspiciously like a set of notes for a future biographer. Compulsively obsessive the habit of making records might have been, but it has put me in touch with the mind of my subject; though it may very well be judged neurotic behaviour by those whose profession it is to make such judgements, to me it makes the character of Moore all the more engaging. In the diaries Moore set down the earth-shaking side by side with the trivial; he gives the reader no clue to help him distinguish between the two categories, and for this reason the diaries are terribly difficult to use.

The reader who knows Moore's philosophical work or, better still, who has heard of Moore's classroom manner, will possibly not be surprised to hear that Moore had an obsessive character. His greatest strength as a philosopher was his patience in pursuing an argument wherever it led and through however many steps it took to arrive there. To be as good as Moore was at this procedure, it is probably helpful to have an obsessive nature. I do not find that knowledge of this detracts from the attractiveness of the man, and cannot imagine any reader finding Moore less lovable because he was a little odd.

In one section of this book G. E. Moore is kept off-stage and scarcely puts in an appearance at all. The reason for paying so much attention to the Cambridge Apostles is that their traditions were of central importance to Bloomsbury and to the story of Moore's own life. These considerations have dictated that the construction of this book should frequently depart from the pattern demanded by the conventions of biography. The image of an hour-glass has – to some degree – determined the structure of this book. In the top of the glass is the sand that represents what Noël Annan has called the English Intellectual Aristocracy; the Cambridge intellectual background; and the history since its foundation in 1820 of the Cambridge Apostles. Moore is represented by the funnel of the hour-glass through which the sand of this long tradition of Cambridge filters into the lower half of the glass, and this represents not only Bloomsbury, but also a great deal of modern philosophy, as well as some specific events, institutions and personal achievements. These would include such aspects of our culture common to both Britain and America as the effect on our literary sensibilities produced by the criticism in newspapers and magazines of Desmond MacCarthy and others associated with him on the *New Statesman*, on the *Sunday Times*, on many small magazines and on several American periodicals. Also in the bottom of the glass I should place the change in our visual sensibility brought about by the writings on art of Roger Fry and Clive Bell, and by their organization of the exhibitions that first introduced to us the work of the Post-Impressionist painters of Europe – some years before the English-speaking world would otherwise have learned of the most important developments in art this century. The revolution in the writing of biography made by Lytton Strachey belongs here; so does his brother James's magnificent translation and standard edition of the works of Freud. There are those who would place in the bottom of this hour-glass the novels and literary criticism of Virginia Woolf and E. M. Forster, and some have even thought there was reason to add the paintings of Duncan Grant and Vanessa Bell* We can certainly place here the work on probability of Maynard Keynes, which is, for the most part, seriously underestimated outside philosophical circles. Leonard Woolf's own political writings definitely belong here, and we should probably be safe in including some at least of the work of Goldsworthy Lowes Dickinson and even G. M. Trevelyan.

On a less elevated level, vestiges of Bloomsbury can still be seen in the English Sunday newspapers, particularly the *Sunday Times* and the *Observer*, where criticism not only of books, but of films and music, is, or was until recently, regularly written by people who were junior associates of the Bloomsbury Group. The *New Statesman* was once thought of as the 'house organ' of the Bloomsbury Group. It is not far-fetched to see the current domestic habits of middle-class Englishmen and Americans as owing a great deal to Bloomsbury's discovery of such things as French provincial and peasant cooking and culture. Roger Fry, Vanessa Bell and Duncan Grant 'discovered' St Tropez at least forty years before Brigitte Bardot. Bloomsbury, whose well-publicized private lives were and still are emulated in the suburbs of New York as well as those of London, created the *climate* in which middle-class families eat for their Sunday lunch *boeuf en daube*, made to an Elizabeth David or Julia Child recipe, on a plain pine farmhouse (American 'life style') table brought from Habitat or New York's Conran shop.

This book effectively closes with the end of the 1914 war, for that date marks the almost complete disappearance of the society and social order of which this book is a description and sometimes, one hopes, an evocation, and also marks a large change in Moore's work. Before the war, only one or two articles from Moore's pen could not be understood and appreciated by any well-educated person capable of following an argument; and the topics he discussed were of at least some general interest. After the war, with one or two exceptions, Moore's work ceased to be accessible to the reader without training in philosophy. The techniques he employed were those of the specialist, and the subjects he discussed grew out of the literature that had accumulated around the problems that interested him. Moore's treatment of these

---

* But, on the other hand, Quentin Bell told me that, in his opinion, Vanessa Bell and Duncan Grant, along with Roger Fry and Adrian Stephen, were the only members of Bloomsbury who did *not* consider themselves followers of Moore.

problems – indeed the very questions he puts – can hardly be understood by someone who is not acquainted with this literature. By 1918 at the very latest, Moore was no longer producing work that could engage a popular following; yet there continued to be 'Mooreists' among the Apostles until well into the thirties, and the earlier allegiance of his admirers in Cambridge and Bloomsbury was not abandoned. His stature as a philosopher grew, along with his influence on other philosophers. He edited the philosophical journal *Mind* in its greatest period. He had become a thorough professional, truly a philosopher's philosopher. And it is to them that we must leave the further discussion of G. E. Moore.

BOOK ONE

I

The 'Intellectual Aristocracy'

Early in the nineteenth century certain families from three distinct groups, those with philanthropic, Quaker or evangelical traditions, began to emerge from their background and to form a recognizable and distinct intellectual élite. As a group they were to influence profoundly the cultural life of the country. At the beginning of the century these families, which produced a large number of professors, tutors and schoolmasters, began to intermarry, since much of their social intercourse was with similar families, and it is natural that marriages should be made between people whose families are acquainted. The rise of their fortunes was parallel with that of the rise of the professional middle class. When the affairs of government and empire became too complicated to be run by the aristocratic ruling class with its traditions of public service, 'members of these intellectual families became the new professional civil servants', Indian and colonial service officials, headmasters, school inspectors, museum curators, editors and journalists. 'Thus', Lord Annan suggests, 'they gradually spread over the length and breadth of English intellectual life criticising the assumptions of the ruling class above them and forming the opinions of the upper middle class to which they belonged.'[1] Members of this intellectual élite persevered in this role of shadow ruling class, emerging from a position of friendly opposition to one of real power by the First World War, which, however, destroyed much of the basis of the social order that many of them and their ancestors had worked to create.

The tie that bound the original families of this élite was philanthropy, but the group had three distinct lines of origin. Many families had been linked to the Clapham Sect, and though their descendants had lost the faith, or never had it at all, the spirit that animated the ancestors was that of the Evangelical Movement. Lord Annan points out that:

'the intellectual aristocracy were imbued with the principles which flowed from that faith. There was the sense of dedication, of living with purpose, or working under the eye, if not that of the great Taskmaster, of their own conscience – that organ which evangelicalism magnified so greatly. . . . There was the sense of accounting for the talents with which Providence had endowed them. There was also the duty to hold themselves apart from a world given over to vanities which men of integrity rejected because they were content to labour in the vineyard where things of eternal significance grew – in the field of scholarship where results were solid not transient.'²

Another line of origin of the intellectual aristocracy was the Quakers, who shared the philanthropic concerns of the Clapham Sect, and a few of whom also had evangelical tendencies. The Gurneys, Barclays, Cadburys, Rowntrees, Frys, Gaskells, Sturges, Hodgkins, Foxes, and Hoares had begun intermarrying in the eighteenth century, and it was from among descendants of these families that Moore's ancestor Joseph Sturge drew his first allies in the agitation against slavery. But as small Quaker traders became important bankers and industrialists, the rigid practices of the Society of Friends began to be felt as unwelcome constraints by some Quakers, who drifted away from formal connections with Quaker meetings, though not from their principles. Quaker separateness, marked by plain dress and plain speech, was already fading in the early decades of the nineteenth century, and the doctrine of following the inner light was actually leading the descendants of some families away from Quakerism itself. This not only made possible an alliance between them and philanthropically-minded evangelicals within the established church, it resulted in the sons of such families as the Gurneys and the Pryors going up to Cambridge where nonconformists were not allowed to take the MA degree until 1871.

The third line of origin was independent of both the evangelical faith and the traditions of dissenting. It was composed of the philosophic radical and Unitarian families whose chief representatives were the Wedgwoods, Darwins, Trevelyans, Martineaus, Huxleys, and Stracheys. Though some of these families had ancestors of evangelical persuasion, by the latter half of the century they no longer derived their social and political opinions from this tradition. Some were Comtean Positivists, some were followers of Mill; some were agnostic, but some remained Church of England. The Wedgwoods neither descended from clergymen, nor produced any; their cousins, the Darwins, were markedly unreligious. This third group was composed of gentlemen: the Trevelyans and the Stracheys were old West Country families with baronetcies dating back a century or two. Both families had an exact sense of their station, which was grand enough; but the intellectual Trevelyans were a cadet branch, and the Stracheys, ruined in the eighteenth century, sent a succession of younger sons to seek their fortunes in India. These families never confused themselves with the real ruling class; indeed many of them were prejudiced against aristocrats, as they could see little merit in being born well. But as Annan says, 'because they judged people by an exterior standard of moral and intellectual merit, they never became an exclusive clique and welcomed the penniless son of a dissenting minister as a son-in-law if they believed in his integrity and ability'.[3]

From all three lines the families that constituted the intellectual aristocracy had in common certain attitudes about work and its importance, about the desirability of higher education, and about the right and duty to follow the dictates of one's own conscience. By the end of the century they had become a bit philistine, and just a bit too earnest; some of the mocking behaviour of the Bloomsbury Group was a reaction against this aspect of their fathers' too blameless characters.

Intermarriage among the families that constituted the intellectual aristocracy was common. Quaker families in particular tended to marry cousins, for Quakers were discouraged from marrying outside the faith, and the number of well-to-do Quaker families from which a suitable spouse could be chosen was not large. It was thought better to marry a first cousin than not to marry a Quaker at all, for they considered themselves a group apart and endogamy was essential to retaining this identity. Non-Quaker members of the intellectual aristocracy also intermarried. The Darwin-Wedgwood-Cornford-Raverat clan frequently held very large gatherings of the extended family; and the presence of Maitlands, Huxleys, Fishers, Keyneses, Vaughan Williamses, Trevelyans, and Peases reminded them that they were part of a world that also included Tennysons, Macaulays, Hodgkins, Arnolds, Penroses, Wards, Frys, Booths, Potters, Stracheys, and Stephens. They knew that this world was privileged, but were proud that it was also civilized. Pleased to have been born into it, they expected to marry another member of it. This they did, either because their parents had arranged it with friends or relations, or because the family circle was so large, and social intercourse so restricted to it, that a young person of marriageable age would scarcely know anyone outside it.

Being born a Darwin or a Wedgwood was reason for congratulation; certainly the elder Darwins and Wedgwoods thought so, and frequently reminded the younger ones that this was the case. Growing up in such a family conferred a self-confidence and assurance that even the great

Some Connections Within the 'Intellectual Aristocracy'

Members of the Apostles are marked with an asterisk.

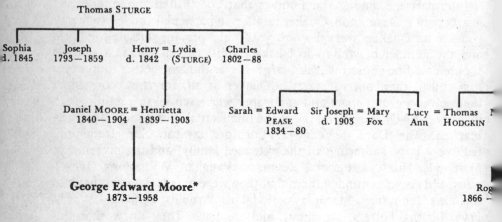

Thomas STURGE

Sophia
d. 1845

Joseph
1793—1859

Henry = Lydia
d. 1842 (STURGE)

Charles
1802—88

Daniel MOORE = Henrietta
1840—1904   1839—1903

Sarah = Edward
PEASE
1834—80

Sir Joseph = Mary
d. 1903   Fox

Lucy = Thomas
Ann   HODGKIN

George Edward Moore*
1873—1958

Rog
1866 –

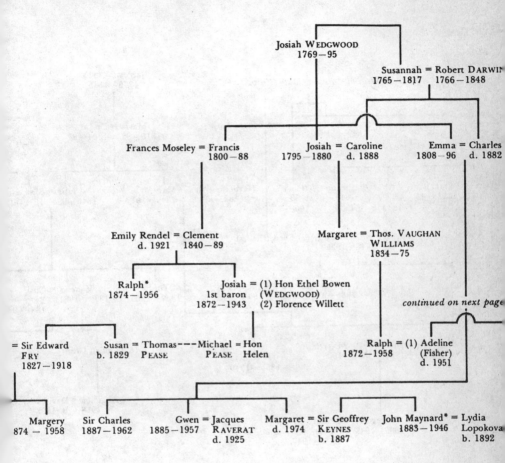

continued on next page

Josiah WEDGWOOD
1769—95

Susannah = Robert DARWIN
1765—1817 1766—1848

Frances Moseley = Francis
1800—88

Josiah = Caroline
1795—1880 d. 1888

Emma = Charles
1808—96 d. 1882

Emily Rendel = Clement
d. 1921 1840—89

Margaret = Thos. VAUGHAN
WILLIAMS
1834—75

Ralph*
1874—1956

Josiah = (1) Hon Ethel Bowen
1st baron (WEDGWOOD)
1872—1943 (2) Florence Willett

= Sir Edward
FRY
1827—1918

Susan = Thomas---Michael = Hon
b. 1829 PEASE PEASE Helen

Ralph = (1) Adeline
1872—1958 (Fisher)
d. 1951

Margery
874—1958

Sir Charles
1887—1962

Gwen = Jacques
1885—1957 RAVERAT
d. 1925

Margaret = Sir Geoffrey
d. 1974 KEYNES
b. 1887

John Maynard* = Lydia
1883—1946 Lopokova
b. 1892

23

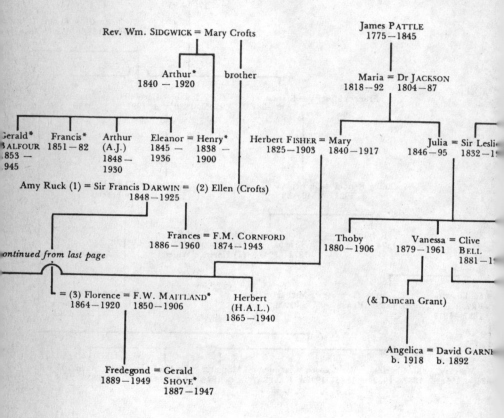

Rev. Wm. SIDGWICK = Mary Crofts

Arthur*
1840 — 1920

brother

James PATTLE
1775 — 1845

Maria = Dr JACKSON
1818—92 1804—87

Gerald*
BALFOUR
1853 —
1945

Francis*
1851 — 82

Arthur
(A.J.)
1848 —
1930

Eleanor = Henry*
1845 —   1838 —
1936   1900

Herbert FISHER = Mary
1825 — 1903   1840 — 1917

Julia = Sir Lesli
1846—95 1832—1

Amy Ruck (1) = Sir Francis DARWIN = (2) Ellen (Crofts)
1848 — 1925

Frances = F.M. CORNFORD
1886 — 1960 1874 — 1943

Thoby
1880 — 1906

Vanessa = Clive
1879 — 1961 BELL
1881 — 1

continued from last page

= (3) Florence = F.W. MAITLAND*
1864 — 1920   1850 — 1906

Herbert
(H.A.L.)
1865 — 1940

(& Duncan Grant)

Fredegond = Gerald
1889 — 1949 SHOVE*
1887 — 1947

Angelica = David GARNE
b. 1918   b. 1892

24

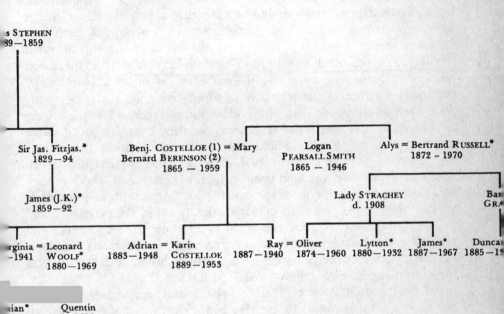

public schools would be hard put to match. Such a child was not only a member of a great family, he was a member of an accomplished and clever family. He was clever himself – his parents told him so constantly – and he would marry somebody clever, as his parents and grandparents had done. Natural selection clearly favoured the Darwins. There was money and education in the environment: a child born into these circumstances was bound to be a creature of promise. Great things were *expected* of such a child. Being a member by right of birth conferred a sense of security crucial to the accomplishment of great intellectual deeds. And with right of birth the crucial factor, there was no way of forfeiting membership – not even, when at university, by espousing daring theories which were sometimes silly. A daring young man, even a silly young man of this class, did not fear to lose the esteem of his peers by advancing bad arguments, for they knew his background, and that was sufficient to indicate the quality of his mind. It is important to note that this intellectual élite is properly regarded as an aristocracy, for one was (and some still are) born into it, and its members possessed the self-confidence usually associated with aristocrats. It was an open-ended group, in that meritocrats could marry into it, and their children would enjoy the security of their uncles', aunts', and cousins' esteem no less than the children of an endogamous marriage. But, as a glance at the pedigrees of this group shows, such a child was likely to make an endogamous marriage himself.

An environment where creative behaviour is encouraged and expected is a great stimulus to creative behaviour, for it is conducive to intellectual boldness and a spirit of adventure. A tradition of such behaviour explains in part why the group has produced such an enormous quantity of men and women of distinction. Although, for a proper assessment of the group's importance one would also have to study in detail the careers of those in this class who made exogamous marriages, it is equally evident, as Lord Annan points out, that 'men of natural but not outstanding ability can reach the front ranks of science and scholarship and the foremost positions in the cultural hierarchy of the country if they have been bred to a tradition of intellectual achievement and have been taught to turn their environment to account'.[4] Such a training has a far stronger effect on the personality when transmitted by family tradition than when inculcated by school or university.

The rise of this portion of the Victorian middle class to positions of cultural and political importance was of great moment for the recent history of England. Many posts of growing influence passed out of the gift of the nobility into the hands of these families, as Annan remarks, though the power of this new aristocracy was limited by the democratic machinery through which such posts of influence were awarded, and for the establishment of which these families had fought. Their offspring naturally gravitated to places and positions where cultural and academic policy were formulated. They preferred Cambridge to Oxford, possibly because the Tractarian Movement frightened evangelical families, and certainly because Cambridge, ever since the Civil War, had the more pleasant associations for nonconformist families. They not only sent their sons (and later, their daughters) to Cambridge, they provided many of the fellows of the colleges, especially Trinity and King's, and it is these undergraduates and fellows who are the special subject of this book. The most brilliant were elected to the Apostles and it was as Apostles that their lives and ideas were to be influenced by G. E. Moore, himself a descendant of a Quaker family that could claim membership of the intellectual aristocracy.

2
Moore's Ancestry, Childhood and Schooldays

No one (to adapt the words of Moore's beloved Jane Austen) who had ever seen G. E. Moore in his infancy would have supposed him born to be a hero. His situation in life, the character of his father and mother, his own person and disposition, were all equally against him. The situation of his childhood and adolescence, and that of his parents' lives together, were determined by a single, pressing circumstance – the wish of his parents to send their sons to be educated at a particular school. The reasons for their choice of school go far to indicate what sort of people they were, and from what background G. E. Moore sprang. The school was a new one, Dulwich College in south London. It was of much the same standing as St Paul's School, and the Moore parents liked what they had heard about its headmaster. With great determination G. E. Moore's parents uprooted themselves to be able to send their sons as day-boys to Dulwich College. In 1871, two years before G. E. Moore was born, his parents had removed from the seaside town of Hastings in Sussex, with its substantial residences and favourable winter climate, to Upper Norwood, a properous suburb of London, then in vogue with the professional middle classes. The houses there were equally substantial, and Daniel Moore nostalgically named his newly built house 'Hastings Lodge'. Daniel Moore was a medical man, and had been in general practice with his brother for some years at Hastings; but after the move to London he gave up the practice of medicine altogether. That he took this drastic step seems, fittingly, to have been due to the ill-health and large fortune of his wife.

Hastings Lodge, to which Daniel Moore moved his growing family, was a large, detached red-brick house, much like the other houses in the new development in Dulwich Hill Park on the western slope of the hill rising to the Crystal Palace, which had been placed in Sydenham in 1854 after its removal from Hyde Park where it had housed the Great Exhibition of 1851. Crystal Palace was the focus of the neighbourhood; it served as a museum for exhibiting paintings, sculpture and architecture, and as a concert hall. Children with tickets could play in the park, and watch the reptilian movements of the huge moving sculptures of prehistoric monsters, placed on the islands dotting the pond near the southern edge of the park. Crystal Palace and the moving statues in its park were paradigms of everything that was new and exciting about the Victorian age; they were the fruit and the flower of applied technology. Equally up to date was the new house down the hill, where the Moore family lived. But although only six miles from the centre of London, Hastings Lodge stood on the site of an ancient wood and it had a half-acre of garden, with three venerable oak trees: only a few years ago this had been a forest. Even then, in the 1870s, there were only twenty-one other houses in Dulwich Hill Park; they were large houses, as they had to be to accommodate a Victorian family and its retainers.

As was the case with most prosperous families of the time, birth control was neither practised, thought of, nor mentioned, and Mrs Moore had a baby almost every year. Daniel Moore's first wife, Anna Sarah Miller, had died in 1867, a year after giving birth to a girl, Annie Harriette. Daniel's family with Henrietta Sturge began with the birth in 1870 of Thomas Sturge, who was followed by a regular succession of brothers and sisters: in 1871, Daniel Henry (Harry); 1872, Henrietta (Hettie); 1873, George Edward; 1874, Helen (Nellie); 1876, Joseph Herbert (Bertie); and finally, in 1878, Sarah Hannah (Sally).

Daniel was the son of George Moore, who had achieved eminence both as a medical man and as an author. Born in 1803 at Plymouth, where his father had followed a semi-medical calling as a dispenser at the local infirmary, George Moore was fortunate to attend lectures in surgical practice at St Bartholomew's Hospital, one of the three London teaching hospitals. Later he studied anatomy in Paris, qualified as a member of the Royal College of Surgeons, and took the degree of MD at St Andrews. Finally he went on to become a member of the Royal College of Physicians.

George Moore was on his way up the steep social and professional ladder, but by the time he neared the top rung he was no longer interested in the ascent. At the age of thirty-five, his health broke down and he settled at Hastings to continue his second career as an author. He wrote four works of homely philosophy and quasi-psychology, intended for a popular audience, and a book of poetry, before becoming the Dr Spock of Victorian England by publishing in 1872 *The Training of Young Children on Christian and Natural Principles*. He followed this with books on theology, the history of religion, many hymns and some short religious poems. The success of his literary pursuits was responsible for a considerable improvement in the fortune of the Moore family. He was moreover able to support his four wives and the seven out of nine children who survived into adulthood by the proceeds of his writing. There is no doubt that he left his son Daniel, the seventh child, by his third wife Hannah Green, not only an interest in medicine and a devotion to the Baptist sect, but a decent amount of cash as well.

Fairly soon after the death in 1867 of his first wife, Anna Sarah Miller, Daniel met Henrietta Sturge, a descendant of one of the great Quaker families. She was a year older than himself and an established spinster by Victorian standards. Henrietta was probably visiting elderly relations at Hastings, where Daniel was living – she tended to go from one old aunt or uncle to another. Her parents had both been dead at least ten years, which meant that Henrietta already had some money of her own when she met Daniel. She and her half-sister were the only children of Henry Sturge and Lydia Sturge, and while the wealth of the family varied from branch to branch, there were no *poor* Sturges.

As was not uncommon in the Sturge family, Henrietta's parents were first cousins. Her father, Henry, was a brother of the famous Joseph Sturge, who is commemorated by a large marble statue in Birmingham. This is not simply because he was one of the city's first aldermen but because he, as much as Wilberforce, was responsible for the universal abolition of slavery in England's colonies. His political life did not, however, consist of this single victory. He also found time to press for abolition in America. Associated with Cobden and Bright in the Anti-Corn-Law League, he gave this up because his interest in the Chartist Movement had led him to believe that complete suffrage was the fundamental problem. In later years he was an active worker for peace, and was one of the three Quakers who went to Russia to call upon the Tsar in an effort to prevent the Crimean War.

Joseph Sturge was still living when Henrietta was a little girl; he must have appeared very grand to her, a patriarch and a great man, a cousin on her mother's side and an uncle on her father's. Henrietta thus had a sense of family as strong and central to her own life as that of any other member of the intellectual aristocracy, or indeed of any member of the English social aristocracy. Henrietta's father had died when she was three, and after the death of her mother sixteen years later, she was probably closest to her uncle George. George, who was much the richest of his branch of the family, had, like his sister, married a Sturge cousin. He had made Henrietta's cousin Jane her aunt by marriage, and Henrietta was one of the many nephews and nieces who paid long visits to the childless George and Jane at their house, Woodthorpe, on Sydenham Hill.

It was to this same area that Henrietta came to live, only a few years later, with her husband Daniel Moore, his five-year-old daughter and their two baby boys. They saw a good deal of their Sturge neighbours, and even more of Henrietta's uncle George following the death of her aunt Jane in 1883. George Sturge spent his last years chiefly in examining the appeals for money which every morning's post brought, and in disposing of his £300,000 estate. He finally arranged for it to be invested, with some of the interest to provide life-time annuities of £104 for about fifty nephews and nieces. (This was the 'Sturge legacy' that was to make it possible for G. E. Moore to continue working at philosophy when he had no academic job.) Daniel and Henrietta Moore were not forgotten by her uncle George, for by 1888 they had moved from Hastings Lodge and had installed themselves and their eight children in George's old house, Woodthorpe.

It is difficult to know what Henrietta Sturge Moore was like. Perhaps this is simply because she was a complicated person, or perhaps because the passage of time has made her traits of character less obvious than they would have been to a contemporary. She could never have been a pretty woman, at best her looks were unprepossessing: her chin was prominent, her eyes were set closely together, and her lower lip was rather thick; she aged badly – late photographs of her show a hard and angular, sharp-featured old woman. But she was not unintelligent and quite well-educated: she was on a *cours* in Paris during the excitement of 1848 and acquired a mastery of French that she later passed on to her own children. Young ladies of serious Quaker backgrounds were not encouraged to cultivate wit and humour, and Henrietta certainly did nothing to obtain these for herself. Following the death of her father, her mother Lydia Sturge settled in France, where her sister Helen married Georges Appia, a Protestant minister from the Vaudois. Lydia had decided views on religion, and these she passed on to her daughters. Having been excluded from the local Quaker meeting for marrying her first cousin, she became more and more attracted to evangelical religion.

Henrietta wrote daily letters to her sister. From these there emerges a pattern of concerns: religion, health and illness, and death. Her letters abound in pious exhortations to see God's will working itself out in everything. Paragraph after paragraph deals with Henrietta's infirmities of body and of mind; for she was subject to lengthy spells of depression. Deaths of relatives are dwelt upon in loving and sometimes grisly detail, with full accounts of the circumstances of the loved one's last moments. Yet such a pattern of morbid concerns was probably not unusual for one in Henrietta's position. A spinster, with no prospects of marriage and children of her own, she was perfectly resigned to a life as companion to a series of ageing and ailing Sturge aunts and uncles.

The wonder is that she was *not* surprised at Daniel Moore's proposal of marriage, which came only a few months after the death of his first wife. While Henrietta did not take an uncommonly long time to decide to accept the proposal, the marriage itself was delayed for four months while she accompanied her brother-in-law, Georges Appia, on a fundraising mission to America. At the time of her engagement she told her sister that she felt 'no ecstasy, no rush of joy'. But her feelings for the doctor soon warmed, and, in a passage that tells us much about herself as well as about Dr Moore, she wrote to her sister on 28 May 1868 from Boston, that

'you must know he is very tall and rather slender, though not such a threadpaper as Mr John Boyes [a relation]. His eyes are blue and although he is short-sighted and obliged almost constantly to wear glasses he has a habit of looking you thro' and thro', so that from the first moment I saw him, I always said, I should be very sorry to have anything to do with him, if I ever wanted to hide anything from him. I believe it is this partly, which makes him so peculiarly clever in his profession; he is extremely kind and a great favourite among the poor, altho' he has a great objection to indiscriminate alms-giving; gentle enough, I think, even to have satisfied our own precious Mamma, and yet firm wherever he feels it his duty to be so. Naturally shy and reserved, yet really sociable and with plenty of good sense, about as capable of saying cool and independent things as ever his father is, ... and from what I have heard, tho' of this I cannot judge myself, one of the most amiable tempers that can be found. There now, aren't you afraid he'll spoil me altogether. I am, I can tell you, especially when I read his tender, loving letters, and feel what a wealth of affection he is already lavishing on his newly found treasure. But then the best of all is, that he is thoroughly a child of God, and that his great aim is, I am sure, to be useful and be conformed to the mind of Jesus.'

(In connection with marriage it is interesting to note that though a woman of twenty-nine, Henrietta had the usual Victorian innocence of even theoretical sexual knowledge. In the popular watering place of Saratoga, New York, she was delighted and fortunate to hear 'a female

Dr lecture on the physiology of women, and say some things which I felt very thankful to have the opportunity of hearing; knowing, as I do, that I have no dear Mamma to give me instructions about things that it may be very desirable for me to know.' [Brooklyn, August 19, 1868.])

Henrietta's religious sentiments were, for a Victorian, surprisingly non-sectarian and free from theological considerations. As a member of a great Quaker family, she was of course steeped in the traditions of the Friends, and in early letters to Quaker relations she uses the 'thee' and 'thou' of plain speech. But the connection of her parents with the family faith had been made tenuous by their exclusion from local Meeting, and though Henrietta occasionally went to and enjoyed a Quaker meeting, she often attended Baptist chapel even before her marriage to Daniel Moore. Evangelical tendencies, passed on by her mother to both her and her half-sister, led her to attend revivalist meetings. The evangelical emphasis on conversion was congenial to her introspective nature, since it demanded that one must constantly search one's heart and mind to see if one really has been converted and reborn. But after her marriage Henrietta began to see the morbid features of such introspection. Seven years after the marriage, in reply to Helen's asking whether she has gone to hear the famous American evangelists, Dwight L. Moody and Ira D. Sankey, whose London campaign in 1875 was the acme of the entire Evangelical Movement, Henrietta wrote on 22 June 1875:

'Daniel is intending to go and hear Moody and Sankey some evening this week; I do not however think I shall accompany him; for whether having thrown myself very enthusiastically into similar revival services some years back, or having in the past given way too constantly to emotional feeling, I find I am obliged to avoid as much as possible everything exciting or likely to touch the feelings; such a little seems completely to rob me of any power of restraining them – besides which, I question very much whether my Christian character would not have been more thorough and strong if I had not indulged too freely in this kind of religious excitement in past years; and I think I have observed similar effects in others; and I cannot go to such a service with a strong doubt as to its legitimacy (at least for myself), or as a simple matter of curiosity.'

In many ways the practice of introspection was Henrietta's vice; but this passage shows that it yielded her an acute piece of self-knowledge: she here explicitly recognizes the pathological aspect of her religious feelings and she actually sees a link between her sentimentality and her ill-health. It would, however, be wrong to think of Henrietta as a malingerer. She is surely right when she says to Helen that 'when you consider how near in age our children are, and how much I have suffered often during pregnancy, I don't think anyone can be much surprised that I have to suffer a good deal in many ways from weakness.' [17 January 1875.] She had borne seven children in eight years, the last when she was thirty-nine years of age, and was no doubt simply worn out from bearing and nursing children. It is no wonder that for most of her marriage she was an invalid. But the chronic ill-health she experienced before her marriage was surely related to her recurring depressions: she simply spent too much of her time enquiring of herself how she was feeling. And in view of her lack of prospects and the life she was leading, it is not surprising that the answer was usually 'not very well'. Anything that encouraged introspection, that encouraged the contemplation of one's own state of mind, was bad for Henrietta's health; and the religious influences she exposed herself to, the Quaker 'inner light', the noncomformist emphasis on the promptings of the individual conscience, and the evangelical demand for personal conversion, all led Henrietta down the dangerous path of self-searching.

Though Henrietta disavowed evangelical religion even before all her children were born, the religious influence remained strong in the Moore household, with important effect, as we shall see, on G. E. Moore himself. Family prayers were held every day and not, as was often the case in Victorian houses, exclusively for the edification of the servants. Twice every Sunday, the whole family went to the nearby Baptist chapel to hear the preaching of the mild and not over-orthodox Mr Tipple. Religion never lost the place it occupied in the Moores' lives, but it ceased, at least for Henrietta, to be a source of unhealth.

Henrietta is a puzzling figure to us partly because she was a type that no longer exists. Since the First World War, a woman in Henrietta's position, orphaned at nineteen, educated, middle-class and well-to-do, would have attempted to create a career for herself outside the confines of family life, and few such young ladies since that time would have considered a career as companion to elderly relations. The particular sort of spinsterish hysteria from which Henrietta seems to have suffered is also a thing of the past. But it should also not be overlooked that to be the sort of invalid Henrietta became after her marriage required a fairly large domestic staff of the sort that hardly existed after the war.

What sort of mother, then, was Henrietta, and how did she influence her children? Owing to her chronic indisposition, the children were in the company of their father rather more than is usual. Henrietta was sorry that by 1873 Dr Moore had no practice at all, but her sorrow was leavened by the thought of her own dependence on his ministrations, and later on by the importance of his presence to the children. In 1875 she wrote to Helen that Daniel 'often gets tired of waiting for work, tho' he keeps himself pretty fully employed in one way or another, and really I can be with the children so little, that if they had not got a Papa who plays with them so much, and is in every way so good to, and watchful over them, I am afraid they would seriously suffer in some ways'. [17 January 1875.] Henrietta was fundamentally a serious person, and while it must be admitted that she lacked the wit and humour that might have made her seriousness more impressive, the concerns she imparted to her children were not frivolous ones.

It was because Henrietta could not stand the comings and goings in a doctor's house, and the hurry and worry of a doctor's life, that her husband gave up the practice of medicine. There were no difficulties about money. Daniel Moore was now free to devote himself entirely to his children, and this he did, teaching them all to read with the aid of Mrs Mortimer's *Reading Without Tears*. He taught the children to write, and took them through the rudiments of geography, arithmetic and English history. At the age of three, each child was given piano lessons by his father, until it could be determined whether the child had any musical aptitude. Thomas Sturge, the eldest boy, was not considered promising, and his lessons were ended soon after they had begun. But Hettie was thought good enough to go on to receive professional musical training, and it was from his father that George Edward first learned to play the piano.

Though the children were not brought up as Quakers, the Sturge connection was important. Once in a while there were family gatherings, with hundreds of Sturges from all over England; their great-uncle George, with exciting tales of his whaling days, lived only a few roads away from Hastings Lodge; and their mother could remember her famous uncle Joseph, whose life was more exciting than any Henty story. Though Henrietta was too ill to spend much time with the children, their father and nurse were always to be found in the house or in the garden; and with seven brothers and sisters there was always plenty of company. Tom and Hettie were delicate and could not always join in games, but George's rather handsome older brother, Harry, was always available – if one wanted to play with him. The three who were closest, Tom, Hettie and George, tended to regard Harry as a slight misfit. They never knew why this pretty, clever child made them feel uncomfortable: it was easier to see why they felt that way about Annie who, as a half-sister, *was* rather different. Tom and George could not help themselves patronizing the unattractive Annie, who even when she grew up had no chin. Both boys were very fond of Hettie and Nellie because of the robust sense of humour that these girls shared, and of Sarah, perhaps because she was the youngest child of all.

If there is little to distinguish the way the Moore family lived from the way thousands of other Victorian families lived, there was also little in the education and early friendships of the future philosopher to herald his distinction or his importance to his later friends. The principal reason for Daniel Moore's having moved his family to Upper Norwood from Hastings, as we have already remarked, was his wish to send his boys to day school at Dulwich College. It was not then the custom, as it was soon to become, for members of Daniel's class to send their sons to school as boarders. There was even some hostility to the great public schools, perhaps because the nonconformist conscience regarded places like Eton, Winchester, Harrow and Rugby as too 'worldly', or perhaps because of residual anti-aristocratic feeling among members of the prosperous middle class, and a tendency to regard these schools as the preserves of the upper classes. Dulwich had not this defect, for, with the exception of the occasional foreign princeling, it catered to the sons of the professional middle classes who lived in the neighbouring red-brick detached houses.

The founder of the original school was the Elizabethan actor Edward Alleyn. Having established the college, he bequeathed to it his huge estate south of London, and a curious feature of his will was the specification that the headmaster must always bear the founder's name. The result was 250 years of mediocre leadership. Originally Alleyn had established a college on these beautiful grounds for a warden, fellows, a chaplain, almsmen and women and twelve poor scholars. While waiting for Lord Chancellor Bacon to grant the charter he had applied for, however, Alleyn changed his mind, and decided that he wanted a college on the lines of Eton and Winchester. Following a delay of nine years, a charter was granted but, to Alleyn's great annoyance, it was for the college he had originally planned. The founder would not have been pleased at the subsequent turn of affairs at his college. Corruption was rife at Alleyn's College of God's Gift, and the great headmaster of Dulwich in Moore's time, A. H. Gilkes, said of his precursors: 'The Warden and Fellows were of little use in the world; they succumbed often, as many people succumb, to the temptations which beset wealth and idleness; they were apt to be self-indulgent, conceited and quarrelsome, narrow in their views and mean in their proceedings; a poor set of people, well clad and well fed, with a varnish of politeness, but often somewhat rotten at heart.'[1] Worse yet, these luxurious men kept down the number of poor scholars, that they might use the money meant for their education for their own worldly pleasures. This situation prevailed until the mid-nineteenth century when the Charity Commissioners interfered, and caused the constitution of Dulwich College to be changed to its present one.

The grounds of Dulwich were large, and the school is still well supplied with playing fields, so that it looks as lushly green as it did in the seventeenth century. The founder (who gave the first performances of *Tamburlaine* and *The Jew of Malta*, and married as his second wife a daughter of John Donne) would have had his renaissance eye pleased by the full-blown Italianate buildings, with definite Gothic influences and an element that must be eastern, built by Barry. In red brick, with its three blocks separated by gravel squares, Dulwich's architecture, though eclectic, is very much that of the traditional Victorian public school. The college lies in the valley at the bottom of Sydenham Hill and Tom, Harry and George Moore would walk (or more often run) the one mile to and from school twice every weekday, passing through the unusually dense oak-wood on the upper slope of the hill just below their own house. Great importance was attached to games at Dulwich, not least because the facilities for playing them were so splendid. And in other ways Dulwich had all the paraphernalia of the public school – prayers, beating and fagging. But prayers, though compulsory, were of a mild Anglican sort, and full chapel was only once a term; this, and its large proportion of day boys, perhaps accounts for some of the popularity Dulwich enjoyed with dissenting parents. The cane was used sparingly, and seldom by boys on each other. Fagging, the practice of making smaller boys wait upon more senior ones, was entirely confined to the four boarding houses. As at St Paul's, a similar school, it was the day boys who set the tone.

The conventions of this all-boy society in the late Victorian era were brilliantly captured by Sir Compton Mackenzie in *Sinister Street*. His hero, Michael Fane, is at Randell House, a preparatory school for St James (St Paul's), so the setting and the age of the boys are very like those of the Moore brothers when they entered Dulwich.

'Within a fortnight Michael had become a schoolboy, sharing in the general ambitions and factions and prejudices and ideals of schoolboy-hood. . . . He was always ready to lam young boarders who were cheeky, and when an older boarder called him a "daybug" Michael was discreetly silent, merely registering a vow to take it out of the young boarders at the first opportunity. He also learnt to speak without blushing of the gym. and the lav. and arith. and hols. and "Bobbie" Rondell and "my people" and "my kiddy sister". He was often first with the claimant "ego" when someone shouted "quis?" over a broken pocket knife found. He could shout "fain I" to be rid of an obligation and "bags I" to secure an advantage. He was a rigid upholder of the inviolableness of Christian names as postulated by Randellite convention. He laid out threepence a week in the purchase of sweets, usually at four ounces a penny; while during the beggary that succeeded he was one of the most persistent criers of "donnez", when richer boys emerged from the tuckshop, sucking gelatines and satin pralines and raspberry noyau.'[2]

Tom and George Moore, with two other boys who were also brothers, C. J. and W. H. Paton, were the founders and only members of the Boomerang Club which they established in 1883, 'chiefly for *Cricket*, *Tennis*, and *Football*, secondly for *Archery* and *Butterfly* and *Moth Collections*.' They later added the achieving of 'Distinction in *Composition*' to the purposes of the club. We know a great deal about the club's activities, and thus about the ten-year-old George and thirteen-year-old Tom, because one of their activities was the production of a paper called the *Boomerang*, which ran to nine numbers, with each boy writing out his contribution himself. The boys maintained a regular schedule of athletic competitions, and had a rather complicated system for determining the progress and prowess of each of the four; the results were listed faithfully in the *Boomerang*, and from them we learn that George Moore was regarded as a footballer of some promise.

Occasionally the *Boomerang* contains signed notices and comments, like the one by Tom Moore in which he said: 'I wish to say that I would like to see better writing by G. E. Moore, at present it is most disgraceful, he has the least to write and does the worst.' (Even when Tom became the famous poet Sturge Moore, his punctuation still left much to be desired.) Sometimes there is school news, as when C. J. Paton reports that 'next term perhaps we shall either have to wear coat tails or an Eton suit, boys over a certain age or height having to wear the coat tails, and perhaps even mortar boards like the masters'. On 18 June 1884 the club held its first debate, on the subject 'Ancient v. Modern Classics'. G. E. Moore's contribution on behalf of the Moderns constitutes the philosopher's very first published argument and reflections on language.

'(1) I think that French and German, being modern languages, are more useful than Latin or Greek. Latin is not in use and no country takes the Latin language as its language. (2) French is easier to learn at the beginning than Latin. I do not know much about German but I expect it is easier than Greek. French moreover has no cases to put after verbs or special verbs to govern the Dative, Ablative, Accusative etc. French also has persons put to the tenses, je, tu, il, etc. while the Latin has not. As I said before, I do not know much about German so I must not pretend to say much about it.

'French also has words for of, to, etc., instead of the Latin cases, so that if you once learnt what "of" was you would always know if you saw it before a word; but in Latin you would have to know how to decline the whole word to know which part of it had "of" put in. There are also in French no declensions, like in Latin, therefore it is much easier; for in Latin each noun is declined differently to that in another declension, while when you have learnt the word in French, to make the Genitive or Dative case you have only got to put the word before the word you want to translate. There in French too is only two genders, so that a word must be made masc. or feminine, while in Latin there are endings in each declension to learn for the genders. In French certainly there are rules for the gender but nothing like so many because there are no different declensions, and because there are only two genders. Also the adjective has not got to be declined with masc., fem., and neut. in each case and number, like it has in Latin or Greek. There is simply a masculine and a feminine, a singular and a plural. I can't think of anything more, so I will stop now.'

Under these two paragraphs it is recorded that 'for this speech G. E. Moore had 18 marks voted him'. In the next debate, a month later, it was George's task to argue the superiority of football to cricket.

At the age of eleven or twelve, G. E. Moore had an experience that had a great effect on his character and which was of decisive importance for the development of some of his intellectual attitudes. At the seaside town where the Moores had repaired for their summer holidays, the young Moore was converted to the ultra-evangelical views of a group of young men who were conducting what they called a 'Children's Special Service Mission', along the lines of a Salvation Army mission.

Such evangelistic campaigns were not uncommon in the late 1870s and eighties, when the Evangelical Movement was at its height; and it is not so very surprising that the young George Moore responded to the blandishments and arguments of the earnest young men who converted him – the fact that his mother had until fairly recently held views of this sort may have been one factor. Young boys on the verge of puberty, who have had some religious instruction from their parents, quite often sense a disparity between what their parents advocate believing and what they actually believe and do. Sometimes they conclude that the parents are defective in religious zeal. Though Dr Moore still held family prayers every morning before breakfast, and though the entire family still went to chapel twice every Sunday to hear Mr Tipple preach, Henrietta and Daniel Moore's interest in revival meetings and the like had waned. They nonetheless encouraged the children in views which laid much stress on the primary importance of 'the love of Jesus'. What more natural than that young George should feel that 'if all that was said in the New Testament was true, and if Jesus was really the Son of God and was still alive (things which, at that time, I did not think of questioning), then we ought far more often to be thinking of Him, and ought to love Him far more intensely, than most people who professed to be Christians (including my own parents) seemed to me to do'?[3]

George tried to think constantly of Jesus, to love Him, and to adopt as a rule of conduct the practice of asking in all doubtful cases, 'What would Jesus do?' He also felt it his duty, if his convictions were correct, to instil them in other people. So he became a boy preacher, handing out religious tracts and arguing with holiday-makers on the beach. It was these activities that caused him a most painful mental conflict, for he felt it was his duty to convert others to the truth, although he genuinely hated making an exhibition of himself in this way. Added to this there was the chagrin of being observed at these activities by the family of two other Dulwich boys, who happened to be having their holiday at the same place. This was definitely not the sort of behaviour expected of a public schoolboy. Obsessed by the feeling that he always ought to be doing more towards spreading the gospel, but experiencing feelings of shame in doing it, Moore concluded that he was 'very deficient in moral courage'.[4]

It was a feature of this intensely religious period, which lasted no more than two years, that Moore never questioned the theological propositions that underlay the evangelical posture he had assumed; at the same time he believed that if they were true propositions (and it never occurred to him to doubt their truth which, after all, his parents' religious regimen seemed to vouch for), then his behaviour was clearly the appropriate response. His *de*conversion came about through his brother Tom's interest in these basic questions of theology and religious belief. Once he had embarked upon discussions of these issues with his sceptical elder brother, then an art student, his evangelical fervour and even his belief in God melted away in the heat of Tom's arguments. George became an agnostic, for he had neither arguments nor evidence to defend any other position, and certainly not his lately-held evangelical views. This, one may surmise, was a crucial factor in his intellectual development, and one not free of emotional repercussions. Following this religious phase and its dissolution Moore never again tolerated, in himself or in anyone else, any but the most rigorously defended beliefs. From the point of view of his later friends and followers, much of Moore's greatness and attraction lay in his single-mindedness about truth. Moore felt that a man might believe any proposition he could defend; but if a belief were challenged, and the defence not adequate, there was an absolute moral duty to no longer believe that proposition. Psychologically difficult as this might be, Moore – in the opinion of many of his friends – *behaved* in a fashion consistent with this. This was the uniqueness, the strength and the force of his character to which so many testify. It cannot be entirely wrong to see the genesis of this attitude in the thirteen- or fourteen-year-old schoolboy shedding his religious faith; and feeling then, not the shame of doing too little to spread the gospel, but the shame of having believed it without having been interested in the arguments for its truth.

An early religious experience of this kind was not without intellectual utility for a future philosopher. Besides its effect on Moore's passionate views on what might be called the ethics of belief, evangelical religion held an advantage for the development of a philosophical turn of mind. The comparable movement within the established church, the Oxford Movement (which so captured the imagination of Compton Mackenzie's schoolboy hero, Michael Fane), tended to lead the adolescent mind to an interest in incense and ecclesiastical vestments. But the evangelical movement within the nonconformist sects cultivated a habit of mind helpful to the philosopher – introspection, or consulting one's own beliefs in order to establish the truth of some proposition. The habit of examining one's conscience by asking oneself 'What would Jesus do?' is conducive to the frame of mind required to enable one to ask oneself 'What is the right (or the good) thing to do?' And it is only a short step from asking oneself what Jesus would do, to the realization that one is not asking an historical question such as 'What in fact did Jesus do?', but a question that means 'What would Jesus have done in these circumstances?' In the end the reflective adolescent comes to see that he is asking a question, not about the habits, motives or inclinations of an individual, but about general *rules* of conduct and behaviour, and that he is appealing to the idea of Jesus as a perfectly moral human being to give him ethical standards. The proto-philosopher might even see that the question is very similar to the more general question of what is the right thing to do in some particular situation, and that the way to go about answering both questions is the same.

From about the time of the conclusion of Moore's 'intense religious phase',[5] his schooling at Dulwich was specialized in a way that violates every modern idea about education. It is amazing that Moore had any general education at all. As we have seen, his first lessons were given by Dr Moore. Then at the age of eight, he followed his brothers to Dulwich. His education was soon restricted to even fewer subjects, and before he had reached the age of thirteen (by which time his 'agnosticism' was settled), he devoted nearly all his time to Latin and Greek.

Moore moved up the school rapidly, so these last six years at Dulwich were spent entirely in the top two forms, two years in the Classical Remove and the final four in the Classical Sixth. He was captain of the school for his last two years. With the exception of a very small amount of time given to the study of mathematics, French and German, Moore spent nearly all his hours at school translating pieces of English prose and verse into Greek and Latin – he had to submit four of these 'compositions' every week. He thus learnt no science at all and hardly any mathematics.* But he did not, in retrospect, regret the narrowness of his education. For one thing, he became acquainted with a great deal of English literature that he might otherwise never have read; and for another, his interests, which consisted only of music and the classics, brought him into contact with four remarkable teachers. 'Each of them, though very different from one another', Moore wrote, were 'men of unusual originality and force of character, with wide intellectual interests.'[6]

The first of these to be encountered by Moore was E. D. Rendall, the music master. He conducted the school choir in which Moore was 'a

---

* He felt he had little aptitude for this, but years later when he was already an accomplished philosopher, he felt the need to make up for this educational lacuna, and tried to remedy it by attending the lectures at Cambridge of the great mathematician, G. H. Hardy.

little boy with a treble voice', and also the school orchestra; in addition he was 'a fertile composer'. He gave Moore some private voice training, in the course of which he introduced him to Schubert's songs; in Moore's last year at Dulwich, Rendall tutored him in organ-playing and taught him the elements of harmony. Rendall's 'general spirit', Moore felt, opened his mind.[7]

Clement Bryans, an old Etonian and Kingsman, was master of the Classical Remove for both the years Moore spent there. He communicated his enthusiasm for the classics to his pupils, and was a stimulating talker with a keen sense of humour. He did Moore two specific good turns: he undertook to give the form German lessons, so they could read the German commentaries on the classics that he himself admired, and at once put them to work on Goethe and Schiller; and he helped Moore improve his English prose style by lending him Saintsbury's anthology for his holiday reading.

Just before his fifteenth birthday Moore was moved into the sixth form where he was taught by W. T. Lendrum (who later changed his name to Vesey) and by the headmaster, the famous A. H. Gilkes. Lendrum, said Moore, 'was a first-rate classical scholar, both learned and accurate, and having, in addition, a very genuine literary taste.'[8] Lendrum was so fine a scholar, Moore thought, that it was unusual for someone like him to be teaching at a school; and it was more fitting his accomplishments when, in 1890, he was elected a fellow of Gonville and Caius College, Cambridge. Lendrum, an Ulsterman who spoke with a slight Irish twang, 'was fastidious, and quick-tempered, and had very violent dislikes'. His strong feelings about English literature impressed Moore, as did the pains Lendrum took 'to be accurate – to get everything *exactly* right'.[9] Perhaps the master passed this trait on to his pupil in whom it was so famously and conspicuously evident.

But Moore regarded Gilkes, an Oxford man and the only one of his quartet of great teachers who had not been at Cambridge, as the most remarkable person he encountered at Dulwich, although, as a scholar, Moore said, Gilkes was not of the same calibre as Lendrum, and his teaching of the classics could not be compared to the latter's. However, some of the boys thought that Gilkes bore a resemblance to the Platonic portrait of Socrates, and, even in his old age, Moore thought there had been some justice in that youthful exaggeration. Gilkes

'produced the impression of being, in a pre-eminent degree, a *good* man – both good *and* benevolent; although . . . he was capable of extreme severity . . . I have seen him angry, and I am very glad that

I, personally, never excited his anger. But, as was, I think, also the case with Socrates, his goodness was rendered more attractive by its combination with a delicious and subtle sense of humour : he was always ready . . . to make quiet fun of us (or of other things) with a charming delicacy.'[10]

The headmaster's intellectual qualities, which Moore regarded highly, were better shown in the subject called 'Divinity', in which he took the entire sixth form every week, than in his teaching of the classics. The sixth formers had to write an essay every week on the subject of whatever Gilkes talked about in 'Divinity'. Gilkes ranged widely – sometimes the subject was theological, but in Moore's essay book for 1891–2 the subjects are often literary, and even include topics like 'Cosmopolitanism' and 'The use and abuse of athletics'. In a wide sense, Gilkes had, Moore thought, 'a very philosophic mind, though I do not remember to have ever seen any sign that he was interested in the sort of technical philosophical questions, with which I have been chiefly occupied and worried for the greater part of my life.'[11]

There were others, masters and boys, whom Moore remembered from Dulwich, but none who influenced him like the four who taught him – and none with whom he was intimate : 'I was indeed rather lonely at school; but this never made me, to any serious degree, unhappy or discontented'.[12] Loneliness is a recurring theme of Moore's adolescence and young manhood, but he never allowed himself to be swamped by this feeling, and it seems seldom to have followed the normal but painful course where the consciousness of being lonely leads to brooding and melancholy. For this escape Moore had probably to thank the fact that though unable to have the ready-made companionship of a boarding-school, he returned home each day to a large and welcoming family. 'On the whole,' Moore summed up this period of his life, 'I enjoyed my life at school, and was very well satisfied with it; and I left Dulwich with a strong affection both for the school as a whole, and for very many people in it.'[13] Dulwich was not for Moore the life-long obsession it became for that other Old Alleynian, Sir P. G. Wodehouse, but at the very least it left no scars, many pleasant memories, and a grounding in the classics so good that for his first two years there, Cambridge had little to teach him.[14]

In December 1891 Moore went to Cambridge for the second instalment of his scholarship examination. From Whewell's Courts at Trinity he wrote to his mother on 13 December 1891 that : 'I have done a most deplorable thing – I spent 5/8 of the 2 hrs. given us for Lat. Prose in turning the piece into Greek Prose. I managed to do it all into Latin in the rest of the time, but I hear from Mr Lendrum . . . that I ought to have shewn up the Greek too.' He nevertheless won the scholarship, and his last days in the sixth form at Dulwich, in the spring of 1892, must have been as satisfactory as his departure from the school was triumphant. He had done considerable credit to himself and to his masters at Dulwich.

August 1892 saw Moore with his brother Tom for the last extended holiday they would have together. This was also the last time the elder brother would have much influence over the younger. George was about to enter a more rigorous intellectual circle than he had known before, and his future mentors would be more sophisticated than his brother Tom; but they must have had plenty to talk about as they set out on their walking tour in the New Forest.

3
Moore at Cambridge: the First Two Years

Just before his nineteenth birthday Moore went up to Trinity. His brother Harry was already there, so naturally the younger man's first introductions were to the elder's circle of friends. As a freshman, Moore could not live in college, so he took lodgings at 17 St John's Street. His first concerns were of course domestic ones, and in the letter to his mother of 9 October 1892 there is a charming picture of undergraduate domestic life.

'My lodgings are two small angular rooms, with two windows for the sitting-, one for the bed-room. They are in the same house with at least three other sets of rooms, I think, and are on the top-floor. A young man waits on me, though I have seen a woman, who asked me if I wanted tea last night. The other, who seemed more pleasant at first than now, though he is quiet and neat, told me that I must get my tea and sugar, but that they would be willing to supply bread and butter ("commons"), porridge at 2d. the soup-plate, and a large set of meat-dishes at 6d each; he said that very many "young gentlemen" had these hot things for breakfast and merely bread and butter or jam for lunch. My washing will be fetched by the college-laundress on Mondays, quite independently of the Landlady; ... As for lighting, I had to choose between gas and lamp; and I chose the latter, thinking it was better for my eyes. My fire seems to smoke badly with this S.W. wind; but I think I shall like my quarters very well. The sitting-room faces nearly due north, the bed-room N.E. Both are moderately decorated. In the former there is even a small-leaved begonia (Wiltoniensis), standing on an ornamental wicker-table.'

Two men had left cards on Moore in the course of his first day, and he had made the acquaintances of two fellow Old Alleynians; the next day he was to call on Dr Verrall with others of his pupils.

'I hope to join the Trinity Boat Club and the Cambridge University

Musical Society; though the former has an entrance fee of £3.3s. A printed notice from it was left at my rooms, together with some score of others, from a tobacconists, a billiard-suite, tailors', grocers', booksellers', etc., which I had not expected.'

A fortnight later, Moore wrote his mother again, to report that his three guineas investment had paid dividends:

'The strangest news I have to tell you about myself is that I am coxswain to an eight! I had not thought of the possibility of this when I joined the boat-club; but on Saturday week, when I was down at the boat-house waiting to be "tubbed", there was a paper stuck to the door on which all members weighing less than 9 st. 6 lb. were asked to sign their names; on a friend's suggestion, I weighed myself there and then, and found my weight certainly not more than 8 st. 11 lb. On Monday, accordingly, I was engaged by a "coach" to "cox" his eight; I have been out with it now 4 times, and answer, as far as coach and crew are concerned, only to the name of "cox". "Coxing" is very pleasant work; but it does not give the exercise, for which I joined the club, it takes time, and it makes cold instead of warm. However I make up for two of these defects by being tubbed and by running all the way home after my work is over; and I think I shall succeed in keeping an average of 7 hours' "serious work" a day, which Mr Gilkes (and Dr Verrall too, I find) considers ample, so that Papa's fears will be groundless.'

The rest of this letter concerns music – is Moore to sing in Dr Mann's choir or in the C.U.M.S.? He decided on the latter, conducted by a genial Irishman, Professor Stanford. He liked Stanford, whom he saw talking 'very volubly at Hall this evening with Dr Jackson, a fellow of this College, who has a great reputation for knowledge of philosophy, but is very fat, and to me, of a very disgusting appearance'. Concerned about lack of exercise, Moore supplemented his (non-) rowing duties by, he claimed, walking thirty-five miles, starting at seven that morning in late October.

Succeeding letters home are full of rowing news, tea parties, visits to relations in the company of Annie and Harry (there now being three Moore siblings up at Cambridge), and on Guy Fawkes' Day 1892, the day after his nineteenth birthday, Moore breakfasted with his brother Harry, 'after which I shaved for the first time: all my showy moustache is swept away'. [6 November 1892.] The letter written a fortnight later, on the 20th, presents a puzzle. In it Moore apologizes for the brevity of the letter, saying that he must make haste because he wants 'to attend a meeting for the Trinity Mission, at which the speaking is to be about 9.15; . . . I send . . . a letter for Tom and an appeal on behalf of the Mission, to which I think that you or papa may be willing to subscribe; it is probably as worthy as any of the private charities for which collections are made at our chapel.' Attendance at chapel was, of course, compulsory, but as Moore claimed that 'long before I left school, I was, to use a word then popular, a complete Agnostic',[1] it is difficult to see why he *wanted* to attend the meeting for the college mission. One can only surmise that the parental pressure was still strong enough and had enough power to ensure that Moore did more than show the mandatory outward sign of religious observance in attending chapel, and felt that he ought, for the sake of good relations with his parents, to pretend to an interest in the doings of the Trinity missionaries. It was, as has been said, his brother Tom who weaned Moore from his juvenile Theism; but Tom was not at Cambridge, and the brother, Harry, who was up at Trinity with Moore, was genuinely religious – indeed he himself became a missionary for a time, and it must be suspected that he paid some attention to the religious welfare of his brother, as well as reporting on the subject to their parents. It is in the area of religious belief and observance, where Moore is known to have held views that differed from those of his parents, that one would have expected to find the first signs of the undergraduate's rebellion; but there were none, and there was no rebellion. It must be remembered that the year was 1892, and that disrespect to one's parents would have been considered, almost universally, morally worse than compromising one's religious non-beliefs. However, the world and the university too were more tolerant of religious vagary than either had been twenty-three years earlier when Sidgwick resigned his fellowship. There was nothing so terrible in the agnostic attending chapel – nor in his holding a fellowship at a Cambridge college. Religion had lost its sting.

By 1892 the Cambridge Conversazione Society, the Apostles, had been in existence for seventy-two years. Each new member was made aware of its history and its traditions in the most palpable way : by signing the same book in which every earlier member had put his signature, and by being given a membership number consecutive with the numbers of all earlier members.

It was during the week of 20 November that Moore first met a man who was to become a life-long friend, Robert Calverley Trevelyan. Bob Trevelyan had been elected Apostle Number 226 in February, and now, in November, he was already vetting Moore, who had been up little more than a month. Moore had been examined for his scholarship by James Duff (Apostle Number 207), and his tutor was Verrall (Apostle Number 174): these two, following the usual practice of Apostolic recruitment, had probably alerted Trevelyan to Moore's presence, and encouraged him to give the younger man the luncheon at which they first met.

On 4 December 1892 there is more rowing news; the boat coxed by Moore had won a race, and there was a dinner in celebration given by 'bow' in 'two's' rooms.

'Yesterday evening I went to the dinner, though I ought to have had dress-clothes. It was the most sumptuous that I have ever seen – some dozen courses, with champagne, claret, port and lemonade, ornamental menu-cards for each person, plate and flowers on the table, two waiters, and all supplied by the college kitchens. I wonder how much it cost! After dinner I had to open proceedings by proposing the health of the Queen; we presented our gift to the coach – two mugs worth 45s.; and almost all the crew spoke to propose or answer various toasts. After that – most uproarious singing, which I accompanied, reading at sight on the piano; the songs were mostly of the style of those in the Dulwich College 6d. book; but there were some sentimental, and they went as low as one entitled "Wot cher", the tune of which you must have heard in the streets, even if you do not know it by name; it is the greatest rival of Ta-ra-ra Boom de-ay. What was most required was a good opportunity for howling and screeching in the chorus. We broke up about a quarter to twelve; I enjoyed myself!'

Having written this paragraph, Moore must have stopped to reflect on what the religious, ascetic, (and he must have known) neurasthenic Henrietta would make of his riotous undergraduate evening. The memory of his enjoyment, and perhaps the pride this studious nineteen-year-old took in being a member of such a fine, hearty company, was discharged by the writing. He wouldn't take it back, or alter the narrative; but the sentiments of the recipient of the letter ought to be considered before it was posted. Would his mother feel proud of her son? Or disappointed in his willingness to drink heavily and carouse with the rowing men? Very likely the latter, but it was too late to apologize for his enjoyment of the evening. So in the subtle way children have of dealing with a difficult parent, Moore excused the events of the foregoing paragraph by tacking on another:

'I hope that this description may be interesting, as giving you a little more insight into the manners and customs of the undergraduate; I have always to choose what to put into my letters out of almost boundless materials, and if this week's view is somewhat brutal, it is perhaps in turn.'

Shortly after this Moore returned to Woodthorpe to spend the Christmas vacation and probably to face a small amount of Henrietta's displeasure for the use he was making of his time at university. The first letter written after his return to Cambridge reveals a lonely, rather solitary boy, who has had to return before the end of the vacation in order to sit his university scholarship examinations, which if won would expand the value of his scholarship to £100 for five years. There is no rowing, and only solitary exercise to be taken.

The examination was to be sat in the senate-house. In filed a stately procession of examiners, one of whom was Jebb, Apostle Number 145, 'with his stooping head and dandified air of resignation, swinging his left arm far backwards and forward', and there was also the public orator, who kept his head erect and had 'the looks of a king'. One examiner had a 'womanly voice', and Moore suspected, though he was not certain, that it belonged to Jebb. The rest of his letter of 15 January 1893 is trivial – difficulties with transporting his baggage and a walk and game of chess with friends – but the tone seems chastened. Had Moore in fact been reprimanded while at home, and decided to write more prudently to his mother in future? If so, he broke his resolve in the very next letter, written on 29 January, in which he boasts of smoking his first cigarette. He is attending both Verrall's and Jebb's lectures; Jebb's audience has fallen because he lectures only on Saturday and Monday, owing, Moore supposes, to the pressure of his parliamentary duties. The two lecturers' 'methods are very different; but I myself find plenty of interesting matter even in the unattractive Jebb'.

In February Moore shows the first glimmer of an interest in politics. He attended

'a meeting about Toynbee Hall, which was addressed by a London County Councillor, such as I had never imagined. He was a genuine workman, like Tom Mann, but not fiery, or with a strong understanding and great power of speech. He was as simple and gentle, as could be, reminding me very strongly, both by personal appearance and by his way of talking, of Mr Cripps. He was a steady Liberal and Progressive; and I could not help thinking much better than before of the London labourers, seeing that they chose him as their candidate. Indeed the whole effect of the meeting was to make me much more hopeful of social reform. The present London County Council seems to be an exemplary body.' [12 February 1893.]

Moore failed to obtain the valuable university scholarship, and one of the examiners, Dr Butler, told him why: 'He complained, as usual, of my English style and the prosiness of my verse compositions.' [12 March 1893.] He was often in the company of Nairn, who was the senior classical major-scholar of his year, and with another man called Barnett they went to one of Mrs Verrall's at homes, where she talked of her paper to the Psychical Research Society on an experiment to do with identifying playing cards without seeing their faces; the results of the experiment were so positive that Mrs Verrall rather thought that the subjects must have had unusually sensitive touch. Moore's first mention of philosophy is casual: 'I went out to breakfast this morning, and had a long discussion about mind and matter: I cannot understand why mind should not be matter, as I am told that it obviously is not.' And in his next letter to his mother, written on 18 March, there is an equally casual attitude to philosophers: 'Last Sunday evening I was taken to Oscar Browning's at home. I did not get any conversation with him personally; but, most of the time, I was listening to McTaggart, a fellow of Trinity for metaphysics, who is very interesting. One man there played a Nocturne of Chopin's very well.' Browning was Apostle Number 142, and J. McT. E. McTaggart Number 212. On the Friday he met his future mentor again when McTaggart spent an hour trying to explain to Moore 'the metaphysical aspect of "time".' And a complete stranger (whose name Moore did not record), hearing of Moore's plan to walk to London, asked if he might join him. Moore agreed to begin on Tuesday morning at 6.15, and ambitiously informed his mother that she might expect him home to supper.

After Easter he went again to 'O.B.'s' at home, and delivered himself of some very harsh nineteen-year-old's strictures:

'He has a great many very precious things but I am not sure that he is not like a big swine among them: however, his rooms are the resort of the most elegant wits of Cambridge. He has a wonderful musical library; but I saw him play with fingers like flabby sticks and with an even fortissimo through a most delicate pianissimo passage in a duet setting of something by Schubert; yet he seemed more clever in slapping the right notes than I should have expected.' [14 May 1893.]

It was time now to decide about rooms for the next year. Moore was entitled to rooms in college, and he decided on a set in Whewell's Courts, at the rather high rent of £8 per term. His first May week was rapidly approaching, and Moore was disappointed that his sister Hettie felt that she had not enough money to come up to Cambridge for the races, and especially for the concerts, one of which was an organ recital in Trinity chapel to be given by M. Saint-Saëns himself.

Moore's sensibilities were not exclusively musical. He had not, at this time, paid much attention to painting or sculpture, but he was not blind to visual beauty, as this account of a long walk near Cambridge shows :

'There were plenty of birds singing, especially larks, at least one of which was hardly ever out of hearing; wood-pigeons also were very common wherever there were many trees. All the hedges are full of wild roses, white and red, some of which are scented; and the green as yet shows no sign of suffering from the long drought. One of the prettiest features in the landscape were plots of vetch, which make large patches of bright crimson; in one place too there was much of a blue flower, which at a distance produces much the same effect as hare-bells and mingled delightfully with the vetch by the roadside.'

He had attended two concerts that week, and writes very full criticisms of each of them. After the last one he went with Trevelyan into the Backs where they heard the nightingale, and Moore treats its song as critically as he did Mr Santley's rendering of the Erl-König :

'The melody seems to me not at all remarkable; only the quality of the notes, especially a series which she sings at intervals crescendo, and which seem produced by drawing in the breath. It was a beautiful night, cloudless, with half-moon and stars shining.'[28 May 1893.]

There is a great gap in the weekly correspondence until 15 July 1893, by which time Moore is installed for the coming long vacation in his rooms in Whewell's Courts, which he is occupied in furnishing and decorating. This hiatus is the greatest pity, for he suddenly introduces five new friends' names into his letter home : the two Llewelyn Davieses – Crompton (Apostle Number 218) and Theodore (Apostle Number 219) – Bertrand Russell (Apostle Number 224), H. G. Dakyns, and Ralph Wedgwood (Apostle Number 227). Of his six closest friends, with whom he had coffee or tea nearly every day, only Trevelyan had previously appeared in the correspondence. On 15 July the Llewelyn Davies brothers introduced Moore to Robin Mayor (Apostle Number 217), whom he describes as 'nephew of the Latin Professor' and 'a Varsity Scholar of King's'.

Having begun his Cambridge social career by dining chiefly with his brother Harry's friends, Moore's acquaintanceship was broadening out in a perfectly natural way. His first friends were Old Alleynians and people with whom he had common interests, like Harris, with whom he played duets, the rowing men he saw most days during term, or Nairn, with whom he read Greek plays at the C.R.S. It was only at the beginning of the summer term that Moore met most of the men with whom he was to have stronger than casual ties. R. C. Trevelyan, 'Bob Trevy', is the first of these names to occur in Moore's letters, and it must be assumed that he introduced Moore to Henry Graham Dakyns Junior and Crompton and Theodore Llewelyn Davies. With the last, Moore went for a walk at the beginning of the May term in the course of which he suggested to Moore that 'love may be better than knowledge'. This so impressed the younger man that he recalled it as late as 1901 when assembling a chronological list headed 'People I See'; this discussion was surely Moore's first serious introduction to philosophy.

Trevelyan had been elected to the Society in February 1893. Prompted by Duff and Verrall, one of his first tasks was to make the acquaintance of the freshman G. E. Moore, to whom he was closer in age than the Llewelyn Davies brothers and Robin Mayor, who were the next Apostles to be introduced to the new 'embryo'. In the course of the long vacation Moore got to know them very well, along with Russell, who had been an Apostle since February 1892, and with Ralph Wedgwood, Ralph Vaughan Williams and Dakyns, all fellow 'embryos'. Moore had something to say about this time of his life in his autobiography:

'Towards the end of my first year I began to make the acquaintance of a set of young students – most of them a year or two my seniors, both in age and academic standing – whose conversation seemed to me to be of a brilliance such as I had never hitherto met with or even imagined. They discussed politics, literature, philosophy and other things with what seemed to me astounding cleverness, but also with very great seriousness. I was full of excitement and admiration. My own part in these discussions was generally merely to listen in silence to what the others said. I felt (and was) extremely crude compared to them; and did not feel able to make any contributions to the discussion which would bear comparison with those which they were making. I felt greatly flattered, and rather surprised, that they seemed to think me worthy of associating with them. I have said that at Dulwich I never became really intimate with any of the clever boys I met there. At Cambridge, for the first time, I did form friendships with extremely clever people; and, of course, this made an enormous difference to me. Until I went to Cambridge, I had no idea how exciting life could be.'[2]

What then, were Moore's brilliant new friends like? Trevelyan, the first of them, was born in 1872, just over a year before Moore. Second son of Sir George Otto Trevelyan and his wife Caroline, daughter of Robert Needham Philips, Liberal MP for Bury, Bob Trevy was thus the great-nephew of Macaulay: he really was born a little Liberal. He was also much the grandest person Moore had yet met: his mother's marriage to his father had been opposed by her uncle, who intended her to marry a peer; from this uncle her father had inherited Welcombe, the large Victorian house near Stratford-on-Avon, which became Bob Trevy's mother's house in 1889; but the Trevelyan estate, Wallington, at Cambo in Northumberland, inherited by G. O. Trevelyan from Sir Walter Trevelyan, was as large and grand an estate as any Whig aristocrat could wish. Bob Trevy had been brought up at Wallington, with Christmas and sometimes Easter holidays spent at Welcombe. At Wallington the three Trevelyan brothers and their father used the thousands of lead soldiers in the private museum there to play their own family war game. The rules were peculiar to the family, and involved campaigns conducted on a Napoleonic scale; one move could take a whole day, and a battle could last longer than the vacation. The Trevelyan brothers were sent to Harrow, then almost a forcing-house for future Apostles, and as the sons of a friend and a fellow Apostle were treated especially well by the headmaster, J. E. C. Welldon (Apostle Number 185) and by E. E. Bowen (Apostle Number 139), Harrow's own lyricist and the author of 'Forty Years On'. Trinity was also a family institution, as Macaulays and Trevelyans had long been Trinity men, and when Bob Trevy went up in 1891, he no doubt found friends of his own as well as his brother Charles's friends – for Charles Trevelyan's time at Trinity overlapped Robert's by one year. By the time Moore met the second Trevelyan brother, he was established in rooms on the first floor of the south-west angle of the Great Court of Trinity. If the two young men had nothing immediately in common, their ancestors had been associated in common causes and crusades of the past, when the Quaker Sturges sought and found allies in the Trevelyans, who were philosophical radicals, and in the Unitarian Philipses.

When they met, Bob Trevy was reading classics. Although he wrote hardly any verse until he left Cambridge, his approach to the ancient authors was less academic than poetic. But his devotion to them was life-long. Russell thought him the most 'bookish' person he had ever met.[3] In his memoirs Eddie Marsh remembered that

'Bob in those days made one think of a charming young woolly bear, all the more charming for not having been too thoroughly licked. The disorderly riches of his mind, which was a junkshop of wisdom and learning, gushed forth in tentative half-sentences, each apologizing for the one before, running out and retreating like mice in a hole, but sometimes achieving a sudden trenchancy – as in his famous rebuke to Dr Verrall, who confessed at their first meeting that he had never read *The Revolt of Islam* all through : "That's sheer indolence of mind." '[4]

There is a perfect portrait of Trevelyan's conversational manner in Lowes Dickinson's *A Modern Symposium* as the poet Coryat, who when asked by the narrator to make his speech

'responded from the darkness, with the hesitation and incoherence which, in him, I have always found so charming.

' "I don't know," he began, "of course – well, yes it may be all very bad – at least for some people. But I don't believe it is. And I doubt whether Audubon [the last character to have spoken, representing Dickinson's great friend, Ferdinand Schiller] really – well, I oughtn't to say that, I suppose. But anyhow, I'm sure most people don't agree with him. At any rate, for my part, I find life extraordinarily good, just as it is, not mine only, I mean, but everybody's; well, except Audubon's, I suppose I ought to say, and even he, perhaps finds it rather good to be able to find it so bad, but I'm not going to argue with him, because I know it's no use." '[5]

Trevelyan, acting as the Apostles' advance scout, probably introduced Moore next to Crompton and Theodore Llewelyn Davies, brothers who shared rooms at Trinity, and who had had the distinction of being elected to the Society only a week apart. Their father, John Llewelyn Davies, was vicar of Kirkby Lonsdale, a respected scholar who had translated Plato's *Republic* for the Golden Treasury series, a broad churchman and follower of F. D. Maurice (Apostle Number 30). He had six sons, of whom Crompton and Theodore were the youngest, and a daughter, Margaret, who became active in the women's rights movement.* Lady Ottoline Morrell got to know the family fairly well, as she often used to call at the rectory when she stayed with her brother Lord Henry Bentinck at Underly. Walking across the park to Kirkby Lonsdale, she would talk to Mr Llewelyn Davies, who impressed her by having been 'a friend of F. D. Maurice and Robert Browning and even Thomas Carlyle. He was a shy, sensitive, reserved man, and had rather a stiff, dry, unsympathetic manner, but after a time I had broken the outer ice. I found this old man, sitting in his little study, a great solace and very interesting.'[6]

Crompton and Theodore were particularly clever, and according to Russell,[7] the scholarships they won allowed them to go through school and university at no expense to their father. Crompton, born in 1868 and the elder of the pair by two years, was especially good-looking (the whole family were handsome) because of his 'very fine blue eyes, which sometimes sparkled with fun and at other times had a steady gaze that was deeply serious'.[8] Both brothers had been at Marlborough, from where Crompton went up to Trinity in 1887 and Theodore in 1888; each won the Bell Scholarship, Crompton in 1888 and Theodore the next year. Crompton was elected to the Society on 9 November 1889, and Theodore on the 16th. Both got firsts in the classical tripos part I in 1891, and Crompton got his first in part II the same year, while Theodore repeated the performance the next year. When Moore met them, the brothers were working on their prize fellowship dissertations; they were to complete their triumphs by both being elected to fellowships in 1894. Neither was to become resident, however, for they had un-donnish ambitions. Crompton had seen something of the world of practical affairs in the spring of 1892 when he was in India, staying with the Lieutenant-Governor of Bengal.

The Llewelyn Davies brothers were among Russell's first friends. When Russell came up to Trinity in 1890 he was not much used to the company of other young men, and Whitehead (Apostle Number 208), who had been his examiner, arranged for him to meet Crompton and Theodore. One of Russell's first memories of Crompton was of an encounter on a dark and winding staircase in college, where Crompton

* A brother of Crompton's and Theodore's had married the daughter of Du Maurier; J. M. Barrie was very attached to her, and when her husband died the elderly playwright adopted her children. This was of course after the university careers of Crompton and Theodore; but the family was not simply a provincial clergyman's brood, as they seem always to have had strong ties to the world of letters.

spontaneously began to recite Blake's 'Tyger, Tyger, burning bright'. When he finished his recitation, Russell, who had never heard any Blake before, was so overcome that he became dizzy and had to lean against the wall for support.[9] 'Hardly a day passed', wrote Russell in his *Autobiography*, 'without my remembering some incident connected with Crompton – sometimes a joke, sometimes a grimace of disgust at meannness or hypocrisy, most often his warm and generous affection.'[10] Russell regarded Crompton Llewelyn Davies as a sort of external conscience; the mere thought of Crompton's disapproval was sufficient to remove any temptation to be less than honest.

Even those like Russell, who counted Crompton one of his three best friends, thought Theodore the more lovable of the pair. Lady Ottoline thought Crompton 'had his brother's intellect but was more reserved and more intensely passionate. What he did say was always something so sincere and so witty and true that it impressed one.'[11] The difference in the brothers' characters is reflected in photographs of them probably taken sometime in the nineties. Crompton, slim, dark, handsome and heavily moustached, is staring directly at the camera. The blue eyes remarked by Russell are heavy-lidded and surmounted by thickly luxuriant dark eyebrows which arch at the temples. Theodore shares with his brother the firm set of the chin and jaw line. But the overall effect of his photograph is altogether softer. Theodore's eyes, for example, are large and soft, even more heavy-lidded than his brother's, but his eyebrows are lighter and somewhat sparse, trailing off to a thin line above the outer corner of the eye. He is handsome, but in a different way to Crompton, for his face is not oval but rectangular, and for all its softness, more angular than his brother's.

Along with Russell, Trevelyan and the Llewelyn Davies brothers, Moore's immediate circle of friends included Henry Graham Dakyns Junior and Ralph Lewis Wedgwood. Dakyns was the son of a classics master at Clifton, 'a Rugby and Cambridge man, who had been tutor to the sons of Tennyson to whom he had been recommended as the most popular man in Cambridge'.[12] Dakyns Senior was a central figure in the circle of homosexual schoolmasters around John Addington Symonds and had numerous points of connection with the Apostles of the 1880s. Graham Dakyns Senior married in 1872 the widow of a colleague at Clifton College. Their son is something of an enigma : he obviously showed much promise when he was up at Trinity, for it is evident from the company he kept that he was regarded as an 'embryo', a potential Apostle; but his brilliance faded, and when his other friends were working for their prize fellowships, Dakyns was working (it would appear from the letters he wrote to Moore) as an engineer in a factory at Newcastle-upon-Tyne.

Given the fact that their ages were similar, Dakyns and Wedgwood probably had a Clifton College connection, for Wedgwood was head of the school in his time there. He was born in 1874, the son of Clement Francis Wedgwood, master potter, and Emily Rendel. Thus on his father's side Ralph was an heir to the Wedgwood fortune and intellectual tradition, and on his mother's side, he was the grandson of James Meadows Rendel, chairman of the Assam Bengal Railway and expert on Poor Law administration, who married Lytton Strachey's eldest sister, Elinor. He was a very handsome and clever young man when he went up to Trinity in 1892; he made devoted and life-long friendships, and handily got firsts in both parts of the moral science tripos. (In 1906 he married Iris Veronica Pawson, who immediately charmed Moore and became his closest female friend; and Moore took an almost avuncular interest in the doings of their children, John and Cicely Veronica, now Sir John Wedgwood, 2nd Bt., and Dame Veronica Wedgwood, OM.)

Young Ralph Wedgwood 'grew up in home surroundings noted for the benevolent yet youthful attitude of [his] father, for the idyllic relationship which existed between [his] parents, and for the candour and liberal outlook which they inspired, alien to so many contemporary Victorian households', wrote George Dow, Wedgwood's biographer in the *Dictionary of National Biography*. Some of this shows in the attractive openness of Wedgwood's face in photographs. His philosophical ability gave him and Moore a common interest that made their affection for each other even deeper. But in the end it was the Rendel blood in him that showed itself: after distinguished service in the First World War, Wedgwood became a railway administrator, ending his career as Chief General Manager of the London and North Eastern Railway, and becoming first a knight and then a baronet.

This concentration on Moore's friends who were Apostles to the exclusion of a detailed description of his academic studies is justified by Moore's own testimony in his autobiography that during his first two years at Cambridge his new friendships were more important to him than his work. Moore said of his work for part I of the classical tripos:

'In this line, in spite of the brilliance of some of my teachers – especially A. W. Verrall – I do not think that I learned anything startlingly new. I had been so well taught by Lendrum, at Dulwich, that my work during these two years at Cambridge consisted almost exclusively in learning more of the same kind of things which he had already taught me.'[13]

Moore only found his vocation through his contact with his friends, especially Russell, who persuaded him to take part II of the moral science tripos for his second part. Before meeting Russell and the other Apostles Moore had had no interest at all in philosophy :

'I had indeed at Dulwich read Plato's *Protagoras* under Gilkes; but I certainly was not then very keenly excited by any of the philosophical questions which that dialogue raises, and I do not think I had read any other philosophy at all. What must have happened, during this second year at Cambridge, was that I found I was very keenly interested in certain philosophical statements which I heard made in conversation.'[14]

Though he took Russell's advice to do part II of the moral science tripos, Moore also decided to 'study simultaneously for the Greek Philosophy Section of part II of the classical tripos, taking two years for the combined courses'.[15] His philosophy teachers were Henry Sidgwick, James Ward, G. F. Stout and, of course, McTaggart; he read classics with Henry Jackson. All but Stout were Apostles.

In the long run, Moore was to owe a great philosophical debt to Sidgwick. But he did not much appreciate him as a teacher. For one thing, he did not find Sidgwick's personality attractive, and for another, his teaching consisted solely of reading his lectures from finished pieces, 'fit for publication as they stood. I think I could have gained more by reading them to myself than by hearing him read them.'[16] From personal contact with Ward, on the other hand, Moore felt he gained more. He made Moore read Lotze, and lectured to him and a very few others on 'metaphysics', which at Cambridge then included all philosophy except ethics. Ward's lectures were more to Moore's taste – indeed more like what his own were to be later : 'he talked; and, while he talked, he was obviously thinking hard about the subject he was talking of and searching for the best way of putting what he wanted to convey.'[17] Moore admired Ward more than any other of those who taught him, 'partly because of his extreme sincerity and conscientiousness, but partly also because of his melancholy. He was a man who found things very difficult.'[18] Moore thought what Ward once said to him was an appropriate motto for Ward's life : *'Das Denken ist schwer'* – thinking is arduous.

Stout's lectures were on the history of modern philosophy from Descartes to Schopenhauer 'and beyond'. Stout was another teacher who simply talked to the undergraduates sitting around his table, and though Moore felt that he did not yet know enough about philosophy to derive maximum benefit from Stout's lectures, 'he was always interesting and exciting'. Stout, Moore thought, had 'a quite exceptional gift for seizing on some particular point of importance, involved in a confused philosophical controversy, and putting the point in the simplest and most conversational language'.[19]

Moore credited McTaggart with quite a lot of influence on his own work. Most of this disappeared (and with it McTaggart's influence on the rest of the philosophical world) when Moore came to disagree decisively with his teacher's idealism. McTaggart was the youngest of the four men whose lectures Moore attended for the moral sciences tripos, and this was certainly one of the reasons he felt closer to McTaggart than to any of the others. They saw quite a lot of each other 'outside the lecture room'. Though McTaggart gave the impression of being quick and clever, what influenced Moore most was, somewhat surprisingly, 'his constant insistence on clearness – on asking the question "What does this mean?" . . . he himself, in his own philosophical works, did not by any means succeed in being perfectly clear'.[20] In fact, McTaggart's lectures on Hegel, which Moore attended, were themselves notoriously opaque, although ostensibly devoted to clarifying Hegel's obscurity; and Moore did not think McTaggart's exegesis of Hegel bore much relation to Hegel's own doctrines: 'certainly Hegel never meant anything so precise'![21]

Henry Jackson taught Moore Greek philosophy for the second part of his classical tripos. Moore acknowledged Jackson's robust and 'forcible personality'; he could be helpful, as Jackson was on occasion to Moore, but he could also be a dangerous enemy – as many younger men discovered to their cost during the First World War, of which Jackson was a vociferous supporter. To Jackson Moore owed his introduction to the chief works of Plato and Aristotle, but to Jackson's own philosophical opinions, Moore felt he owed 'scarcely anything'.[22]

The interest of Moore's undergraduate career lies, in his own phrase, 'outside the lecture-room'. All clever undergraduates at Oxford and Cambridge learn more from each other than they do from the dons. That is true now and it was true when G. E. Moore, in his second year, was elected to membership of the Cambridge Apostles. Here Moore found his true peers, and to them he was from the beginning more teacher than pupil.

Up to this point the Apostles have been mentioned only briefly, but I have given the membership numbers of those whom Moore had already met before he was elected a member himself. They included his tutor Verrall, his scholarship examiner Duff and Oscar Browning, as well as some of his own contemporaries.

When an Apostle went down from Cambridge, he still kept his links with the Society, as membership was for life. These links spread across England and through the generations. It is possible to trace the overlap and influence of Apostle upon Apostle from the Society's inception in 1820 until today. However, here I shall try to single out and write about only those members who were important to the Society, those who had particular influence, those who enhanced its flavour and those who knew or influenced members who had some connection with G. E. Moore. For instance William Johnson was elected an Apostle in 1844; he is mentioned here because he later taught at Eton and recommended Oscar Browning for election when he went from Eton to Cambridge – and G. E. Moore attended Oscar Browning's 'at homes'.

A likely candidate might be elected an Apostle at about twenty years of age – seldom in his first year. The Society had probably been fore-warned of his intellectual merit by schoolmasters who had been Apostles in their own days at Cambridge. Otherwise a tip might come from an undergraduate's examiner or tutor, or the word might be whispered in the appropriate ear by a boy's father or brother. He was most likely to have come from Eton or Harrow, and to be at either King's or Trinity. Once elected a member he attended weekly meetings, listened to original essays read by other members, discussed these at some length, and later he read papers to his fellow members himself. At these meet-ings he encountered not only his contemporaries but older members as well. The latter might drop in to attend metings at Cambridge, and many came to the annual dinner held in London. Sometimes, too, papers by older members might be read at meetings if a current member had not had time to write one. Older members were also important for the help they could offer when an Apostle had gone down from Cambridge; they were sources of jobs, patronage and contacts. The circle was wide, influential and particularly powerful in politics and the law, in literary London and in education.

Many people – from Lytton Strachey to Jonathan Miller – have credited Moore with inventing the dialectical procedure of clarifying the question to be asked before attempting to answer it. In fact, though Moore may have perfected the technique, he certainly did not invent it – it had been a tradition of the Apostles since at least 1824. Among other general attitudes that have come to be associated with Moore were several that were common to 'Cambridge humanism', and which were shared by Apostles such as Sidgwick, McTaggart and Lowes Dickinson. A belief in rationality and the power of reason was the chief of these. All these philosophers believed that men's minds could be changed by rational argument, and that belief could affect action, so that it was in the power of mankind to decide rationally to follow a certain course of action. This turn of thought was deeply ingrained in Bloomsbury. Indeed, when Keynes in his memoir says that he has come to accept the validity of some of D. H. Lawrence's criticisms of himself and his Cambridge friends, what he means is that under Moore's influence they placed *too much* reliance on reason, and did not allow for such ir- rational phenomena as, for instance, artistic and poetic inspiration.

By looking briefly at the history of the Apostles, we can begin to un- tangle the web of Moore's influence and see how much of what he passed on was Apostolic tradition, what modifications were made to it by his contemporaries, and what was his own, unique contribution. For example, a great many of the ideas of *Principia Ethica* were first developed by Sidgwick – a debt Moore frequently and happily acknow- ledged. And Moore's own papers for the Apostles were the principal vehicle for the development and transmission of his own ideas; it is only by examining them that we can trace the spread of his influence.

BOOK TWO

4
The Apostles

The Apostles, also called 'The Society' or to give that group its proper name, the Cambridge Conversazione Society, was founded in 1820 by George Tomlinson, who later became the Bishop of Gibraltar. The Society was not at first a secret society, and its initial membership was not so distinguished as it was later to become when both its proceedings and its members' names were secret. But from the time of its foundation there were rituals associated with Apostles' meetings. The 'brother' to whom the lot had fallen the previous week would read aloud a paper on an assigned topic. He, as the 'moderator', would read standing on the 'hearthrug', and afterwards lots were drawn to determine the order in which the other brothers would speak. Each took his place on the hearthrug when his turn came to speak. Following this ceremony, a question would be put to the vote; by the mid-nineteenth century the convention had grown up that the proposition to be voted on must not bear an obvious relation to the matter of the evening's paper, but it generally sprang from the paper or the discussion which followed, and the framing of the question often displayed a sophomoric cleverness. 'Whales' – sardines on toast – were consumed with coffee, and the rites were repeated to determine the topic and the reader for the next week.

Election to the Apostles was for life. Whether undergraduate or don, every Apostle was obliged to attend every meeting in term when he was resident in Cambridge. It was possible to be released from this obligation by undergoing the ceremony that came to be called 'taking wings', after which the Apostle became an 'angel' and was free to come to meetings whenever he liked. This practice grew out of an earlier one of bestowing honorary membership on those who were no longer able to attend meetings regularly. Some angels regularly availed themselves of the opportunity of meeting new members, or of inspecting young men, 'embryos', who were being considered for membership. The induction ceremony was called 'birth', and the new member's sponsor sometimes referred to as his 'father'. In its rites, secrecy and neo-Kantian argot that made the society 'real' and the rest of the world 'phenomenal', the Apostles were a typical undergraduate debating club and typically silly. However, through most of its history, this group was distinguished from all other such societies by the outstanding intellectual capacities of its members.

Contact between active Apostles and angels was common, and often beneficial to the careers of younger men. Few brothers who were ambitious for academic posts ever failed to receive them. Early politically well-connected Apostles had included Sir William Harcourt (1827–1904), one of the most important politicians of the last quarter of the nineteenth century. His contemporary in the society was the Hon. Edward Stanley (1826–93), the future Lord Stanley and 15th Earl of Derby, who experienced the signal honour of being offered the throne of Greece. As he held ministerial office under both Disraeli *and* Gladstone, he had considerable patronage at his disposal, and like Harcourt, he tended to find his Parliamentary Private Secretaries from among the ranks of younger Apostles. In the early 1900s an Apostle who aspired to be a writer might be lucky enough to read a paper to an audience which included Desmond MacCarthy.

Tennyson and Hallam were among the Society's most celebrated members, and the famous verses from *In Memoriam* are the first description in print of an Apostles' meeting. Tennyson revisits Cambridge, and comes to the rooms in Trinity of his beloved Arthur Hallam, where he discovers that:

> *Another name was on the door.*
> *I lingered; all within was noise*
> *Of songs, and clapping hands, and boys*
> *That crashed the glass and beat the floor;*
>
> *Where once we held debate, a band*
> *Of youthful friends, on mind and art,*
> *And labour, and the changing mart,*
> *And all the framework of the land;*
>
> *When one would aim an arrow fair,*
> *But send it slackly from the string;*
> *And one would pierce an outer ring,*
> *And one an inner, here and there;*
>
> *And last the master-bowman, he,*
> *Would cleave the mark. A willing ear*
> *We lent him. Who but hung to hear*
> *The rapt oration flowing free*

> *From point to point, with power and grace*
> *And music in the bounds of law,*
> *To those conclusions when we saw*
> *The God within him light his face, . . .*

While somewhat idealized, this is recognizable as a description of a meeting of the Apostles' Society.

The Society was larger in its first decade than it was ever to be again in its history; there were seventy-two members elected in the twenties, whereas for the rest of the century there were never more than thirty-one 'births' in a single decade.

Though the Society was to become, if not anti-religious, militantly non-Christian, those first members of 1820 had a distinctly clerical cast; of the twelve, nine took holy orders. While it must be remembered that the university was not then open to nonconformists, and that dons had to be clergymen to hold a fellowship for more than seven years, this is still a high number. Clearly an interest in religious questions was something the original members had in common. In its first year nine of the Society's twelve members were at St John's College, but several other colleges were represented by the next year, and soon the centre shifted to Trinity, where it has remained ever since, though with stiff competition from King's.

J. F. D. Maurice

In its fourth year, the Society elected, as its thirtieth member, John Frederick Denison Maurice (1805–72), the 'father of Christian Socialism'. He went up to Trinity in 1823, but after seven terms, unsure of his allegiance to the established church which was required of those taking the triposes, he abandoned the normal university course of classics and migrated to Trinity Hall where he sat the civil law classes of 1826–7. He inclined to several sorts of religious heterodoxy, and took the unusual step of continuing his education at Oxford, where he entered Exeter College to prepare to take orders. Maurice settled his doubts sufficiently to be ordained and to accept the chaplaincy of Guy's Hospital, which he held from 1836 to 1846. For part of that time he was also professor of English literature and history at King's College, London, where he lectured from 1840 until his dismissal in 1853 for his unorthodox opinions about eternal punishment. Near the end of his life, the educational establishment, if not the religious one, recognized Maurice's great stature by appointing him Professor of Moral Philosophy at Cambridge in 1866. Always industrious, Maurice found time to write for the *Westminster Review*, the *London Literary*

Chronicle, and the *Athenaeum*, which he edited for a short time; to write his novel, *Eustace Conway*; to issue a flurry of pamphlets on religious controversies; to quarrel with Dr Pusey; and to found the Working Men's College movement.

Maurice had a great effect on the Society; indeed according to his entry in the *Dictionary of National Biography*, he was (with John Sterling) co-founder of the Apostles. And in his official biography, edited by his son, it is remarked that in 1834 'at the annual dinner of the "Apostles' Club" they this year toasted him in his absence three times; first, as the author of the Club itself; second, as having taken orders since the last meeting; third, as the author of *Eustace Conway*'.[1] He was, of course, not the actual founder of the Society, but the meaning of the compliment paid him at the 1834 dinner was clarified in a letter from a later Apostle, Arthur Hallam (at the time of writing, aged nineteen) to W. E. Gladstone: *

> 'The effect which he has produced on the minds of many at Cambridge by the single creation of that Society of Apostles (for the spirit though not the form, was created by him) is far greater than I can dare calculate, and will be felt, both directly and indirectly, in the age that is upon us.'[2]

The intellectual discipline which allowed the Society to survive the nineteenth century and pass on into the twentieth was established by Maurice. In fact, the Society as it existed in the time of Bertrand Russell and G. E. Moore, when membership was often the most important influence on a man's life, was Maurice's creation. The emphasis on sincerity and rationality, the hallmark of the modern Apostles, was introduced by the young man who took the inferior course in civil law to avoid having to affirm or renounce his membership of the established church; in view of the genuineness of his doubt, he was as unwilling to leave the church as to profess to be a member.[3] This action was a compound of conscience and logic. Maurice was not *certain*; he only doubted. Had he been certain, a public gesture would have been required of him. But mere doubt obliged him to keep his silence and sacrifice his own career rather than shake the faith of others. When at last he decided that he could not subscribe to the Thirty-sixth Canon, Maurice did not take his degree in civil law and had his name removed from the college books, giving up the possibility of a fellowship at Trinity Hall.

* During Maurice's brief time at Oxford, the future prime minister fell under his influence and founded an Oxford society modelled on the Apostles. It, or its successor, still exists and is called simply 'The Society'.

He was the first of several Apostles whose religious agonies caused them to take unpleasant practical steps. Subsequently, finding himself able to believe in the dogmas of the church, Maurice not only took orders at Oxford, but recanted publicly and published *Subscription no Bondage*, which was against abolishing subscription to the Thirty-Nine Articles.

The following passage from Frederick Maurice's *Life* of his father describes a Society so much like the later Society and with such strong parallels to what has been called G. E. Moore's 'philosophical method', that it is astonishing to consider that it was written in 1872, the year before Moore's birth.

'Now supposing a youth, educated under conditions which induced him to adopt an unusual set of phrases [namely, the jargon of the Unitarianism of several members of Maurice's family, which Maurice's son compares to public school jargon] to be thrown into intimate association with a great number of young men just at the time of life when anything out of the common is most sure to be freely challenged, what would necessarily happen?

'First, of course, that the exceptional man would have continually to give an account of his peculiar expressions, and would in all probability be forced for the first time in his life to consider what he did actually mean by them. Secondly, that he should begin to ask "for change" for the expressions he found so freely used around him. Thirdly, that having once begun this process and having found that he and others learnt a good deal by it, the thing should become habitual with him.

'Now it happens that this was just my father's case.'⁴

The younger Maurice was not an Apostle, and therefore this account must have been given him by his father's contemporaries in the Society. From what is known of Maurice's sharpness and his fellows' dullness, it is more likely that they acquired this habit of close questioning from Maurice than he from them. And when, much later, G. E. Moore demands of someone that he be precise as to what question he is asking, it is this dialectical tradition of the Apostles that Moore is exemplifying.

John Sterling

The changes Maurice effected in the Society occurred too early in its history to be called a renaissance; but with the help of hindsight it appears to us rather as though the group had only found its true course with the election of Maurice. After him in 1825 came John Sterling, the subject of Carlyle's famous biography, who exemplified that consummate product of the ancient English universities: the man who dies on the verge of middle-age with a brilliant future behind him. Like Brian Howard, Cyril Connolly and Robert Byron, and like many of the characters of Evelyn Waugh's novels, this type achieves fame as an undergraduate and his promise is so great that his fame remains undimmed by his lack of success after his university years. Sterling and Brian Howard fall into this category, as they failed to live up to the expectations the world entertained for them as undergraduates, but there were also those like Arthur Hallam, Julian Bell and John Cornford who died so young that there were few achievements to be assessed. But they are all essentially variants of the same character, a character well represented in the Apostles. This was bound to be the case, for an undergraduate's promise was the chief criterion by which he was evaluated for membership.

After Cambridge, Sterling looked to a career in public life as the likeliest avenue to worldly success and fame, and after a very brief time as secretary to an association promoting the opening of trade with India, he embarked upon literary journalism. With his fellow Apostle F. D. Maurice, he purchased in 1828 the copyright of a literary paper, the *Athenaeum*, and for a short time its contents were distinctly improved. Commercially Sterling's management of the paper was not a success; but his position as its editor launched him, a fledgling of twenty-two, into the centre of London literary life. At his lodgings in Regent Street, Apostles would meet John Stuart Mill and Sterling himself would frequently call upon Coleridge in his lodgings on Highgate Hill.

Sterling was ordained a deacon in the Church of England, he published a novel, wrote some poems and reviews, travelled for his health and married. From his life and non-career, two interesting points about the Apostles emerge: first that many Apostles of his time maintained their contacts with each other throughout their lives; and secondly that Sterling introduced many of his fellow Apostles to literary London. He was at the centre of a web of contacts between former Apostles and some of the leaders of the cultural life of the country.

One way in which Sterling served to introduce his fellow Apostles to a wider world was his foundation of a dining club in 1838. First called the Anonymous Club, its name was soon changed to honour its founder. James Spedding (Apostle Number 67), its secretary, wrote to William Bodham Donne (Apostle Number 56):

'Sterling has been endeavouring to get up a club which is to exist for the purpose of dining together once a month. The dinner is to be cheap, the attendance not compulsory, the day and the place fixed, and the members chosen unanimously from the witty, the worthy, the wise and the inspired – and it is hoped that the Society will sooner or later combine within itself as much of the wit, worth, wisdom and inspiration of the age as can live together in Apostolic harmony.'[5]

The Sterling Club aimed to introduce the benefits of the Cambridge Apostles to a larger public.

Later Maurice, who had first refused membership, joined; and eleven years after its foundation, with a membership of seventy or eighty, the club became embroiled in controversy over the late John Sterling's personal views, and acceded to Maurice's wish that it change its name; thereafter it was known as the 'Tuesday' or 'Dinner' club.[6] It was a remarkable group that Sterling had gathered around him, including artists, writers, statesmen and the two greatest English thinkers of the day, Carlyle and John Stuart Mill.

Tennyson, Hallam and the Early Victorians

The Society's Georgian period was unremarkable, most of the clever young men chosen becoming lawyers, divines or politicians of no great importance, until the election in May 1829 of Arthur Hallam, whose early death has made him a legendary figure to readers of English poetry: it is 'Tennyson and Hallam' who are mentioned most often as forbears in the memoirs and biographies of later brothers. Tennyson's assertions that he 'seemed to tread the earth as a spirit from some better world' and that he was 'as near perfection as mortal man can be', were not untypical of the feelings of those who had known him, but during his lifetime he received more affection than praise.

Hallam read five papers to the Apostles; won the declamation prize; and, grim omen of *In Memoriam*, edited a reprint of Shelley's *Adonais*. After going down from Cambridge, he prepared for a career as a chancery barrister, and began to translate Dante's *Vita Nuova* and the sonnets, but never finished because of his sudden death in Vienna at the age of twenty-two. Gladstone's epithet on him was: 'All comprehensive tenderness. All subtilising intellect.'

Thus far in sketching the history of the Apostles, there has been little reason to raise the question that was to become, much later, of such importance to the Society – that of homosexuality. Tennyson's contemporaries were not slow to put a homosexual construction upon his poem about Hallam: Charles Kingsley found precedents for the friendship in those of Jonathan and David, Damon and Pythias, Socrates and Alcibiades, and Shakespeare and the young man addressed in his sonnets.[7] Benjamin Jowett also raised the issue of Shakespeare's sonnets, and sailed so close to the wind that Tennyson's son felt compelled to trim Jowett's remark for his memoir of his father, to prevent misconstruction.[8] Professor Ricks tells us that, when in 1839, Henry Hallam, Arthur's father, deplored the passion depicted in the sonnets, he may have been delivering a hint to Tennyson concerning *In Memoriam*; Tennyson seems to have understood this when he said: 'Henry Hallam made a great mistake about them: they are noble.'[9] Brian Reade, in his anthology, *Sexual Heretics: Male Homosexuality in English Literature from 1850–1900*, is convinced of the sexual nature of Tennyson's passion for Hallam and of his poem, and he points out[10] that *The Times* reviewer at the time of the poem's publication in 1850 seemed to have thought the same thing. Professor Ricks quotes from the same review (which may have been written by Gerard Manley Hopkins's father) as evidence that the poem was received as homosexual. The reviewer complained that he found in the poem 'amatory tenderness', and asked of some verses (in LXXIV), 'who would not give them a feminine application?'.[11] As Professor Ricks points out, this rather vitiates the usual defence of Tennyson, exemplified by Professor Gordon Haight's reference in his biography of George Eliot: 'The Victorians' conception of love between those of the same sex cannot be understood fairly by an age steeped in Freud. Where they saw only pure friendship, the modern reader assumes perversion. . . . Even *In Memoriam* for some, now has a troubling overtone.'[12] *The Times*' reviewer was not steeped in Freud; nor was Tennyson's son, Hallam Tennyson, when he edited the memoir of his father in the 1890s and attempted to suppress any hint of homosexuality. The Apostles of the generation of Strachey and Keynes, who, if not exactly steeped in Freud, later became familiar with his views, assumed that the relationship of Tennyson and Hallam was homosexual. But then Strachey and Keynes found homosexuality everywhere, and were particularly pleased to think that the Society should have a homosexual tradition.

It is unlikely that we shall ever know whether the relationship of Tennyson and Hallam was homosexual in any way we would now recognize, but from the point of view of those Apostles immediately after Moore, it either provided a tradition of homosexuality or at the very least provided them with a pretext for inventing such a tradition. Tennyson was on the Society's books only from 31 October 1829 until 13 February 1830, when he resigned because he could not bring himself to read his paper on 'ghosts'.[13] In the memoir, Hallam Tennyson tells us a bit about the sort of topics debated by the Apostles in his father's time:

> 'Three questions discussed by the Society were: (1) Have Shelley's poems an immoral tendency? Tennyson votes "NO". (2) Is an intelligible First Cause deducible from the phenomena of the Universe? Tennyson votes "NO". (3) Is there any rule of moral action beyond general expediency? Tennyson votes "Aye".'[14]

The Victorian age had begun in name as well as in fact by the summer of 1841, when the young queen had been on the throne exactly four years, and the Society was twenty years old. It had survived long enough for all its members to regard it as a permanent institution and to treat it with reverence and respect. But the early brilliance of the Apostles had been succeeded by a decade of dimness. Indeed the brothers were having trouble in upholding any of the Society's traditions. Perhaps they felt their inferiority to the brothers of the past or perhaps they felt that religious controversy was less important, for they now widened their field somewhat and looked more to future lawyers and schoolmasters and less to future divines.

The first Victorian member to become distinguished was the legal historian Henry Sumner Maine, and he was followed by the famous schoolmaster, William Johnson. Maine later encouraged many legal luminaries to be chosen for the Apostles, and Johnson was one of the first manifestations among the Apostles of the brilliant homosexual schoolmaster, a major strand in the membership which was to run from the 1840s right through to modern times with its peak in the 1880s. In the early period many of these headmasters and housemasters were post-Arnoldian stalwarts; later they were to link up with the Bohemian homosexual literary life of London and the decadent and aesthetic worlds of John Addington Symonds, Simeon Solomon, Walter Pater and Swinburne.

Johnson came to King's via the usual route of Eton and is best known to history as the author of the 'Eton Boating Song'. On graduation he became an assistant master at Eton, which post he held, as was usual, in conjunction with a fellowship at King's, for twenty-seven years. These connections were terminated abruptly in 1872, when he also changed his name by deed poll to Cory. This was almost certainly because of a homosexual scandal involving two of his aristocratic pupils, the future Viscount Halifax and the future Lord Rosebery. Cory contributed a great deal to Eton and King's and was later influential in making Oscar Browning an Apostle. Browning was also to be a schoolmaster at Eton and a don at King's; indeed, as we have seen, he was still active in Cambridge when G. E. Moore came up.

The Society now entered one of its vigorous periods with nearly a full complement of clever young members. They had become fairly unpolitical and solidly middle-class, but now the brothers changed course, and began electing young men from less bourgeois and more sophisticated families. In consequence, the Society had as members several future politicians.

The policy of recruiting from among the sons of the aristocracy and sophisticated upper middle class seems to have taken firm root by 1847, when the Honourable Edward Stanley was elected. He was to hold high office, being Secretary of State for India and Foreign Secretary under Disraeli. In his elder statesman years when he had succeeded to the title of the 15th Earl of Derby, honours were heaped upon him and he became successively Lord Rector of the universities at Glasgow and Edinburgh, and finally Chancellor of the University of London: an example of an Apostle with a powerful, wide-ranging career who fully justified his early promise.

Elected a week after Stanley and also from a political family was James Fitzjames Stephen, the elder brother of the better known Leslie, father of Virginia and Vanessa. Curiously, the younger brother, Leslie, was not made an Apostle. This inexplicable bias against the cadet branch of the Stephens was maintained for two generations: J. F.'s son, J. K. Stephen, was elected but his cousin, Leslie's son Thoby, though handsome, charming and brilliant, was not.

Stephen's career culminated in a high court judgeship. Besides his extremely distinguished legal career, he was a prolific journalist, contributing to *Fraser*, the *Cornhill*, *Pall Mall Gazette* and the *Saturday Review*, which was largely the product of former Apostles, and one of the most brilliant of Victorian weekly magazines.

The *Saturday Review of Politics, Literature, Science and Art* first appeared in November 1885, partly to combat the influence of *The Times* and partly to give some occupation to A. J. B. Beresford Hope who had inherited a vast fortune from his step-father. Beresford Hope engaged John Cook as a professional editor and encouraged him to recruit Cambridge men to contribute articles. Cook recruited Maine who in turn introduced two fellow Apostles, Vernon Harcourt and Fitzjames

Stephen. Beresford Hope then recruited his former tutor at Trinity, J. W. Blakesley, who was also an Apostle. In all, six Apostles contributed to the first number of the *Saturday Review*. Soon the Apostles controlled the paper and in it they put over their common views and causes. But reading through the various numbers, it appears to be old-boy ties which brought them all together, rather than uniformity of opinion, although they did have many social and political views in common. The *Saturday Review* was sometimes used to further the careers and interests of older Apostles, and the younger men seem to have used the paper less as a pulpit than as a rung on a very worldly ladder.

Henry Sidgwick

In the academic year 1856–7 the Apostles made two elections of great importance to the future direction and character of the Society. The first of these was to be the most influential Apostle between F. D. Maurice and the advent of G. E. Moore: Henry Sidgwick (1838–1900). Sidgwick (Apostle Number 138) was born in Yorkshire and attended Rugby school where, although he disliked and had not the physical aptitude for games, he proved himself a prodigy at his studies. When he went up to Trinity in October 1855, Sidgwick had little ambition save to succeed in his examinations and become a fellow of his college. But on 15 November 1856 he was elected to the Apostles, an event, said Sidgwick in an autobiographical fragment, 'which had more effect on my intellectual life than any one thing that happened to me afterwards'.[15] The Society had then been in existence thirty-six years, 'old and possessing historical traditions', but it lacked exuberance and perhaps vitality too. The traditions of the Apostles, though, had not been lost in the slough of mid-Victorian complacency; the zeal of the early Apostles might have diminished,

> 'but the spirit, I think, remained the same, and gradually this spirit – at least as I apprehended it – absorbed it – absorbed and dominated me. I can only describe it as the spirit of the pursuit of truth with absolute devotion and unreserve by a group of intimate friends, who were perfectly frank with each other, and indulged in any amount of humorous sarcasm and playful banter, and yet each respects the other, and when he discourses tries to learn from him and see what he sees. Absolute candour was the only duty that the tradition of the Society enforced. No consistency was demanded with opinions

previously held – truth as we saw it then and there was what we had to embrace and maintain, and there were no propositions so well established that an Apostle had not the right to deny or question, if he did so sincerely and not from mere love of paradox. The gravest subjects were continually debated but gravity of treatment, as I have said, was not imposed though sincerity was. In fact it was rather a point of the Apostolic mind to understand how much suggestion and instruction may be derived from what is in form a jest – even in dealing with the gravest matters.'[16]

Sidgwick had formed the ambition to take both the classical and mathematical triposes – no mean feat even then, as they had to be sat within a few weeks of each other, and could not, therefore, be prepared for at separate times. When, after many visits to his rooms by relative strangers vetting him for the Society, he was finally asked to join, he was reluctant to accept the invitation, as he was worried about the effect a standing engagement for every Saturday night might have on his tripos preparations. Sidgwick did join, however, and his member-ship in the Apostles not only put the triposes into perspective, but fired in him new intellectual ambitions.

'After I had gradually apprehended the spirit as I have described it, it came to me that no part of my life at Cambridge was so real to me as the Saturday evenings on which the Apostolic debates were held; and the tie of attachment to the Society is much the strongest corpor-ate bond which I have known in life. I think, then, that my admission into this society and the enthusiastic way in which I came to idealize it really determined or revealed that the deepest bent of my nature was towards the life of thought – thought exercised on the central problems of human life.'[17]

It was thus that Sidgwick became the most important moral philosopher between Mill and Moore. But he did get his double first anyway – as 33rd Wrangler and Senior Classic* in 1859, and crowned this achieve-ment by also becoming first Chancellor's medallist. He was immediately elected into a fellowship, and remained active in the Apostles for over five years, until November 1865. Sidgwick put a good deal of emphasis on what membership of the Apostles did for him; the benefits he con-ferred on the Society can be measured by the fact that in nine years of

---

* In Cambridge terminology, men who got firsts in the mathematics tripos were called Wranglers. The Senior Classic was the best first in the classics tripos. Internal rankings in class lists persisted until the turn of the century.

membership he read thirty-two papers, more than one each term. He also served as twenty-eighth secretary. Sidgwick was in fact to remain at Cambridge the rest of his life and continued to attend the Society's meetings and to influence new generations of its members. As Moore readily remarked, many of what were hailed as the most original ideas in *Principia Ethica* actually had their source in the works of Sidgwick.

In his autobiographical fragment, Sidgwick lays great stress on the orthodoxy of his religious views, even when he was most under the influence of J. S. Mill. It was not until he began reading Renan in 1862 that he first experienced religious doubt. By 1869 he had become agnostic, and no longer felt he had the right to keep his fellowship, as college fellowships were closed to any but those who professed the established religion until, two years later, parliament passed the Test Act of 1871. He resigned, but kept his lectureship in moral sciences until 1875 when he was made Praelector of Moral and Political Philosophy, and eight years later Knightsbridge Professor of Moral Philosophy; in 1881 he was made an honorary Fellow of Trinity, and in 1885, sixteen years after his resignation, resumed his ordinary fellowship. In fact Gladstone's decision to abolish religious tests had been influenced by Sidgwick's resignation. It was also an event of great importance for the Apostles. In spite of the great number of future clergymen whom the Apostles had always had among their members, there had been times in their history when religious questions had not much interested the group. There had even been brothers, such as Maurice, who departed from orthodoxy and suffered the consequences; but it was Sidgwick's resignation of his fellowship that marked the beginning of the non-religious strain in the Society. With suitable irony, future generations of Apostles would refer to Sidgwick as their Pope.

Sidgwick was a proponent of every sort of university reform, including the admission of women. Accordingly he supported a scheme for providing lectures for girls at Cambridge, which culminated in the opening of Cambridge's second women's college, Newnham Hall, in 1876, the year in which he married. His wife was Eleanor Mildred Balfour, sister of the future prime minister; she became President of Newnham in 1892. By 1881, Sidgwick had carried his point and women were admitted to the university and permitted to sit examinations. For two periods, from 1882–5 and 1888–93, Sidgwick was President of the Society for Psychical Research, which led to his interest in what were considered fraudulent experiments, and to an acquaintance, unusual for a Cambridge don, with the theosophist, Madame Blavatsky. Nonetheless, as there was a fad for para-psychology in Cambridge and London at the time, neither the one nor the other much damaged his philosophical reputation.

Oscar Browning

In 1857 there burst upon the Apostles a hurricane in the shape of Oscar Browning (1837–1923). O.B., as Browning was often known, maintained a lifelong connection with the Society and introduced many of its members to the wider world beyond Cambridge. Just as he was a prime mover in the making of the modern King's College, so he guided the Apostles' move from one era into another. The son of a Buckinghamshire brewer, Browning's connection with Eton began in January 1851 when he entered that school as a colleger. His tutor was William Johnson (Apostle Number 112). As a schoolboy, he conceived literary ambitions that were to endure, without satisfaction, his whole life long. He was not happy at Eton; by contrast the years at King's were bliss. In his autobiography, *Memories of Sixty Years*, he wrote that while he was instructed at King's, 'education was given me at Trinity. Here I found a cultivated society devoted to intellectual aims, respecting each other and themselves, courteous, affectionate, and dignified.'[18] When many years later O.B. returned to King's, he resolved to make over King's in this image, and to some extent he succeeded in doing so. The picture he gives of King's in 1856 is noteworthy :

'As I have before said, the new men of our years came up to King's with the consciousness of beginning a new era. We had no respect for those who had preceded us, and I am bound to say that they did not deserve respect. Their morals were loose, but better than those of an earlier generation; they had little care for intellectual pursuits, their talk was of the sport, in which they imagined, or tried to make others imagine, they had spent the vacation. I confess that I was a conceited prig. . . . The by-laws of our society were peculiar. Although we were all Etonians, any mention of Eton at the dinner table was forbidden, and was punished by social ostracism. I was naturally ambitious, was anxious to make my mark in the University, especially at the Union, this wounded my fellow students in their tenderest part; I was solemnly warned that if I continued to speak at the Union I should be sent to Coventry. I did continue to speak, and the penalty was inflicted.'[19]

The union was important to him for it was there he met the men who gave him entrée to Trinity and the Apostles. There had not been an

Apostle from King's for fourteen years before his election, and that single brother from King's was O.B.'s unfortunate tutor William Johnson. O.B. subsequently became president of the union, the first Kingsman to hold the office for nineteen years.

In the spring of 1860 he returned to Eton where he flourished for fifteen years. His actual work of teaching the classics to his students he seems to have performed perfunctorily while, to the anger of the old Eton party, he set about the reform of Eton. He introduced his pupils to the study of history and English literature, and he opposed the undue emphasis on athletic pursuits. His personal fortune also flourished, for a master at Eton in those days could make between £2,000 and £4,000 clear profit from his house. In his house, however, boys were well fed and watched over with a civilized attention to physical comfort. Unfortunately, O.B. took a personal interest in them also, and by 1874 he was forbidden by the Headmaster, Dr Hornby, to have any intercourse at all with the boys, especially George Nathaniel Curzon, the future Viceroy of India. O.B. ought to have been more careful, for he had before him the example of William Johnson.

Dismissed from Eton, O.B. resumed his fellowship at King's, but at enormous financial loss; not only was his mother's position as house matron and hostess now gone, but his income fell from £3,000, to £300, the amount he formerly spent every year on his library alone. Yet on his return to Cambridge he immediately created for himself the style of life that made him a legend – the most famous don of his day at Oxford or Cambridge.

E. F. Benson, the author of the 'Dodo' and 'Lucia' books, writes in his delightful *As We Were*, that O.B. 'was a tragic instance of such stupid jokes as nature plays when, after she has formed by means of cosmic pressures and secular incandescences some noble gem, she proceeds with a silly giggle to plant a fatal flaw in the very heart of it. He was a genius flawed by abysmal fatuity.'[20] On taking up his life-fellowship at King's and receiving an appointment as a lecturer in history, he proceeded to design and construct institutions devised to facilitate contact with the undergraduates. On Sunday nights King's was filled with O.B.'s guests: dons and undergraduates from other colleges, musicians, literary men, even 'sporting gents from the Athenaeum', as well as handsome sailors and blacksmiths' lads. And, of course, there were Apostles.

While O.B.'s interests in the working classes were often of a sexual nature, he did perform many acts of kindness to individuals not so fortunate as to be undergraduates, and he was popular with the workers in the constituencies where he stood as a parliamentary candidate. He believed education to be a crucial factor in the social and economic mobility of the underprivileged, and for better or for worse, he pioneered the teacher training movement, becoming the first principal of the Cambridge Day Training College.

Moore's was nearly the last generation of Apostles directly influenced by the social mannerisms and political radicalism of O.B. For in his later days at King's O.B., says E. F. Benson, 'could no longer acquire information through the medium of speech; he could only soliloquise'.[21] His effect on King's and the university was considerable, in that it led to greater respectability for the study of history and politics; but he was not a good teacher. By his friendships, his often outrageous behaviour and his style, however, O.B. gave to G. E. Moore and his contemporaries a taste of the 1890s, as those years were experienced in London literary circles.

A rising star at the union had come to the attention of the Society, and, almost as soon as term began in October 1859, George Otto Trevelyan was elected to the Apostles. He had come up to Trinity in 1857 from Harrow, and later he distinguished himself in politics and as an historian of note. In the next generation two of his three sons were elected Apostles and were contemporaries of Moore's. G. M. Trevelyan wrote a delightful passage in his memoir of his father. After listing his father's friends, he says:

'Most of them were members of the Apostles society. At that time Henry Sidgwick, with his eager thirst for the impartial truth on all subjects was its heart and soul. My father, though a more exotic philosopher, was proud and happy to attend its meetings.

'This group of Cambridge friends was not a mutual admiration society; a society for mutual criticism would be nearer the mark of description; strong individualists, with nothing in common but the Victorian attitude towards life and morals, and the liberal attitude towards moderate reform usual among young university men in the sixties, each carved out his own path in the world towards an ideal chosen by himself, and each spoke his mind freely in criticism of the others without the least danger to friendship. My father's gifts as a young man were such that too easy admiration from his closest college friends would have been very dangerous; he never got it and he never sought it.'[22]

The Later Victorians

The Apostles were now entering upon a new golden age, comparable, perhaps, to that enjoyed by the Society when Hallam and Tennyson were members. Their discussions during the mid-sixties were dominated by the arguments that followed the publication of two books in 1859: Mill's *On Liberty* and Darwin's *Origin of Species*. The publication of these books was an intellectual watershed, and the intellectual streams of the rest of the Victorian age were to flow from them. The sixties constituted a period of transition between the unsettling of certain early-Victorian fixed attitudes about society and religion, and the final rejection of these 'settled creeds' in the seventies, when they were replaced by the sort of liberal posture the Apostles had assumed for generations.[23] The intellectual climate, largely created by members of the 'Intellectual Aristocracy', was growing more congenial to the Apostolic mind – some of the new warmth being due to the intellectual labours of earlier Apostles as scientists, philosophers and liberal scholars and theologians. Mill and Darwin were not themselves members of the Society, but Henry Sidgwick was a disciple of Mill and, though the early clerical Apostles seemed to have passed over Charles Darwin for membership, they did elect his brother Erasmus. (In the same way those dim Apostles of earlier days had failed to elect Macaulay, but did choose his much less illustrious cousin, Kenneth.)

By 1863 the battle of the evolutionists against the creationists had been joined by the publication of Huxley's *Man's Place in Nature*, with its 'popularization' of Darwin. And in 1864 Charles Kingsley slandered Newman in his review of Froude's *History of England*, prompting Newman to respond with his *Apologia pro vita sua*. It was an exciting and creative time: Arnold, Browning, Carlyle, Dickens, Mrs Gaskell, George Eliot, Huxley, Meredith, Spencer, Tennyson, and Trollope all published in 1864; and posthumous works of Praed and Thackeray appeared. In poetry something quite new was happening. George Meredith published *Modern Love* and three years later Swinburne published *Atalanta in Calydon*. (Moore was an avid Meredithian and closely annotated his own volumes of Meredith, especially the verse.)

Spring 1865 saw the election of Frederick Pollock, a man of stature equal to that of the greatest Apostles of the past; indeed many thought him the most comprehensively learned man of his time. An authority on contract law and equity, he also wrote a life of Spinoza before becoming Professor of Jurisprudence at Oxford at the early age of thirty-eight. A succession of legal posts and honours followed, as did a flow of important books. Pollock's approach to the law was deeply philosophical: it was his ambition to define the nature of legal concepts, and he succeeded in encouraging the study of jurisprudence and conferring new prestige on the law itself. Later he got to know G. E. Moore and sent him perceptive comments on *Principia Ethica* when it first came out, showing that the dialectical reasoning in which Moore's argument was couched was well-known to him.

November 1865 was a momentous time for the Apostles, for their 'pope' resigned. Almost exactly nine years after his election, Henry Sidgwick, Moore's teacher and philosophical mentor to whom he was to owe so much, 'took wings'. The remarks that F. W. Maitland (Apostle Number 182) made about Sidgwick as a teacher are, with almost no qualifications, applicable to the role he played in the Society.

> 'I believe that he was a supremely great teacher. In the first place, I remember the admirable patience which could never be out-worn by stupidity, and which nothing but pretentiousness could disturb. Then there was the sympathetic and kindly endeavour to overcome our shyness, to make us talk, and to make us think. Then there was that marked dislike for any mere reproduction of his own opinions which made it impossible for Sidgwick to be in the bad sense the founder of a school. I sometimes think that the one and only prejudice that Sidgwick had was a prejudice against his own results. All this was far more impressive and far more inspiriting to us than any dogmatism could have been. Then the freest and boldest thinking was set forth in words which seemed to carry candour and sobriety and circumspection to their furthest limit.... I believe that no more truthful man than Sidgwick ever lived. I am speaking of a rare intellectual virtue.'[24]

These were the qualities Sidgwick displayed in his intellectual leadership of the Apostles. Some of these traits he no doubt developed from his own membership of the Society, others were Sidgwick's contribution to remaking the traditions of the Apostles. His formal resignation did not of course mean that he ceased altogether to attend Saturday night meetings; it simply exempted him from the obligation to attend every meeting that took place while he was in residence. As Sidgwick did not actually leave Cambridge at all, future generations of Apostles were to be enriched by his influence.

The first three new members elected by the Apostles in 1873, in their bid to bolster up their numbers and morale, did not have very extensive or long-lived contact with the group, but the next newcomer was one of those devoted and conscientious members, who, making his career at Cambridge, influenced generations of Apostles to come. He was Arthur Woolgar Verrall (1851–1912), who was to become a celebrated scholar and tutor to G. E. Moore. The importance to him of his election to the Apostles has been recorded by his memorialist:

> 'One event, which occurred early in his University Career, he spoke of at the time as "the best thing that ever happened to me in my life". This was his admission to a private but not obscure society, consisting of graduates and undergraduates, which met and still meets, for intimate discussion of any and every subject. Dating at least as far back as the time of Tennyson, it counts among its members, I believe, many of Cambridge's most distinguished men, and Verrall always considered that he owed more to his membership of this "glorious company" than to any other influence of Cambridge life.'[25]

Verrall's contribution to raising the Society from its slump can be measured by the fact that he read nineteen papers in his six years of active membership, and he never ceased attending the Society's meetings so long as his health permitted.

He became one of Trinity's most illustrious lecturers, and pioneered a movement in the teaching of the classics that is so universal today that it seems hard to believe that the practice was different only a hundred years ago: this was the treatment of classics as literary works of art, rather than texts in a dead language presenting various problems of scholarship. Verrall's sense of what made for drama was evident in his famous editions of Euripides and Aeschylus, and it is today hard to realize that those who listened to his lectures on those writers' works were startled to hear the lecturer attack various cruces and suggest emendations on the grounds that a solution was to be preferred if it enhanced the dramatic action of a play. It is perhaps to Verrall's new treatment of the classics that we today owe the many splendid productions of them that we are privileged to see even in our commercial theatre. The man who introduced literary criticism alongside textual criticism in the teaching of the classics was an obvious choice for the first chair in English literature at Cambridge. This Verrall was offered, and in spite of being crippled with arthritis, he accepted in 1911 the King Edward VII Professorship of English Literature.

Wit informed all Verrall's talk in the lecture room or at the dinner-table, and he was, according to so competent a judge as Lytton Strachey, a great conversationalist. Verrall's influence on the Apostles was a curious one: he had no taste for the sort of metaphysical speculation so characteristic of the Society's discussions, and always preferred consideration of the concrete to that of the abstract question. Further, as his friend Bayfield wrote, 'he was not, by modern standards, a very learned man; he knew the ancient writings that deserve to be called literature up and down, but he was a little impatient when he was made to attend to archaeological lore. Not of course, that he either despised or neglected it; but his private name for it was "stuffage".'[26] In what, then, lay the brilliance of his teaching, praised by so discerning a former pupil as G. E. Moore? Again, Bayfield on Verrall: 'What he loved to analyse was the intended qualities of technique and design, and all the unconscious effects of style. He realized that a Greek play, for instance, must be interpreted primarily from itself, not buried under a load of more or less relevant learning, still less used as a text for a general disquisition on grammar.'[27] It is difficult for those who have seen the New Criticism and other modern movements come and go to appreciate that the breathing of new life into the very dry bones of the Greek and Latin classics was a work begun by Verrall, less than a century ago. It is fortunate for our literary culture that it was Verrall, and not the more typical dry-as-dust don, who was chosen to initiate the study of English literature into academic respectability.

In 1882 he married Margaret de Gaudrion Merrifield, a brilliant classicist herself, who was remembered with affection by Verrall's students and by her own at Newnham. Mrs Verrall was very much of her age and place. Like so many Cambridge dons and their wives, her great interest was the work of the Society for Psychical Research and she led her husband and her daughter into these tangled webs.

The Apostles were supremely rationalist and not given to crankiness, but, like many perfectly serious senior members of Cambridge society during this period, they became interested in para-psychology. The Society for Psychical Research was socially respectable and the subject fascinated many of the intellectual aristocracy. Indeed it was one of the first common causes which they had shared since their fathers' enthusiasm for the abolition of the slave trade. Many of these intellectually astute people had been brought up with strong religious beliefs in childhood, and as they had grown older and had lost these beliefs in the age of Darwin, they seem to have replaced their religious yearnings with the hope that para-psychology would give a scientific foundation for a belief in the immortality of the soul.

It was through the Society for Psychical Research that Freud's work was introduced to England, in 1893, in a paper by F. W. H. Myers. And it was as an undergraduate that James Strachey attended a meeting of the SPR in the first decade of this century, and heard a paper by Freud read; this stimulated the interest in psycho-analysis that resulted in his standard edition of the works of Freud.[28] In *The Edwardian Turn of Mind*, Samuel Hynes remarks that 'none of the discreditable aura of table-tipping in darkened rooms seems to have attached itself to the Society, and its membership lists during the Edwardian period might well be the lists of the members of some rather intellectual West End club, or the pew-holders of a fashionable church'.[29] Hynes suggests two reasons for the success of the SPR. The first is that 'at a time when English society was still stratified and, within those strata, homogeneous, the founders of the Society were so impeccably acceptable, so very Cambridge and well born, that they carried their social position with them, even into the séance'.[30] Secondly Hynes sees the SPR as a rebellion against Victorian materialism, both in the precise sense of philosophical doctrine, and in the wider sense of a preoccupation with the manufacture and acquisition of material objects. Members of the SPR sought in its activities liberation from Victorian materialism, most in the hope that the conclusions of its research work would restore to them the consolation of religion denied by Victorian science; but others (like William James) merely seeking empirical knowledge without the metaphysical underpinnings of theology and earlier philosophy. Some (like Oliver Lodge, at first) regarded it as a scientific challenge to explain the phenomena that concerned the SPR by ordinary physical laws.[31] The most poignant case, however, was that of the SPR's first president, Henry Sidgwick, whose interest in para-psychological phenomena might be seen as the aftermath of the religious crisis that led to the resignation of his fellowship. Unable to ground his belief in personal immortality by philosophical argument, Sidgwick devoted much of his time to the SPR in search of empirical evidence for the existence of the soul. This search was, of course, an admission of philosophical defeat.

The subject of education had been of special concern to the Apostles at every stage of their history, and now, in their sixth decade (1870 marked their jubilee), the topic must have been discussed with increasing frequency. Prussia's success in war and among the nations of Europe was widely attributed as much to her schoolmasters as to her generals, and in 1870 parliament finally passed an Education Act, which extended literacy to every class and every region of the country. Outside parliament, measures taken to broaden education included the foundation in 1873 of 'university extension' by James Stuart (Apostle

Number 162), who had resigned from the Apostles the year before. Not only did an Apostle found this movement, but the project and its subsequent developments were always dear to individual Apostles, who could be relied upon to participate as fully as possible. University extension, explained by G. M. Trevelyan (Apostle Number 230), meant:

'The Universities sent out some of their best men to lecture to audiences at a distance from their walls. This movement stimulated local demands for higher education, led to the formation of some of the local University Colleges, and ultimately assisted the formation of those new Universities in great industrial centres which so strongly differentiate the higher education of our day from that with which our fathers had to be content. The Extension lectures also led, in the twentieth century, to the further development of tutorial classes for working-men, and to the Workers' Educational Association.'[32]

Founded in 1873, the year of Moore's birth, the movement was still vigorous twenty-five years later when Moore lectured on Kant at the Passmore Edwards Settlement. It is not far-fetched to see this particular line of education as a special Apostolic project, for which, the Society being secret, no credit could be claimed.

Although the membership records indicated ten members for this year, Walter Leaf (Apostle Number 184) thought that in his time as an Apostle the true active membership was seldom more than six or seven. But visits from 'angels' were frequent, and

'thus there was established a continuous Apostolic succession, and at the same time those who were residing in Cambridge or who came up for the week-end visits made full use of the permission to keep up their bonds of fellowship, and a valuable link between different generations was formed. The most constant attendant at our meetings was James Stuart, a young mathematician lecturer at the College, full of initiative and, under the influence of that remarkable woman, Mrs Josephine Butler, ready to dedicate himself to various causes which, to tell the truth, did not greatly appeal to most of us. At that moment he was throwing himself heart and soul into the movement known as University Extension, for the spread of academic teaching on a democratic basis through local lectures. Here we all sympathized; many of my friends became lecturers . . . and I myself was swept into it on the administration side as soon as I settled in London. Stuart, I think, deliberately used the Society for propaganda; but he was always a clever and amusing debater. He subsequently married a wealthy wife, bought a newspaper and sat in Parliament, obtaining a Privy Councillorship. But he was too impracticable in his ideas to attain the position which his abilities seemed to assure him.'[33]

It was also in the seventies that women's colleges were founded at Oxford and Cambridge, and the leading roles taken by individual Apostles, especially Sidgwick, in the great cause of education for women has been noted already.

But the change which most affected the Apostles, because it most affected Cambridge, was the Universities Test Act of 1871, a reform as bold as any made by Gladstone. Without this reform, G. E. Moore and many of his contemporaries could not have made careers at Cambridge, and might therefore not have sought admission at all. Acts of 1854 and 1856 had opened Oxford and Cambridge to dissenters, but they were still ineligible to take the MA or any divinity degree, and so unable to hold any college fellowship or any university post. Thus the ablest of nonconformist men were unable to contribute to the intellectual life of the nation, except in the ministry of their own denominations. Trevelyan estimated that this bar affected half the nation, and would have proved disastrous.

'The clerical and celibate character imposed on College Fellows, the almost complete supersession of the University by the individual colleges, the close character of the elections to Fellowships, and the prevalence of absenteeism and sinecureism, rendered them incapable of meeting the demands of the new age, particularly in non-classical subjects, humane or scientific. Such impotence in the higher sphere of the intellect and research must eventually have ruined the country in peace and in war, when matched against foreign rivals who valued scientific and educational progress. The timely reform of Oxford and Cambridge by Act of Parliament saved the situation.'[34]

The salvation of the universities by the Test Act, however, proved to be the undoing of the dissenting movement, as the articulate young men, who had enriched the nonconformist ministry, were now co-opted by the universities.

University reform was by no means completed: the dons were still celibate and would be required to remain so for another decade, but control by the established church was ended for ever. In the previous year Gladstone had stopped the practice of patronage in the home civil service by initiating competitive examinations as the normal means of entrance. Young men at the university could now choose freely among the careers for which their abilities best suited them, to the benefit of the nation as a whole. For new generations of Apostles this was to open up great vistas of private accomplishment and public service.

James Ward

In March 1876 the Society elected a rather unusual man, James Ward (1843–1925); at the time of his election he was thirty-three years old, and already a fellow of Trinity. Born in Liverpool, the son of a merchant, he left school early and was articled to a firm of Liverpool architects; after a time he gave up his apprenticeship to prepare himself for the Congregationalist ministry at Spring Hill Congregationalist College, Birmingham from 1863 to 1869. For a year while he should have been pastor of Emmanuel Church at Cambridge, he studied instead at Berlin and Göttingen. There he changed his theological views, and rather than go to Cambridge as a dissenting minister, entered Trinity as an undergraduate in 1871. In 1872 he was a twenty-nine-year-old scholar of the college, and two years later took a first class in the moral sciences tripos. His fellowship, which he could not have held before the Test Act passed four years earlier, followed in 1875.

At Trinity, Ward had begun by doing research in the natural sciences; as a philosopher he was later to criticize those who try to deal with philosophical problems from the point of view of the physicist; so it is interesting but not surprising that in his own career his interests now changed from natural science to psychology. In 1881 he was appointed a lecturer, and in 1886, he published his famous *Encyclopaedia Britannica* article which transformed British psychology. The prevalent view among British psychologists conceived of the mind in terms of an analogy with atomic physics, where ideas, like atoms, are attractive or repellent to one another. Ward suggested substituting for this associationist picture of mind a biological model, where the mind is not merely the passive recipient of sensations but actively pursues and desires sensations in order to become 'expert by experiment'.

About 1894 Ward began to be interested in philosophy itself and lectured on 'metaphysics', which in Cambridge then included all philosophy save moral philosophy. Moore, who was his pupil at the time, remembered attending Ward's lectures with two or three other students. They sat round a table in his college rooms, and listened to him think aloud; for although he always had a large notebook open before him on the table, he did not read his lecture, but actually talked to his small audience. While a student in Germany, Ward had himself attended the lectures of Lotze, and he in turn set his pupil Moore to write essays on Lotze's *Metaphysics*, the chief distinguishing feature of which was its incorporation of science as part of philosophy, rather than as a way of looking at the world which is opposed to philosophy.

Ward then turned his attention fully from psychology to metaphysics, led in this direction quite naturally by his criticism of Cartesian dualism. He was not a materialist, nor was he happy with the solution to the Cartesian problem that treats the internal spiritual domain as more fundamentally real than the external, material world; still less did he like the current solution at Oxford that treated both as appearances of the absolute. The limitation of the physicist, Ward thought, is that he is inevitably led into treating his own necessarily abstract creations – atoms and molecules – as though they had an existence of their own independent of the existence of mind. The natural scientist, if he is to get on with his work, cannot call into question the ultimate reality of his abstractions; but it is just because they are abstractions, and not concretely experienced things, that the 'objects' of the scientist are not 'real', and that the scientific attitude must treat physics as though it were all there is to metaphysics.

The way out of these intellectual attitudes that falsify reality, Ward thought, was by means of a discipline that does not abstract from experience, but is instead a record of experience : history. 'History offers us facts, individuals, purpose and meaning, progress or decline, all that we miss in the world of mechanism.'[35] History deals with individuals, the opposite of abstractions, and it deals with individuals in their own environments; the unity of the individual and his environment, in all its rich diversity, must be the starting point for any account of reality, just as it is the starting point of any historical narrative.

In his excellent passage on Ward's philosophy, John Passmore says that Ward was thus able to maintain

'that there can be no sudden leap, no sharp break in continuity, between mind and matter. The materialist recognizes as much, but materialism, according to Ward, can make nothing of the striving, valuing individual : for to understand the individual, he thought, we must make use of that kind of category of purpose which the materialist discards. But if we suppose that the environment, too, is purposive, spiritual, then, Ward tells us, all difficulties in relating man to his environment will vanish. We can understand at once, and otherwise cannot understand at all, how it happens that the mind discovers in its environment the possibility of fulfilling its ideals. This does not mean, Ward hastened to point out, that we must abandon the idea of scientific law : we come to see, however, that a law is a product of mind, of our way of dealing with the environment.'[36]

While Ward's teleological message is clear enough, it is not evident whether he means to substitute monism or pluralism for Cartesian dualism. (As Passmore says, the difficulty with Ward is 'to decide what he really meant to say on the issues of central philosophical importance';[37] or, as Moore said in his autobiography, 'I thought, and still think, that his thinking was apt to be often very confused.'[38]) In fact, Ward indicated, in the last of his long series of Gifford Lectures, that while he was sympathetic to a version of pluralism in which reality consists of a plurality of minds in harmony and in conflict, he did not feel that this sort of pluralism could give a complete account of experience; and so, in the end, his *The Realms of Ends* (Gifford Lectures at St Andrews, 1911) has to appeal to the discarded theism of his youth. Ward could not prove the existence of God, but always extolled theism as an ideal, because the existence of God could alone provide a tidy solution to the metaphysical problems with which he had struggled in the decades since he gave up the Congregational ministry.

In May 1880 the Society elected its two hundredth member. It was now sixty years old, and this milestone must have induced many of the Apostles to reflect on the reasons for the Society's survival. Surely one of the reasons for this extraordinary success was, in fact, the élitist traditions of the Society, and the care exercised in the choice of new members. With three exceptions, it had been fully ten years since any member had failed to be in the first class list of his tripos. In the seventies four out of ten Senior Classics had been Apostles.

The Edwardians

In the autumn of 1882, two young men were elected who seemed different from their immediate predecessors, livelier and more worldly. Walter Raleigh and Henry Cust were, in their different ways, precursors of the Edwardian era that began when they reached their thirties.

Walter Alexander Raleigh was the fifth child and only son of a Congregationalist minister and his wife, who was the sister of the Scottish judge Lord Gifford, founder of the Gifford Lectures in Natural

Theology. Young Walter was educated first in Scotland then at University College School, University College, London, and finally King's, Cambridge. He enjoyed himself as an undergraduate and must have been a source of pleasure to his friends and fellow Apostles, for he was blessed with a strong and original sense of humour. Indeed, six weeks after his election, he read the Apostles a paper on this subject. It was called 'Laughter from a Cloud' and the question it set was: 'Is sense of humour or personal integrity more potent for pleasure to its owner?' The maturity of the style of this essay is the more impressive because its author had just turned twenty-one.

Raleigh begins by saying that the alternative he has posed in his question may not be a real one:

> 'In the first place I am bound on my own behalf to advocate the former of the qualities; for I can hardly come forward to recommend the pleasures of personal virtue to the brothers, when each, whether he has intimately revelled in them, or resolutely forgone them, can declare the naked truth.
>
> 'In the second place the alternatives may not be genuinely inter-exclusive, and some brother may be disposed to assert that he is both good and funny.'[39]

It was, no doubt, Raleigh's possession of a keen sense of humour that led the other members to set him his topic, and so what may be his maiden speech to the Apostles is something of an apology for his own character. The argument is conducted with a certain lightness which must have been disagreeable to the more earnest sort of Victorian reformer, of whom it is unlikely that many still remained as active members of the Apostles. Although James Stuart returned to Cambridge from time to time to recruit Apostles to his University Extension project, Raleigh's paper can be taken as an indication of waning interest in Stuart's sort of activism. Raleigh went on:

> 'In trying to show that the man who enjoys the pleasure of humour to the utmost is prevented from being vicious as everyday people are vicious, I have just indicated that he is not improbably a person of high moral endowment. But as he cannot be very wicked neither can he, it would seem, be very good. : . . For although his moral vision is clear and extended, he has nothing within him which urges him to action, his life is purely aesthetic, he is neither Reformer nor Hero.'[40]

The break with Victorianism is shown in another way in this paper, which is a model of how to be serious without being solemn. Both the subject and treatment herald a new intellectual mood or approach in the Society. Raleigh, deriding optimism, dismisses by implication the very Victorian idea of progress. He teases Tennyson for hoping for that 'far-off divine event to which the whole creation moves' which consoled the poet for the loss of Hallam, and says that 'the multitude believe, not the truth, but what will be, or what they think will be, best for them'.[41] And he goes on to castigate William Kingdon Clifford (Apostle Number 165) because in his *Unseen Universe* the earlier Apostle had rejected the orthodox doctrine of immortality of the soul only to substitute an equally optimistic view of immortality by which we live on in our descendants and in the memories of those we have benefited. Raleigh justifies this digression by claiming that the chief difference between the humourist and the 'man of virtue' is that the latter is an optimist.

> 'He has an intense conviction that human nature is high and holy, and he is made uneasy by the obscenity of the humourist; he is over-whelmed by the importance of life and the weightiness of its issues, and accordingly the humorous treatment of these things seems to him irreverent; he is eager to reach truth as a means of progress, and humour to him seems painfully independent of truth.'[42]

Raleigh goes on to explore humour's moral function, as the humourist 'can hardly avoid a true and extended view of the moral universe',[43] and he concludes by asking 'why Nature gives less scope for humour than society?'[44] and then answers his own question by asserting that nature avoids society's error of sacrificing the means to the end, as every object is an end in itself.

> 'But the creations of man, especially in cities, are nothing apart from their end, so that an umbrella floating about, say, on the sea, and evidently not serving its purpose, is nothing. Nothing, I say, but here the humourist steps in and amends this; he contemplates it for a moment, enjoys the situation, and, by so doing, completes its destiny, rendering it ludicrous.'[45]

His essay is a splendid example of the sort of paper the Apostles read at their meetings, and perfect evidence of the great change taking place in the Apostles, heralding the change over the next ten years in society as a whole.

In May 1883 the Apostles elected Henry John Cockayne Cust. Harry Cust, even more than Walter Raleigh, represented a new type of undergraduate. He was a model Edwardian, worldly, rich, clever, handsome and rakish; 'the Rupert Brooke of our day', Lady Horner called him.[46] Through his grandfather, an aristocratic parson, Cust became heir to the barony of Brownlow. He was sent to Eton and then to King's, after which he not only became a barrister in England, but presented himself in Paris for the *Baccalauréat en Droit*, and passed out head of the list. In 1890 he was returned as Unionist MP for Stamford, and held the seat for five years. He was expected to make a great political career, but in 1892 at a dinner party he met William Waldorf Astor, who had just bought the *Pall Mall Gazette* from its Liberal owner. Astor was impressed by the young man's conversation and offered him the editorship, and, though he had no experience whatever of journalism, he accepted on the spot. For the next four years the *Pall Mall Gazette* became the finest evening paper England has ever seen. The paper had had a chequered political career from its foundation in 1865 and this record continued after 1896 until its amalgamation with the *Evening Standard* in 1923. Henry Yates Thompson (Apostle Number 147), though himself a Liberal, had earlier sold the paper with no care as to the politics of its new proprietor, causing distress to his own party who regarded it as an invaluable organ of Liberal policies. Now that Astor proposed to turn the paper Conservative, what better choice than a Unionist MP as editor? But Harry Cust was repeatedly to favour the progressives in his own party, and by the expedient of refusing to print any of Astor's intended contributions to the paper, succeeded in forcing Astor to sack him.

Cust's formula for improving the *Pall Mall Gazette* was a simple one: employ the best contributors. The staff of professional journalists was suddenly augmented by names such as Alice Meynell, Robert Louis Stevenson, Rudyard Kipling, W. E. Henley, Sir Frederick Pollock and H. G. Wells. Cust's humour was legendary, and his handling of hecklers at political meetings was a source of both amusement and despair to political reporters – it was hilariously funny but delivered too rapidly to record.

Cust was a true man about town and belonged to the smallest and most exclusive club of all: the Crabbet Club named after Crabbet Park where Wilfred Blunt played host to Cust, Curzon, George Wyndham, Lord Crewe, Esme Howard, George Leveson Gower and a very few others, for a week every year 'to contend in games, in talk, and in verse competition, the prize for which, voted at dinner, was a Georgian silver goblet, inscribed "Crabbed age and youth cannot live together".'[47] Of the Apostles who came to manhood in the nineties, Cust and Alfred

Lyttelton alone were also members of the Souls, a clique of glittering men and women who, while in 'Society' were nevertheless interested in literature and art as well as politics. Another respect in which Cust was typically Edwardian was his womanizing. Cust had a lengthy liaison with the Duchess of Rutland. No scandal attached to this very Edwardian union: the scandal was all reserved for Cust's marriage to Nina Welby, the story of which is recounted in Enid Bagnold's autobiography.

Raleigh with his un-Victorian mind and Cust with his un-Victorian ways stood for a change in the Apostles, though Cust was much too worldly to make a serious impression on the Apostolic character. There were to be no more Victorian Apostles after the election of Raleigh and Cust. The idea that the history of the race was a story of untrammelled progress was being questioned; and the popular morality of late Victorian times had begun to be openly flouted. However, the basis of this morality had not yet been challenged, for Cust, like Raleigh, was a product of social evolution; the revolution was yet to come. It was made, many people thought, by the work of G. E. Moore.

A. N. Whitehead

In 1884, with the membership of the Society very low, Alfred North Whitehead (1861–1947), a young fellow of Trinity, was elected. Whitehead's family came from Kent where they had lived and 'been clergymen, ever since about the time of the landing of St Augustine in that county', claimed Bertrand Russell, Whitehead's most eminent pupil, who thought that 'something of the vicarage atmosphere remained in his ways of feeling and came out in his later philosophical writings'.[48] Whitehead had been at Sherbourne school, and as a young man the influence of Cardinal Newman had caused him to consider converting to Catholicism, though this episode probably indicated his genuine concern with religion more than it showed a real inclination to Rome. Originally a mathematician, Whitehead was later to find in philosophy much of what he had earlier sought from religion. Whitehead read twelve papers in the three years he was a member. He kept his fellowship at Trinity for life, but in 1910 he gave up his lectureship to exchange it the next year for one in applied mathematics and mechanics, which he held with the readership in geometry at University College London. Then in 1914 he accepted the professorship of mathematics at Imperial College, London, which he held until 1924 when he made the momentous decision to leave England to become professor of philosophy at Harvard University, where he stayed until 1937. Whitehead's distinction as a mathematician had been recognized long before he went to Harvard; as early as 1903 he became F.R.S., in 1914 he sat on the Council of the Royal Society, and for the following two years he was president of the Mathematical Association and of Section A of the British Academy. These honours and many others followed the publication in three volumes from 1910–13 of *Principia Mathematica*, the great work on which Whitehead collaborated with Russell so fully that Russell later felt it impossible to distinguish his own contribution from Whitehead's.

It is somewhat curious that Whitehead does not figure at all in the biographies and memoirs of the Apostles who were contemporary with him. He does not seem to have formed any close friendships, even with his fellow Apostles, and seems to have been known, if at all, as a mathematician, without much influence until the time of Moore and Russell. Following his marriage to Evelyn Wade and Russell's to Alys Pearsall Smith, the two couples frequently lived together, so that Russell knew him very well indeed, and was more than a little in love with his wife. Russell has extolled Whitehead's phenomenal capacity for concentration, and he often remarked that Whitehead was a perfect teacher.[49] Moore referred to him as a philosopher 'to whom I owe not a little and whom I regard with the warmest feelings of affection'.[50]

Russell, too, had reason to be grateful to Whitehead, for when Russell went up to Trinity in 1890 a friendless aristocrat who had never been to school, Whitehead told the younger Apostles to look out for him, as his examination papers were so good. As a result, in his first week at Trinity, Russell made his first friends, and these friendships lasted his whole long life. But long collaboration and sharing of houses gave Russell knowledge of Whitehead's character that few other men had, and not all of it was pleasant:

'Whitehead appeared to the world calm, reasonable, and judicious, but when one came to know him well one discovered that this was only a facade. Like many people possessed of great self-control, he suffered from impulses which were scarcely sane. Before he met Mrs Whitehead he had made up his mind to join the Catholic Church, and was only turned aside at the last minute by falling in love with her. He was obsessed by fear of lack of money, and he did not meet this fear in a reasonable way, but by spending recklessly in the hope of persuading himself that he could afford to do so. He used to frighten Mrs Whitehead and her servants by mutterings in which he addressed injurious objurgations to himself. At times he would be completely silent for some days, saying nothing whatever to anybody in the house. Mrs Whitehead was in perpetual fear that he would go mad. I think, in retrospect, that she exaggerated the danger, for she tended to be melodramatic in her outlook. But the danger was certainly real, even if not as great as she believed. She spoke of him to me with the utmost frankness, and I found myself in an alliance with her to keep him sane. Whatever happened his work never flagged, but one felt he was exerting more self-control than a human being could be expected to stand and that any moment a breakdown was possible. Mrs Whitehead was always discovering that he had run up large bills with Cambridge tradesmen, and she did not dare to tell him that there was no money to pay them for fear of driving him over the edge. I used to supply the wherewithal surreptitiously. It was hateful to deceive Whitehead, who would have found the humiliation unbearable if he had known of it. But there was his family to be supported and *Principia Mathematica* to be written, and there seemed no other way by which these objects could be achieved.'[51]

Principia Mathematica, the greatest single contribution to logic since Aristotle, and the basis of modern symbolic logic, was an attempt to show that all mathematics could be reduced to logic, using few primitive symbols, few axioms, and few rules of inference. Whitehead's teaching duties were too great for him to spare much time for the actual construction of the book, so it fell to Russell to write out the proofs. Early on Whitehead had criticized harshly Russell's draft of the beginning saying, 'Everything, even the object of the book, has been sacrificed to making proofs look short and neat'.[52] Russell accepted the advice of his old teacher, and began on a different tack. The amount of labour was incredible but recognition of the work's importance was immediate. For ten years after its publication Whitehead continued his mathematical work, but his interest in philosophy grew; and in 1924 he went to Harvard. He had had some interest in philosophy since the early nineties, when he joined Lowes Dickinson, Russell, McTaggart and other Apostles in what they called an 'Eranos' for the discussion of philosophical problems.*

* Dickinson says that McTaggart was the leader of the group,[53] which continued for some years; so it is to be presumed that Moore was also a member.

At Harvard Whitehead published *Science and the Modern World, Religion in the Making, The Aims of Education, Nature and Life, Process and Reality* and several other philosophical books in which he expounded an organic philosophy that owes more to McTaggart's idealism than to the work of Russell or Moore. The obscurity of Whitehead's prose, and the host of neologisms he called into being, have not prevented his books from being read, but they have tended to restrict their influence to those who are not philosophers. His attempt to formulate a 'unified scientific religion' was of no interest to Russell or Moore. Russell and Whitehead drifted apart first philosophically, then personally because the older man greatly disliked Russell's anti-war position and activities in the First World War. Whitehead and Moore remained in contact – though they were never very close and though they moved in opposite philosophical directions. At Harvard, Whitehead often wrote to Moore, asking that he take on American post-graduate students or publish articles in *Mind*, and Moore seems always to have complied graciously.

Whitehead was a popular teacher at Harvard and is still remembered by his former students. He was one of the founders of the Society of Fellows, which exists to free its junior fellows from the tyranny of the American Ph.D., by conferring academic status and yet allowing them to pursue their research outside normal university and departmental regulations.

Whitehead's intellectual stature was acknowledged by making him a Fellow of the British Academy in 1931, by a host of honorary degrees and by the award in 1945 of the Order of Merit.

Goldsworthy Lowes Dickinson

The great agricultural depression that began after 1875 had worsened by 1884; indeed English agriculture had collapsed. G. M. Trevelyan says that the downward trend was accelerated by several bad crops, but that the cause of the catastrophe was the opening up of the American prairies as sources of corn which new developments in transport made available to the English market.[54] This resulted in the overthrow of the landed aristocracy and the permanent urbanization of the vast number of Englishmen who had formerly been agricultural workers. Equally great was the effect of the depression on the colleges of Oxford and Cambridge, which derived nearly all their revenues from agricultural rents. King's annual income from endowments in the 1870s was £30,000; by the eighties, nearly all this was gone. Reforms involving the opening of the college to non-Etonians and provision for poor students were severely threatened.

They were not scrapped immediately, however, and one of the leaders of the movement to rescue them was the next Apostle to be elected, Goldsworthy Lowes Dickinson (1862–1932), who insisted that the value of fellowships, which was £280 at the time he was made a fellow, be reduced and cut again until they were only £80 a year. The party of self-sacrifice led by Lowes Dickinson succeeded in making sure that scholarships were not cut until the dons' salaries reached this minimum figure, and some of the reform scheme was salvaged.

From 1901 and for some time following his death in 1932, Lowes Dickinson was well known in Britain and America as a writer and broadcaster, and also as the spiritual father of the League of Nations. Lowes Dickinson's pretensions as a philosopher were crushed quite un- intentionally by Moore's own work, yet Lowes Dickinson had, like McTaggart, a personal influence over Moore as an individual. For example, it was through Lowes Dickinson and McTaggart, his seniors in the Society, that the romantic idea of Apostolic homosexuality was transmitted to Moore. Despite Moore having undercut his own philo- sophical work, Lowes Dickinson continued to influence Moore even as late as 1914, when Moore made the dramatic gesture of accompanying him to a founding meeting of an anti-war organization.

Lowes Dickinson was born in 1862 at Hanwell, a suburb of London which was a country village at the time of his birth. His father, Cato Lowes Dickinson, was a moderately successful painter, and a genial man; his mother died while he was in his first year at King's. He seems to have had a happy childhood, typical of a middle-class child in the 1860s, and there seems to be nothing in the family background to explain his having developed shoe fetishism well before puberty. He only became aware that he was also homosexual when he was at Cambridge, and even managed to get through Charterhouse, at that time a 'hothouse of vice', with no experience of homosexuality and hardly any interest in it.

He was shy at first, and the efforts of his elder brother to introduce him to his own set at King's were not a success; Lowes Dickinson set about his university career as though it were merely a continuation of school, conscientiously but mechanically reading and attending lec- tures. But after his mother's death during his first year, he conceived a sudden passion for Shelley, not – he says – as a poet, but as a vision- ary. He began to write poetry himself and, also through the influence of Shelley, to interest himself in politics. In 1884 he went abroad to

Germany and returned to Cambridge in the autumn with very little idea of what he was going to do with himself, though he was thinking in a half-hearted way of working on a fellowship dissertation. It was now, in February 1885, that he was elected to the Apostles. In the next few years when the most active members were McTaggart, Roger Fry and Nathaniel Wedd, Dickinson became devoted to the Apostles.

Though still lacking a métier, Dickinson's interests and the direction in which they would take him are indicated by a paper he read to the Society, 'Shall we elect God?', which was known to several generations of Apostles after his own time. The *mise-en-scène* of the paper is an Apostles' meeting in heaven, and the active members were Goethe, Hegel, Turgenev and Victor Hugo. The brothers were considering the topic that occupied so much of the time of the earthly brethren : whom to elect? Someone had proposed that God should be considered for membership, but a number of objections were raised. The vote had not yet taken place when there was a knock on the door, and He enters. In a trice God deals with all their objections. Noël Annan summarizes the action that takes place :

> 'He tells them that their doubts are mistaken : they cannot refuse to elect him. He is all they believe in, all they see, all they deny, all they affirm : he is the doubter and the doubt and the founder of their Society. They still remain unconvinced and, since his face is hidden by his cloak and hat they ask him to reveal himself. As he does so they all recognize him and each calls him by his name – Goethe "Das Schöne!" Turgenev "La Vérité", Hugo "L'Idéal", Hegel "Das Absolut".'[55]

This paper points up the attraction idealism had for Lowes Dickinson, and how important he felt it to be at least to attempt to reconcile the notions of perfection that every man in fact has, however difficult any man may find it to articulate his notion or even name it. This yearning for such reconciliation reveals Lowes Dickinson's view of human nature, and provides a thread of consistency from which can hang nearly all the words and deeds of his entire life.

Lowes Dickinson had met Roger Fry (Apostle Number 214) in London before Fry's election to the Apostles in 1887; but now he realized that his feelings for Fry were not strictly those of friendship. In this year, which was Fry's last at Cambridge, the two were continuously together. Overlapping this fairly chaste love affair was another with Ferdinand Schiller, a businessman who was soon to join his father in the family business in India before returning to London to work in the

City. He was the brother of Max and Canning Schiller, the first an eminent KC and the other the most famous of the Oxford pragmatist philosophers. In 1888 there was a house party of Schiller, Lowes Dickinson, Fry, and McTaggart at Gersau, where the Schillers had a house on the lake of Lucerne. Schiller and Lowes Dickinson went again to Gersau in 1893, and Lowes Dickinson was now rapturously in love with Schiller, who was only in Europe on holiday from India.

The affairs with Roger Fry and Ferdinand Schiller ended their passionate phase with shared and permanent feelings of affection. Not so Lowes Dickinson's next affair, with a King's undergraduate called Oscar Eckhard, which began in 1909, by which time he was forty-seven and famous. This was stormy, but difficulties were bound to come into his life as the men he was attracted to were always heterosexual. His last two great loves, Peter Savary and Dennis Proctor, though still heterosexual, were much more amenable, and Lowes Dickinson was mostly happy and always in love – 'if the word love', as he says in his autobiography, 'may be used of a feeling continually thwarted on the physical side'.[56]

In 1895 the fellows of King's had failed, by one vote, to renew Lowes Dickinson's fellowship, but he was immediately made librarian, a post that carried a fellowship with it. From 1896 to 1920 he was lecturer, and held his fellowship until his death.

The Society, reduced to seven members in May 1886, now elected one of those men who was to dominate its proceedings for some time. This was the philosopher John McTaggart Ellis McTaggart, the foil against whom Moore and Russell worked out their own philosophies. In early days, both men were inspired by McTaggart's intellectual example and wished to be his disciples, but the association ended with something very like the destruction of McTaggart's philosophy.

J. McT. E. McTaggart

There are still those at Cambridge who remember McTaggart in his last years, a fiercely reactionary don with the crab-wise walk of the agoraphobic. It is not difficult to trace the growth of McTaggart's foibles and opinions, and it is worth looking briefly at his childhood and schooldays. His father, Francis, who died in 1870 when 'Jack' McTaggart was only four, was the descendant of distinguished lawyers, scientists, and rich merchants, who were themselves descended from Wiltshire yeoman farmers who can be traced back to the fourteenth century. By birth Ellis and not McTaggart, Francis's father had married Susan Mc-

Taggart, whose brother, a rich baronet, settled his fortune on his nephew on condition that he assumed the name McTaggart. Owing to Francis McTaggart's early death, the children were brought up by their mother, also an Ellis, who was her husband's first cousin. Mrs McTaggart, the daughter of a country rector, was a professed agnostic, and this affected her son's views: at the age of six he is reported to have told an uncle that he did not believe in an after-life, and he was supposed to have been sent away from his preparatory school at Weybridge for arguing against the Apostles' Creed and denying the existence of God.

McTaggart's peculiar walk was also noted early in life: Lowes Dickinson, who assembled and wrote most of McTaggart's biography, reports that an informant told him that, as a child, 'he used to walk out alone, walking sideways and swinging a stick and hold long conversations with himself and was known to the village children by the name of the "Loonie" '.

Lowes Dickinson comments:

'This curious gait was very familiar to all who knew Jack in later life and was commonly attributed to his habit of keeping close to a wall to avoid the kicks of his school-fellows; but this note suggests that it derived from an earlier date. And there is reason to suppose that he had a slight curvature of the spine.'[57]

McTaggart's second school was Caterham, where he was excused playing games after a display of passive resistance to compulsory football by lying down in the middle of the field and refusing to move. His dress was untidy and his boots often mis-matched. He seems to have been tolerated by the other boys, who regarded him as peculiar but did not persecute him. In 1880 he left Caterham and was privately tutored, and by this date, aged thirteen, he had begun reading Kant.

Two years later he was sent to Clifton, though he was completely ill-suited for a public school. Trouble and pain there was, as reported by Roger Fry, with whom McTaggart had the good fortune to become intimate at Clifton:

'He was sheltered by no indulgent doctor's certificate and duly appeared on the football field, but appeared only to stand, a limp, melancholy, asymmetrical figure, which showed no sign of awareness of what was expected of a player. To kick such a loafer into the scrummage was at once the duty and pleasure of an energetic back, but the figure merely sidled a few paces off and stood once more in dejected solitude. It was found that however often this process was repeated the result was always the same; no force could make McTaggart's body go through the rudimentary semblance of taking part in a game of football. The spectacle was altogether too demoralizing to be allowed and McTaggart got off all games for no more officially valid reason that that it was impossible to make him play them.'[58]

Worse than his refusal to take part in the most important aspect of public school life were his views which 'outraged every standard of schoolboy decency'.[59] McTaggart was not only a self-proclaimed atheist and materialist, but a republican. He was once 'tried' at Clifton for his republican sympathies, when he lamented that the madman who had attempted to shoot the queen was not a better shot. McTaggart insisted on cross-examining the witnesses to his transgression, which he did to such good effect that the trial was halted, but the boy was convicted anyway. Fry remembered that 'the punishment was not ... very barbarous, and indeed McTaggart's complete incapacity to resist any attack made him an unsatisfactory butt for physical violence'.[60] Though his republican sentiments were well known, Fry thought McTaggart avoided talking about his atheism because 'being for the time an inmate of a Christian school he owed to it a debt of loyalty which forbade any criticism of its tenets'.[61] McTaggart himself, however, attributed his unpopularity at school to not being a Christian; and even when they were at Cambridge, Lady Fry, Roger's mother, doubted whether McTaggart was a suitable friend for her Christian son.[62]

In spite of his radical opinions and his refusal to take part in games, McTaggart was by no means entirely cut off from the life of Clifton. He was the mainstay of the debating society, where he found a willing and ever-increasing audience for his unpopular views, and he wrote poems and papers, sometimes on philosophical subjects, for *The Cliftonian*. Boys and masters alike came to recognize his worth and the high order of his intellect. Dickinson remarks that 'since he could not be bullied into conformity he must be made into an institution himself and thus digested, without serious inconvenience, to the standards of the community. Jack thus became a legend and a new cause for congratulation to the school. They had produced the limit of oddity'.[63] McTaggart produced more trouble for his school than had any public schoolboy since Shelley. But by the time they left Clifton together Roger Fry had detected in McTaggart an attitude that goes some way to explaining the conversion of this youthful radical to the reactionary he was soon to become. Having made his peace with Clifton, writes Fry, 'there grew up in him not only a deep and lasting loyalty to the institution, but a romantic attachment to the whole public school system and to all the patriotic emotions which it enshrines'.[64] Loyalty was the sentiment McTaggart seemed to feel most deeply all his life; and, strangely for a philosopher, he would time and again make the logic-defying leap from loyalty to one particular instance of an institution, like Clifton, to loyalty to the institution itself, in this case the public school system.

Another aspect of public school life that did not fail to make its mark on McTaggart was schoolboy romance; Lowes Dickinson makes it clear that in 1882 or 1883 McTaggart experienced a sentimental attachment to an older boy. His affection was returned, and the friendship lasted for McTaggart's lifetime.

The president of Trinity College, Oxford, hearing of McTaggart's intellectual eminence, attempted to recruit him for the college; but his suit failed, and in the autumn of 1885 (Lowes Dickinson gives the date wrongly as 1886) McTaggart went up to the other Trinity College, where he read for the moral sciences tripos. He was nineteen years old. In May of his second year he was elected a member of the Apostles, joining the brothers Arthur Hamilton and Henry Babington Smith, Walter Raleigh, James Duff, Whitehead, Dickinson, and the inactive Herbert F. W. Tatham. It was only with McTaggart's election that Dickinson began to take any great interest in the society. McTaggart, who read eighteen papers before he resigned exactly five years after his election, made a great impression on all the brethren. Lowes Dickinson was just coming to the realization of his homosexuality, and he and McTaggart had this in common as well as an interest in philosophy. McTaggart, in a paper that was to be prized and often re-read by future Apostles, re-introduced into the Society's discussions a topic that seems to have been dormant for some years. The paper, 'Violets or Orange Blossom?', was a defence of homosexual love, and it remained famous long after it disappeared from the Ark (where the Society's records were kept and papers sometimes deposited) and was lost.

Not much is known about McTaggart's years as an undergraduate except that he became a scholar in 1888, and in the same year he got a first in the moral sciences tripos with distinction in metaphysics. The other subjects of the tripos were moral and political philosophy, psychology, logic and methodology, and political economy. Lowes Dickinson wrote that 'in the latter, then abstract, pseudo-science McTaggart had a thorough grounding and his opinions on economics throughout his life were determined by it. He was always a brilliant and doughty dialectician on the anti-socialist and free trade side.'[65] The debating activities he had begun at Clifton were continued at the Cambridge Union, and he was president in 1890. In 1891 he won a prize fellowship at Trinity.

His eccentricities extended beyond his opinions; he was as famous for riding his heavy and ancient tricycle as for his breakfast and luncheon parties, where the conversation was as hearty as the fare was meagre. Every Sunday McTaggart observed the procession into the university church (which as a non-Christian he hardly ever attended himself), looking for ecclesiastical improprieties and complaining when they occurred. He now developed his life-long but unbelieving attachment to the church, which culminated in full-blooded anti-disestablishmentarianism. Once when Lowes Dickinson asked him about the House of Lords, McTaggart said that the only reform he favoured was the addition of those bishops who did not sit there at present. His Toryism was developing in the same direction as his previous radicalism, and when he was a don at Cambridge its light blue coloured all his opinions.

McTaggart's greatest Cambridge friends were Nathaniel Wedd (Apostle Number 215), Lowes Dickinson and Roger Fry. At the close of each summer term the quartet used to row down the Thames from Lechlade. Dickinson remembered that

'those days were a wonderful blend of fun and sentiment. McTaggart bubbled over all the time. He could not row, of course, but we made him do so. "Time, Bow" said the cox and McTaggart replied "Space". He read aloud or quoted Dickens, whom he knew almost by heart. The long stretches choked with rushes and reeds above Oxford; Abingdon, where we would pass the night and lie in the hay by the river; the wonderful wooded reach between Pangbourne and Maple Durham; the Hill at Streetley which we climbed at sunset; the locks with their roaring water; teas in riverside gardens; a moonlight night at Shipley; the splendid prospect of Windsor and ices in the famous tuck shop; it all lingers still in my mind after forty years, and the ghost of McTaggart rises up inspiring and enchanting it all, witty, absurd, sentimental, adorable.'[66]

Sometimes the company included Ferdinand Schiller, whom Lowes Dickinson, himself then in love with Schiller, calls McTaggart's greatest friend.[67] After taking his degree in 1888 McTaggart went with Dickinson and Fry on the party to Schiller's mother's house at Gersau, and repeated the visit with the same party five years later.

McTaggart spent 1892 and 1893 in New Zealand. On his return he settled down to being a don at Trinity where he was appointed to a lectureship in 1897. The year before his appointment he had published his first book, *Studies in Hegelian Dialectic*, which shows how far he had moved from his youthful materialism. With Whitehead, Russell and Dickinson, McTaggart formed the 'Eranos' for the discussion of philosophy. All the participants were at that time inclined to idealism. A privately printed essay of 1893, 'Further Determination of the Absolute', shows that McTaggart was already developing the ideas for which his studies of Hegel were meant to provide the underpinnings. He believed in the immortality of the soul, reincarnation and something quite like a heaven without God. From the workings of the Hegelian dialectic he hoped to deduce a satisfactory rationale for these beliefs. McTaggart was one of the last major philosophers to construct a systematic philosophy to justify beliefs that he already held to be true. The keystone of these beliefs was his interpretation of the Absolute as a state of communion of immortal souls in the perfect love of friendship – a heaven with no need of a God. Reincarnation was implicit in McTaggart's early ideas, for he thought that friendships were made by the recognition of souls we had known in another existence, so that the basis for friendship was never fortuitous.

On 12 June 1898 McTaggart sailed to New Zealand for his second visit. On his first he had met a woman called Margaret Bird (who was usually known as Daisy) and he had corresponded with her after his return to England. By January 1899 she and McTaggart were engaged. McTaggart wrote to Wedd on 24 January 1899 that Miss Bird, who was then aged thirty, had been a nurse for the last three years; that she was very clever, although she had only a high school education; and that she was in fact almost Apostolic, as she was fond of metaphysical discussion and of schoolboys. Wedd was assured that McTaggart's marriage would mean no change in the pattern of his friendships, as his new wife would simply be an addition to his friendships and not a replacement for any of them. He told Wedd that he had re-read 'Violets or Orange Blossom?' and that he still held the pro-homosexual views he expressed in that Apostles' paper. Finally, he added, neither his work nor his devotion to Trinity would suffer by his marriage, for his fiancée had agreed that he should carry on dining in college as much he had done when a bachelor. The marriage took place in New Plymouth on 5 August 1899, and McTaggart and his bride sailed for England in October.

Of this period in McTaggart's life, Dickinson says:

'From the time of his marriage onward, McTaggart's main object was to accomplish the task he had set himself of demonstrating by reason the truth which he already believed. . . . it is essential to remember that, if he was a philosopher by nature and choice he was also a lover and a husband, a devoted son of Trinity and of Cambridge, a paradoxical wit, an enthusiastic epicure, and a whole-hearted British patriot. The combination is unusual, but it was his, and all these qualities were somehow reflected in his appearance, now becoming corpulent, his uncouth walk, his devotion to college and university business, and the pained expression which distorted his features when he heard a bad argument or an opinion which he considered heretical.'[68]

Anyone who has had occasion to take notice of the several volumes in which McTaggart worked out his philosophy of absolutism, and the volumes of comment on them and explication of their doctrines by C. D. Broad, will appreciate that only a very superficial glance at that philosophy is possible in a short space. Dickinson raises the most important point when he says that 'the origin of McTaggart's philosophy was not in his intellect but in his emotions'.[69] In support of this assertion he goes on to quote a passage from McTaggart's unpublished *The Further Determination of the Absolute*:

'What is the concrete and material content of such a life as this? What does it come to? I believe it means one thing, and one thing only – love. When I have explained that I do not mean benevolence, even in its most impassioned form, not even the feeling of St Francis, I shall have cut off one probable explanation of my meaning. When I add that I do not mean the love of Truth, or Virtue, or Beauty, or any other word that can be found in the dictionary, I shall have made confusion worse confounded. When I continue by saying that I mean passionate, all-absorbing, all-consuming love, I shall have become scandalous. And when I wind up by saying that I do not mean sexual desire, I shall be condemned as hopelessly morbid – the sin against the Holy Ghost of Ascalon.'[70]

Having ruled out love as *philia* and having explicitly denied that the love he means is *eros*, McTaggart is left with love as a sort of *agape* without God or a Christ. This notion of love, an emotion that McTaggart seems to have felt, bears a stronger resemblance to the New Testament meaning of love than to any other; so here we have the fundamental motive for the construction of McTaggart's whole speculative philosophy – a near-paradox – Christian love without a godhead. By the time McTaggart came to philosophy as a profession, he was already certain of the truth of several propositions – e.g. those about the communion of souls in perfect love, and those concerning immortality and reincarnation of souls. The task he set himself as a philosopher was to *prove* their truth, by systematically deducing them from higher-order propositions. Thus he was drawn to Hegel, for he hoped that in elucidating Hegel's philosophy, he would work out and ground his own. There were few ever who thought his interpretation of Hegel correct – many indeed hoped to find in McTaggart's interpretation something better than was actually in Hegel.

C. D. Broad, McTaggart's executor and author of a two-volume study of McTaggart's philosophy, felt called upon to defend McTaggart's undertaking against several charges that it had been better not done at all. Among these was the argument, widely accepted by philosophers, at least since the First World War, that speculative philosophy is a futile pursuit and ought simply to be ignored. To this Broad replied:

> 'If McTaggart's philosophy were merely the expression of his personal reaction to life, and if the deductive form in which he clothed it were merely "the finding of bad reasons for what he believed on instinct", it would express the reaction of an extraordinarily original and sensitive personality endowed with a singularly acute and powerful intellect. As such, his system, and the arguments by which he claimed to demonstrate it, would justify the most careful and sympathetic consideration.'[71]

Broad does not, however, admit the charge of the fundamental futility of the enterprise, simply on the grounds that the Vedantists, Plotinus, Spinoza and Hegel had all held some form of Absolutism, and that even if Absolutism is nonsense, it is worth investigating the very similar nonsense independently talked by so many intelligent men of different types and traditions. Sidgwick is purported to have taken a similar view of McTaggart's work. When reading McTaggart's fellowship dissertation on Hegel, Sidgwick is reported to have said, 'I can see that this is nonsense, but what I want to know is whether it is the right kind of nonsense.'[72]

G. E. Moore had a good deal of personal contact with McTaggart and, as is well known, was for a time greatly influenced by him. In 1894, aged twenty, Moore became an Apostle and listened to McTaggart's lectures for part II of the moral sciences tripos. In his autobiography, Moore has left the most vivid picture of McTaggart as a philosopher, and the passage is worth quoting at length:

'Of the four men, whose lectures I attended for the Moral Sciences Tripos, I think I was undoubtedly most influenced by the youngest, McTaggart. This may have been partly due to the fact that I saw a good deal more of him outside the lecture-room, and partly also, perhaps to the fact that he was nearer to me in age. He produced the impression of being immensely clever and immensely quick in argument; but I think that what influenced me most was his constant insistence on clearness – on trying to give a precise meaning to philosophical expressions, on asking the question, "What does this mean?". That he himself, in his own philosophical works, did not by any means always succeed in being perfectly clear, has, I think, been conclusively shown by Broad, in his *Examination of Mc-Taggart's Philosophy*; but how clear he was, as compared to the majority of philosophers! And what immense pains he took to get clear, even though he did not always succeed! McTaggart used often to use the word "woolly" as a name for a characteristic of some philosophers to which he particularly objected. "Woolliness" was, of course, incompatible with the kind of clarity at which he aimed; and one of his objects in aiming at clarity was to avoid "woolliness". But a philosopher might, of course, be obscure without being "woolly". Hegel, for instance, I do not think McTaggart would have accused of being "woolly", though he would certainly not have denied that he was very obscure.'

It was McTaggart's lectures on Hegel that Moore attended in 1894, and he goes on to say:

'I think it can fairly be said that what McTaggart was mainly engaged with was trying to find a precise meaning for Hegel's obscure utterances; and he did succeed in finding many things precise enough to be discussed: his own lectures were eminently clear. But I think that most Hegelian scholars would agree that many of the comparatively clear doctrines which he attributed to Hegel were very unlike anything which Hegel could possibly have meant – certainly Hegel never meant anything so precise. After these two years in which I was obliged to read some Hegel, I never thought it worth while to read him again; but McTaggart's own published works I have thought it well worth while to study carefully, and have both written and lectured on particular points in them.'[73]

McTaggart was, naturally enough, a great admirer of his idealist counterpart at Oxford, F. H. Bradley. (He told Moore that, when Bradley entered the same room, he felt 'as if a Platonic Idea had walked into the room'.[74]) It was while working on a passage of Bradley's *Logic* that Moore first developed the ideas that were to lead him and Russell to shatter McTaggart's idealism and to leave his dialectical method a shambles. Dickinson reports that although McTaggart was never able to counter their criticisms, he did not allow his philosophical disputes to cloud his friendships. And with Moore, McTaggart attempted to remain always on the best possible terms.

Roger Fry

McTaggart's schoolboy friend, Roger Eliot Fry (1866-1934), had loathed Clifton, his public school, since his first day there, but during his second year he went to some lengths to make a new friend, and this friendship was to alter his schooldays and his later life as well. Fry's study mate at Clifton, 'an exceedingly prim and conventional schoolboy. The very personification of good form', attempted one day in 1882 to relate the bizarre appearance of a new boy in the lower fourth: 'Words failed to describe its strangeness – the shock head of hair, the long twisted lank frame, the untidy clothes, and above all a peculiarly crooked gait which made it appear that McTaggart was engaged in polishing the limestone walls of Clifton College as he sidled along their surface.' Several boys in the audience laughed heartily at this description of the future philosopher as a small boy, but Fry did not:

> 'I was already conscious of so deep a revolt against all schoolboy standards that my heart warmed to the idea of any creature who thus blatantly outraged them. Here, I thought, in one so marked out as a pariah, was a possible friend for me. I deliberately sought him out. . . . My intuition was more than justified; that ungainly body contained a spirit which became the great consolation of my remaining years at school, and no Sunday evening walk for all that time was ever shared by anyone but him.'[75]

Lady Fry, as was remarked above, was much concerned about the effect this friendship with the precociously agnostic McTaggart would have upon her son's Christianity. (Though Roger Fry was to claim that he did not know about McTaggart's position on religion when they were schoolboys – thus making Lady Fry's knowledge of his agnosticism rather mysterious.) Fry was the descendant of at least eight generations of Quakers. He was the second son of Edward Fry and Mariabella Hodgkin, then, as now, famous Quaker names, and his family tree also included Eliots and Howards. Sir Edward Fry was one of the last generation of nonconformists to whom Oxford and Cambridge were in effect closed, and so he could not entertain the ambition of becoming a scientist. He chose the law only because it gave him the opportunity to go to University College, London. His Quakerism, as that of his wife, was life-long and deep, though not uncritical. Late in life he wrote that 'miserable questions about dress and address and the disputes about orthodoxy produced a chasm in my feelings between myself and systematic Quakerism which I have never got over'.[76] A strong, if not strict Quaker, Sir Edward was rather contemptuous of the common run of humanity, and the regime at his home in Highgate was rather harsh. Distinguished as barrister, judge and international legal negotiator, he was more pleased with his fellowship of the Royal Society than with his knighthood, and probably valued his work as an amateur botanist more highly than his position as a judge on the Hague Tribunal. His wife was hardly less rigid. Both were to be tried sorely by the early career of their son.

At first everything about this career looked perfectly calculated to make his parents happy. He went up to King's in 1885 to read for the natural sciences tripos, and it seemed for a long time as though the father's thwarted ambitions were to be fulfilled by the son. From the earliest days, though, there had been a double strain in Roger's interest in science, one part of which his parents failed to detect. As a child he had been given a square yard of his very own in the back garden at 6 The Grove, Highgate. Roger was enthralled by a poppy that had wandered into his patch of garden, and his mother was thrilled by this early interest and botanized endlessly on Roger's poppy – while Roger contemplated not its stamens and pistils, but its brilliant redness. Encouraged by his parents to sketch flowers to heighten his powers of observation, Roger was, of course, developing his draughtsmanship.

At his prep school, Sunninghill, there was little enough beauty, only the 'shrivelled pine trees and dirty heather' which Virginia Woolf regarded as being emblematic of the school,[77] and Roger came to see the headmaster, Mr Sneyd-Kynnersly, as a sadist, excited by the endless series of beatings in which Roger, as head boy, was always called to participate. Clifton, a new public school with limestone buildings, was hardly more beautiful; but there were no floggings and instead of the aristocratic little boys of Sunninghill there was McTaggart. Curiously, Fry and McTaggart had rather little in common: Fry pursued his science lessons seriously and was happiest in the laboratory, while McTaggart knew nothing about science, and it held no interest for him;

religion in the form of the headmaster's sermons was their chief topic of discussion. Yet that must have been bloodless talk, for McTaggart was reluctant to say anything that would disturb Fry's belief in Christianity.

The social position of the Fry family needs stressing. Sir Edward was keenly aware of his position as the leader of the gentry in Highgate, and one of the few welcome visitors to the neighbouring noble house at Kenwood. Sir Edward believed firmly in respectability, and held the comfortable view that Providence had arranged that earthly rewards should reflect a man's merits. This, of course, entailed social and political views, and Roger was obliged to accept these along with the family religion. 'Outwardly pious and even priggish' was Virginia Woolf's judgement of the young Roger Fry.[78] But it was a very different young man who went up to King's in 1885, shortly to put aside his piety without fuss and without giving pain to his parents. In spite of Fry's and McTaggart's insistence that the revolutionary did not attempt to convert the other, it must, at least partially, have been the influence of McTaggart that liberated Roger Fry from the chains of his family's creed.

Though he thought that he had done badly in his examination, Roger Fry won a two-year exhibition to King's in December 1884; it was the only award made to a scientist. However, Fry had links with Trinity from the very beginning of his university career, for he shared rooms with McTaggart in a lodging-house. It was thus no accident that they also shared the first friends they made at Cambridge – Schiller, Wedd, Dickinson, Headlam and C. R. Ashbee. Fry met the famous dons of King's, the notables of Cambridge, and he even rowed. Social life was much more to his taste than the occasional forays of a schoolboy into the society of his parents' London friends, and, most importantly, his surroundings were no longer ugly; in place of the dreariness of Sunninghill House and Clifton there was now King's College chapel and the Backs of Cambridge.

When Edward Carpenter, the social reformer and homosexual apologist, visited Cambridge, he was described by Fry to his parents as once 'one of F. D. Maurice's curates'[79] in order not to cause them alarm. In fact Carpenter had a great effect on Roger Fry, as he did on many undergraduates, persuading them to read Walt Whitman and to think seriously about the prospect of democracy in England. Virginia Woolf gives more credit to Carpenter than to McTaggart for changing Fry's political views,[80] and it is certainly true that Fry's letters home first began to challenge his parents' opinions after he and Dickinson had stayed with Carpenter at Millthorpe. Carpenter was a propagandist for a certain sort of homosexual love, exemplified by his own life with his working-class lover. This, too, had an effect on the young Cambridge men, and soon Dickinson realized that he was homosexual and in love with Roger Fry. Fry acknowledged Lowes Dickinson's passion to the extent of indulging his boot-fetishism and allowing a certain amount of petting. Fry, who was very open and un-neurotic about sexual matters, is supposed to have suggested to Dickinson that they might have (what would have been in that context) more orthodox sexual relations, but Dickinson was too inhibited.

The first thing that Fry did on election to the Apostles in May 1887 was to break its rules by telling two people – his mother and his non-Apostle friend Ashbee – of his triumph. Being asked to join the Apostles was 'rather a priding thing, though I do not know whether I shall like it much', Fry wrote his mother. Fry told her it was 'a society for the discussion of things in general. It was started by Tennyson and Hallam I think about 1820, and has always considered itself very select.' After this bit of mis-information, he went on to say that 'it consists of about six members. McTaggart and Dickinson belong', he wrote, and 'It is an extremely secret society, so you must not mention it much'.[81] As Lady Fry did not at this time much care for either McTaggart or Lowes Dickinson, Fry probably felt that he ought to impress a bit more upon her the distinction conferred by membership. So he wrote her again on 26 May 1887, two days before his formal initiation.

'Since I last wrote I have been partially initiated into the Society I mentioned before, i.e. I have seen the records, which are very interesting, containing as they do the names of all the members which include nearly everyone of distinction who was at Cambridge during the last fifty years. Tennyson, I think I told you, is still a member and there are references to the society in *In Memoriam* which none but the duly initiated can fully understand. Thompson, the late Master of Trinity, Baron Pollock, Lord Derby, Sir James Stephen, Clerk-Maxwell, Henry and Arthur Sidgwick and Hort are all (or have been) members, so that I feel much awed by becoming a member of so distinguished and secret a society – it has a wonderfully secret ritual the full details of which I do not yet know but which is highly impressive. The most awful thing is that on June 22 there is a great dinner at Richmond at which Gerald Balfour is President and I (woe is me) as being the newest member am vice-president and have to make a speech. I suppose that theoretically it is very wrong of me to tell you all this, but you must tell no one but father. The full initiation ceremony takes place next Saturday.'[82]

Virginia Woolf records that Fry's speech at the annual dinner was successful – his jokes were funny and the president as always complimented the newest member, who was by tradition the vice-president, on his speech. After the dinner Fry and nine others rowed down the river and reached Putney at 2 a.m.[83] The first of Fry's eleven papers was called 'Shall we obey?' and Virginia Woolf thought it 'typical of the general run'.[84] She said of the Apostles that: 'the society of equals enjoying each other's foibles, criticizing each other's characters, and questioning everything with complete freedom, . . . became the centre of Roger Fry's life at Cambridge.'[85] Mrs Woolf, while not able to consult the records of the Society, made some guesses about the subjects discussed at their meetings:

'It is difficult to suppose that Baron Pollock, Lord Derby, Sir James Stephen, Clerk-Maxwell and the Sidgwicks ever discussed the music of Bach and Beethoven or the painting of Titian and Velázquez. There is no evidence, apart from McTaggart's early reference to Rossetti, and from one visit in his company to the Royal Academy, that the young men who read so many books and discussed so many problems ever looked at pictures or debated the theory of aesthetics. Politics and philosophy were their chief interests. Art was for them the art of literature; and literature was half-prophecy. Shelley and Walt Whitman were to be read for their message rather than for their music.'[86]

The collective interests of the Apostles had not changed much since the time of Hallam and Tennyson; nearly sixty-five years on, many of the young men still believed 'that social service of some kind was the only end worth pursuing'.[87] But Fry 'had come to be sceptical. Not only was he hiding from his friends as a guilty secret his doubts about political activity – he was hiding from his family another secret; that art, not science, was to be his job.'[88]

Fry had not neglected his proper work at Cambridge. In the 1888 natural science tripos the examiners placed him in the first class in both parts I and II. His success of course exacerbated his dilemma, for the way was now open to him to achieve his father's ambition for him – a fellowship and a career as a man of science. However, Fry took the advice of his friend John Henry Middleton, the Slade Professor of Art at Cambridge, and stayed on at Cambridge for a few more terms; during this time he brought together art and science by a combination of dissection in the laboratory and painting the male nude under Middleton's supervision. He also worked half-heartedly at a fellowship dissertation. His first attempt was purely scientific, his second combined his two interests and was called 'On the Laws of Phenomenology and their Application to Greek Painting'; both were failures. But neither a fellowship, nor a scientific education, was what Roger Fry sought from Cambridge. What he looked for, and what he required, he got from his friendship with other students and his membership of the Apostles, which continued until November 1891.

In the winter of that year he had travelled to Italy with his friend, Pip Hughes, the son of Thomas Hughes. In Rome Fry looked seriously at pictures and sculpture, increasing not only his knowledge but his critical resources. He also went out into society. In Rome he lunched with contessas; but in Venice in May he met John Addington Symonds, the friend of so many earlier Apostles, and Horatio Brown, '*the* authority upon early Venetian painting'.[89] Symonds was now leading an openly homosexual life, and according to Virginia Woolf, set out deliberately to shock Roger Fry. He succeeded, for Fry wrote to Basil Williams that 'Symonds is the most pornographic person I ever saw but not in the least nasty . . . he has become most confidential to me over certain passages in his life. He is a curious creature – very dogmatic and overbearing in discussion, but with nice humane broad views of life.'[90] In 1892 Fry set off for Paris to study at the famous *Académie Julian*, where he shared rooms with Lowes Dickinson, and between them they managed to miss almost every exciting feature of the nineties in Paris. Fry was a little more adventurous than Lowes Dickinson – he managed to hear Wagner at the *Opéra* and to frequent the *Chat Noir* – but he failed to see a single picture by Cézanne. One could hardly have guessed the importance France and its cultural life would come to have for Roger Fry.

It was still 1892 when he returned to London to share a house with R. C. Trevelyan, Moore's future friend who had yet to be elected to the Apostles. Fry had not shown remarkable talent as a painter at Julian's, but now, having been given George Moore's *Modern Painting* for review, he found his métier as a critic almost at once. In 1894 he was back at Cambridge giving university extension lectures, and his career was under way. He was in a fortunate position, for his own interests coincided with the expanding interest in early Italian painting and the beginning of the international trade in art. In 1894 he returned to Italy and began to acquire expertise in Italian painting. It is not known when he first met Bernard Berenson, but Berenson's Cambridge connections through his wife Mary, sister of Logan Pearsall Smith, were so numerous that a meeting was inevitable. The rapid progress of Fry's career is well known – his writing for the *Burlington Magazine* and the fame it brought him; his association with J. P. Morgan and his curatorship at the Metropolitan Museum of Art, New York, followed closely by the offer and his refusal of the directorship of the National Gallery in London. Life in America was something of a shock, but Fry's contribution to the museum came at an important time in its history, and he is as responsible as anyone for the excellence of its European collection.

One reason for his leaving America was that he missed, and feared for the health of, his wife. He had married Helen Coombe, a fellow-artist in 1896, but subsequently they were separated for a long time. She had a history of mental instability and in 1907 she suffered a serious breakdown. Fry then returned to England and decided to move his household, his wife, their two children and his wife's nurses, to the country at Guildford. Soon he had builders at work, constructing to his own design the house that he called Durbins. Owing something to Italian Renaissance palace architecture and something to the work of Mansard, the house stood in grounds designed by the great gardener, Gertrude Jekyll, and ornamented with sculptures by Eric Gill.

The setting was perfect for Fry's already splendid collection of pictures, sculptures and books. However, domestic tragedy overwhelmed the pleasure of moving into the new house, for Mrs Fry was now declared incurably ill. She scarcely lived at Durbins and spent the rest of her life in institutions. The law as it stood at that time prohibited Fry's remarriage until her death.

Fry's emotional life now became turbulent: it is evident from his early history that he was a passionate man, often in love, but seldom without difficulties even in the most orthodox circumstances. Fry's association with what was to become the Bloomsbury Group almost began with a love affair. As an Apostle, albeit of an older generation than the Bloomsbury Apostles, Fry was part of the background from which Bloomsbury emerged, and he was certainly aware of the group of younger Apostles to whom Vanessa and Virginia Stephen regularly played hostess, as he was of Lady Ottoline Morrell's salon at 44 Bedford Square. He had known Desmond MacCarthy (Apostle Number 231) well enough to ask him to be the secretary of his first Grafton Galleries exhibition in 1910, and in the same year he met Clive and Vanessa Bell, and Duncan Grant. Clive Bell had not been elected to the Apostles and Grant was not at Cambridge, yet they were central to Bloomsbury.

Fry's association with the Bloomsbury Group can be said to date from this time.

Roger Fry was the greatest single influence of this century on both the practice and appreciation of the visual arts in the English-speaking world. Through his Grafton Galleries exhibitions of 1910 and 1912, he introduced to most Englishmen the modern movement in the arts that emanated from the continent, and through his writing he made possible the ease with which we today accept Picasso on the same artistic footing as Rembrandt. It must not be forgotten that this was not achieved without a struggle, and that it was Roger Fry who led the fight. Furthermore, though his Omega Workshops project lasted only from 1913 to 1919, it left a permanent and progressive mark on English taste in design and interior decoration. Despite his pre-eminence as a critic, Fry always preferred to think of himself as a painter.

Much of Fry's achievement was made possible by the breadth of his acquaintances and friendships, most obviously his close connections with French artists and critics. But Fry was also an unequivocal member of the Bloomsbury Group. In the twenties and beyond this conferred a cachet that made Fry's work easier, for as many memoirs of the period testify it was to the Bloomsbury Group that young people interested in the arts looked for leadership. This raises the question of the influence on Fry's thought of his junior, G. E. Moore. There is almost no mention of Moore in anything written by or about Roger Fry, and in view of Bloomsbury's much-acknowledged dependence on Moore this omission is puzzling indeed. There are a few exceptions to this silence. One is Clive Bell's remark in *Old Friends* that 'Roger Fry, . . . whose authority was quite as great as that of Lytton Strachey was definitely anti-Moorist'.[91] J. K. Johnstone's view in *The Bloomsbury Group* contradicts this, for he states that Fry shared some of Moore's philosophy and went on (with Clive Bell) to derive an aesthetic theory from it :

'All their experience, and the whole of Moore's philosophy, taught them that art is an intrinsic good – "one of the chief organs", as Roger Fry puts it, "of the spiritual life" – which is valuable in and for itself and needs no other justification. This is the central belief of Bloomsbury's philosophy : a belief in art for art's sake.[92]

. . . . .

'Since . . . Moore believes good taste to be very important to morals, and since the appreciation of beauty is the most essential constituent of the good that he describes, a theory of aesthetics is necessary to complete his ethics – Bloomsbury provided this theory. Its principles were set forth by Roger Fry, with some help from Clive Bell.'[93]

Against this, Michael Holroyd writes that 'Roger Fry, whose aesthetic principles J. K. Johnstone claims were closely integrated with Moore's work, and in a sense completed it, actually dismissed *Principia Ethica* as "sheer nonsense".'[94] The business of tracing influences is a very tricky one, and it would be foolish to dismiss out of hand the complicated web of influences woven by Johnstone; but it must be noted that it is Johnstone's own construction and rests on inferences drawn by him from texts by Moore and Fry. The little evidence that does exist points to the opposite conclusion.

There are certain verbal similarities between Moore's work and Fry's, and there are definitely assumptions held in common. One of them is that 'states of mind' occupy a special position in the underpinnings of philosophy. In *Principia Ethica* Moore argues that it is only states of mind that are good in themselves (i.e., not as means to something else). In a dialogue between himself and Prince Mirsky which took place in 1925, Fry modified the use of the expression. He endorsed Charles Mauron's dictum that 'the subject-matter of psychological science – the successive *états d'âme* of which our psychological existence consists – is also the stuff in which the literary artist works.'[95] Though the concept of a state of mind is nearly the same one, it was considered by Fry at this date to be a basic concept of psychology, whereas Moore treated it in *Principia Ethica* as part of the subject-matter of ethics. Though Bloomsbury was much given to crediting Moore with the discovery of the importance of states of mind, that is of course only very generally true. Both Moore and Fry derive the distinction between states of mind and actions from the same source: the Cambridge humanism represented by Sidgwick, McTaggart and Lowes Dickinson. Moore probably absorbed the idea of the paramount importance of states of mind from the generation of Apostles to which Fry belonged. Similarly, there is no reason to credit Moore, as Johnstone does, with the re-discovery of the autonomy of the work of art; the idea itself is as old as Aristotle, and there is no age in which it has been forgotten, though often it has been misunderstood and sometimes held to be false.

Fry was seven years older than Moore, and it is from this fact that a less murky picture of their relationship emerges. Probably the two men had met by 1894, when Moore was elected to the Society, for Fry was often in Cambridge that year, giving his university extension lectures and designing the furniture for McTaggart's rooms. By this time Fry's career as a critic had got under way, and he must have looked on the twenty-one-year-old Moore with the amused tolerance of an older, more sophisticated man. Fry's greatest friends, it must not be forgotten, were philosophers – Lowes Dickinson and McTaggart – the very pair Moore was to dethrone. Fry was both sympathetic to the views of Dickinson and McTaggart and very loyal; he would not easily change those views when Moore began to oppose them, nor would a unified chorus of praise for Moore from Bloomsbury alter his earlier loyalties. Personal relations between Fry and Moore were conventionally warm : the only letter Fry seems to have written to Moore (in June 1913) begins 'My dear Moore' and ends 'Yours ever'; clearly they were not strangers. But there cannot have been many opportunities for Fry to succumb, as had the younger Apostles such as Lytton Strachey, Leonard Woolf and Maynard Keynes, to the spell of Moore's conversation and presence.

Nathaniel Wedd and Robin Mayor

Before Fry's election there had been several formal resignations from the Apostles, so that he, Lowes Dickinson and McTaggart had the Society to themselves from December 1887 until February 1888, when they elected the man who regularly made them a foursome on their boating parties and non-Apostolic late-night discussions. This man was Nathaniel Wedd (1864–1940). E. M. Forster, who was deeply influenced by Wedd, said that it was through him that he could best imagine King's in the late eighties. 'Wedd was then cynical, aggressive, Mephistophelian, wore a red tie, blasphemed, and taught Dickinson how to swear too – always a desirable accomplishment for a high-minded young don.'[96]

Wedd's feeling about religion ran strong and deep. Its strength can be seen in a phrase from a letter of 13 September 1898 to his friend Frederick Bulmer, where he refers to 'the High Church *Doctrines* about the Presence and all the bloody swinish bunkum that the prize idiots of the two Universities use to cloak their erotic tendencies'. The depth of his feeling is reflected in another letter to Bulmer, written on 1 February 1894, when the latter had recently stood for Parliament. Wedd wrote :

'I was amused to see the numbers of people who referred to you and your views as Christian : it is this that occasionally inclines me to wish to retain the Church. J.C. stands for most of the things I believe in and he is connected at least etymologically with the Christian sect: I admit that historically the connection is very slight: but as this institution, though pharisaical (and so anti-J.C.) in the past, believes that it has some real affinity with the person in question, we may play on that and really nobble it for him in the future.'

Wedd's parents were freethinkers who allowed him to choose his own religion, and as a child he went shopping in a sort of supermarket of religions, rejecting the Baptists, Methodists, Evangelicals, Congregationalists, Roman Catholics, and even the established church. He settled on a humanist sect run by an American, Moncure Daniel Conway, who read aloud poetry and philosophy, and played bits of serious music, at South Place Institute in Finsbury.[97] Not surprisingly Wedd was a political radical as well as a determined atheist by the time he came up to the university.

Wedd got a first in the classics tripos and was also Chancellor's Medallist. Just after his election to the Apostles he became a fellow of King's, and he spent the rest of his working life teaching classics at King's, Queen's, and Newnham (of which he was an early supporter). Lowes Dickinson said of Wedd,

'his teaching was universally admired by his pupils. But he was more than a teacher. He gave up all his time and energy to the undergraduates, was at home to them at all hours of the night, stimulated, comforted, amused, and generally maintained the best tradition of King's, that of friendship and intimacy between undergraduates and dons, but overworked and oversmoked himself so that in the end he fell seriously ill and many years of his life have been frustrated.'[98]

So devoted was he to his teaching that he published nothing save his edition of Euripides' *Orestes* in 1895, but he did become a co-founder of the *Independent Review* in 1903, and wrote occasional pieces for it. In his youth his views were Fabian, and like his fellow Apostles he admired Shelley, Shaw, and Edward Carpenter. Forster felt that Dickinson, 'Roger Fry, J. E. McTaggart, and Nathaniel Wedd were originally drawn together by their passion for philosophy, and they were fired by a belief which McTaggart at all events never abandoned: the belief that philosophy explains the universe'.[99] Wedd, however, seems to have abandoned that belief for there is no record of his being at all interested in philosophy after his time as an Apostle. Like McTaggart he was happily married – in 1906, to Rachel Evelyn White, who was lecturer in classics at Newnham; and though never so reactionary as McTaggart, Wedd too ended up a Tory.

With his attractive, drawling voice and unending supply of blasphemous oaths, the young Wedd was a joyful companion, and for several months in the spring of 1888, the Apostles were a merry band of best friends.

The chief interest of the Apostles at this time was philosophy and McTaggart was the guiding spirit of the group, so the next Apostle to be elected was truly a passionate philosopher, Robert John Grote Mayor (1869–1947), always known as 'Robin', from Eton and King's. His son, Andreas, also became an Apostle, and one of his daughters, Theresa, married an Apostle, Lord Rothschild.

As he was deeply interested in philosophy, Mayor was naturally much influenced by Moore. But as he was four years older than Moore, he was in the position of McTaggart, Lowes Dickinson and Fry, who admired but never became really intimate with the younger man, as did the next group of Apostles, who included the Llewelyn Davies brothers, C. P. Sanger, Russell, the Trevelyan brothers and Desmond MacCarthy, all of whom regarded themselves as belonging to the same generation of Apostles as Moore. Membership of Moore's inner circle is probably best indicated by having been invited to come on Moore's annual reading parties, and Mayor was invited (and came) twice. The fact was that, while Moore liked and respected Mayor, he was not greatly impressed by the latter's gifts for philosophy. When after Mayor's death in 1947, Moore was sounded out about the possibility of publishing posthumously Mayor's philosophical work of his retirement (which appeared in 1951 with the title *Reason and Common Sense*), he did not feel able to encourage the project.

Robin Mayor was one of the last Apostles of the nineties not to be an intimate friend of Moore's; certainly he was the last important and philosophically-minded member not to be captivated by the spell of Moore. So it is appropriate that we finish this examination of the Society with the election of Robin Mayor in 1889, and introduce the remainder of the members as they appear in the undergraduate career of G. E. Moore.

BOOK THREE

5
Moore as an Apostle

On Saturday 10 February 1894, the Apostles met to hear Roger Fry read a paper on 'Must a Picture be Intelligible?' Now aged twenty-eight, Fry had taken wings two and a half years earlier. Following his not very successful career as an art student, he had recently discovered his vocation as a critic. His choice of topic reflected his new-found interest on this occasion, which celebrated his return to Cambridge as a university extension lecturer. The older Apostles in his audience were his great friend McTaggart, the 'pope' of the Apostles, who, at the age of twenty-eight, was then a Prize Fellow; Wedd, a thirty-year-old bachelor don, who had been a fellow of King's for the past six years, and lectured in classics at Newnham as well as at King's; Robin Mayor, who at the age of twenty-five was soon to become a fellow of King's and begin reading for the Bar; and Malcolm MacNaghten, also twenty-five, who a month earlier had received his call to the Bar and was visiting Cambridge this evening. One of the Llewelyn Davies brothers was also present; at this time both Crompton and Theodore were Prize Fellows of Trinity, in their mid-twenties.

The younger Apostles present to hear Fry's essay included C. P. Sanger, who was twenty-three and an Apostle of two years' standing. Sanger had just been Second Wrangler the year before, and was now preparing for part II of the moral science tripos (in which he got a first) and reading economics with Marshall. Bertrand Russell, who had been elected an Apostle a week after Sanger, had been Seventh Wrangler, and was now reading for the moral science tripos as well. Bob Trevelyan, then a Trinity undergraduate, had been an Apostle for one year, about eight months longer than Ralph Wedgwood, who was preparing for the moral science tripos, in both parts of which he was to get a first. The newest Apostle present at this meeting was Eddie Marsh, who had been elected only a fortnight earlier. Marsh was an undergraduate at Trinity, and would soon get firsts in both parts of the classics tripos.

When Fry had read his essay, the Society divided on the question: 'Must a Picture be Intelligible?' Mayor, Wedgwood and Fry voted an unequivocal Yes. Sanger, Russell and Marsh voted No. McTaggart joined them in the negative, but added enigmatically, 'It had better be'. In the neutral lobby were MacNaghten, Trevelyan, one of the Llewelyn Davies brothers, who noted he was 'with McTaggart', and Wedd, who commented 'No, nor unintelligible'.

Following the ancient traditions of the Society, it was not until after the debate on Fry's paper that the brothers proceeded to the evening's other business, the election of the twenty-year-old George Edward Moore as the newest Apostle. Moore was reading for the first part of the classics tripos, in which he got a first later that year. And it was now, persuaded by Russell that he had talent as a philosopher, that Moore was also beginning to attend lectures for the moral science tripos. Moore had met several of the younger Apostles who elected him towards the end of his first year; at the time of his election he was in his fifth term at Cambridge. With Marsh, the Llewelyn Davies brothers and Trevelyan Moore had in common an interest in classics; with Wedgwood, Sanger and Russell, an interest in philosophy.

It was, of course, McTaggart's opinion that counted most heavily in deciding whether to elect a young man to the Apostles, and early in 1893 Russell arranged for Moore to meet the great man, as Moore mentioned to his mother in the letter of 18 March 1893. Russell gave Moore and McTaggart tea, and Moore recalled that 'McTaggart, in the course of conversation had been led to express his well-known view that Time is unreal. This must have seemed to me then (as it still does) a perfectly monstrous proposition, and I did my best to argue against it. I don't suppose I argued at all well; but I think I was persistent and found quite a lot of different things to say in answer to McTaggart.'[1] This meeting, so momentous for the subsequent history of philosophy, must have gone well; for Moore passed his vetting, and a year later was elected to the Apostles.

Moore had, and continued to have, friends outside the circle of the Apostles, including Ralph Vaughan Williams, Maurice Amos, and particularly H. G. Dakyns, with whom he breakfasted every day during his third year at Cambridge. But in the lists of friends Moore was given to making, the names of other Apostles figure most frequently. One likes to think that the philosophically fruitful meeting of Moore and Russell would have taken place even if the Apostles had not existed; but it seems that Russell and Moore first met because the latter had been called to the attention of the former by the Apostles. In the long vacation of his first year, Moore noted in the list he called 'People I see', that he got 'to know Russell, Crompton, Mayor, Wedgwood, V. W. [and] Dakyns very well'. All the men in this list save the last two were members of the Apostles.

By the time of his election Moore seems to have been on fairly familiar terms with McTaggart. After their first meeting in Russell's rooms, they encountered each other frequently at Oscar Browning's 'at homes', and on other social occasions; and Russell had persuaded Moore to attend McTaggart's lectures on Hegel in 1894. As Moore had managed to argue with McTaggart on their first meeting, he cannot have felt too keenly the age difference of eight years, or even the difference in status that separates the undergraduate from the young don.

At Moore's first meeting of the Apostles on 17 February the subject was 'What ought Cambridge to give?', and Moore's first vote in the Apostles differed from that of Russell, who had nominated him for membership. Russell felt that one ought to acquire 'specialized knowledge' from one's time at Cambridge. Moore simply voted for 'pleasure'.

Moore created a sensation at his first meeting, and the occasion was evoked by Russell, in a hitherto unpublished letter of 18 February 1894 to his fiancée, Alys Pearsall Smith:

'Yesterday Moore made his début in the Society, and the scene was so perfectly wonderful and unprecedented that I would give anything to be able to describe it adequately. He spoke perfectly clearly and unhesitatingly, and at first with no sign whatever of nervousness (which makes most people dumb at their first meeting). He looked like Newton and Satan rolled into one, each at the supreme moment of his life. I had said (we were discussing the Cambridge education) that our training up has produced such a profound scepticism about everything that many of us are unfitted for practical life: Moore said that was the one great gain from education: at least, he said, we are not so far unfitted as to be unable to earn our bread: we should therefore spread scepticism until at last everybody knows that we can know absolutely nothing.

'At this point he was overcome by hysterical laughter (everybody else had been laughing a great deal all the time), and turned his back to the room and rested his forehead on the mantelpiece. When he had recovered, he went on, in the same attitude: this universal scepticism will no doubt produce the dissolution of society, which I should welcome; as people would then be forced to build up knowledge again empirically, and *this time it would probably be recorded*, and would not require to be done a third time. . . . [in original] All this he meant as earnestly as the most intense eagerness could make him : at one point he said : scepticism cannot destroy enthusiasm, there is one which will always remain, and that is the enthusiasm for scepticism. And to see him say it no one could doubt his utter conviction of the truth of what he was saying. We all felt electrified by him, and as if we had all slumbered hitherto and never realized what fearless intellect pure and unadulterated really means. If he does not die or go mad I cannot doubt that he will somehow mark himself out as a man of stupendous genius.'[2]

Russell's claims about Moore were large, so large that they could not be accepted whole, even by the adoring Alys, who did not regard herself as an intellectual, and was usually content to defer to the opinions on such matters of her devoted 'Bertie'. But while Alys did not doubt that in Moore Russell had discovered 'a man of stupendous genius', she jibbed at accepting that Moore's enthusiasm for scepticism was sincere. In her reply to Russell of 20 February 1894 she put just this point. Russell wrote back from Trinity College on Wednesday morning, 21 February :

'I don't see why thee doesn't believe in Moore's enthusiasm for scepticism. Thee would if thee could see his eyes. He has strong passions and emotions, but hardly those of a human being : they are all intellectual and critical. It is he who argued in the teeth of the wind. I find it impossible either to like or dislike him, because I have seen no trace of humanity in him yet: but there is an odd exhilaration in talking with him : his criticism is like the air of the High Alps.'[3]

Though we do not know who else was present at the Apostles' meeting on the evening of 17 February, we cannot doubt that they all 'felt electrified' by Moore, or that Moore's performance on this evening was to be repeated many times over; for it was this power to 'electrify' that was the source of Moore's influence over so many generations of Apostles. So vivid is Russell's picture of the beautiful young man we know from his photographs, turning 'his back to the room' and resting 'his forehead on the mantelpiece' while recovering his composure, that one can imagine his audience at the same moment, taking advantage of the pause to draw breath themselves. These letters from Russell provide at least some explanation of the fascination exerted by the young

Moore, the force of his personality that so many other writers have remarked but failed to explain, and they are therefore key documents in the difficult task of unlocking the enigma of Moore's character.

On 24 February Sanger read a paper to the Apostles called 'Which Wagner?' The contrast was between Richard Wagner, the composer, and Adolph Wagner (1835–1917), the German economist, and the Apostles were being asked to choose between music and economics, i.e. between art and social reform. Russell wrote to Alys the next day that Sanger supported the side of art, and so did McTaggart, 'merely because it appears at first sight the less virtuous course, and he has a childish love of naughtiness.'[4] Moore voted with them, for what struck Russell as a misguided but less frivolous reason: 'Because he is a Stoic and thinks happiness doesn't depend on externals such as food or clothing. Teach the East-ender to appreciate art and he will be happy. Moore is colossally ignorant of life.'[5] In his comments about the conduct of the discussion, Russell revealed something about the tone of the Society's debates, and a great deal about how the sides lined up:

> 'Crompton and I maintained very fine emotions were to be got out of identifying yourself with any great movement, even if it did have some practical utility, but I differed from Crompton in thinking it would be a gain if one could devote oneself solely to the pleasures not directly dependent on benevolence. (These include love.) The discussion was hopelessly unsatisfactory, as all discussions on practical questions always are.'[6]

Moore, who was reading classics at the time of his election, had his first sustained introduction to philosophy at the Society's meetings. Indeed the normal mode of discussion was philosophical – there were even recognized philosophical ploys: 'McTaggart ran his Absolute, as usual', wrote Russell to Alys and he protested that either it served no purpose to invoke the machinery of the absolute, or else that the absolute pointed to the opposite of McTaggart's conclusion. But Marsh 'being new, and not knowing the trick' was overwhelmed by McTaggart's dialectic and was 'half converted'. 'The odd thing about the Absolute', Russell pointed out, 'is that it always goes against the Chronicle, whatever that paper may happen to say. Also that when anybody else uses it McTaggart says it can't be used.'[7]

On 28 February Russell wrote to Alys on the subject of his forthcoming paper on electing women to the Society. The letter is revealing of the attitudes to sexual questions among the Apostles of this time:

'We of the Society set ourselves to face everything even if it does lead to temporary morbidness, and most of us would think a good deal about such things if we didn't talk of them : and my own experience is that nothing is so powerful as frank and fearless discussion for destroying morbidness produced by solitary brooding. And young men understand their sexual natures much better than girls, often only too well; and have to endure a great deal of by no means profitable talk, to which a better sort is the only antidote. I think nothing but want of frankness makes discussion on sexual subjects unwholesome : and that certainly would not be found in the Society.'

Russell then goes on to tease Alys about her two great passions, religion and the cause of women's rights. 'It is altogether a misfortune that women are so tied to sex, but no one is to blame except thy friend the Deity, who is much the worst enemy the advocates of women's rights have to contend with.'[8]

On 3 March Russell finally delivered the paper on 'Should we like to elect women?' which he called 'Lööberg or Hedda?'* Crompton Llewelyn Davies, Trevelyan, Wedgwood, Marsh, Moore, Mayor, Sanger and Russell himself voted Yes. A solitary No came from Lowes Dickinson. In the next day's letter to Alys, Russell described the meeting :

' – I may as well begin with an account of last night's meeting I suppose : on the whole it was *extremely* successful from my point of view. We divided on Should we like to elect women? and everybody voted Yes, except Dickinson, who is not of the active Society. Most people were of course very ignorant and were inclined to accept my psychology on trust : thanks to thy suggestions everybody seemed much impressed by the paper, and Crompton this morning was very complimentary about it. I didn't lose my temper with anybody fortunately, though I got a little annoyed with Dickinson in his discussion as he was inclined to doubt the possibility of apostolic women. Everybody almost [sic] thought (and I think rightly) that the apostolic nature is usually more passionate than the average, but that the occurrence of love would not matter. Moore said he was entirely in favour of it and the only thing which made him doubt was that my paper was so specious. I was too lazy to re-write it, but I added two pages at different places in the middle, which I enclose. Wedgwood [who appears not to have voted in the division] discovered the point I mentioned, that my end contradicts the beginning, but I invented

---

* In 1970 the Apostles did elect their first woman member.

a subtlety which reconciled them. – I was very glad Marsh knew the facts [that Russell was in love with Alys], as I should have been sorry so good a joke should be wasted: all through the discussion everybody except Crompton (who guessed) was saying how could I tell? I had no experience, and should find love very different from what I imagined it: at least that was Dickinson's line: he himself is as ignorant as he supposed me to be. However I think the analysis in my paper convinced most people I had somehow learnt to understand about it. The discussion convinced me that it is now merely a question of time, of waiting till enough of the older members have died, and that all new ones are likely to be in favour of it.'[9]

On Russell's own admission, Moore was right to find his paper 'specious', at least in one sense; for Russell had much earlier noticed the contradiction spotted by Wedgwood. Unable to resolve it, he had resorted to sophistry – the invented 'subtlety' – and simply cobbled the paper together as best he could. Russell put this fault down to laziness; Moore was later to come to think this tactic of Russell's dishonest.

The Apostles of this time were keenly interested in aesthetic questions; this is shown both by the next subject for discussion, 'Is any art criticism possible?' and by the topic for 28 April, 'Shall music and drama combine in the expression of emotion?' Those present for what was presumably a discussion of the opera were Mayor, Russell, Moore, Trevelyan, Sanger, Wedgwood and Marsh.

On 12 May 1894 Moore presented his maiden essay, an effort entitled 'What End?', which perhaps grew out of the discussion of 17 February, when Moore had voted for 'pleasure', for Moore has indicated that the subject of his paper was 'Hedonism'. This paper, which is muddled, confused and confusing, is nonetheless a document of great importance; first, because it shows that Moore, who was sitting part I of the classics tripos practically at the time of its delivery, was already interested in and familiar with contemporary philosophical questions. Secondly, this first foray into philosophy is important because Moore's later refutation of its principal thesis is one of the main strands in the development of *Principia Ethica*. On the first point 'What End?' must be the result of Russell's encouragement of Moore to do philosophy, for it was in this, his second year, that Russell

'urged me strongly to do what he had done and to take Part II of the Moral Science Tripos for my Second Part; and if he had not urged me, I doubt if I should have done so. Until that year I had in fact hardly known that there was such a subject as philosophy. I came up to Cambridge expecting to do nothing but Classics there, and expecting also that afterwards, all my life long, my work would consist in teaching Classics to the Sixth Form of some Public School – a prospect to which I looked forward with pleasure.'[10]

'What End?' is the paper referred to by Russell in his autobiography where he speaks of 'a paper which began: "In the beginning was matter, and matter begat the devil, and the devil begat God." The paper ended with the death, first of God and then of the devil, leaving matter alone as in the beginning. At the time when he read this paper, he [Moore] was still a freshman, and an ardent disciple of Lucretius.'[11] Russell's memory played him false on this occasion, for nearly everything in this passage is incorrect, except for the slightly misleading mention of Lucretius. Moore was not a freshman and his paper began with a general introduction which was, in the fashion favoured for Apostle's papers, irrelevant to the body of the essay, and not with the parody of Genesis with its memorable whiff of juvenile blasphemy.

It was Moore's second paragraph which opens 'In the beginning was matter and then came the devil', and which carries on with a Lucretian materialist catalogue until God is introduced in the fifth sentence. By implying that the subject of Moore's essay was a defence of Lucretian materialism, Russell has misled his readers wildly, for the subject of Moore's first philosophical effort is ethics.

The point of the Lucretian account of matter which Moore gives is to introduce sentient beings into the universe; it is all a bit of a joke, as is the introduction of a God compounded of equal parts of Plato and Hegel:

'In the beginning was matter and then came the devil. First we have gases, minerals, chemical combinations: of these I have nothing to say. Next we have vegetables, possessed of what is called life, and having needs which must be satisfied else death comes. Of this kind of life I am not speaking in this paper. Next comes the first animal organism and with it appears God; whom we find to be a dual not a trinal unity. God is life, and his two indivisible components are consciousness and will. His presence is shewn by the movement of the whole of his own body or by internal causes undiscoverable to science. The lowest animal I conceive [has] both will and consciousness, and one thing which puts them into connection is two abstractions – pleasure and pain. Either pleasure or pain or both are always to be predicated in some degree of every state in which consciousness is; and *will*, without which life cannot go on, is always being prompted by desire to avoid pain and seek pleasure.'

Moore gives his hearers the first hint of what he is trying to argue when he says, 'I need only go thus far in the history of the world to make it plain what I mean when I say that the desire for pleasant states is inseparable from life.' What he is seeking to establish is the truth of the doctrine of psychological hedonism – the thesis that, as a matter of fact, the end of all actions of conscious beings is an experience of pleasure. Moore also wants to argue in this paper for the truth of ethical hedonism, that what we *ought* to do is what will result in pleasant experiences:

'I now come to the practical question: How are we to help the person with will become conscious, and therefore wishing help, to decide what course to pursue? With his unconscious will I have told him that he is always aiming at pleasant states, though even there he is sometimes thwarted by the devil; but how is he to satisfy himself that he is not in some particular instance being so thwarted, being turned off the *right* road, the road in which he will realize himself, that is will continue to live with the greatest intensity and in accordance with the general development of life in the universe?'

Moore does seem to be aware that there is a difference between psychological and ethical hedonism, and he does seem to want to argue that both are true; but he does also seem to be aware, as he comes near the end of his essay, that he has not succeeded in establishing by argument the truth of ethical hedonism, and so he attempts to ground the case for ethical hedonism in the nature of the perfection of God: 'The end to which we tend, the perfection of God, would be consciousness without will or desire, and with all pleasant states of the greatest possible intensity not succeeding one another but all together.'

Implicit in, but confused with, Moore's arguments for psychological and ethical hedonism, is another thesis, that of the truth of 'the selfish philosophy', egoism; and again one must distinguish between psychological egoism – that, as a matter of fact, what every organism aims at is its *own* welfare (pleasure), and ethical egoism – that what one *ought* to aim at is one's own well-being. This last Moore covers with his use of the concept of self-realization. Since it is possible to be incorrect about what will in fact give one pleasure, Moore finds it necessary to postulate the existence of 'pseudo-consciousness', which is sometimes responsible for misleading us, as when we commit not the sins, but the mistakes of drunkenness and fornication: 'I have here treated with the two of the most primitive of the so-called pleasures – wine and women:

they are really, no doubt, causes of pleasant states but in taking them we may be sacrificing that more pleasant state of being in harmony with the world-development.' It is this last phrase that encapsulates the position Moore is trying to work out in this paper : egoistic hedonism – that what we should aim at in all our actions is our own pleasure. Following what he understands to be the position of McTaggart and Hegel, Moore regards the ultimate state of pleasure as 'being in harmony with the world-development'.

Thus we can see the point of Moore's Lucretian pastiche, and how he reached the conclusions of his paper, which must have startled his audience.

> 'That [idea] on which I lay least stress is the classification of pleasures. I am mainly anxious that that of pleasure, desire and will as always attendant upon consciousness should be recognized. And I was also bent on shewing that "self-realization" was the same thing as this pleasure after which we are necessarily always striving and ought always to strive. It follows also from my reasoning that both Sidgwick's ethical axioms are untrue.'

Among Moore's audience for this paper were four philosophers, Sanger, Wedgwood, Russell and Mayor. They must have been surprised by Moore's last sentence; for not only did Moore fail to mention Sidgwick anywhere in the body of his paper, but he actually seemed to be in agreement with one of the more important parts of Sidgwick's thought, his ethical hedonism. No doubt the debate after Moore's reading of his essay made it clear that Moore felt he was taking a more radical line than Sidgwick, as he conjoined to Sidgwick's hedonism the doctrine of ethical egoism.*

It was precisely to avoid ethical egoism that Sidgwick, in his *Methods of Ethics*, felt bound to adopt the second of his two axioms, i.e. the principle of benevolence. Moore was certainly correct in 'What End?' in thinking that his espousal of ethical egoism was inconsistent with

---

* Historians of philosophy have for long wondered whether Moore's influence on Russell was the greater, or Russell's on Moore. It is interesting to note in connection with this question that the conclusion of Moore's paper of 12 May was prefigured by Russell in a letter to Alys Pearsall Smith written on 25 February : 'I am also carrying on an ethical controversy as to ethical axioms : I have revolted from pure hedonism which has annoyed Sidgwick.'[12] It is clear from this that Russell not only interested Moore in philosophy in general, but also directed Moore's interest to specific topics in philosophy.

Sidgwick's axioms, and this has a great bearing on Moore's own philosophical development leading up to *Principia Ethica*.

A later formulation of Sidgwick's second axiom, 'as a rational being I am bound to aim at good generally – so far as it is attainable by my efforts – not merely at a particular part of it', makes it clear that the axiom is intended to be opposed to ethical egoism.[13] Sidgwick was desperate to avoid ethical egoism, for he felt it was self-contradictory; that in seeking to attain my own ends I must necessarily thwart the ends of others, and they in turn thwart mine, so that it is not *logically* possible to attain my own ends if I seek to attain my own ends. C. D. Broad comments on this point in his essay in *The Philosophy of G. E. Moore*: 'Sidgwick's axiom is equivalent to the assertion of ethical neutralism and ... ethical egoism is inconsistent with it.'[14] But Broad is concerned to show that ethical egoism is not self-contradictory. In 'What End?' Moore had assumed that ethical egoism was true; he later came to agree with Sidgwick that it was self-contradictory, and the struggle against ethical egoism is one of the main-springs of *Principia Ethica*. Broad went on to say that in *Principia Ethica* 'Moore simply assumes, in common with Sidgwick, that there must be a certain state of affairs which is *the* ultimate end at which *everyone* ought to aim; shows that ethical egoism is inconsistent with this assumption; and then unjustifiably accuses ethical egoism of being *self*-contradictory.'[15] The assumption of '*the* ultimate end at which *everyone* ought to aim' is, of course, the chief point of 'What End?', which was Moore's first venture into philosophy. Moore later came to deny its ethical egoism, but in its great assumption he persisted throughout his career as a philosopher.

Though as a mature philosopher Moore denied flatly the ethical egoism of his first philosophical essay, this does not, of course, mean that the early work was shoddy or insincere. It is probable that in the first flush of enthusiasm for his new subject the arguments against ethical egoism given above, which he later came to accept, simply did not occur to him, just as it seems not to have occurred to him to give arguments *for* that position, the truth of which, as we have seen, he merely assumed. If we look at the philosophical faults in this paper from a biographical standpoint, it would appear that the young man was trying to reconcile too many disparate strands of thought, and did not see the possibility that they might clash. It is obvious that Moore was trying to reconcile the Epicurean hedonism he had absorbed from his reading of Lucretius, with McTaggart's reading of Hegel, which assimilated the egoistic principle of self-realization to 'being in harmony with the World Spirit'. In his desire to be faithful to his classics while making a gesture of allegiance to his new master, McTaggart, Moore seems not to have anticipated the possibility that they might be in conflict. Of course Moore must have wished to make a big noise on the occasion of his first paper for the Apostles; to ensure this he resorted to the devices of classical rhetoric, and reserved his bombshell conclusion for his final sentence. There is no reason to be surprised that a young man with a classical education should present his argument in this way, but it is still surprising that a novice philosopher should manage to deal with such a prodigious number of substantive philosophical issues when making his début. It is no more than the privilege of maturity that Moore should later change his mind and, on reflection, come to agree with Sidgwick.

In the debate that followed Moore's paper on that Saturday evening in May 1894, it was evident that his hearers had taken the chief points of his argument – and disagreed with them. The question on which they divided was, 'Are all martyrs voluptuaries?' That is, in even the most extreme case of self-sacrifice, does every person act only to procure his own selfish pleasure? Are we all, even those of us who choose voluntarily to die in the cause of an ideal or religious belief, egoistic hedonists? Marsh, Sanger, Wedgwood, Russell and Mayor all voted No. Moore stuck to his guns and voted Yes, all martyrs are voluptuaries, '*voluptas* being understood as synonymous with happiness and pleasure'. Bob Trevelyan registered an inclination to side with Moore, and the Society moved on to its other business of the evening, the election of Theodore Llewelyn Davies, who had not taken up residence when he got his fellowship, as an honorary member.

Moore had by now created a role for himself in the Society, one in which he was assured and comfortable, and able to argue as an equal with his elders. Though McTaggart, for example, was one of Moore's teachers, the traditions of the Society itself required that they regard themselves as being on an equal footing in discussion. Moore was very active in these discussions, as is shown by a letter from Sanger to Russell about the meeting of 26 May, a fortnight after Moore's first paper: 'We had a very long and rather large meeting last night with Dickinson and Wedd present and, of course, we disagreed with the greatest vigour. Moore was, I think, even more splendid than usual and, in addition was not so brutal to those who failed to agree with him.'[16]

Moore and Russell decided to take a break before their triposes began and go on a walking tour in Norfolk.

'I am going to the sea tomorrow with Moore, who also has a Tripos (the Classical) beginning on Monday. We mean to walk 15 miles a day till Saturday, on which day I have to be back to dine at the Lodge [Pembroke Lodge, Russell's home]; but I daresay we shan't walk quite so far really. I feel sure that our whole talk will consist in my trying to persuade him that the phrase "unconscious will" is meaningless, which doubtless seems to thee a very frivolous topic, as indeed it does to me.'[17]

This last phrase sounds an ominous note for the future of Moore's and Russell's friendship, and in the event they did not talk exclusively of that 'frivolous topic'. Instead there was another sort of talk, which Moore found disturbing and distressing.

'Moore and I came back yesterday morning, having walked 40 miles in two days without perceptible fatigue, and I am indeed "disgustingly healthy" by now, but also very sleepy. We made friends with a man we met in the hotel, who was very well informed in various matters and a very good linguist, but whose talk consisted almost wholly of his own and his friends' immoralities. Moore is very ignorant, so I drew this man out for Moore's instruction and my amusement, and he poured forth beastly stories, one more horrible and disgusting than the other, till Moore could hardly contain himself. Afterwards Moore was tremendously excited, and realized for the first time what men are. He was merely an average specimen, but Moore said he was the most wicked man he had ever met or even read about, and couldn't have a spark of good in him, which was amusing. Moore said he had never known till this hour what it was to hate a man, that he had hated one other for a similar reason, but not nearly so much as this one. I tried to persuade Moore most men were just like that, and to shew him the man had only talked because I encouraged him and pretended to be just as bad myself; and I think Moore has really learnt a useful lesson and will take reformers and such people more seriously in future. I shouldn't wonder if Moore would have murdered him if they had been much longer together. What made him particularly mad was that, on discovering he had read some indecent classical authors (for his work) the man persisted in regarding him as a sly dog, a very deep person, who hid all sorts of wickedness under an innocent exterior. The whole thing, when I could conquer my disgust, was most amusing, and but for me Moore would never have found him out, as they would only have talked of architecture and history.'[18]

The strange light in which Russell unwittingly reveals *himself* in this extraordinary passage cast a shadow over his relationship with Moore. Russell had 'amused' himself by toying with Moore's innocence – a highly remarkable form of seduction. He had tried to infect Moore with his own view of man's nature – which in spite of his carefully non-Christian upbringing was that man is essentially a sinful creature in need of 'reform'. Russell's enthusiasm for political movements of the Left must have sprung from this conviction; it was this conviction that allowed him to be in fundamental sympathy with Alys's disposition, though he explicitly disavowed the religious conclusions she drew from the sinfulness of human nature. This deep conviction of something that almost amounted to a belief in original sin caused Russell to take some noble stands and utter some well-justified, ringing protests in his long life: from the First World War to the war in Vietnam Russell was on the side of the angels because he secretly believed in the devil. But there was something nasty, even dishonourable, in seeking to give Moore 'instruction' by tampering with what was his greatest virtue, and the quality for which so many people – even in his youth – loved and revered him, his innocence. Moore's outrage at the talk of the foul-mouthed man in the hotel was Dostoevskian in its intensity, but so was the innocence Russell sought to deprive him of. Moore was already suspicious of the quality of Russell's intellectual integrity; his doubts about it grew. So did his dislike of the man who exposed him to an unpleasantness he himself probably considered trivial, but which upset Moore emotionally as well as intellectually. No doubt Russell genuinely forgot what happened on this occasion – certainly the letter quoted above was not available to him when he wrote his *Autobiography* – the version of this episode given in that book is meant to serve as an example of Moore's purity, but it is meant also to be an amusing story. The comparison with Russell's own earlier version of the encounter makes one wonder whether Russell's memory or his morals were the more culpable:

'In the world of intellect, [Moore] was fearless and adventurous, but in the everyday world he was a child. During my fourth year I spent some days walking with him on the coast of Norfolk. We fell in by accident with a husky fellow, who began talking about Petronius with intense relish for his indecencies. I rather encouraged the man, who amused me as a type. Moore remained completely silent until the man had gone, and then turned upon me, saying, "That man was horrible." I do not believe that he has ever in all his life derived the faintest pleasure from improper stories or conversation."[19]

If Russell did remember more of the story when he re-told it in his *Autobiography*, then perhaps he censored some of the less attractive details because he felt – quite properly – guilty.

After the horrors of their walking tour and their triposes Moore and Russell attended the Society's annual dinner at the Savoy Hotel on 13 June. As the newest member Moore served as vice-president, and was obliged to make a speech. On this occasion he met several older Apostles who were no longer active. G. H. Blakesley was then a distinguished barrister of forty-eight. James Parker Smith, aged forty, was a Liberal Unionist MP. Walford D. Green, who had been active in the Apostles two years earlier, was twenty-five years old, reading for the Bar, and preparing to stand as Conservative candidate for Wednesbury. A. H. Smith was thirty-four, and an Assistant Keeper at the British Museum. A. H. Clough was a thirty-five-year-old barrister. Henry Yates Thompson, at fifty-six the oldest Apostle present, had sold the *Pall Mall Gazette* two years earlier, and was then concentrating on improving his great manuscript collection. Stephen Spring Rice was at age thirty-eight already quite high up in the Treasury. Marlborough Robert Pryor, aged forty-five, was a country gentleman with important business connections. Harry Francis Wilson, who was devoted to the Apostles, was, aged thirty-five, at the beginning of his great career as a colonial administrator, Walter Raleigh was thirty-three and Professor of Modern Literature at Liverpool. William Wyse, thirty-four, was Professor of Greek at University College London. H. H. Turner was, at the early age of thirty-three, Professor of Astronomy at Oxford. Theodore Beck, aged thirty-five, was back temporarily from India, where he was principal of the Anglo-Indian College of Aligarh. John Fletcher Moulton, aged fifty, was then Liberal MP for South Hackney. Sir Frederick Pollock Bt. was at forty-nine the Corpus Professor of Jurisprudence at Oxford. W. H. Macaulay, in his late thirties, was bursar of King's College, Cambridge. Edward Conybeare was fifty-one, the vicar of a Cambridgeshire parish church and a writer. Gerald Balfour, aged forty-one, was Conservative MP for Leeds. Other older men present Moore already knew from Cambridge: Wedd, Verrall, Henry Sidgwick, Ward, Duff, McTaggart and Whitehead. In addition there were the active or recently active Apostles of, or nearer to, Moore's own generation: Crompton and Theodore Llewelyn Davies, Mayor, MacNaghten, Sanger, Russell, Trevelyan, Wedgwood and Marsh.

They were mostly distinguished academics, with whom the twenty-year-old Moore was probably comfortable, having encountered many of them already at Cambridge.* But the 1894 dinner must have been the first time Moore was in the company of politicians, several of them rising men on the brink of office, and others with connections to the great world of the Treasury, the City, and the press. The very lack of comment in Moore's notes and jottings about that time of his life inclines one to think that he took it all in his stride, being neither impressed nor disdainful of those whose careers took them outside the university's cloisters and quadrangles. As he addressed the more than thirty past and present Apostles who attended the dinner, Moore must have cut an interesting figure; he was, we know, extraordinarily handsome, and his cleverness was well known to those who were his examiners, teachers and contemporary Apostles. To the less academic and more worldly Apostles at the dinner Moore might well have recalled their own youthful selves. A good many of them had read classics too, and could possibly see in their undergraduate vice-president a future lawyer, politician, civil servant or connoisseur. To the others Moore was no doubt a future academic; but as far as we know he still thought of himself as an embryo schoolmaster.

About a week after the dinner came the news of Moore's first in part I of the classics tripos. Congratulations came from Verrall in a letter dated 22 June: 'Let me begin by congratulating you on your division in the Tripos, which was most magnificent, though I regret that those phenomena and buzzing chimaeras Nairn and Barnett should have been thought worthy of comparison with the Sidgwick-hunting McTaggart-bewildering "hammer of the angels".'

Moore had had an active social life in the spring of 1894, full of travel and visits. In March he went to Belgium and Holland with Bob Trevy. Also in that month he seems to have *walked* from Cambridge to London. Crompton Llewelyn Davies stayed one night with the Moores at Woodthorpe in April, and he and Moore attended a concert together at Dulwich. In May, presumably after his tripos, Moore went to Hunstanton where he stayed two nights with Russell, and the next month to Dakyns at Haslemere, where he played the piano with the great Joachim.

* Though not completely comfortable, as is shown by a letter to Moore from A. W. Verrall written five days after the dinner: 'What in the name of Hades, Tomlinson Bishop of Gibraltar and all other brethren and Angels, do you mean by addressing me as "Dear Sir"?'[20]

1. Moore in early manhood

2. Moore's father, Daniel Moore

3. Moore's mother, Henrietta Sturge

4. Moore at about seventeen

5. Moore's brother Tom

6. R. C. Trevelyan ('Bob Trevy')

7. G. M. Trevelyan

8. Theodore Llewelyn Davies

9. Crompton Llewelyn Davies

10. Bertrand Russell and his wife Alys Pearsall Smith in 1894
(*Collection Mrs Barbara Strachey Halpern*)

11. Oscar Browning   12. Goldsworthy Lowes Dickinson in 1910

13. Leonard Woolf with Moore in June 1914

14. Lytton Strachey and Saxon Sydney-Turner in 1914
(*Photographed by Ray Strachey, Collection Mrs Barbara Strachey Halpern*)

15. Ralph Wedgwood (seated) and
Ralph Vaughan Williams

16. Desmond MacCarthy

17. Roger Fry in 1915

18. Oliver Strachey, Moore and
Maynard Keynes, 1914

(*Photographed by Ray Strachey, Collection Mrs Barbara Strachey Halpern*)

19. The Cambridge University Moral Science Club in 1915 (MAs only).
Moore is standing on the extreme left, Russell is standing second
from the right and McTaggart is sitting on the extreme right.

20. A. R. Ainsworth

21. Ludwig Wittgenstein
(*Photographed by Dorothy Moore*)

The reading parties which were to play so large a part in Moore's life began in July of this year, when he went to Skye for five or six weeks with Wedgwood, George Trevelyan, Maurice Amos, Vaughan Williams and Moore's brother, Bertie. The plans were made well in advance, as is shown by Wedgwood who wrote:

'I hope you are not starting too impatiently at your philosophy, as I shall not be beginning it till I get to Skye: At present I am busy at Psychology. The Books I am going to bring are Locke's Human Understanding, Fraser on Locke (the Serial Edition), Berkeley (Dialogues and the other thing), and Descartes. Pollock's Spinoza I will get and am willing to get two or three more if you will tell me what you have got. I have ordered Windelband's History, which Stout says is the best.'[21]

In addition to reading, the young men holidaying on Skye indulged in Moore's favourite recreation, long walks. But on one of these he injured his knee so seriously that it continued to trouble him for some months. By October it had healed, and Moore was able to walk to Haslemere with Theodore Llewelyn Davies and Bob Trevelyan.

The Society were considering electing George Macaulay Trevelyan, now in his second year and reading history. He was already intensely political – which the members of the Society were not. To Russell, Sanger reports that 'we are quite divided about George Trevy – that is to say Marsh and Wedgwood are in favour of him, and I am, on whole, neutral but Moore thinks that most of our discussions would not interest him'.[22] The question of electing George Trevelyan was fairly urgent, for there were only about four Apostles whose regular attendance could be counted upon; this made it difficult to produce a paper every week, so while they were dithering over the younger Trevelyan, they were very glad of Russell's offer to come up and read them a paper. He suggested the title 'Cleopatra or Maggie Tulliver?', which was accepted without demur, and read to the Apostles on 3 November. The subject was passion, and the members divided on the question 'Duty or Passion?' with Moore, Marsh and Dickinson unequivocally voting for duty. Russell voted on both sides, appending the comment 'according to circumstances' to his vote for duty. For passion were, with Russell, Sanger, Wedd and McTaggart, who added: 'on the distinct understanding that it is of no practical importance'.

Sex in its various and interesting forms now became the Apostles' chief interest. After Russell on passion there came, on 10 November, Moore on love and friendship in a paper entitled 'Achilles or Patroclus?'

Moore's choice of the most famous homosexual lovers in all literature for his title suggests that the homosexual tone of the late eighties still persisted in the Society. This tone was a purely verbal matter, a tradition that in the discussion of sexual questions it was obligatory to make the humorous assumption that all sexual relations were homosexual ones, so that even heterosexual love had to be treated as only a special case of the Higher Sodomy. There can be no doubt that the tone was set, and the convention upheld, chiefly by McTaggart and Lowes Dickinson, for with the exception of Eddie Marsh, there were virtually no homosexuals elected to the Apostles during the nineties. In the late 1850s and early sixties there were overt homosexuals like Oscar Browning, Roden Noel and Arthur Sidgwick among the Apostles, but we do not know whether in their Saturday night meetings they discussed the merits of various schoolboys and the other questions that so exercised them in their private correspondence; still less do we know what sort of language they used in their essays and debates. They may have left a legacy of homosexual jargon to the men of the eighties, but it matters little for the Apostles of the 1890s; by then it was fashionable to be 'campy'. It was the heyday of Oscar Wilde, after all, and the Apostles had no monopoly on posing as sodomites. And in the case of Moore, posing it certainly was. As we shall see, Moore did not seem to realize that homosexuality existed in modern times before he was recruited by the Apostles.

The mannerisms of 'Achilles or Patroclus?' are, then, attributable to the traditions of the Society, and Moore's second Apostles' paper would be of little biographical interest, were it not for the presence in it of a theme that recurs in Moore's thought, a theme that finds its grandest expression in the famous chapter on 'The Ideal' in *Principia Ethica*. This is the emphasis on love and friendship in the passage that was to strike the Bloomsbury Group so forcefully: 'that personal affections and aesthetic enjoyments include *all* the greatest, and *by far* the greatest, goods we can imagine'.[23] Moore summed up 'Achilles or Patroclus?' thus: 'It is shewn that in love we obtain the highest of human goods. And then it is maintained that such love may be felt for one other human being in a completeness so great as to deserve setting this quite apart, as the one final end of life.'

In *Principia Ethica* Moore is not so insistent on the singularity of the object of love as he was in this essay; but the key idea of personal affection as a good or an end in itself was certainly present in this early effort.

'Achilles or Patroclus?' begins with the usual jokey defence of the choice of title. The subject is to be ' "friendship" in general', but the question may be interpreted whether the rich, high-born, famous lover, Achilles, or his less-advantaged beloved, Patroclus, 'had the preferable lot?' Moore says he is going to argue that the perfection of their friendship levelled their differences. He adds that this raises another question – a red herring to us, but to the Society the spice that was the necessary ingredient of any paper read to them. This was 'how far in friendship it is necessary that one party should be active (*erastés*) and the other passive (*erómenos*), and what effects on the happiness of each follow from this activity or passivity – in sodomy or otherwise'? Before getting down to the actual argument, there remains a gesture to be made – a sort of salute to McTaggart:

> 'I have not resisted my impulse to try to connect the subject with the whole theory of the universe: and before I step on to this to me forbidden ground, I must throw a sop to the dragon who guards it. I cannot plead any right to enter: but I only beg McTaggart, if I am quite on the wrong track, to say so very clearly.'

It is unlikely that there was any dissent from McTaggart, for the idea of perfect friendship was an important part of his own notion of Heaven without God; though Moore's treatment of the subject owed a good deal more to McTaggart's teacher Sidgwick than to McTaggart himself. The procedure Moore adopted in 'Achilles or Patroclus?' has Sidgwickian echoes that are to be heard again in *Principia Ethica*:

> 'In order to prove friendship so immensely valuable ... it seems necessary in some way to define the "good" and show the relation of friendship to it. Now let consciousness be analysed into 3 parts, the will, the intellectual, and the emotional. Which of these is it, or all, whose perfection gives us the end of life? The will may be rejected, as only the efficient cause, or perhaps the accompaniment of the other two. The highest function of the intellect is to perceive the whole of what is and the whole of what should be (which perhaps are not different) – that is to know the true and the good. This mere knowledge it seems to me impossible to regard as an end in itself – certainly, if it be so, it is different in kind from any of the ends which we practically pursue: these are all satisfactory states of emotion such as could only accompany knowledge, not be identified with it. There remains the emotional faculty, the perfection of which I cannot but consider as the final end of all life: it is on the activities of this faculty that pleasure (the most obvious of practical ends) attends,

and on its perfect activity, I conceive, attends happiness, which is a perfect and complete pleasure.'

If we substitute 'good states of mind' for the phrase 'satisfactory states of emotion', it is evident that one of the chief tenets of *Principia Ethica* is already present in this early paper. (This may fairly be regarded as a refinement of Sidgwick's conclusion, 'that the only Good that can claim to be so intrinsically, and at the same time capable of furnishing a standard of conduct, is Perfection or Excellence of conscious life'.[24] But how much clearer than the master's is the young pupil's formulation!)

It should be noted that in 'What End?' Moore thought, what he was later to deny in *Principia Ethica*,[25] that pleasure is the *sole* good. In 'Achilles or Patroclus?' he thinks pleasure is the *highest* good – happiness 'is a perfect and complete pleasure' – but not necessarily the sole good. Happiness makes its first appearance in Moore's second Apostles' paper – the word is not mentioned in the first – and this was to make his views more flexible, as 'happiness' carries fewer overtones of selfishness than does 'pleasure', a point taken by Sidgwick himself. While Moore has not, in 'Achilles or Patroclus?', abandoned Egoistic Hedonism – that would have been a very radical change of mind in the short interval between May and November – his thought is already progressing steadily in the direction of his mature work.

But we must remember that it is only with hindsight that we can regard Moore's early Apostles' papers as apprentice works; to his audience these landmarks in his philosophical journey, though no doubt understood *as* philosophical points, were parts of the argument of the ostensible subject of 'Achilles or Patroclus?' Thus Sanger wrote to Russell on 11 November 1894:

> 'Last night Moore read on friendship and Trevy, Mayor and Theodore came up so that we had a very good meeting. Wedgwood and Mayor differed from the rest of us in thinking that the fact of copulation made an essential difference whereas we thought that love and friendship graduated into one another and that copulation was of secondary importance. But we differed further and a great deal as to how far it was important, symbolically or otherwise.
> 'Theodore was very good and Moore's paper very clear.'[26]

Sanger's description of the discussion following Moore's paper is a very good indication of how, in an Apostles' meeting, nothing was ever quite what it seemed to be. The division Sanger alludes to was on the question 'Are solid friendships the best?', with Mayor and Wedgwood voting Yes, and Bob Trevelyan, Sanger, Theodore Llewelyn Davies, Wedd, Marsh, Moore, Dickinson and McTaggart voting No.

Moore invited this trivialization of his subject by tacking on to his real argument a paragraph that was foreshadowed by his earlier talk of 'activity' and 'passivity' – 'in sodomy or otherwise'. It must be stressed that this was expected by his audiences, because it was sanctioned, indeed demanded, by tradition. It is therefore not at all clear that the attitudes expressed in this paragraph were absolutely genuine : Moore may very well have delivered himself of these priggish propositions about sexual practices with his tongue implanted very firmly in his cheek.

'It will, I think, now be plain from my description that the passion with which my paper deals, may be felt equally between either man and woman, man and man, or woman and woman; and therefore may be called either friendship or love. It will also be plain that both parties must be active and both also passive in all the essential acts of their relation : ... I will take an important example. In copulation one party is active, the other passive; and this act has been exaggerated in importance as if in it was exhibited the chief [part] if not the whole of love. I take it, on the other hand, that sexual pruriency is to be very clearly distinguished from that sympathy, which I have laid down as the basis of love. It is necessary that this pruriency be indulged for the begetting of children; and, though for a man and woman who truly love one another copulation will be disagreeable, yet, they will share this as they share other trials and troubles, alleviating the unpleasantness by the consciousness of their sympathy. But, unfortunately, copulation like other low pleasures, has attractions for most people : so that they pursue it for its own sake, forgetting the highest pleasure of love, which alone and the means to it they ought to pursue. Hence comes that monstrous unnatural vice of copulating with a woman more often than is necessary for begetting children : hence also sodomy and sapphism, the indulgence of a desire for which, stunts or kills the capability, inborn in every human being, of enjoying the happiness of true love.'

We know from other papers that Moore did hold conventional views on sexual matters that would have been unpopular with his fellow Apostles, but the vehemence with which he denounces sexual acts in this paper (and the fact that Sanger did not bother to mention this in his account of the meeting to Russell) was obviously meant to tease his hearers, and show that he was quite capable of poking fun at his own views by exaggerating them.

The extent to which it was the practice of the Apostles to divorce the subject of the essay read to them from the question voted on subsequently is forcefully shown by the next week's meeting. McTaggart was the reader (or 'moderator') and the question for the vote was, 'Is indigestion an ultimate reality?' The actual subject revealed by Sanger's customary letter to Russell was very different: 'Last week McTaggart read his old paper on "Crumpled Roseleaves" about evil. We were rather unable to discuss it because of our ignorance of philosophy, but McT was very good and did not once use the word dialectic in the discussion.'[27]

With 1894 coming to a close, few of the brothers had the time or energy to produce papers, but Moore, with part I of his tripos behind him and not too much pressure on him to prepare for his second part, was better placed than some of the others to do some extra-academic work. And there was inclination too, for he had obviously taken something of a beating when he read 'Achilles or Patroclus?' So for the last meeting of 1894 on Saturday 8 December, he read 'Shall we take delight in crushing our roses?' in which he candidly defended 'a conventional view of sexual morality, such as in your nostrils will, I fear, savour rankly of puritanism and prudery. I own that I chose the subject with a view to justify my own feelings, and I have found the task very difficult.'

At least since the days of Hallam and Tennyson the Society had had a tradition of candour, and it is well known that no subject was taboo on Saturday nights. But so open and honest was Moore in this paper, that it is difficult to believe that the Society had ever before heard a paper so breathtakingly candid or so sweetly innocent. And yet it was really intellectual toughness that caused Moore to cast aside the secrecy that even the most extrovert people preserve about their own sexual experience, and make a gift of his most intimate confidences to the brothers present that night. He wanted his hearers to be able 'to judge whether I am speaking from prejudice or rationally', so to the Apostles he confessed in detail his own sexual experience and the shame he had felt – all and solely in the interest of getting at the truth. In a delicate manner he alluded to masturbation and to his own virginity.

In defence of his feeling, the legacy no doubt of his Quaker and evangelical forbears, that lust is base and copulation vicious except when done with the intention of procreating, Moore adduced the emotion of shame, which every human being has experienced at some time or another in connection with sexuality. Shame he took as the mark of the badness of the emotion of lust and the action of indulging it.

Like Prince Myshkin's willingness to discuss anything about himself – his fits as well as his feelings – his *ability* to bare his soul, Moore's willingness to reveal his shame as well as his innocence in this Apostles' paper, gives us some insight into what was so remarkable about his character, this trait that is so often testified to, but so difficult even to describe.

To an audience consisting of Marsh, Russell, Sanger, Crompton Llewelyn Davies, Wedgwood, Dickinson and McTaggart, seven men of varying ages and temperaments, for whom he felt varying degrees of affection and intimacy, Moore exposed his soul; and this in 1894, a time when such conversation would have embarrassed a doctor or a priest. And this he did because, even at the age of twenty-one, he was intellectually scrupulous; it was because the *argument* required it.

Speaking of the universality of lust and the frequency with which it is felt, Moore admitted:

'I think it is possible that I may exaggerate this prevalence, because of some peculiarity in my experience: the very shame, which I take to be my witness of the badness of the thing, makes it very difficult to obtain conclusive evidence – innocence is almost indistinguishable from hypocrisy, even while the minds of the innocent and hypocrite are at the greatest possible distance from one another.'

Moore did *not* regard his own condition as one of innocence, but of ignorance:

'When I came up to Cambridge, I did not know that there would be a single man in Cambridge who fornicated; and, till a year ago, I had no idea that sodomy was ever practised in modern times. My discoveries on these points have naturally brought the subject very much before my mind, and perhaps made me attach an undue importance to it; though I had been long familiar with the extent of the vice in Greece and Rome, and had often read of it merely to indulge my lust.

'Here may conveniently come in one thing, which I wish to be carefully understood, . . . Ignorance and innocence, I should distinguish as carefully as any one of you, and am very anxious that the present ignorance of the nature of lust, especially in girls, should disappear. But at the same time my own experience has led me to think that there is great danger of lust itself being mixed with the desire for knowledge about it.'

At the conclusion of this startling paper, the question put to the vote was 'Must copulation be lustful?' Moore could hardly have been surprised that everyone present voted against him and answered No, except for McTaggart, who said: 'Yes. But lust is good in its place.' With his good humour unruffled and intact, Moore inscribed himself Yes, 'but not hereafter'. Having with those words recorded a moral victory, Moore retreated to Woodthorpe to spend Christmas with his parents.

The first Apostles' meeting of 1895 seems to have taken place on 26 January. Marsh read, and reported to Russell that it was

'a very interesting subject which I couldn't express in words, tho' people saw what I meant – something like this; when there's an ideal duty on one side a practical good on the other, which ought you to follow? Sanger and I thought that if you were a fine enough person you could do as you pleased. Moore of course disagreed; his "continuous exposition" was rather remarkable; his main point was that the only thing of the least importance is to be a fine character, and that landed him in the statement that everyone who's ever going to be a fine character is so the moment he's born, and that nothing that happens afterwards can make the least difference. So you see he's not much changed. We aren't any nearer to thinking of new members.'[28]

Russell was in Berlin with Alys, whom he had married in December, to attend economics lectures at the University of Berlin, but Sanger wrote on 17 February asking a question about physics and geometry, which had arisen out of his reading of Lotze with Moore. 'I can't understand it,' wrote Sanger, 'but it amuses me. Moore takes it quite seriously and finds that metaphysical difficulties keep him from getting bored.'[29] Sanger continues his letter:

'At the Society last night Raleigh, who had come up to lecture at Newnham, read a smart amusing paper about profanity and indecency. We concluded that they both existed (most of the Society rather thought that it was impossible to be efficiently profane) and that indecency was a question of style (in the widest sense). Finally we divided, about evenly, on "Is the reader or the writer obscene." It was a good meeting, Whitehead, Wedd and Wyse came.... We're thinking very seriously of electing George Trevy: but we can't find anyone else.... The most interesting varsity thing is the appointment of the new history professor.* The betting on O.B. is slowly receding, but it is difficult to see who Ld. Rosebery can possibly give the appointment to. The standing joke is, of course, "O.B. or not O.B. that is the question?"...P. S. Marsh has got a Chancellor's medal and Moore a varsity scholarship.'[30]

Raleigh had not been an academic star at Cambridge, so his choice of career was not an easy one, and for a time seemed to lie between journalism and a minor academic post. When the latter was offered him in 1889, at Manchester, he seized it, but strangely enough he was there only a few months. A. C. Bradley had just left the professorship of English literature at Liverpool for the chair at Glasgow, and the imaginative Liverpool electors chose as the great critic's replacement Raleigh, aged twenty-eight, and the author of only a single paper on Browning. At Liverpool Raleigh flourished, married Lucy Gertrude Jackson, and wrote some of his most famous, though now rarely read, books: *The English Novel*, *Robert Louis Stevenson*, *Style*, and *Milton*. In 1900 he again succeeded Bradley, this time to the chair at Glasgow. While there he published *Wordsworth* and *English Voyagers*, and was so successful he was invited to be Oxford's first professor of English literature only four years later. Raleigh actually founded Oxford's English school, and for this, on the joint recommendation of Balfour and Asquith, he was knighted in 1911, becoming the second Sir Walter Raleigh.

On 23 February a paper was read on 'Is happiness a test of progress?' and the Society finally made up its mind to elect G. M. Trevelyan to membership. They had been debating this election since early autumn, and it seems that Moore was responsible for the delay, for, as Eddie Marsh wrote to Russell, 'Moore who knows him better than anyone else has scruples.'[31]

In the next essay, probably generated by the discussion following Raleigh's paper of 16 February, Moore found something to engage his philosophical attention in the fact that Raleigh was able to be 'amusing' on the subject of profanity and indecency. Moore read a paper on 2 March on humour and was probably inspired to write it by reflecting on what he therein calls the 'charm of the indecent'. Riding his puritan hobby-horse, as usual, it must have struck Moore as puzzling that the indecent should be funny. Intuitively he felt indecency to be a bad thing; humour, a good thing; why should there be a natural or at least

---

* The appointment to the Regius Professorship of modern history was in fact the imaginative and bold one of Lord Acton.

frequent conjunction of the two? He called his paper 'Can God be serious?', which was another way of asking whether humour is a good thing.

> 'I am using serious as a negative predicate, denoting the absence of that particular emotion of which laughter is usually the sign, and which as it has no name, I will in future, for convenience, call "sense of humour". By God I mean a being which should be perfectly good, if such a thing is conceivable. And what I want to know is whether such a God could laugh; whether a sense of humour is consistent with perfect goodness.'

Moore had for some time been attending McTaggart's lectures on Hegel; this paper shows him trying to come to grips with the chief philosophical problem posed by the Hegelian philosophy, the nature of the absolute; it further shows that Moore, though a willing pupil, could not bring himself easily to accept his master's teachings. Moore jibbed at the idea that we could *know* any of the attributes of a perfect being; the only predicate we *know* we can apply to a perfect being is 'goodness; and that by itself scarcely differs from non-entity'. This remark he addressed personally to McTaggart (although he may not have been present to hear it), and it allowed Moore to draw a conclusion that savoured of the sort of paradox of which the Society was so fond: 'Since God, then, is absolutely indeterminate, I cannot say if he has a sense of humour; though I may safely declare that he may *not* have it – that he may be serious.' Humour then is not a necessary good, as it would be if it were an attribute of a perfect being; it is a contingent good, and the object of Moore's paper was 'to determine as far as possible, under what circumstances and in what degree a sense of humour is good'. Proceeding to an analysis of humour itself, Moore defines it by noting that

> 'an universal mark of it seems to be contrast in some form or other, whether between a person's present state and that in which he previously was, or between his opinion of himself and his actions or character as they appear to other people, or between his professions and his real beliefs or nature; or again in the juxtaposition of words or ideas, not commonly associated together. But the essence of humour cannot lie in this contrast, because the same contrast may produce quite different pleasurable or painful emotions'

and he instances the pain of tragedy and the pleasure of comedy as emotions resulting from opposite contrasts.

In language that curiously foreshadows that of *Principia Ethica* Moore concludes: 'Nothing, then can be said to be essentially humorous – humorous for all persons and at all times. The sense of humour is a distinct simple emotion, as are love and hate, and, like them it is excited now by one thing, now by another.' This reasoning leaves Moore free to distinguish the proper object of laughter from the improper one, and to deliver a little homily on inconstancy of affection, lack of sympathy with the thing or person laughed at, even the possibility that the person who is too easily moved to laughter shows 'an incapacity for any strong emotion', culminating in an attack on indecent humour – an attack intended to discomfit those in his audience who had evidenced their relish of indecent humour in the discussion after Raleigh's paper.

'It is a bad kind, as being founded on a renunciation of all attempt to be reasonable and consistent. This is when we laugh at the contrast between our desires and a restraint which we have been taught to respect, without understanding why the restraint is desirable or accepting it as right. We leave our minds undetermined on a matter which in practice we recognise as most important, and we laugh, in folly, at the contradiction, which we will not apply ourselves to solve.'

Moore, conscious that he has once again tried to justify what he already believes, ends his paper with an apology.

'I am very much ashamed that this paper is so short and so bad. I wished to make out a system which could be applied to all views and cases; but I have failed altogether and despair of the utility of adding a good deal more matter which I had collected, without giving it shape, or even of trying to summarise what I have already written and to make it consistent. For some time past I seem to have been unable to think.'

While Moore no doubt meant this, it was part of his personal charm that he could see something funny in his mental fogginess. He ends his paper (employing the convention that all great thinkers of the past were to be regarded as honorary Apostles): 'if there is any excuse in precedent, perhaps I may claim the protection of our great brother Aristotle, who seems also to have found the manifold too many for consistency when he wrote us his interesting paper on Ethics.'

Dividing on the question, 'Is Humour infinite?', Marsh, Wedgwood, and the two Trevelyans joined Moore in voting Yes, while Sanger,

Wedd and Dickinson voted No. The evening ended with Moore accepting election as the Society's forty-ninth secretary, an office he carried out with dedication for several years.

The success of the reading party on Skye in the long vacation of 1894 led to its being repeated in the Easter vacation of 1895 at Seatoller in Cumberland. The same group, Amos, George Trevelyan, Wedgwood. Vaughan Williams and Moore, joined together once again, to walk, read, and – remarkably in view of the weather – to bathe. This time the band of friends kept a log book, which shows how they structured their days and their conversations. They recorded in it each day the name of the last to rise and of the 'president' who presided over their discussions, as well as the topic for discussion, the state of the weather, the type of expeditions undertaken and the identities of those fearless enough to bathe. In the book are poems, parodies and drawings, specimens of undergraduate wit composed by three future holders of the Order of Merit (Moore, Trevelyan and Vaughan Williams), a future judge and eminent legal scholar (Amos), and the future head of the London North Eastern Railway (Wedgwood). Wedgwood, Vaughan Williams and Amos were preparing for their triposes; Moore's and Trevelyan's reading served less urgent purposes. The five were intimate friends, and had much in common besides being on their second reading party together. The two Ralphs were cousins; three of them, Moore, Wedgwood and Amos were reading moral sciences (all were to get firsts); they were all keen walkers; Moore shared Vaughan Williams's passion for music; and three were Apostles. The secrecy of this last matter must have strained relations slightly with Amos and Vaughan Williams, for Moore, Wedgwood and Trevelyan would have been obliged to be guarded in their conversation in front of the other two.

Among the entries in the log book are engaging glimpses of the participants' characters and habits. For example, there is the fragment 'Theophrastus Revised' in the hand of Amos, which comments on Moore:

> 'The balance of this acute intelligence is never (or very rarely) disturbed by that striving for a bald logical consistency which diverts more formal minds from speculative rectitude. Neither does he take any pleasure in controversy whose end lies only in itself. Being singly concerned with the interests of the intelligence, it may be doubted if he knows so much as what he eats – whether it be flesh or fish,

bread or even butter. Nor will it ever be said of him that he cunningly by a pretence robs widows of their mite.'

In one respect Moore may have found the members of this party more congenial than he would have found a party composed entirely of his fellow Apostles. Each of the young men present inclined at least slightly to Moore's own romantic, Victorian sentiments about love and sex: there was none among them tinged by the Apostles' fashion for talk of 'sodomy'. Indeed their contributions to the log book show them more inclined to view themselves in the romantic troubadour tradition. There was so much about knights and mediaeval scholars in their tales and verses, that Amos felt the need to supply a modernist antidote, a comic tale of passion called 'Paris in Camden Town'. Ralph Vaughan Williams, for example, was at this time something of a dandy, good-looking and very interested in girls. Nonetheless, he had a deeply romantic disposition and, though he even admired those 'freer' than himself, he valued purity – in himself and in women.[32] To Vaughan Williams, Moore's puritanical views were more sympathetic than the Apostles found them. It may be that all the members of the reading party were self-consciously and humorously aware that they differed in this way from their other Cambridge friends who held more 'advanced' views, for one of Amos's contributions to the log book, a pastiche history of the Seatoller party, was called 'An Examination of the Ancient legend of the "Secession of the Prigs" – otherwise known as the Seatoller Saga'.

As for the reading, G. M. Trevelyan wrote to Vaughan Williams, who had had to leave early, that: 'We have set up an institution of reading Shaker in the evening. . . . Moore reads very well indeed.'[33] And to his elder brother Bob, Trevelyan wrote about private reading: 'Moore reading Jane Eyre and novels chiefly, and I all sorts of jolly books, . . . I never had a jollier time. The party suits itself very well, we get on splendidly; it is even a greater success than the Skye party. There is not the slightest distance between Moore and Wedgwood that there was at Skye. . . . and Moore and I have also walked across to Grasmere and Rydal, we being the Wordsworthians of the party.'[34]

This walk took Moore and George Trevelyan to Dove Cottage, where first Wordsworth and then De Quincey had lived. There they met an old woman who had known Wordsworth, and from among the various pictures of the poet hanging in the house, she pointed out the one that bore the greatest likeness to him. The young men proceeded to Rydal Mount, passing a farmhouse where Coleridge had lived; their Lake Poets' pilgrimage completed, they returned to Seatoller by a long and difficult route which Trevelyan, always a fanatical walker, insisted upon.[35]

By 30 April, Moore had been back at Trinity for some time, and wrote to his mother that he was moving into larger rooms which had formerly been occupied by his friend Dakyns. In the same letter he speaks of deeds and papers written in a near-unintelligible legal jargon, which he has signed and had witnessed. As he had reached his majority by then, these documents must have related to his Sturge inheritance, and it would have been then that he became possessed of the private income that was to make it possible for him to pursue his career as a philosopher in the years to come when he had no academic post.

With George Trevelyan and two other undergraduates, Moore was invited to dine at Newnham with the Sidgwicks. His description of the evening to his mother includes both a glimpse of the domestic life of the Sidgwicks, and an interesting comment on Sidgwick as a philosopher. He wrote on 30 April 1895:

'The professor is immensely interesting and amusing: he always has plenty to say, wandering on gently from topic to topic, with shrewd remarks and plenty of witty anecdotes; I wish it were the same with his lectures, but they generally seem three times as long as anybody else's, and are very difficult to follow. He is so familiar with his subject and all its side-issues, that he does not make its skeleton clear enough, being continually engaged in arguments on details. This is also the fault of his book on "Methods of Ethics". Mrs Sidgwick (Arthur Balfour's sister) is very nice; what little she said was worth hearing, but it was little because her husband flowed continuously.'

Henrietta Moore seems to have remonstrated with her son that he was not doing enough work, and this provoked the interesting reply of 26 May 1895:

'I am afraid I am an idler by nature and should find any work troublesome: I have certainly as much real interest in my present work as I ever had in my classics; the difference is that there I had the stimulus of set tasks and regular habits, which is wanting now; I can only console myself by hoping that, when I do work now, I work more effectively (I certainly do at times) and looking forward to a time when I shall have exchanged the difficult business of learning for the much easier one of teaching.'

Increasingly interested in Sidgwick, Moore reported to his mother another encounter with him.

'Last Friday evening, after taking my French pupils [two students from the Albert Institute whom he was coaching in French language], I went to the sole meeting for this term of the Moral Science Club, at which Prof. Sidgwick read his annual paper – this time on the lessons of socialism to economics. The paper was only of a theoretical interest, shewing three points in which exaggerated doctrines of socialists, on the one side, had moderated exaggerated views of economists on the other. Throughout he shewed himself very sceptical of the practical worth of socialistic schemes, and derided the Germans in general, and particularly on this point. He stammers very badly at times; and unfortunately I had been warned that some people were coming who would be likely to laugh; accordingly I caught the very first chuckle, and, being very liable to that kind of infection, could scarcely restrain myself, and that only by grimacing. Hence I could not attend as well as I wished.'

Theodore Llewelyn Davies was in Cambridge, staying with the Verralls. They went together to a garden party on 25 May at the house of their fellow-Apostle Ward, and there Moore partnered at tennis a Miss Sturge, a distant cousin of his from Bristol, who was reading moral science at Newnham. He continued his letter to his mother : 'I thought she seemed distinctly dis-agreeable – the kind of person who would take a morose delight in snubbing everyone, and that without any superiority to justify her : but I hope I may have been mistaken. She said she had always heard of us that we shut ourselves up at home and did nothing but study.' Much more agreeable was the warm spring weather, which allowed Moore to join a party to bathe at Byron's Pool, and afterwards dry themselves in the sun, lying in the long green grass dotted with buttercups; he remarked that the flatness of the Cambridge landscape was an advantage, for it seemed to make the grass grow richer, and often the view was cut short abruptly by hedges and trees.

On 5 May 1895 Moore had read his first paper to the Trinity Sunday Essay Society on the subject, 'The Socratic Theory of Virtue'. The Society met on Sunday evenings, 'for the discussion of subjects connected with Religion', but in the Easter term 1895, its members included McTaggart, Amos and G. M. Trevelyan, and it is clear that 'religion' was by then interpreted in the widest possible sense, so that it included not only ethics, but psychology and even literary criticism.

In this essay Moore dealt with the paradox arising from the Socratic identification of virtue and knowledge, which he set out in his own translation of the famous passage from Xenophon : 'If any man, then, knew what was so, he would not choose any other kind of action; but if any man did not know what was fair and good, he could not do it, but must fail, even if he tried.' Moore pointed out that 'when we say "wickedness" we surely don't mean "ignorance" ', and that therefore 'common sense . . . is at issue with Socrates; and the object of this paper is to explain wherein they differ.'

Moore continues by summarizing the doctrine as expressed in Plato's *Protagoras*: 'We always do what we know to be good, says Socrates; when men sin it is only because they have committed an error of judgement.' He then raises Grote's objection that it is futile to defend this doctrine by giving a new sense to the word 'knowledge'. But this is precisely what Moore does do: he says that he feels that Grote, as opposed to Hume, would allow us to say that we *know* that the sun will rise tomorrow as it has always done in the past, not merely that we *believe* it.

'We believe that the sun will rise to-morrow, because we have observed and do observe no event, except what does not appear to have prevented it from rising before. But when we say that we believe or know we ought to work, and yet continue to do nothing, are we not then mis-using the words "believe" and "know", because all our observations are not now in harmony with those which formerly led us to conclude that work was good? We have a desire to continue idle; we so far believe that idleness is a good; and therefore we do not completely assent to the proposition that it would be good for us to work.

'My point is then that for every "knowing", properly so-called, this assent of the will, which constitutes true belief, is necessary: this is equivalent to saying that every condition, upon which the truth of our hypothetical proposition depends, is absolutely fulfilled, because nothing contrary is present to the mind.'

Moore now accepts the distinction between the theoretical syllogism, in which assent to the premises necessarily leads to assent to the conclusion, and the practical syllogism, in which belief in the premises necessarily leads to action. He does not accept the validity of the practical syllogism uncritically, but defends it by saying that it is rare for us to reason from premises to which it is possible to assent whole-heartedly: 'There are presented to us but few premises, which force such absolute assent; we cannot exhaust the conditions implied in them: and in these cases our assent is determined more casually by probabilities, or may receive force from habit.'

In the case of conscious decisions to act, Moore says, there is only one certain premiss – of which he will speak later in his paper; the other premisses gain their force from memory of previous experience, from the effect on the imagination of desires, or from habit. Few premisses are certain, so few conclusions of the practical syllogism are certain; in the rare cases when we do have the necessary knowledge, Moore thinks, our will assents with 'full force' and the 'act of assent at once leads to external action'.

Moore had not yet begun the serious philosophical study of Plato and Aristotle, and this might be the reason that he did not attempt to give an example of a necessary practical syllogism; had he made the effort he might have concluded that he could not think of one in which certain premisses led to a necessary conclusion which in turn resulted in immediate action. He might then have been less content to accept parity between the theoretical and practical syllogism. But several of the points he goes on to make are interesting for his future philosophical development:

'If then this analysis of knowledge be correct; if the assent of the will is necessary for every judgement, and in practical matters this assent implies action: then it is Grote and Aristotle, who err with the vulgar, in giving the name of knowledge to an act, not completed by that belief, which they commonly recognise as necessary to knowledge. The Socratic doctrine may have been a half-truth, in that it did not explicitly state the part played by will in all cognition: but it is a half-truth only in the sense in which it is a half-truth to say of a curved line that it is concave, in which statement the whole truth that it is also convex is fully implied. The common distinction between ignorance and wickedness is valid, only if it pretends to correspond to the distinction between a theoretical and a practical judgment; it is only utterly at fault when it goes on to assert that a man may do wrong knowing that it is wrong: since it is impossible that his will can have given complete assent to the theoretical judgment that his action is wrong, without enforcing the contrary action.

'.... But what is the criterion of truth in a judgment of what is good? I said above that there was only one premiss of certain truth for a moral judgment; and what this is Socrates again has said in the Protagoras. Pleasure is good; when we do what is pleasant ... we do well; that a particular thing is pleasant we know by intuition, it is a fact to which the will gives necessary assent; and the possibility of error lies only in the impossibility of deciding accurately the degrees in which different things are pleasant – especially because here an immediate pleasure is at an immense advantage over one that is distant, because it is forcibly presented to our imagination by desire, whereas we can, in general, but feebly imagine a future good. That good is pleasure, is well known to be difficult of proof: but I think it may be made plainer by pointing out certain errors commonly made by the many who deny it. Some say that certain *things* are good: but if they analyse their meaning, they will surely find, that those are good only as means to certain good states of mind. It is harder to convict those who speak of certain states of mind as good in themselves, as Plato did of "knowing" and Aristotle of "speculation". But here again a close analysis will shew that no state of mind is unaccompanied either by pleasure or by pain; and that it is this accompaniment alone which can form a motive to the will, may, I think, be made more probable by the mere use of language, which often expresses an unconscious analysis more correct than that which is afterwards substituted by the conscious efforts which try to correct it. For instance, we use "preferable" to express a comparison within both the classes of "good" and "pleasant"; whenever we attempt to evaluate states of mind, as it is our nature to do, the idea of the good or the pleasant is implied: so that when we say that the good is the pleasant, we only mean that our judgments of worth have some common basis, and that we prefer to call this pleasure, as more immediately intelligible. As for the differentiation implied by the coexistence of both words, that may be explained as meant to express the felt difference between the quality of violent physical emotions, which pleasure most obviously accompanies, and those more intellectual states, wherein it is harder to perceive it. And it is the common identification of pleasure with the quality of sensual emotions only, which causes the blind outcry of some teachers, both ancient and modern, at a doctrine which only signifies a deeper search for the discovery of conceptual truth, not any disparagement of the practical worth of their half-concepts of conscience or of faith.'

In this extraordinary fusion of Socrates and Sidgwick we can see yet again Moore's preoccupation with the basic ethical questions he was to deal with eventually in *Principia Ethica*, especially his concern with the issue of hedonism. But here for the first time intuition makes an appearance, and in this paper, unlike 'What End?', he does not attack Sidgwick's utilitarianism. It was almost one year exactly since he delivered the earlier paper, and clearly some of his views had changed, though not perhaps those on conventional morality, which he had defended to the Apostles in 'Shall we take delight in crushing our roses?' For he ends his Sunday Essay with a not very rigorous defence of the morality of the common man. Reverting to the question of why we think the honest workman morally superior to the drunkard (with which judgment the Socratic doctrine of virtue being knowledge conflicts), Moore says:

'It is certainly improbable that the honest workman has made a conscious calculation of the way to get the greatest pleasure, while he lives in this world or a next: he has probably accepted an abridgement in the trust that nothing essential is omitted; he is one of the faithful; his guide is conscience and conventional morality. He is better than the drunkard in that conscience and conventional morality, being derived from the long experience and search of former times, is likely to be right in the main. And so we also must take the greater part of our judgments in faith from the same teachers; but the importance of the Socratic doctrine lies in this, that it would leave to faith as little as it can. Its danger is that, by opening all moral conduct free to speculation, where no certain knowledge can be reached, it may lead narrow men to very wrong conclusions, and conclusions often changed: meanwhile these men may think that they are broadminded champions of freedom; they have, they say, no respect for principle; the frequency with which they change their minds and the many inconsistent things they do, shew how unprejudiced they are.'

The warning of this last paragraph about the effect of liberating narrow men from conventional morality by means of the Socratic doctrine has an odd prophetic ring to it. It is reminiscent of the passage in Keynes's memoir, 'My Early Beliefs', in which he endorses Wittgenstein's remark that the young men liberated from conventional morality by their reading of *Principia Ethica* lacked 'reverence'. Moore read that passage when the memoir was published after Keynes's death. Did he remember then that fifty years earlier, when he was only an undergraduate, he had seen the danger inherent in the rejection of conventional morality, and that he would himself be given the credit (or blame) for making the rejection possible? Probably not. But where Keynes said, 'We had no respect for traditional wisdom or the restraints of custom. We lacked reverence ... for everything and everyone', Moore has remarked in the margin of his copy, that the two things are 'utterly different'.

On 25 May Moore as secretary read an old paper from the Ark, Clifford's famous 'Lay Sermon – Success', and Crompton Llewelyn Davies took wings. A week later, Moore read a paper on solipsism, idealism and materialism, called 'What is matter?' (Moore dated the paper 24 May 1895, but delivered it on 1 June.)

This paper was a landmark in Moore's philosophical development, for in it he abandoned the 'Lucretian' materialism to which he felt drawn in his years as a classical scholar for 'such poor idealistic system as I can construct in its place'. Several considerations prompted the writing of this essay. Moore listed them as:

'(1) The difficulty there is in our belief of the real coexistence of sensible things in space. (2) The argument against solipsism. (3) The dependence of our knowledge of the existence of other persons upon our knowledge of the existence of that other real being, which we may call "matter". (4) The immortality of the soul.'

'What is matter?' begins with the usual Apostolic God-baiting: ' "I am" said God to Moses, and upon this existential proposition he based his claim to the respect of the children of Israel ... But also, at the same time, God added a predicate and turned his assertion of existence into an assertion of relation: "I am that I am".' The banter continues, until Moore has got to his point.

'It may indeed seem that in this proposition he merely justified the form of the first logical principle, that of identity, and did not advance far upon that road of conception, the assertion of relation between different real things, which is travelled by the curiosity of men, when they seek to explain and to know. But God did not say "I am I"; and in the phrase "that which I am" he implied the possibility of other real existences, to which he bore that mysterious relation symbolized by the metaphysical copulation, – or at least he implied the possibility of determinate aspects of himself.

'I, too, like God, will venture to say that "I am": but I do not feel so sure that "you are" or that "it is"; and the object of this paper is to search out what reasons I have, beyond the common practice of men who recognize three personal pronouns, for believing these other existential propositions.'

Moore proceeds to rehearse the argument of 'our much-to-be-regretted brother, George Berkeley' that the being of the fountain in

Trinity Great Court 'consists in its being perceived: its *esse* is *percipi*'.
But Moore finds

'the difficulty of common sense which Berkeley has not sufficiently
explained to me. I cannot help believing that the fountain is in the
Great Court now, though I do not perceive it: nor am I satisfied by
the answer that, maybe, someone else is perceiving it; for I can
perfectly imagine its being there without anyone perceiving it. And
if you say, as Berkeley does say, that my imagining this is what
constitutes its [. . .] being, I answer that I have a general belief in
the existence of a world consisting of all that I have ever perceived
and much more beside, derived by inference of myself and others,
without at all imagining the particular things in it.

'Is the strength of this common belief sufficiently explained by the
only undoubted fact which remains to explain it, namely the fixed
order of our perceptions in experience? It is very hard to think so:
and this, I suppose, is the difficulty which Mr Mill meant to overcome
by saying there existed a permanent possibility of sensations. But this
existence, again, can only be understood as the validity of the law
that perceptions will recur in a certain order, which is no real existence at all but only an abstraction from the content of our minds; or
else possibility must mean "condition" for possibility, that is, some
real existence, which, by coming into certain relations with us,
causes our perceptions, but is itself quite different from the content
of these perceptions.

'The latter (conditions being variously defined) is now the accepted
view of philosophy.'

Moore says that he is convinced, now, of the existence of Crompton
Llewelyn Davies, in the room; though, because Crompton is sitting
behind him, he has no perception of him. And he points out that each
of his hearers is equally convinced of the truth of some similar propositions, which amount to more than asserting that if Moore were suddenly to turn around, he would see Crompton. Rather

'I do believe, rightly or wrongly, in the coexistence in space of certain
sensible qualities, not perceived by me, but which yet are of a nature
which I admit only to be a content of my own mind.

'I also believe similar qualities to persist through time, though not
perceived by me.'

From the example of water in the basin that turns into ice on a
chilly winter night, Moore points out that we all suppose that the water

has gradually changed into ice, though the occupant of the room was asleep and there was therefore no one to perceive the change taking place. Berkeley, insisting that all we have are two isolated perceptions, one of water and one of ice, would have it that 'if the one has changed into the other at all, the change was instantaneous, and neither water nor ice existed while I was sleeping'. The patent absurdity of this leads us to

'believe in the continuity of a system of motions in infinite space through infinite time; and the question is are we mistaken in this? and is all the world merely a product of our mental activity, which, for the sake of convenience, has come to represent all its possible perceptions as parts of an existing whole, conceiving all its finite perceptions as produced to infinity, instead of merely believing, as it ought, that its perceptions have occurred in a definite order, whence it is possible to calculate in what order they will hereafter occur?

'The latter view, which looks upon the order of my given perceptions as the only real existence, which, however, by its orderliness, suggests to the mind imaginary completions, is, so far as I can see, incapable of disproof; and in this solipsism I thought, when I began to write, that I should have to rest. But the course of my discussion has led me to see a probability that other things, of whose dependence on myself I am not conscious, do exist.'

It is the defects he found in Berkeley that led Moore

'towards a more satisfactory explanation of the ordinary conception of the world. To sum up: I know, as he says, nothing immediately but my own perceptions, which are parts of me, are in my mind; but in the mere fact that these perceptions are ordered, I should not, as he does, find any reason for thinking that anything exists except myself – who am the unity of the perceived manifold: thus all his arguments would lead me only to solipsism. But there remains the strange empirically given fact, which he does not sufficiently explain and which is still a great difficulty to me, that the order of my perceptions and the combining power of the percipient have somehow forced upon me the belief that there persists through time an infinite ordered universe, independent of my perception of it, and made up of qualities, which I only know as capable to exist within a mind – namely the qualities which I perceive. I grant to Berkeley that I must be wrong in believing that this world is composed of such qualities, though I cannot help thinking so, and not satisfied at being forced to have this false idea though I am (as one "Lotze" says "the impression is overwhelming"). But I think that this belief, though part of its content is false, constitutes a probability, not a proof, that there is at least some other existence beside my own: that not only "I am" but also "it is".'

Moore's determination to derive an idealistic philosophy from these arguments, makes it very difficult for him to analyse the subject of this second true existential proposition.

'It cannot be matter, in the sense of something extended in space, since extension in space is only in my mind. It cannot be a mere possibility of sensation; since possibility is an abstract term and denotes only a property of some real thing, which is able to become something else. It is certainly something which *is able to* be perceived by me, but *is* not always so perceived, and this something is not explained by Berkeley's crude notion, that it is the perception of an infinite mind, external to my own; since I have no experience of how the perception in one mind could be transferred to another, and certainly from the nature of my own mind, to which my perceptions appear inseparably to belong, I should conclude it was impossible.'

For the existence of other minds Moore produces an argument based on a curious variation of the argument from analogy. In observations of other bodies in space

'I perceive signs, such as I am conscious of producing in my body and which are directly connected by will with my thought, that is, with myself, whose existence actually such as I know it I cannot doubt. And I have no reason for doubting that these signs may be produced by a self similar to my own: since I know that such a self can exist, and since it is not a mere perception, but only inferred from perceptions, as is that real something, at whose nature I cannot guess. In any case it is unhappily only through my perceptions that I can know anything of you; and I should have no reason even for believing that you are, unless I had that probable argument that something is. Thus the third person is logically prior to the second.'

Thus far in his paper Moore has dealt with three of the four points mentioned above. Berkeleyian phenomenalism is nudged aside because of the strength of our common sense 'belief of the real co-existence of sensible things in space', but this is conjoined with

McTaggart's idealist denial of the reality of space – 'extension in space is only in my mind'. And this leaves open the possibility of valid arguments for another of McTaggart's views, Moore's fourth point, the immortality of the soul.

'Finally I should like to say something more about that first person, with which I began. All this world of colours and sounds, figures and motions is, we have seen, only the manifold, which it, this spirit, unifies. Now there comes a time when it ceases to declare itself to other similar spirits through these appearances. It is said to die, because that body disappears through which it makes these communications and through which in turn it receives the perceptions which declare to it the existence of other spirits and of that other unknown existence. But this fact is no proof that it itself ceases to exist. We have no reason for thinking that every being need declare itself through our perceptions: no being is in space and therefore we need not look for a place in space wherein this disembodied spirit may be. It may still exist, though we with our forms of perception can get no knowledge of it: and perhaps it there may have a more direct knowledge, such as we cannot conceive, of the other spirits and things which exist along with it, whether they are still such as continue to exhibit themselves to one another through our present forms of perception, or have ceased, like it, or not begun to do so.
'I am painfully conscious that in this paper I have surpassed myself in the saying with great effort of that which everyone else knew already. Its chief interest is for myself in that it signifies my departure from the materialism, which I once thought I could uphold, and sets out (I fear not even plainly) such poor idealistic system as I can construct in its place. I have committed an offence inexcusable in a brother – that of proffering no paradox, that is, as Clifford says, nothing new, which is not included in common belief and therefore difficult to believe. To those of the brethren, who have at all studied philosophy, it will be plain how much I have borrowed; though indeed I have modified the loan, by borrowing without intelligence. I scarcely dare to hope that anyone will disagree.'

The weakest point in the argument is, of course, precisely Moore's abandonment of materialism (as opposed to his mere assertion of the idealist view of time and space); for, instead of arguing against the fundamental 'reality' of matter, he has simply *denied* its reality in the sense of extension in space (on idealist grounds), and made the 'reality' of matter a necessary explicit assumption: 'our knowledge of the existence of other real persons' depends upon 'our knowledge of the existence of that other real being, which we may call "matter" '. Moreover, the only grounds Moore gives for assuming the existence of matter are that it *can* be inferred from the orderliness and recurrent patterns of our perceptions, and that it *must* be assumed to explain our knowledge (if indeed knowledge is possible) of the existence of other persons. One wonders what McTaggart made of his pupil's first essay in idealism. The record shows that the question put to the vote after the discussion of Moore's paper was 'Are we certain there is anything else?' McTaggart in fact voted Yes, as did Crompton Llewelyn Davies, Marsh, MacNaghten, Dickinson, and Sanger and Trevelyan, who showed their grasp of Moore's paper by the first's comment, 'But I have no reason for thinking so', and the latter's gloss on that, 'Exactly so'. Wedgwood and Moore himself voted No; Moore had, after all, given no grounds for being *certain* that solipsism is false or that matter exists.

All this year McTaggart had taken a large part in the Society's proceedings, and on 8 June, the last meeting of the academic year, he followed Moore's attempt at adapting and adopting his idealist views by a paper of his own. This was a splendid presentation of his paradoxical views on religion which resulted in voting on the question 'Do we want an efficient church?' McTaggart of course voted Yes, with Wedgwood and Mayor, the latter explaining his vote by adding, 'To save us from an efficient Salvation Army'. Moore could not bring himself to travel quite this far with his newly acknowledged mentor, and voted No, along with Trevelyan, Marsh and Sanger.

On 12 June at the Savoy Hotel, Moore attended his second annual Apostles' dinner, at which was present a striking cross-section of members of the Society from its several periods. Henry Sidgwick and Edward Bowen had been active as long ago as the mid-1850s. There were five Apostles from the sixties, six from the seventies, three from the early 1880s, and from the late 1880s there was the trio of Lowes Dickinson, McTaggart and Fry, along with Mayor and the Llewelyn Davies brothers. The more recent brothers of the nineties present were Sanger, Russell, MacNaghten, the Trevelyan brothers, Marsh and Wedgwood. The vice-president's speech would have been given by G. M. Trevelyan, the newest Apostle, and indeed the only new man elected in 1895.

Moore took the Society's secrecy seriously – he had never told his parents of his membership. At the same time he was accustomed to write frequently to his parents and to account – truthfully – for his whereabouts. He had not seen his parents for some time, and he was now in the awkward position of having to explain that he had been in London but had not called in at home, without either breaching a secret or telling an untruth. So when he wrote to his mother that week on 15 June he told her some of the truth: 'I stayed with the Davies's at Westminster on Wednesday and Thursday evening, and spent all my time seeing various Cambridge people.'

To make up for this, and for not having written earlier, Moore related to his mother fully the events of the week preceding the Apostles' dinner. On the Wednesday Vaughan Williams took him to a concert, on Friday he attended the boat races in company with Dakyns, and with Dakyns's father (now reformed and no longer the homosexual crony of Symonds and Arthur Sidgwick, but a respectable family man), mother and sister, who were staying with Professor and Mrs Sidgwick. That evening Vaughan Williams hosted a Seatoller reunion supper in his rooms, with everyone present except George Trevelyan. This was the last time for such an occasion, because 'Amos and V.-W. are going down this term'. On Saturday, 'after tea V.-W. and I gave a performance in my rooms, to Sanger, who had come up for the concert, and Marsh, of Schubert's unfinished symphony, which was to be played on Monday, and the first two movements of his Symphony in C.' Moore's letter closes with news of examination results. Dakyns had got a third, 'of which I am very glad, since there seemed some chance that he would not get an honours degree at all'. Vaughan Williams was in the second class, 'which is better than we much hoped', and Marsh got a first with distinction in his classics part II, 'as might have been expected'.

After the dinner Moore returned for a few days to Trinity to make preparations for the summer vacation, which he planned to spend away from Cambridge. Here he received the news that his parents had sold their house, Woodthorpe, at auction; he hoped that the large house had made more than the £1,500 a neighbour had received for his.[36] A few days later he called in at Woodthorpe for a meal, en route for a five-day visit to Russell at Friday's Hill, an elaborate house and farming estate, on the border between Surrey and Sussex.

Russell's family had opposed his marriage vigorously; not only were the Smiths American and nonconformist, but Alys's generation had a whiff of scandal about them. Her sister Mary had left her husband, a barrister called B. F. C. (Frank) Costelloe, and was living with Bernard Berenson, whom she did not marry until Mr Costelloe's death in 1900. The thin veil of respectability thrown over the affair would not have been difficult for even Moore to penetrate. Their brother Logan was a very nineties figure, 'campy' and aesthetical in the Wildean manner. In

1895 he was an aspiring man of letters, but had no success until the publication of his *Trivia* series of pithy paragraphs and anecdotes after the First World War.* The Russell ménage was completed by Alys's parents. Her father, Robert Pearsall Smith, had by now lost his faith but not his social aspirations; he was suffering from senility by 1895, which impaired his reason but not his snobbery. In America he had been known as plain 'Mr Smith', a preacher, but he was Mr Pearsall Smith in England where he had originally come as a fashionable evangelist, and had assembled a fine collection of aristocrats in his circle of acquaintances. His wife Hannah was amused by his predilections, and did not disapprove of her household's worldly social life despite her remaining a pious, plain-speaking Quaker. Alys was more like her mother than any other member of her family.

The bizarre group of people Moore met when he came for his annual visits sometimes included the whole Pearsall Smith family and Mary's husband, Frank Costelloe, who had remained friendly with Hannah and continued to live very near the Pearsall Smiths both in London and in the country. On his first visit Moore met Ray and Karin, the daughters of Mary and Frank Costelloe.

Russell had waited over six months after the wedding to invite his friend to meet his new wife again; which is perhaps not to be wondered at, as he could not have been eager for Moore to meet his new in-laws. What would have disturbed Moore most, Robert's snobbery, Hannah's piety, Mary's adultery or Logan's affectations? All that can be said was that Moore emerged from the visit with a good deal of sympathy for Alys, and that when the doomed marriage finally broke up, Moore felt that Russell had behaved very badly indeed to Alys.

In addition to philosophy, Moore and Russell must have discussed Germany, for the Russells had recently returned from their long visit there to study German social democracy, and Moore was just about to leave for Tübingen, where he hoped to improve his command of the language.[37]

Moore arrived in Tübingen during the first week of July, having stopped en route to see 'Köln cathedral, which is very disappointing. I stayed Tuesday night at Heidelberg, which is ditto.'[38] On the Thursday he called on the Frorieps, family friends who helped the young man

---

* At the age of thirty he was already embittered by his lack of fame, which he made up for in later years by playing the literary lion and employing 'secretaries' who included Cyril Connolly and Kenneth (Lord) Clark. Logan also had more than a touch of the family madness, *folie circulaire*, and a visitor was likely to find him either wildly elated or deeply depressed.

find lodgings and provided him with an introduction to Professor Sigwart, a philosopher whose lectures Moore wished to attend. The other purpose of his visit was to improve his German, and he had lessons from the elderly Dr Riecke, with whom he lodged. Of his hour-long German lessons he told his mother:

> 'This consists of my reading in German a few verses of German poetry (my pronunciation he never corrects) and then translating them into English, asking him the meaning of any word I don't know, which he either explains in German, or translates into French or English, with the help of a dictionary. He makes any remarks which the words suggest to him, and the German conversation I thus get is perhaps the best part of the lessons. They are scarcely worth the price – 10 marks for 6 lessons: for he has scarcely any idea how to pronounce English, though he understands an English book pretty well: but the lessons were pressed upon me by him and his wife, and I think they are so poor as to be very glad of the money.
> 'I still understand only disconnected sentences at Sigwart's lectures, and so miss everything that is really important: but I fancy he is better than I thought at first. I called on him on Sunday morning with an introductory card from Prof. Froriep (it is the proper thing here between 11½ and 12½ on Sunday to make 10 or 12 calls of about 5 minutes each), and he has since written to ask me to supper next Friday.'[39]

Moore also had an introduction to Sigwart from Ward, who had advised him to listen to the German philosopher's lectures on Kant at the University of Tübingen – of which the most famous graduate was Hegel. Moore also attended a few lectures on Plato by Professor Crusius – delivered at seven in the morning. He later said that 'this visit advanced my knowledge of German very considerably, but, so far as philosophy was concerned, it had, I think, no effect on me at all. I did not really understand German well enough (nor perhaps Kant either) to be able to profit from Sigwart's lectures.'[40] In fact, this was probably Moore's introduction to Kant, a philosopher who became increasingly important to him for the next few years.

Moore spent five weeks in Tübingen, not only listening to lectures and having German lessons, but swimming, playing the piano, going to church to hear the music and to try to puzzle out the sermon, and going to parties, where he was given huge quantities of cold meat, beer and cigars. He felt at the time that his conversational German probably benefited more from his social life than from his lessons.

Moore had arranged to meet his sister Hettie and brother Tom in Munich for the Wagner season at the opera there. He decided to travel to Munich by way of Ulm, Friedrichshafen on Lake Constance, and Davos, where he was the guest of Maurice Amos and his mother for a week. Their house, he wrote to his mother on 21 August, 'like all in Davos, was splendidly fitted: electric-light, panelling, and everywhere double windows and doors'. Moore especially enjoyed the alpine scenery, and did not mind the climate. It was the climate that brought his friend Amos to Davos to convalesce – presumably from a respiratory ailment – and Moore found him better but still weak.

Moore's social calendar was very full that summer. Immediately after leaving Germany he went for a week at the beginning of September to stay with the Llewelyn Davies family at Kirkby Lonsdale in Cumberland. His parents had now vacated Woodthorpe and Moore went to them in Devon for a fortnight, and then on to Newcastle to stay for a few days with his friend Dakyns. Henry Graham Dakyns Junior was about to embark on a somewhat unusual career for the son of his father. Dakyns Senior, the positivist schoolmaster at Clifton with whom John Addington Symonds had been in love, had married and produced several children, of whom Arthur and Henry Graham Junior had been undergraduates at Cambridge. After leaving Cambridge, the latter stayed for a time at the family home at Haslemere while searching for a profession. He decided on engineering, and was apprenticed to Parsons and Sons of Newcastle-upon-Tyne, a firm of electrical engineers. It must have made a dramatic change from Haslemere, where the Dakyns family was used to entertaining Russell, Moore, Sanger, the Davieses and others of their sons' friends, and Dakyns's correspondence to Moore over the next year is full of tales of industrial injuries he sustained in the course of his apprenticeship. On this occasion Moore and Dakyns seem not to have stayed long at Newcastle, for on 17 October Moore wrote to his mother, 'I think my out-of-dooring in the Lakes was very good for me: I certainly came away in excellent health.'

6

Moore's Philosophical Apprenticeship

Moore began the new academic year by moving to rooms in O, Old Court. He was now working almost exclusively at philosophy, and on 17 October he wrote to his mother:

'I feel I am making progress with my work, though my hours and methods are very irregular and the vastness of the detail is still far too much for me. However, this term I shall have to keep more to the point as I have regular papers on Ethics and on McTaggart's Hegel lectures to do. Dr Jackson is going to read some Aristotle with me, and I shall read some Plato by myself. So that my hands will be full. McTaggart has given 3 lectures already, all quite clear and good, and this morning he just began the real difficulties, which was splendid. He has conversation classes once a week, for questions, and Sidgwick will also give some on Ethics: to both of which I look forward. – I have also promised to read two papers this term, one to the Moral Science Club, and the other to the Sunday Essay Society, so that I shall have something to think of "out of school" too. And the last straw is having to do compositions for Verrall, by way of practice for the Chancellors' Medal: only I'm afraid the camel is more likely to break the last straw, and perhaps to throw off some of his other loads too, than to have his own back broken.'

Moore assured his mother that he was not neglecting his exercise; he played fives ('which makes me sweat like the walls of my staircase in wet weather, though perhaps the simile won't appeal to you'); nor his music – in fact he was practising Schumann sonatas. Other news was that both Russell and Sanger had got their fellowships, and that friends who were up this term included Wedgwood, George Trevy and Marsh. Moore's only new acquaintance was Wedgwood's younger brother, Felix, 'very nice and one of the funniest persons I ever saw – red hair, and the ugliest of faces, and perfectly astonishing vivacity'.

With his birthday looming in early November, Moore wrote to his father from Trinity on 30 October 1895 that the only present he wanted was the vocal score of 'Parsifal', the one major opera by Wagner that he had not heard at Munich. This letter to Dr Moore is mostly about music, but it contains one amusing passage which shows Moore stepping gingerly in order not to give offence to his Baptist parent:

> 'My chief piece of news is that I have begun to take dancing-lessons. Did I tell you I was going to? I hope you won't disapprove. I may not ever have much chance of dancing; but it was very provoking at Wedgwood's not knowing how, and it is such splendid exercise and altogether so delightful. Wedgwood goes with me to learn, though he already knows a good deal: without him I should not have had the courage. But the ladies who teach are very nice.'

Moore then switches abruptly to the less contentious subject of music, and says of the playing of Leonard Borwick, whom he has just heard in concert, that 'his execution is not quite up to the standard of Paderewski and the other London stars; but he combines it with better taste than they have, so that I think I prefer him to anyone'.

Moore's complaint to his mother that he did not work hard enough is difficult to credit. He was to accuse himself of this vice nearly all his life, but, in fact, he must have been working extremely hard and very efficiently. In that same letter of 17 October 1895, he had told her of his promise to write papers for various societies, and in early November he read his paper to the Moral Science Club. He told his mother in a letter written on 13 November that 'it went off very well. It was a very small point, but I had to maintain it for an hour; and succeeded, though three people attacked me as hard as they could. Then McTaggart and Stout came up, and endorsed me in the main, and they made the rest of the evening go very well'. Then on 24 November Moore delivered the second paper he had mentioned to his mother, the one for the Sunday Essay Society on the subject of aesthetics.

Because ethics and aesthetics have an obvious connection, as dealing with evaluative concepts; because the Bloomsbury Group included several artists; because of Clive Bell's explicit debt to Moore; and because Moore published so little of direct relevance to the field of aesthetics, there has long been intense speculation concerning his views on aesthetics. There has even been a book on the subject called *G. E. Moore's Analyses of Beauty*,[1] by Teddy Brunius, a Swedish philosopher who attempts to reconstruct Moore's views from his published work. The nature of the enterprise is revealed by the book's sub-title, 'An Impasse and a Way Out'. The author states the 'impasse' concisely: 'If G. E. Moore's analyses of beauty are ingenious but nevertheless blind alleys in aesthetics, it is because of the lack of an empirical basis of his analyses and a blind confidence in the language of common sense using the word "beauty" as a term that is able to be used in a precise way.'[2] The 'way out', Brunius feels, is indicated in Moore's summaries 'Wittgenstein's Lectures in 1930–33', collected posthumously in Moore's *Philosophical Papers*, 1959. Like virtually everything that has been written on this subject, Brunius's book was done without benefit of Moore's actual writings on aesthetics, which range from the Sunday Essay of 1895 to several Apostles' papers on topics concerned with aesthetics.

The remarkable fact is that Moore dealt with at least one of Brunius's objections in his first venture into aesthetics: his 'confidence in the language of' the common-sense use of the word 'beauty' was by no means 'blind'. Moore began his Sunday Essay with some considerations on whether the etymology of the word 'aesthetics' from the Greek for 'sensation' reveals anything essential about the modern use of the word, and concluded that it does link the term with the object of sensation, as opposed both to the object of cognition and the object of the will. Having made his gesture to Kant, Moore moved on to dispose of a particularly grotesque view of art as imitation, which he managed to find in Macaulay, whom he accused of committing the fallacy of 'regarding the imitation as the same with the object imitated'. Moore did not demolish the mimetic theory of art altogether, and did not even consider the more sophisticated version of it to be found in Aristotle, for example. The real purpose of his essay was to quarrel with more modern subjectivist theories of aesthetics.

'In short, this modern theory that all art is form, is exclusively subjective. It denies that an object is beautiful in itself, but it does not see that it is not even an object in itself. It is just as true to say that a sunset is beautiful as to say that a sunset exists. I would therefore try to define the beautiful as that with regard to which you have a specific emotion, the nature of which can only be discovered by looking into yourself, whenever you say that an object is beautiful, and finding what you mean thereby. But I must also maintain that this emotion is not merely yours, and capable of attaching itself to any object whatever, but that some objects are by their very nature more capable than others of exciting it. When you say that a particular red is beautiful, you mean that you feel a pleasant emotion in contemplating it; and that emotion at once constitutes it a different object: it is no longer that particular red, to be distinguished only by intellectual marks; it is no longer given you only as an object of knowledge, but actually *given* as an object of feeling.

'But different people think different things to be beautiful, and the same thing is thought ugly by one person and beautiful by another; how then can you say that that same thing *is* beautiful or ugly? I must reply by a question: Is it the same thing? When the two people say "beautiful", they have to some extent the same notion: else the word "beauty" would be utterly without meaning, and we should never pass such a judgment at all. When, therefore, two people say of a thing, one that it is beautiful, and the other that it is ugly, the thing of which they are speaking is not the same thing. Part of the thing is the same, else they could not understand one another: but part also is different, since for one the fixed notion of beauty is wrapped up in it, for the other its opposite.

'But how are we to judge between them? If they are asserting opposite propositions about different things, they are not contradicting one another. But they are contradicting one another; and are also asserting opposite propositions about the same thing. We can only decide between them by shewing that in the very notion, which makes it possible for them to contradict one another, there is implied that which makes one of them wrong and the other right. In other words, we must make the bare notion of beauty determine itself, and decide for itself with what other marks it is consistent and with what it is inconsistent.

'But can we do this? We shall be told: "there is no disputing about tastes". But it is a curious thing that, though we are constantly being told this and may even think we are convinced of it, we do nevertheless dispute about tastes and contradict our theory by our practice. More than this we are even amenable to reason on the point, and may be convinced that a thing which we had taken for ugly is beautiful: which seems to shew that our taste is in a sense rational, and has laws of its own, which may be expressed. Indeed, it follows from the fact that we attach any meaning at all to "beauty", that beauty must have a nature of its own, absolutely definite, and which therefore excludes certain objects and must include others; and further that this definite nature may be known, but though certain that we can know it, yet perhaps we can't; for we find we can't do everything which we know we can do.'

It would be as well to pause here to suggest a clarification of the last sentence of this passage. Moore seems to have thought it obvious that 'we can't do everything which we know we can do', and that the proposition required no argument to make us see its truth. Perhaps what Moore meant here was 'we can't do everything which we know *how* to do'. For example, we may know how to bake a cake or repair a motor car, but be unable to do so because we have no flour or lack the requisite tools, or have just sprained a wrist. Read like this, Moore's remark is a truism, but not trivial: he might mean that the judgment of beauty is a rational one, one on which people of opposed views could reach agreement and on agreed grounds; but that there is some obstacle of language or of experience, or just of articulateness, that prevents us from making those grounds explicit.

Though Moore has stated that 'beauty must have a nature of its own, absolutely definite', he has not claimed or implied that the nature of beauty must be everywhere the same, for every beautiful object; merely that every beautiful object must have something in common by virtue of which it is judged to be beautiful. He has allowed this much to the subjectivist, beauty-is-in-the-eye-of-the-beholder position, that he cannot be held to a simple essentialist position that would make beauty a definable quality of *objects*. Nor has he actually said that beauty is the property that all works of art have in common. So far in this paper Moore may be seen to be inclining to a position with respect to 'beauty' compatible with his later position that 'goodness' is a simple indefinable property, *not* a property that can be deduced from the nature or qualities of beautiful objects. He does not, therefore, in the passage that follows, commit what he was himself later to call the 'naturalistic fallacy', for he does not claim that beauty is a natural property of objects.

'I can only suggest the following as a possible guide to some definition of beauty. Emotion in its simplest form is pleasure, though we do not then call it emotion: it is mere feeling. But this cannot exist by itself and therefore demands that it should be pleasure in something – a pleasure. The simplest form of this seems to be pleasure in a sensation, which is pleasant; such as may be indicated by an insect walking on a striped paper, and preferring some colours to others. Thus the higher pleasure, or emotion, ought to be capable of representation as the pleasure in a lower pleasure: and the more simple emotions, such as love or fear, would therefore seem to be lower than the artistic emotion. Without them it could not be; we cannot see beauty in a landscape, unless we have loved a woman. When, however, we have the emotion of beauty it may apply itself to any object at all, even though that object be identified only with a very low emotion; but it would most fully be itself when applied to the emotions which come next in order below it, and these must at all events be human emotions. Thus a man is essentially more beautiful than a tree, because his nature, as emotion, is higher. This is the sense in which beauty is truth; the more completely rational is also the more beautiful.

'Thus the artist is the man who has the crowning and complete emotion, that which embraces and transforms all others. If he has this, he must be able to express it, since it cannot exist in him, unless it have the distinctive marks which characterize it, and these are also the means of expression. His work is his emotion, and seems more beautiful to us than things in nature, because *they* are merely our emotions, whereas by virtue of our sympathy we can make his ours.'

This paper for the Sunday Essay Society is, after all, not a mature work, and it would be fruitless to offer too vigorous a defence of the many and confused ideas it contains. But it does seem to be the precursor of several major themes of *Principia Ethica*; and it does not seem to be open to the charge that it ignores the difficulties in the ordinary use of the word 'beauty'.

In telling his mother about the two papers he had to prepare for delivery in November, Moore had not told her about all his extra-curricular obligations. On 6 November he attended a meeting of the Apostles at which George Trevelyan read a paper, 'Is it dangerous to learn facts?' Moore voted Yes, 'because facts without thought are absolute superstition'. Wedgwood also voted Yes, against the Noes of Theodore Llewelyn Davies, Mayor, Marsh, and the moderator who added, 'Facts need thought'. Then on 30 November Moore read to the Apostles his third paper of the month, which he called *Éthos ethismós*, and began: 'The object of this paper is to enquire into the relation between habit and moral character'. 'That there is some connection between them', he continued, 'will be admitted.' Having apologized that he has 'no paradoxical view to advocate', he immediately goes on to formulate one:

'Aristotle says "For virtue it is of no small importance to be habituated in this way or in that from one's very infancy; it is of very *great* importance indeed, nay all-important". Well, if it is, is this a satisfactory state of things? For us, above all men, who are not phenomena, but the elect? We feel that we are gods, creators of ourselves, and can we consent to a view which seems to make us creatures of habit? I should like to deny that habit had anything at all to do with goodness; to assert my freedom, and say that I can do anything by my own power, and that that power is in no sense given me by others, least of all by nature. Otherwise I seem to have no merit in being what I am.'

While conceding that Aristotle did not mean that habit is all-important in the sense held by a modern determinist, Moore nevertheless finds the statement distasteful even as a 'partial truth'. He gives the example of a new boot conforming to the shape of the foot after it has been worn several times, and remarks that it would be odd to say that the boot has acquired the habit of being comfortable. In fact

'I think this view must seem ridiculous, if we take it seriously; and it is taken seriously, and must be so taken, by consistent "Determinists". The fact is, that when McTaggart says his door has a habit of opening itself, he is using a metaphor, and that is even why the expression pleases us. In all cases of inorganic objects, such as boots and doors, some external cause for their motion can be assigned in accordance with physical laws; and in no such case can the term habit be applied. Only objects, which seem to have their cause of action inside them, objects which have wills, can have habits.'

Moore is prepared to admit that animals, and to a lesser extent plants, can be said to have habits. He claims that in attempting to explain the tendency of the Virginia Creeper 'to climb up the walls of houses', 'science has abandoned mere physical laws, and refers to "adaptation to environment" as an explanatory principle, whereby it recognises that some things have a power of adapting themselves from within'. Of course, it is the ultimate aim of science to reduce the case of this sort of adaptation to the purely physical case of the adaptation of the boot to the foot; but science has not yet succeeded in effecting the reduction of the phenomenon of life to physical causes; 'and if the movement there is really from within, as [most rational scientists] are bound so far to admit, they never will'. Moore thinks 'habit' too strong a word for the Virginia Creeper's tendency to climb the walls of a house

'because its power of adaptation is so very limited. Science has shewn that it depends almost entirely on its environment; if a plant is acclimatized, it therewith changes its nature: it is not the same plant, which has one habit in one set of circumstances and another in another. Habit may be a second nature; but the bother with plants is that if they get a second nature, they lose the first: and though it is doubtless very vexing to Mother Nature, that they have a nature of their own at all, she yet has power enough to limit them to one.'

The case of animals, Moore thinks, is easier, for a dog has a much greater power of adaptation than a Virginia Creeper, though

'the tolerable claim that science has made to explain animals, rests on the fact that an animal's nature can only be the same through change within narrow limits: a great alteration in environment causes either extinction or else a new species. However, I'm afraid I can't deny that common use has sanctioned the application of the term "habit" to dogs: there was a dog which had a habit of going to church on Sundays, and broke himself of the habit for good reasons.'

What is the dialectic Moore is trying to set up? It is in the first place a conflict between Aristotle and Kant. Moore is reading Aristotle's argument, that 'it is from being virtuous that we act virtuously, and acting virtuously makes us more virtuous', as a statement that a good moral character is the result of consciously setting out to acquire good habits, or of having good habits forced upon one, or at least inculcated, by education and upbringing. He finds in this version of Aristotle's ethical doctrines an evident conflict with Kant's version of free will, meaning that within us which is not determined by external forces, our noumenal being which is not subject to the laws of the phenomenal world. Moore tries to resolve this conflict in a synthesis that involves saying that human beings (as opposed to animals) consciously *choose* to cultivate good habits, so that our will voluntarily surrenders some of its power, and in so doing preserves its essential freedom.

This strategy leads him into strange by-ways of argument, couched in odd language which is reminiscent of the philosophical idiom of Kant, Hegel and even Schopenhauer. Moore himself apologizes for seeming 'misty and metaphysical'. Once again he has found himself saying some peculiar things in a manner not entirely congenial to himself, in order to reconcile a classical insight with a more recent one, and in the resolution of the conflict there are very strong traces of McTaggart's influence.

Moore's last paragraph recapitulates his entire argument. In it he piles paradox upon paradox, in the best German manner, and then proceeds to draw from his quarrel with Aristotle's classical view of habit and morality a thoroughly romantic conclusion. Throughout this paper Moore has displayed a very dry wit, particularly in his comments on the habits of dogs. While he was certainly concerned here to effect a genuine rapprochement between Aristotle and Kant, the reader ought to attempt to imagine Moore delivering this last paragraph with his tongue somewhere in the area of his cheek :

'the first question was about the relation of habit to moral character, and so far I have said nothing directly about this. Our dog has habits but he has not character. He acts with regularity in the phenomenal world and these actions may be contrary to his nature, and yet not end in his extinction, because these habitual actions were imposed on him by a higher will. He can only have habits in so far as he is domesticated : his will is still unconscious. In us the difference is that our habits are not only willed by us, contrary to our nature, and in accordance with a higher will, but that higher will is felt also to be ours, before we make it so by willing its will. It is our nature, and we know what our nature is. It is in virtue of this that we have character. A man has not a good character, unless he has good habits : it is his nature, which he consciously robs of its nature, by fixing it in reference to phenomenal objects, keeping so all the good in it, which his phenomenal existence allows him to keep, but just not that which makes it character not habit. This, again, Aristotle notices when he says it is from being virtuous that we act virtuously, and acting virtuously makes us more virtuous. But he does not draw the conclusion that the being virtuous has a certain priority; which is why I objected to him. What we aim at is to have character without habit, and this is what we cannot have. Hence it is that I cannot perfectly approve a man who acts rightly without any appearance of struggle. He is generally taken to be the perfect man. He has struggled to form good habits, and having done so, he acts upon them with ease and pleasure. He fills as well as can be his position in the world. But surely he should remember that his position in the world is not his only position. He is far better than the innocent, because he has had a struggle. He has developed his will to the best the world allows. But he has not therefore made it one with his character, which is above the world. There should always be in his mind that it is his nature to make the world and that he should have made it other than it is; not only made the best of it as it is. Among all the good habits which we are to form we should certainly not neglect the habit of indecision.'

The Apostles who heard this paper showed their appreciation of its intricacies by voting on the question, 'Can we carry good habits too far?' George Trevelyan voted Yes with Moore; Wedgwood and Marsh voted No; and McTaggart professed himself neutral.

On Wednesday, 11 December, Moore attended the Trinity 'com-mem.' feast, the annual dinner of about eight courses to commemorate the benefactors of the college, at which speeches were made, madrigals sung in the hall, and too much eaten and drunk by everyone. Moore reported the occasion to his mother on 15 December, in a suitably censored version:

'The chief visitors, who spoke, were Viscount Peel, the late chairman of the Commons, and the Earl of Crewe, the late lord-lieutenant of Ireland. Peel was nice in looks and manner, but his speech dull and empty. Lord Houghton [Moore's fellow Apostle, Richard Monckton Milnes] spoke better; but the Master who spoke three times, as usual, in his last speech was much the best. We were rather disgusted at the dinner by a man next me, who got drunk, and kept making remarks in the speeches. Afterwards Dr Jackson held his usual 'at home' in the two big lecture-rooms, and I stayed up there till ½ past three in the morning, when the last under-grads went away, and then till ½ past 4 with a number of others in another scholar's rooms. I did not feel the worse for it next day.'

This is a good example of the growing distance between Moore and his parents, of how he could not write with absolute frankness about an episode that would not have amused those very Victorian evangelicals. For he amplified upon the evening's events in a letter written on 14 December to Ralph Wedgwood:

'I did not drink any whiskey at Commem.: I tried brandy and soda instead, and liked that better. But, though both Marsh and I stood the champagne very well, we were very much discommoded by someone next to me, who did not – namely Rumsey. This fine mathematician's wits were completely gone, before the speeches began. He broke his dessert plate into a dozen or 20 bits with his knife, and then announced to the company in a loud voice and with a smile, that he could not well break it into any more. He threw bits of pine-apple and grapes at the choir-boys; and brought in "bugger" in every other sentence, or perhaps 2/3. Finally in the speeches he made loud comments; asked who was speaking; and offered seriously to bet me sixpence it was the Earl of Crewe on his legs at the moment.'[3]

The Christmas holidays began for Moore on Monday, 16 December, when he went to stay until the Friday with the Wedgwoods at their house in north Staffordshire, Barlaston Lea, near Stoke-on-Trent. He wrote his parents on 22 December that he had enjoyed himself there: 'The place is in rather nice country, though the weather did not make it enjoyable. I did a good deal of work there, especially some Greek and Latin verses, as a test in which I satisfied myself.' Dr Moore had evidently not been too severe over the issue of the dancing lessons, for Moore felt able to write unabashedly that 'we had a small dance on Tuesday evening at the house of their uncle'. He continued:

'Wednesday afternoon I went a walk in the Duke of Sutherland's park, and on Thursday we went to Stoke ... to see the Wedgwood Pottery. The latter was very interesting, as Frank, the brother of my Wedgwood, who manages the works, shewed us all over and explained the processes very clearly. They employ about 700 hands, including women and children and now do a great deal of ordinary china, earthenware, and tile manufacturing, beside the particular sort of ware, low white reliefs on a particular coloured ground (jasper, they call it), for which they are famous. Flaxman made the designs of these for Josiah Wedgwood. The marks of all the workmen who help to make it, and of the firm, are on each piece of ware which goes out. Frank seemed to know all the workmen very well by name; I believe he is very much liked; he was elected head of the poll for the district school board; and his father was a very good master and very popular.'

This letter was written to Moore's parents in Mentone, where they were spending the holidays, from 39 South Grove, Highgate, the family's new house, which Moore thought in good repair and well managed, though his sister 'Hettie does a good deal of waiting herself'. He tells of seeing the Llewelyn Davieses for breakfast at Westminster, and Dakyns, who was down from Newcastle. Christmas itself Moore spent with what was left of his family at Highgate, and on Boxing Day he went to the Dakyns family house at Haslemere, leaving on the Saturday to go to the Trevelyans at Welcombe, near Stratford-upon-Avon. That he found this an exciting experience can be told from the tone of his letter of 12 January 1896 to his father:

'Welcombe is a huge and very grand place, newly built in red brick but a very decent imitation of Elizabethan style. There were seven or eight of us there at a time, but we only lived in one wing. Sir George and Lady Trevelyan were away in Rome, and thus was a party got up by the eldest and youngest sons [Charles and George]. Most of the people I knew before – Crompton Davies, Amos, the other Trevy, and Dickinson, a King's don, who has just brought out a political history of modern England. Miss Llewelyn Davies, who is leading in the woman movement (especially cooperation), was also there two or three days, and is very nice; also Graham Wallas, of Fabian and School Board fame, whom and his views I did not much like. There was talking, reading, and piano-playing, on a very good old Broadwood grand . . . The country, and Shakespeare's town, rather disappointed me; but not far off, in Arden Forest, I walked to see the most splendid house I ever saw, Hampton Lucy, in a most beautiful park.'

Moore's rather cryptic comment on Graham Wallas hid a great deal of hostility. Wallas, who was thirty-eight at the time of their meeting, was then a lecturer at the London School of Economics, which he had helped to found. He was already the author of some socialist tracts, and was interested in educational psychology. He had the not uncommon failing of several of his Fabian colleagues of being too convinced of his own importance. Just how much this annoyed Moore becomes apparent from his correspondence with Ralph Wedgwood. From Welcombe, Moore wrote on 1 January:

'Graham Wallas is a beastly fool; that's what I have most on my mind. Hasn't he a sneaking air of conceit as if he thought he knew everything? And so he does; a specimen of Oxford culture, with a retreating chin! He has no idea of what real science is; everything is to subserve his wretched utility – educating the masses! Educate them into what? He cannot tell you. – He is a blind leader of the blind, eminently stupid; a man with a muckrake who, in the name of thought and learning, would destroy real thought and learning off the face of the earth if he could. I wonder that such a man should be so well liked by apostles. He's no apostle – a man without humour, without affection, without respect. His heart is as dry and as grey as his head and hair. He has a fixedly low point of view, and laughs at what signifies the heaven which he never even peeped into, as if there were nothing more ridiculous on earth.

'I dare say you'll be surprised at my violence against one who appears to be a thin, quiet, unoffending gentleman; but I have been

disappointed. He has not true modesty, he has not a very fine understanding; and though cleverer than the average he is worse than a
lump of wood in having turned all his vigour to the cause of "utter un-
intelligence". You may take my word for it that he is really duller
than all the rest of the company here except Charles Trevy; his
talents are merely specious: and yet he thinks he could direct the
energies of men like Marshall and McTaggart and Sanger! McTaggart
seems to him merely perverse; and yet, by his own confession,
Wallas's only argument against him was to say that it was a question
of words between them! That, I believe, is *never* a just plea. A man
may be in the right to assert that there is no *likeness*, where his
opponent sees one, but *never* to assert that there is no *difference*.
That means merely that his understanding is deficient.

'Almost the only touch of Headlong Hall we've had has come from
me: I must own it, though it seems to my shame. The others are
only too agreeable to one another. But twice I have set Dickinson
laughing by what he thinks absurd paradoxes (oh! he doesn't understand Hegel); once in arguing with Charles, and once, at first sight,
with Wallas, when I had been cooking in silence my anger and
tedium at his supercilious stupidities.

'Charles Trevy is a blundering ass and a snob! I use hard words;
but I wonder at his reputation too. The fact is I'm in a miserable
condition, unable to work and able to do wrong; but unable to repent.
I would like to be modest, but I see some merit in hating; and I think
I am right here, if I know truth at all; and after all I don't think I
know everything. . . .

'Crompton was only here two days, as splendid as ever; but he
rather damps me, because he can't make many words of it. . . .

'For the rest, Dickinson is really very nice, full of good stories and
always ready to say something with sense in it: but he bores me a
little. George is very silent and ascetic; but he has shewn no temper,
and took me a walk today for which I was very thankful: . . . But
Bob is the joy! He is exquisitely funny (unintentionally).'[4]

Wedgwood answered from Barlaston on 7 January:

'I am afraid you didn't care for your visit to Welcombe, and unless
Sanger's breezy views have done something to cheer you, an early
return to Cambridge will have made you a premature misanthropist.
. . . I agree with you in not thinking much of Charlie Trevelyan; he
is cut out to be a party hack and thinks himself deserving of a higher
destiny. But what can you want better than the "education of the

masses"? It's such a simple thing too that one can turn on the most ordinary University Graduate to do it, and all that is required is a little money and a large distribution of Wordsworths. It is a highly entertaining view of life from a distance, but perhaps it is unpleasant to be beset by it at a dinner-table. Did they sketch out a course of popular lectures for yourself and McTaggart which should "teach philosophy to the man in the street"[?]

'I am sorry Graham Wallas is a fool; I had hoped better of him. But I do think it was a little hard to spring one of your paradoxes on him the first time you heard him; after all he is only an Oxonian, and not fit at once for the strong meat of the Hegelian philosophy, and you have a way of putting the toughest dishes before a beginner, which as Amos would say is less prudent than characteristic.'[5]

Moore replied by return of post:

'I believe it is best to "strike the iron while it is hot": – don't despise me for my proverbs, as Lord M. says to his knavish nephew in Clarissa; it was a chief merit of that excellent young lady to be sententious.

'Perhaps you will think the iron never need be struck at all; but you accuse me of a tendency to misanthropy, and I am much at fault if you do not shew infinitely more in this very letter. You sneer; but I am furious, and that shews that I am not indifferent, and hence have a positive basis of admiration for some human qualities. Do not imagine you will reply effectively by saying you do not care, if you are cynical. I am not sure it was generous to take advantage of a weakness which I knew of.

'Wallas persisted in treating me like a child, which made me try to behave childishly in his presence; and you may make what you like out of that as a confession that wounded vanity was the secret of my dislike – I wish indeed you would make a paper on hypocrisy out of it: but I warn you I don't believe it's the truth.

'He did not propose any work for *me* to do. What he wanted was a *first-rate man* (Bradley in his eye) to discover (a priori, if he could; he didn't seem quite certain whether that or statistics were the better method: I recommended the latter) whether memory was improved by learning by heart; in order that Mr Wallas might apply the results to his school-children in cultivating their memories. This was the real business of psychology; and this, he conceived, was the nature of Darwin's work. I hope family feeling will make you a little warm at this, if you weren't before.

'I dare say you are right that I did not enjoy myself at Welcombe, though it was very impressive; I don't know my own mind well enough yet. But it was much my own fault: I was demoralized; I did not work, and the company did not stimulate me. I did get the latter advantage with Sanger, who agreed with me about Wallas's set in general, except Bernard Shaw: but I believe I should hate him worse than any; I have read one wicked writing of his. He also made me feel that I did not know everything, which, though I always think it, I'm afraid is too rare.'[6]

Sanger and Moore had discussed Shaw, Wallas and the Fabians on Sunday 5 January, when Moore rounded off his holidays by staying one night with Sanger at Weybridge. He then went up to Trinity on the Monday to prepare for his examinations, and found himself rather lonely, as term had not yet begun, and none of his friends was up.

Moore's outburst against Graham Wallas is revealing of his character. At the end of 1895 and the beginning of 1896 Moore was serving his philosophical apprenticeship; his masters were McTaggart and more especially Hegel. While Moore's rage at Wallas appeared to be untypical of his temperament, the quality of his rage, and the grounds for it, give us the greatest insight into his character. The grounds for Moore's hatred of Wallas have never been so well explored as they were by a writer who had once himself been a young Hegelian (in quite a different sense, of course), Dostoevsky. There is a passage in *The Idiot* in which the narrator interrupts his story to comment in his own person on a class of characters, to whom, in Moore's view, Graham Wallas belonged:

'The arrogance of the simple-minded, if one may use such an expression, assumes quite amazing proportions in such cases; all this sounds incredible, yet you come across this sort of thing every moment. This arrogance of the simple-minded, this total absence of doubt in his abilities by a stupid man is excellently portrayed by Gogol in his wonderful character Lieutenant Pirogov. Pirogov never doubts that he is a genius or, indeed, that he is superior to any genius. He is so certain of it that it never occurs to him to question it; he does not question anything, anyway. The great writer was in the end forced to give him a thrashing to satisfy the outraged feelings of his reader ... And how many Pirogovs have there not been among our writers, our men of learning, our propagandists? I say "have been", but of course we have them still.'[7]

Quite clearly Moore saw Graham Wallas as a Pirogov, 'a beastly fool', with 'a sneaking air of conceit as if he thought he knew everything', a man whose 'talents are merely specious' yet who 'thinks he could direct the energies of men like Marshall and McTaggart and Sanger!' There can be very little doubt that from his very different point of view Dostoevsky would have regarded Wallas as a Pirogov figure. Whether or not this is a correct or fair estimate of Wallas's character is beside the point. What is relevant is the Dostoevskian quality of Moore's rage, and the light it sheds on his own character: it is a quality of hatred that can only be felt by the pure in spirit, the dislike of the innocent for the corrupt. Dostoevsky's narrator digresses on the character of Pirogov in order, ultimately, to highlight the contrast with Myshkin. Moore's innocent disgust with Graham Wallas was worthy of Myshkin. And Moore was *like* Myshkin in his pure hatred of the kind of man he took Wallas to be.

In January 1896 Moore was twenty-two and in his fourth year at Trinity. He had a good first in part I of the classics tripos and had won the Craven Scholarship. Not only had he attained the highest academic honours available to a man in his position; he had also acquired a new academic interest – philosophy – which engaged his interest more deeply than the classics had ever done. He was slim and handsome, though perhaps he had not enough vanity to realize how attractive he was; and after less than two years' membership, he was already a central figure in the Apostles. He ought to have found his life exciting. But the autobiographical notes he made sometime later seem to imply that he found his existence somewhat flat. His social life, it is true, was confined almost entirely to his own college. Even the Apostles' active membership was then exclusively at Trinity – with occasional appearances on Saturday nights by a quartet of angels from King's: Dickinson, Wedd, Mayor and Furness. Moore dined, he wrote, 'with George Trevy, Lloyd, MacCarthy, Buxton' and saw 'hardly anyone but Wedgwood, Felix and Marsh'. Moore's real complaint was that he made few new friends this year. He did not really become friends with MacCarthy, on his own reckoning, until the spring of 1896, by which time Wedgwood was preparing to go down. Dakyns had left Cambridge earlier, and at first Moore wrote to him regularly. But his social life the previous autumn had not really been that bleak: he had taken dancing lessons with Wedgwood, and George Trevelyan had taught him to ride a bicycle; the latter skill was soon to be a source of very great pleasure and satisfaction. One cannot help wondering whether the lack of opportunity to exercise the former skill may not have contributed something to this winter's discontent.

Moore was part of an all male but not homosexual society (with the possible exception of Marsh), and he was not uninterested in sex – at least in the discussion of it. The blue-stockings of Newnham and Girton were at this time heavily chaperoned, and men of Moore's class and background did not consort with women outside their own class; in the nineties middle-class undergraduates generally left this sort of *louche* behaviour to their upper-class counterparts. Moore's dissatisfaction may very well have been due to that most common of causes, repression and frustration of the burgeoning sexual drive.

At twenty-two frustrated romantic sensibilities may be an even more potent source of dissatisfaction than sexual frustration itself; there is often left over from adolescence the yearning for a special friend, one particular friend, and this kind of intimacy Moore does not seem to have enjoyed with anyone in 1896. The need for such a relationship was to grow rather than diminish with increasing maturity, and in Moore's case these feelings found their expression first, when later that year he began his life-long friendship with Desmond MacCarthy, and again two years or so later with Alfred Ainsworth, and finally twenty years later when he married Dorothy Ely in 1916.

Moore's life now began to take on a pattern: Apostles' meetings in term; reading parties and visits in the vacations; and though he still felt, as he was to do all his life, that he was not doing enough work, Moore had this year his usual bag of academic successes and honours.

Crompton Llewelyn Davies wrote to Moore from London on 18 February 1896 that he had read a paper the night before to the Aristotelian Society; Bernard Bosanquet had been sympathetic, but other members were 'taken aback by its Germanism'. Crompton asked Moore to show the paper to McTaggart and anyone else who might take an interest, and goes on to say that Russell had been elected to the Aristotelian and was going to read a paper to them on the *a priori* in geometry. All this philosophical activity was to culminate in Moore's reading his first paper to the Aristotelian Society in October. This letter, which is addressed to 'My dear GEM of purest ray serene', ends with the writer asking 'Is there any reason to believe with Rossetti that

> 'Whatever there is to know
>
>   That we shall know one day.[?]

'It seems to me true that knowledge grows and cannot cease growing, except by the collapse which McTaggart loves to imagine.

'Till then, I am your knowing Crompton.'[8]

On Saturday, 22 February, Moore read his first paper of the new year to the Apostles. It was called 'Are we hypocrites?', and begins:

> 'When I asked this question I meant the "we" to stand for England. I can remember nothing to quote for the assertion, but yet I think this charge has probably been more often brought against us than any other nation. We are all supposed to be hypocritical in pretending to care for justice and protection of the weak in international relations, while we really care only for our own interest; our puritans were commonly charged with hypocrisy even by their own countrymen; and the same charge is now made against what is known, at least in the Society, as the purity party, and I do not think such a charge was ever brought against so large a body in any other nation : . . . the matter was brought home to the Society the other day, when I heard our brother Wedd call our brother McTaggart "a holy humbug". Is McTaggart a holy humbug? This will serve for my question as well as the other. I do not think he is; and in shewing this, I hope to place McTaggart in the same class with those with whom he would least like to be associated, and to vindicate the whole by distinguishing their common quality from that hypocrisy which is too often confused with it, and shewing it to be, far from a vice, the highest quality which a nation can possess, and the chief source of any greatness which England may be thought to have.'

The episode that occasioned Wedd's remark was this : McTaggart had been walking one Sunday in Neville's Court; his party included Russell, who had been smoking his pipe when the party was encountered by the vice-master, and McTaggart had expressed his distress that a member of his party should be seen by the vice-master of Trinity to be smoking within the boundaries of the college on the sabbath. When he heard of McTaggart's having been upset, Wedd ridiculed McTaggart as a 'holy humbug'. This was, of course, merely one more example of McTaggart's habitual but always startling respect for institutions in which he could not believe. Moore could hardly maintain that the atheist McTaggart's concern over an infraction of the rules concerning sabbath observance (so unimportant that the vice-master himself probably did not notice that Russell was smoking) was not hypocrisy – so Moore attempted to vindicate hypocrisy itself, to argue that hypocrisy is not always vicious :

> 'It is always well to have and profess admiration for a virtue which we have not, and which we know we shall not shew, provided that

knowledge does not accompany a resolution not to have it. The opposite view supposes that though you cannot touch pitch without being defiled, you may thrust your hand into a jam pot without getting any sweetness on it. It is better to have a white sepulchre to cover your rotting bodies, provided it be known that the rotting bodies are there, than to have the rotting bodies exposed to give you typhoid. Honesty does not consist solely in complete conformity of outer with inner; rather the outer may well be in some points better than the inner, that so it may increase it into a better conformity: provided the outer be not to the inner, like the bull to the frog.'

The vote was taken on the question *Si peccas, peccandum fortiter?*, a waggish twist to Luther's *Esto peccator et pecca fortiter*, Be a sinner and sin strongly. The only votes recorded were two Noes, Moore's own and that of Marsh, who scribbled something in Greek – perhaps *hékista*, absolutely not! – adding, in English, 'McTaggart is a *holy* humbug'. McTaggart's is the only other vote recorded – neutral.

It might be objected that in this paper Moore wavers between a defence of hypocrisy as not being itself a vice and distinguishing hypocrisy from something else – the assumption of a character or virtue not one's own, which as it can lead to the acquisition of the better character or virtue, is no bad thing. Somebody evidently did make this point in the discussion following the paper, for on the following Saturday, which was Leap Year's day, Moore read another paper on hypocrisy in which he tried to sort out the confusion of the first paper, though he ended in even greater muddle – for the reader the specious clarity of the first paper is much to be preferred to the tangled and complicated reasoning of the second attempt.

Though devoted now to philosophy, Moore's classics were by no means rusty, and in March, before the vacation, he was further rewarded by an honourable mention for the Chancellor's Medal. He spent the beginning and end of the Easter vacation with his parents, first at Upper Woburn Place and later for a few days in April at Bournemouth. In between he was part of a three-week reading party at Penmenner, which consisted of Wedgwood, George Trevelyan, Maurice Amos and Vaughan Williams. They were joined at Easter by Crompton Llewelyn Davies, C. P. Sanger and Verrall.

Moore did not entirely enjoy this party in Cornwall. He confided to Marsh on 12 April that, though he could not say exactly *how* disagreeable he found the reading party, he could say who made it so – George Trevelyan:

'In general I find this estimable personage intolerable. I spent the first
week alone with him and Wedgwood, . . . I did not like even to be
in the same room with him. It was better when the others came, . . .
I even sometimes admired him, from sympathy with their admiration. But the tragedy came at the end. When he went away, he said
to me: "I'm afraid you found me very disagreeable sometimes; I
have been rather ill: I hope you didn't mind." I muttered that of
course I didn't; but he must add something more . . . to the effect that
he hoped I had liked his company. I stood absolutely dumb for a
minute, and then he desperately seized my hand and said goodbye,
but I dared not look in his face. . . . I could not think of anything
consoling; and I doubted the expediency of honestly saying, I disliked
him very much and I hoped I should see as little of him as possible
for the future: and indeed I should like to see him sometimes talking
to other people. . . .
'For the rest, I did not like VW so much this time: he seemed
more querulous and ill-humoured, and he couldn't walk fast.
'Amos went off exceedingly well: he can really be amusing sometimes, whether you see it or no; and I had the pleasure of brow-
beating him soundly on that very subject of pleasure.'

Moore went on in this letter to tell Marsh some 'indiscreet' and very
funny tales about his family:

'I left with the last on Thursday and stayed two nights in my pater-
nal town of Plymouth, in a circle of old and young ladies, the normal
descendants of that stock from which we are a most distressing
sport. I saw much that was worthy of Jane Austen. One perfectly
delicious old lady was delighted beyond anything to find that there
was some hard roe in the breakfast herrings: she said she could
hardly believe it was true; they had deceived her so often. . . .
'The extraordinary cleverness of my family, of which we were
speaking last term, has been recently exemplified in the most un-
mistakable manner by my brother D. H., who has broken off his
engagement in the most sudden and peremptory manner for no other
reason than that he did not like the lady well enough. I can assure
you that nothing but great intellect could have produced quite the
same effect. It is well-known to be antagonistic to constancy, and
Friedrich Nietsche [sic] thinks it much preferable. It is his 'master
morality', here curiously illustrated in a Christian.'[9]

Marsh in reply said that he would be sorry if Moore had had an open breach with Trevelyan, particularly because this would make for awkwardness in the Society. This provoked Moore to write from High-gate on 17 April 1896:

'I am either a very bad judge or a very false witness for I do think you take that particular interview with George (the name is appropriated to him, so I am glad I hate it to begin with: you will please to note that I am G. E. or George Edward; I would follow your example and drop the first entirely, were it not that truth and family pride and your own prior claims forbid it) — I think you take it much too seriously. I never thought or meant to hint that there was any question of "a breach". My dear Sir, the end of it was that he *forgave* me; that is how I took it: and it has even occurred to me that I may have heightened his esteem by my honesty in not profess-ing satisfaction where I felt none.'[10]

This letter runs to eight pages, of which six are occupied with Moore's relationship to George Trevelyan. Under the teasing surface of his re-marks to Marsh, there is the desire to be exact and precise — not about George Trevelyan's character — but about Moore's feelings about Trevelyan. In his correspondence with Marsh, Moore is striving to describe with accuracy his own state of mind about his personal rela-tion with Trevelyan; this sort of activity is one that fills the pages of the correspondence of, say, Lytton Strachey, who quite clearly got the habit from his mentor, Moore; for the origins of this Bloomsbury prac-tice one need look no further than this letter from Moore to Eddie Marsh.

At the beginning of May term 1896 the Apostles elected Desmond MacCarthy as their 231st member. One week later, on 9 May, Mac-Carthy attended his first meeting of the Society, when he heard Marsh read a paper on suicide. To the question, 'May a man make away with himself?', Marsh and Sanger answered Yes. Wedgwood assented, add-ing, 'The judgment of an individual being generally nearest to God's', and so did Trevelyan, with the qualification that: 'A wise man is a better judge of what is good for the state than the state is generally.' MacCarthy voted No, 'Except to save life or the state,' as did Moore, who added: 'Only the state, or its deputy, may dispose of life, however wicked, hurtful or painful; and it is only justified in so doing, if it be or has been hurtful to its own or that of another man.'

At the end of the May term 1896 Moore had received his examina-tion results: a first with distinction in part II of the moral sciences tripos, though only a second class in the Greek philosophy section of classics part II. It was obvious that the young man who had been content to be a schoolmaster could now aspire to a more lofty academic career.

7
Working for a Fellowship

With his success in the triposes, Moore's undergraduate career came to an end. He spent the next two years, from autumn 1896 to 1898, working for a Trinity Prize Fellowship. Fellowships were awarded by dissertation and Moore decided to write one on Kant's ethics, a design encouraged by Ward. He wrote nothing during the summer of 1896, but spent his time reading Kant and the commentaries. Moore described his work in his autobiography:

'During the first of these two years the part of Kant's ethical doctrines with which I was chiefly concerned was some of the things he said about freedom. He seemed to me to say or imply that each of us had two "selves" or "Egos", one of which he called a "noümenal" self, the other an "empirical" self, and he seemed also to say or imply that the "noümenal" self was free, whereas the "empirical" self was not; and what I wrote during this first year can, I think, be described as, in the main, an attempt to make sense of these extremely mysterious assertions. I found something which seemed to me at the time to give them an intelligible meaning, but I have no doubt that the meaning I found was as far or further from anything which Kant actually meant, as was McTaggart's interpretation of Hegel's "Absolute Idea" from anything which Hegel meant. The substance of what I wrote on this topic was published shortly afterwards as an article in *Mind*, entitled "Freedom"; and, though I have not looked at that article for a long time, I have no doubt that it was absolutely worthless.'[1]

Moore was certainly being too modest when he wrote of this early work that it was 'worthless'; but its interest, even to professional philosophers, is somewhat limited. His second year of research produced, Moore wrote,

'a much more profitable line of enquiry, though one which had a much less direct connection with Kant's Ethics – had, indeed, a more direct connection with the *Critique of Pure Reason* than with the *Critique of Practical Reason*. It seemed to me that it was extremely difficult to see clearly what Kant meant by "Reason". This was a term which occurred not only in the title of both these works, but also frequently in the text, and, as it seemed to me, in a very mystifying manner. What on earth did Kant mean by it? He must be referring, more or less directly, to something which was to be found in the world, and which could be described in other terms. But to what exactly? This was what I set myself to think about; and it led me to think first about the notion of "truth", since it seemed to me that, in some of its uses at all events, Kant's term "Reason" involved a reference to the notion of "truth"; and, in thinking about truth, I was led to take as my text a passage from the beginning of Bradley's *Logic*, in which after saying that "Truth and falsehood depend on the relation of our ideas to reality", he goes on to say that the "meaning" of an idea consists in a part of its content "cut off, fixed by the mind, and considered apart from the existence" of the idea in question. It seemed to me, if I remember right, that the meaning of an idea was not anything "cut off" from it, but something wholly independent of mind. I tried to argue for this position, and this was the beginning, I think, of certain tendencies in me which have led some people to call me a "realist", and was also the beginning of a break-away from belief in Bradley's philosophy, of which, up till about then, both Russell and I had, following McTaggart, been enthusiastic admirers."[2]

In this passage Moore had been *grievously* modest. As a twenty-four-year-old postgraduate student he had in the course of his work begun the trend that was to extirpate the neo-Hegelian philosophy, represented by McTaggart and Bradley, that dominated academic philosophy in Britain and America.

Moore had failed to win his fellowship in the first election; he was not surprised, for Trinity Prize Fellowships were greatly coveted and hotly competed for; it was normal for even an outstanding candidate to receive his fellowship only on his second attempt. The Board of Electors, with Ward as their philosophical adviser, could not fail to recognize work of the quality of Moore's second submission, and so he was elected, and in the autumn of 1898, took up his Prize Fellowship, which was then given unconditionally for a period of six years. It carried a 'dividend' then of about £200, and if the fellow chose to reside in college, a set of rooms and free dinners in hall.

Whilst working on his dissertation Moore remained very active in the affairs of the Society. Only two new members were elected in these two years. The first, in November 1897, was Austin Smyth (1877–1949), a Trinity man who got firsts in both parts of the classics tripos, and became a Prize Fellow himself when he was already working as a clerk in the House of Commons, where he was librarian for nearly thirty years. The second election, in February 1898, was that of the mathematician Godfrey Harold Hardy (1877–1947). Owing to the success of his book *A Mathematician's Apology* (in the introduction to which C. P. Snow said its author had 'star quality'[3]), G. H. Hardy is one of the few of his profession to have become a household name. He was born in Cranleigh, Surrey, where his father was a prep-school master; despite their cleverness neither of his parents had been able to afford to go to university. When Hardy went to Trinity in 1896, it was from Winchester, where he had known Austin Smyth; his tutor was Verrall. Hardy associated himself with many of Russell's views, both on mathematical philosophy and on politics; like Russell, he was a conscientious objector in the First World War.

Moore's contributions to the Apostles during the two years he was working for his fellowship included the first paper of the academic year 1896–7, 'Is Beauty Truth?', delivered on 31 October. To an audience consisting of only Fry and MacCarthy, Moore read a very long paper, from which developed the question for the vote, 'Can feeling include cognition?' Fry said Yes ('In pious hope'), and Moore echoed his answer, but MacCarthy voted No. Moore concluded this paper: 'I have ventured to put forward a theory [of the identity of truth and beauty] which, as I have stated it, is full of inconsistencies, absurdities and misunderstandings.' While it is difficult to disagree with Moore's own remarks on this paper, it is interesting to note that the terms in which he conducts the argument can be interpreted so as to make it similar to his arguments in *Principia Ethica* denouncing the naturalistic fallacy: 'I cannot see by what possible logical necessity we can be driven from the emphatic assertion "This is" to the assertion "This is good." The judgment of value and the judgment of existence seem to be logically without connection'.

After spending Christmas with his family at Cheriton, Moore read on 23 January 1897 a paper concerning categories, called 'Can we mean anything, when we don't know what we mean?' Moore intended this as an essay in certain problems of idealist philosophy; he meant to deal with the sort of questions that concerned McTaggart: 'in what sense "abstracts" were real, what was the difference between the particular and the universal, and whether the universal might not be distinguished from the general'. But Moore found himself unable 'to run down the hares I had started'. This is another illustration of Moore's temperamental inability to become an idealist philosopher. He *wanted* to be a disciple of McTaggart – the heart was willing – but he could not bring himself even to discuss those questions that were of burning interest to the neo-Hegelian philosophy. Instead, he found himself wondering how to analyse statements of value, such as 'I love Susan' and 'Port wine is good', statements which, as Moore says himself, are of more concern to Sidgwick than they are a contribution to McTaggart's enterprise. In this paper, as in his second year's fellowship work, Moore, while hoping to fortify McTaggart in his idealist stronghold, is in fact bringing down the whole edifice. He was temperamentally a realist.

The last third of this paper contains a discussion about the meaning of 'good' which is quite similar to the opening chapter of *Principia Ethica*, though, naturally enough, the treatment here is briefer, more tentative and simpler than in his mature work. Moore considers attempts to analyse 'good' in terms of 'pleasure' and seems to conclude that no such analysis can be adequate; that though we do mean something by propositions like 'That port wine is good', we do not know what we mean – in the sense that we cannot provide an analysis of the statement. In a tantalizing last paragraph, Moore says:

'I ought to have left myself more time to consider possible difficulties consequent upon the theory that a reference to pleasure, or some sensible quality, is involved in the meaning of good: as for instance, how, then, we could say that pleasure itself was good? but I hope enough has been said to sustain the position, that we may mean something by good even though we do not know what we mean.'

Sadly for the historian, McTaggart was not present for the reading of this paper; indeed, Lowes Dickinson was the only philosopher present to vote on 'Can we mean anything, when we don't know what we mean?' Raleigh, with, we may suspect, more wit than understanding voted Yes ('But it commits us to nothing'), and was joined in the Yes lobby by George Trevelyan, Wedd and Moore himself, while Mac-Carthy and Dickinson voted No.

For the rest of the year Moore's papers were ostensibly on religious subjects; as the topics were chosen by the members at the end of one meeting and in advance of the next, they may well have been urged upon Moore *because* of his lack of genuine interest in religious questions. Moore managed invariably to turn the choice of topic to his own uses, and quite often produced a good joke, as when in his paper of 27 February, having been assigned the topic 'What is belief in God?', he read a paper on epistemology in which God does not put in an appearance until the last paragraph. Moore here argues that to distinguish between knowledge and belief is to be committed to various 'metaphysical' doctrines, as the state of mind of a person who *knows* something may well be indistinguishable from the state of mind of a person who merely *believes* the same thing – though he *thinks* he knows it.

McTaggart read a paper on 13 March 1897, about two years before his own marriage, which resulted in a double question: (1) Shall we marry the people we love? (2) Shall we love the people we marry? The only vote of interest was McTaggart's own No to question (1), because 'It is wasteful to flush sewers with whisky'.

Following a visit to the Russells at the Millhangar in June, and short sojourns with Bob Trevelyan and Ralph Wedgwood, Moore spent the long vacation of 1897 at Cambridge, working on his dissertation. In September he repeated some of the summer's visits, and then on 13 November Moore read a paper on 'What is it to be wicked?' He was to read this paper again with only minor revisions on 15 November 1902, when he was finishing *Principia Ethica*, and if this excellent little essay is not a direct ancestor of that book, then at least there is nothing in it that is inconsistent with Moore's later thinking. It even begins with the typical Moorean qualification 'But I should like to make it quite plain what the question is'. He goes on:

> 'The main point is this: That "good" does mean something; that though perhaps we cannot tell what things are good, yet it is certain that everything must be more or less good or bad; and that, if a thing is good, it is good, and that fact cannot be expressed in any other way. To say this just amounts to denying that the notion of goodness is a mere convention.'

There then follows a refutation of moral relativism and an affirmation of the 'objectivity' of good: 'some things at all events must *be* either good or bad. I don't profess to know much more about what this means; but I do think you must contradict yourself if you deny it.' In the main this paper is a comparison between Greek and Christian views of morality; the former being that 'there is but one *kind* of goodness and badness, and all good things differ from one another only in their degree of goodness', and the latter, with its notion of sin involving a difference in kind. There is also some consideration of the Socratic claim that no man knowingly does evil, which Moore is inclined to accept. The last section of the paper is heralded with a still youthful blaze of blasphemy, as Moore announces, 'But what I want to ask to-night is whether Mr Christ or Mr Paul had any more to tell us after Plato had taught us [the objectivity of good].' The question put to the vote was 'Oysters or devils?' which is perhaps intelligible as a play on the names of the savoury dishes served after the sweet course, angels (oysters) on horseback and devils (chicken livers) on horseback. To this surreal question Moore replied Oysters, 'Devils being the last antithesis, and having the worst of moral forms'. G. M. Trevelyan was Neutral, because 'I am not at all certain that all individuals of one class are superior to all individuals of the other'. To confuse things further, McTaggart voted for 'theological' Devils : 'There are many worse things than wickedness and innocence is one of them.' Smyth voted for Devils, and so did MacCarthy, who added, 'Although oysters are not so irritating'.

On 19 February 1898 the Apostles had a gala meeting, with a paper delivered by one of its oldest members, Henry Jackson, who had been elected thirty-five years earlier. A full dozen, MacCarthy, McTaggart, Maitland (who had himself been an Apostle for twenty-five years), Wedd, Russell, Mayor, Moore, Trevelyan, Smyth and both Llewelyn Davieses met that night, and Jackson read on 'Shall we write and re-write and re-write again?' To cap off this celebration, Moore once again proposed G. H. Hardy for membership; this time, one year after he had first refused, Hardy was willing to accept the honour, and the meeting concluded with his election.

Moore read on 26 February a paper on selfishness. The question was 'Is it virtuous to wash?', which grew out of Moore's illustration : 'For the Jews in the desert it was no doubt an effort to keep clean; the act of washing was for them a virtue : but for us, with baths in Whewell's Courts, it is no longer so.' Moore's point was that virtue as an end in itself could not be pursued as a goal by the Jews in the desert, so they made a virtue of something that was actually only a *means* towards a virtue, and were unable to make the distinction between an end, 'which must be the same for all and always', and the means to an end. Most of this essay is not philosophically interesting, but near the end, where the ostensible subject is egoism versus altruism, Moore deals with that age-old question in a peculiar way that foreshadows the importance he will attach to personal relations in *Principia Ethica* : 'To be in the right relations with the right persons is all that can here be good; and if you are so, you do not do one thing for self and another for them, but all simply for the sake of the whole that is you and them and what is between you.' In the vote, Sanger, Smyth and Mayor said Yes, it is virtuous to wash, as did Trevelyan, who appended, 'Not discussing the merits of washing but meaning by it all the qualities for which the Anglo-Saxon is peculiar in history'. MacCarthy and Hardy voted No, and so did Moore, who had the last word: 'It is only necessary.'

Dickinson on 5 March read a paper that led to the question, 'Is any event necessary?' The responses indicate the growth of Moore's philosophical dominance of the group, for Russell and Moore voted Yes. Russell added: 'Every event must be, but I cannot see that any event is.' And Moore responded, 'If it must be, it is; and what does it matter what Russell can see?' Smyth was Neutral, while Hardy and Whitehead voted No. Russell decided to vote on both sides of the issue, and to his Yes he added a No as well. Dickinson himself voted that no event was necessary, with the portentous qualification, 'None except my conversion by Moore'.

A week later McTaggart again read his paper 'Does youth approve of Age?' Yes: Trevelyan, Smyth, MacCarthy and McTaggart. No: Moore, Russell, Hardy and Sanger. It is interesting to note the presence of Russell at so many Apostles' meetings in the winter and early spring of 1898, for it was at this time that Moore's work on his dissertation was leading him away from Hegelianism, taking Russell with him on the road to realism.

The Easter vacation of 1898 marked the beginning of a tradition. As we have seen, there had been reading parties from time to time in this vacation, organized by Moore or by one of his friends. This year a reading party was held at Wingate, organized by Moore. The participants were at first MacCarthy and Smyth, followed by Bob Trevelyan and Sanger. This was the first of a series of reading parties held at Easter which persisted until the outbreak of war – except for 1906 and 1910, when Moore's arrangements broke down. Not all the members of all the parties were Apostles – there was one non-Apostle, Donald Robertson, in 1901 and another, Dakyns, in 1905; these were Moore's reading parties, and Moore invited whom he liked. (Moore's dislike of Russell was so great in 1903 that he could not bear the prospect of Russell being included in the reading party, and this resulted in a painful row.) Being invited to one of Moore's reading parties, said Leonard Woolf,[4] represented membership in an 'inner group' of Apostles, who were 'special' disciples of Moore; this inner circle included most of the Apostles who were to become members of Bloomsbury – Woolf himself, Lytton and James Strachey, Keynes, MacCarthy, Harry Norton and even Roger Fry, the single notable omission being E. M. Forster; but it also included men who were only on the fringes of Bloomsbury like Gerald Shove, Rupert Brooke, J. T. Sheppard, Mayor, Bob Trevelyan, Sanger, the Llewelyn Davies brothers and Ralph Hawtrey. The most constant members of the party were Ainsworth (whom Leonard Woolf described as Moore's 'lieutenant'), and Moore's best friend, Desmond MacCarthy. Though Moore had not yet come to feel so strongly against Russell in the early years of the reading parties, and though Russell more than once asked to be invited, he was in fact *never* a member of any of Moore's parties.

The annual dinner in 1898 was again held at Brown's Hotel and the oldest Apostle present was Oscar Browning. Moore spent the long vacation at Cambridge again; he had learned that he had won his fellowship, and it was to begin in October. Ward had replaced Sidgwick on the Board of Electors and Sidgwick had cautioned him to be certain to speak warmly enough of Moore's work to ensure that Moore got his fellowship. Moore commented on this that 'Ward, although he had secured my election to a Fellowship, was not very happy about me. When I went to see him after the election, he told me he thought I was too sceptical, and that I seemed to take a pride and pleasure in picking holes in accepted views: this he did not like, and he compared me in that respect to Hume.'[5] Ward intended no compliment by making this comparison, for until his re-appraisal by the logical positivists in the twentieth century, Hume's reputation as a philosopher stood much lower than it does today.

Lowes Dickinson's reputation as a 'publicist' (as he was happy to call himself) was based on his published works, and for a time this reputation was very great. His *Letters from John Chinaman* was a bestseller. E. M. Forster, remarking on 'fashion's barometer', emphasized 'the very high level touched by the mercury about 1905. It looked then as though Mr G. L. Dickinson would easily beat Pater and Gobineau, and even creep up towards Voltaire and Mr Bernard Shaw.'[6] Lowes Dickinson's first three books, *From King to King* (1891), *Revolution and Reaction in Modern France* (1892), and *The Development of Parliament in the Nineteenth Century* (1895) were strictly historical, but with *The Greek Way of Life* (1896) he broke new ground. That book was an introduction to Greek civilization for those who had no Greek.

The book was conceived to help readers to a fuller appreciation of the Greek mind than is ordinarily obtainable by those whose only access is through translations. The book was a great success, and went through more than twenty editions. Intended as a popular book, it extended Lowes Dickinson's reputation beyond Cambridge, even as far as America.

Lowes Dickinson and Moore had corresponded on philosophical matters in 1897, and on 17 December the older man wrote to Moore to suggest a way out of the difficulty that Moore had found in Kant's notion of freedom (in his article 'Freedom' in *Mind*, published April 1898). There Moore had found a discrepancy between Kant's assertion of theoretical freedom of the will in the noumenal realm, and his attempt to establish practical freedom of the will in the phenomenal realm. In Moore's view Kant had departed further than he realized from ordinary usage in asserting the former, which he simply should have allowed to stand as a special sense of 'freedom of the will', and not have attempted then to connect it with human volition. Thus Kant would have avoided the problem of establishing a 'valid connection between the notion of Transcendental Freedom and that of End or Good'. Moore's article was connected with his fellowship dissertation, and Lowes Dickinson must have read one of the copies of it circulated before publication. Lowes Dickinson wrote that he thought he had found a fundamental criticism of Moore's argument that tended to reinstate Kant's attempts to connect the two senses of freedom of the will; it lay in the psychological 'feeling of being a cause'. He remembered, no doubt correctly, that Moore would probably 'object to all my language, but also probably you will see my point'. The letter was written during the vacation from his father's house in London, and concludes with an open invitation to tea or supper.[7]

But by the following summer Lowes Dickinson's intercourse with Moore was having more serious consequences for him. In a letter of 20 August 1898 to R. C. Trevelyan, we catch a clear intimation of some of the reasons why Lowes Dickinson was shortly to give up philosophy:

'– I'm fagged to death – result of a metaphysical talk with Moore. What a brain that fellow has! It desiccates mine! Dries up my lakes and seas and leaves me in arid tracts of sand. Not that *he* is arid – anything but; he's merely the sun. One ought to put up a parasol – I do try to, one of humour, but it has so many rents in it. Oh dear!

Surely I once had some rivers? I wish you were here to water me. All poets water. They are the rain; metaphysics are the sun; and between them they fertilize the soil.

> Yours so far as there is anything of me,
>
> G.L.D.'[8]

8

Moore's Time as a Prize Fellow of Trinity: 1898-1904

Whilst a Prize Fellow, said Moore, 'I was living in a set of Fellows' rooms on the north side of Neville's Court – a very pleasant place and a very pleasant life.'[1] His first philosophical work after completing his dissertation was some articles for Baldwin's *Dictionary of Philosophy and Psychology*: 'Cause and Effect', 'Change', 'Nativism', 'Quality', 'Real', 'Reason', 'Relative', 'Relativity of Knowledge', 'Substance', 'Spirit', 'Teleology' and 'Truth'. Though a great deal of work went into writing these articles, Moore was not proud of them, and said they were 'extraordinarily crude, and were very far from giving a really adequate account of the use of the terms in question'.

The results of his second year's dissertation work, which marked his abandonment of the idealist philosophy, were published in substance in *Mind* for April 1899, under the title 'The Nature of Judgment'. Apart from some book reviews for professional journals, this piece was the most difficult article Moore wrote during this period of his life. It was, and still is, virtually inaccessible to readers without training in philosophy. But its importance can be seen from a few sentences of Russell's in a famous passage of *My Philosophical Development*: 'It was towards the end of 1898 that Moore and I rebelled against both Kant and Hegel. Moore led the way, but I followed closely in his footsteps. I think that the first published account of the new philosophy was Moore's article in *Mind* on "The Nature of Judgement". Although neither he nor I would now adhere to all the doctrines in this article, I, and I think he, would still agree with its negative part – i.e. with the doctrine that fact is in general independent of experience.'[2]

In 1899 Moore had his first experience of lecturing. He gave two courses of lectures at the Passmore Edwards Settlement in London, the first on Kant's ethics, and the second simply on ethics. In the audience for the first lecture was Moore's brother Tom – now known as Sturge Moore. He sent his notes to his younger brother for his comments and corrections, and they were returned with whole pages covered in

Moore's neat writing. But Sturge Moore was not really of a philosophical disposition. When, much later, his correspondence with W. B. Yeats was published, his brother found Sturge Moore's remarks on philosophy nearly as dotty as Yeats's own. The second course of lectures was of very great moment:

'It was in writing the course on Ethics that I developed the main outline of *Principia Ethica*; but *Principia* was almost entirely a new, and was a much longer, work, and the latter part of those six years was mainly occupied in writing it. I found this an extremely troublesome business. I write very slowly and with great difficulty; and I constantly found that I had to re-write what I had written, because there was something wrong with it. Of course, even after all this alteration, there still remained an immense deal that was wrong with it; but I did not see that clearly at the time, though I constantly felt vaguely dissatisfied.'[3]

In the years of his fellowship, Moore also wrote and delivered several papers to the Aristotelian Society, and did a bit of editing of a professional journal. He summed up these years by saying:

'Taking everything together, I think I did a respectable amount of work during my tenure of this Fellowship. *Respectable*, I think; but I am afraid, not more than respectable. I cannot claim that during this period I worked *very* hard, nor perhaps as hard as I ought. Indeed I do not think that for any considerable period of my life I have ever worked very hard, except perhaps for four or five years while I was at school. The fact is that, by disposition, I am very lazy; and there is almost always something which I would much rather be doing than working: more often than not, *what* I would much rather be doing is reading some novel or some history or biography – some *story* in fact; for stories, whether purporting to be true or avowedly mere fiction, have a tremendous fascination for me. The consequence is that I have always been having constantly to struggle to force myself to work, and constantly suffering from a more or less bad conscience for not succeeding better. This state of things seems to me so natural, that I find it difficult to believe that it is not the same with everyone; and if it were the same with everyone, it would not be worth mentioning – it would go without saying. But I have met with facts which seem to me to suggest that, unintelligible though it may seem there are some people who don't need to struggle so hard as I do to make themselves work, and are not so constantly or strongly tempted to do something else. Perhaps such people form only a small minority; but, if there are any of them at all, it is perhaps worth mentioning that I have never, since I grew up, been one of them.'⁴

When he wrote these words in 1941 and 1942 Moore's commitment to the secrecy of the Society was absolute. Nonetheless, as the Apostles' meetings and his less formal contacts with individual Apostles were crucial to his work as a philosopher – during these years he knew hardly *any* philosophers who were not Apostles – he permitted himself an oblique reference to his fellow Apostles:

'Certainly during these six years I spent a very great deal of time in reading novels and in talking to friends. But a good deal of the time spent in the latter way was by no means without profit for my philosophical work. I have already mentioned that during part of these years I had a good deal of discussion with Russell; and I also learned a good deal from discussion with other friends. To mention one particular instance, the whole plan of the last chapter of *Principia* was first formed in conversation with a friend.'⁵

The name of that friend was Hugh Owen Meredith (1878–1964), E. M. Forster's greatest friend and one time lover, who was elected to the Apostles in May 1900.

Moore's attendance at Apostles' meetings remained constant after his election to his fellowship and he continued to act as secretary until January 1901. In November 1898 Moore read a paper on lovers' quarrels, '*Amantium querellae (sic)*'. (The 'sic' was because when he had offered topics to be chosen Moore had misquoted a line from Terence's *Andria* (33, 23) '*Amantium irae amoris integratio est*'.) A mere bagatelle, the subject and Moore's treatment of it are trivial even by the Apostles' most lax standards, but it does contain some interesting asides on love and friendship, including some remarks of biographical interest: 'Things are said of [love], of its strength and its effects on almost everything a man may think or feel, such as I have certainly never been able to observe either in myself or others: . . . For myself I have seen in it nothing but what differs in degree, and in no very marked degree, from ordinary friendship.' Moore professes himself dismayed by 'the apparent absurdity of the causes which seem to have such great effects'. He says he thinks it completely unreasonable to think that the people he likes must be *better* than other people, yet among lovers this sentiment is a 'commonplace'. And this puzzles him because it does not apply with the same force to one's own taste in works of art, for example : 'I can admit with tolerable equanimity, that other works of art may be as good as those I like; that something may be said for other people's preferences in this matter : but that is simply because I do not care half so much for any work of art as for many people.'

At the last meeting before the Christmas break, Ward addressed the Society, asking 'Do we wish to be all one God?' The two Trevelyans voted No, as did Hardy and Moore, who added, 'I recognize a difficulty, but I do prefer to be myself.' The fact that this apparently sophomoric discussion was initiated by the fifty-five-year-old Professor of Mental Philosophy might indicate that the actual proceedings of the Society were not so juvenile as the records of them would lead one to believe.

The Christmas vacation of 1898 found Moore making a by now customary visit to Bertrand and Alys Russell at Millhangar; then he went to Desmond MacCarthy and his family at Kensington Park Gardens. Moore had become deeply involved in the MacCarthy family's affairs, and it was to Moore that Desmond's mother turned when she was worried about her son and needed a confidant. When in 1906 MacCarthy married Mary Warre-Cornish, Moore was a trustee of their marriage settlement, and he stood godfather to (apparently both) their son Michael and daughter Rachel (now Lady David Cecil). Following Moore's visit to the MacCarthys, Desmond MacCarthy spent Christmas itself with Moore's family in Devon.

On the appointed day for the first Apostles' meeting of the new term in 1899, 21 January, there was no paper prepared, so Moore gave a supper to Dickinson, Russell, Marsh, G. M. Trevelyan, MacCarthy, Smyth and Hardy. These suppers in lieu of papers occurred increasingly frequently in 1898 and 1899; when only two or three Apostles were involved, as was usually the case, a supper might have seemed a painless alternative to preparing a paper; but when, as on this occasion, the host had to wine and dine seven guests, the expense must have been considerable. The following week Moore must have been ill or away from Cambridge – it was the first Apostles' meeting he had missed for years.

The Society met on 4 February 1899 to hear Moore read an interesting paper entitled 'Do we love ourselves best?', which was an impassioned argument – a tirade almost – against ethical egoism, the position he had adopted in 'What end?', the first paper he had read to the Apostles. Moore says that he detects a tendency to abandon egoism – formerly, he says, accepted as a truism – in favour of the recognition that 'we do sometimes love our neighbours'. He calls this a 'great advance'. Turning to the claim that egoism, though not *in fact* the only motive for action, is in some 'metaphysical' (i.e. more profound) sense true, he writes:

> 'Now for myself, I must admit that when I understand a thing is true or not true, I wish to stick to it. To do so may make speculation more difficult and of much less absorbing interest; but nevertheless I do not *like* to contradict myself, if I can help it. I cannot therefore take it to be true that self-love is the only motive of our actions in any sense whatever, either common or uncommon, shallow or profound.'

Moore concludes that we can only properly be said to love others and not ourselves at all. More interestingly, he is here groping towards the notion of love of others as something that is good as an end in itself and not as a means to some other end: 'Love of others is a thing of very great value, and it may be very strong although it does not lead to any actions. There is, indeed, no reason why it should; to test it by results is quite absurd.'

For the vote, the Apostles stood Moore's question on its head: 'Can we hate ourselves as much as other people?' Russell and MacCarthy thought Yes; Hardy, Smyth, Sanger and Moore said No.

Russell, who was resident at Cambridge that term, gave a paper the next week. It resulted in two questions being put to the vote: (1) 'Is matter beautiful?' (2) 'Is matter good?' On question (1) all present, Moore, both Llewelyn Davieses, Hardy and Russell himself voted Yes. On (2) Moore and Crompton Llewelyn Davies voted Yes, while Theodore, Hardy and Russell voted No. Moore commented on both questions: 'The whole thing is absurd, the question has never been raised.'

Moore *was* cross. For Russell read 'Was the world good before the 6th day?' to refute the view that beauty is good as an end. But of course that is not what Moore had argued – only that love of others is good as an end in itself.* This was the first public indication of the breach between Moore and Russell that could only widen if Russell was capable of misrepresenting Moore's views to those who had heard them in the first place. Russell's paper begins:

> 'Our brother Moore has been engaged, by order of the Society, in

* The first mention of 'beauty' in Moore's paper was an example: handsome persons, he argued, cannot be said to admire their own beauty in the sense in which they can be said to admire the beauty of another person. The second was a distinction between the object of love and this action or that, which 'serves somewhat to enhance its beauty'.

a heroic work, involving the very highest degree of danger and difficulty. He has been endeavouring – I believe with success – to corrupt still further (an arduous task) the morals of those phenomena who frequent the shallow abyss known among the shadows as "The London School of Ethics and Social Philosophy." As the glory of God is enhanced by the damnation of the wicked, by which they are rendered still more wicked than they intended to be, so the glory of the Society is enhanced by increasing the phenomenality of phenomena. And as it is the mark of the Society to be wise and good, so it is the mark of phenomena to be foolish and wicked. Moore has been endeavouring then, to render these shadows even more foolish and more wicked than they naturally are. That this is difficult is certanly undeniable; but the difficulty seems to have been successfully overcome. For according to an emissary, sent by the Society to report upon Moore's success, he persuaded the assembled phenomena that their so-called lives were of such value to each other, that, if they saw one of the wise and good drowning, they ought not to risk death in an endeavour to save him. The danger of Moore's mission, however, was even more overwhelming than the difficulty, and has, I fear, been less effectively avoided. It is well-known that whatever is dangerous for a brother is unreal, and that contact with the unreal may entail fatal consequences. What, then, was my horror, when I discovered that these views, designed for the corruption of the nonexistent, had – I shudder at the thought – infected our lamented brother himself. To free him from these dreadful toils is my purpose tonight.'

One can imagine Moore's annoyance as Russell went on, perhaps with an obvious touch of malice in his voice :

'Moore contends that God, when he looked down upon the world in its early stages, was right in maintaining it to be good – that it was already good in and for itself, and would have continued so even if God had not been looking. A world of matter alone – so says our misguided brother – may be good or bad. For it may certainly be beautiful or ugly, and beauty is better than ugliness. It cannot be said – so the argument proceeds – that beauty is good only as a means to the production of emotion in us. For we judge the man who is moved by beauty to be better than the man who is equally moved by ugliness. This judgment can only be valid, if beauty is good *per se*; for in this case, the man who enjoys ugliness more is to be condemned for liking what is bad. But if beauty were only good as a means, ugliness would be equally good if it produced the same effect; this, however, is manifestly false. Hence beauty is good *per se*, and a purely material world, with no one to contemplate it, is better if it is beautiful than if it is ugly.

'Such is the argument, which, though invented for the further perdition of shadows, has alas! deceived our brother himself. Let us now endeavour to persuade him that this sophism, like the world of matter, can only be good as a means, and must never be taken as an end.'

Russell goes on in this paper to accept what was to be the main assumption of the last chapter of *Principia Ethica*, that the only things that are good in themselves are states of mind (Russell calls them 'psychical states'). But he then claims that our ethical judgement that the man who enjoys beauty is a better man than one who enjoys ugliness implies the validity of hedonism – which would discomfit Moore. This, because the only difference in the states of mind of a man perceiving beauty rather than ugliness, is that the former carries greater pleasure.[6]

The 'sophism', of course, was entirely Russell's; his paper, as Moore made clear in his comment on the vote, badly misrepresented the views Moore had expressed the week before. One has to wonder how Russell could have had the cheek to distort Moore's views so much *in Moore's presence*. The teasing at the beginning of Russell's paper Moore could have accepted with equanimity – even if it were not entirely good-natured; but attributing to him views he did not hold was a slight Moore could never have borne. Russell must have intended to give offence. According to James Strachey (as reported in Michael Holroyd's *Lytton Strachey*), 'Russell resented the greater influence exerted' over their fellow Apostles by Moore, and Frances Partridge told of Desmond MacCarthy's saying that Moore 'felt that his own patient, inquiring method of analysis was seriously disrupted by Russell's quick-fire, censorious and – so Moore sometimes felt – invalid arguments'. Holroyd goes on to say that Russell 'seems to have returned Moore's cerebral disapprobation'.[7]

On the first Saturday in March, Sanger read a paper which resulted in the question, 'Can moral philosophy provide any antidote for unhappiness?' Hardy, Marsh and Moore thought it could, with Moore adding the qualifying remark, 'I think it does to me, but I don't know if I think it ought.' Mayor, Smyth, the Llewelyn Davies brothers and Sanger voted No.

Two days later the Apostles held a meeting that was extraordinary in two senses: both for its timing, coming so soon after another meeting, and for its subject-matter. In Hardy's absence, Moore read a paper by him on metageometry. The question put was sensible – 'Is space probably Euclidean?' In fact only Moore and Russell were present to debate the question, and maths was never Moore's strong point; it is doubtful that he had heard of Lobachevsky or Riemann before that evening, so Russell had a decided edge. Moore voted that space 'is certainly Euclidean, but not demonstrably by me at present'; Russell of course voted No.

The reading party for 1899 was held at Gunnerside; besides Moore, it consisted of MacCarthy, Mayor, Sanger and Bob Trevelyan. Back at Cambridge, Moore defaulted on his paper of 22 April and instead gave supper to Dickinson, Smyth and Hardy. A week later he had, after a fashion, got his paper ready, and he read 'Vanity of vanities'. Here Moore asks the question (which he says Sanger touched on last term), 'What, on earth, people live for?' and says it is the 'only thing which occurs to interest' him. Moore then wanders Apostolically around the edges of his subject – he is not sure what he means by the question he has raised, and it is improper therefore to expect others to answer it; and he half-heartedly raises other questions, like 'How can people believe what is false?' and 'How can people desire what is not good?' He then settles down to defending, without much warmth, the view that 'there is nothing worth living for'. In the vote Smyth, Dickinson and Mayor disagreed with him, while Sanger and Hardy took his side, and MacCarthy voted on both sides of the question.

In May Moore changed the subject – to sex. On 27 May he read a legendary paper, which is unfortunately missing, that resulted in the question 'Is self-abuse bad as an end?' (In the records of the meeting, Moore has crossed out 'or only as a means?') Only Hardy and Mayor agreed with Moore that masturbation was bad as an end; Smyth, Roger Fry, Bob Trevelyan and Lowes Dickinson voted No. In a letter that shows how seriously he took the Society's debates, a distinctly annoyed Moore wrote to MacCarthy on 30 May 1899, that he was sorry Mac-Carthy hadn't come last Saturday chiefly

'because of the meeting. I read, a very long paper, about sexual matters – as frank a paper as George Trevy's: I wanted to know what Smyth and Hardy thought, and, having to write, there was nothing else I could write so much about with so much interest. And the division sickened me. The question was: Is self-abuse bad *as an end?* and the majority said No. Bob Trevy certainly did not know what he was saying; and I think that Fry and Dickinson were too innocent to know: but Smyth – he revolted me most, but perhaps he also did not understand. The division was not on the practical question, which divided you from us last time; but I wrote my paper so as to exclude that, and thought I had put the thing *in itself* so strongly that nobody could differ from me.

'I see now how I might have put it stronger; and in fact Fry, the chief of the opposition, was largely on practical issues; but still I hate the result and have been thinking of it ever since (at least 10 times more than I usually do). It was a great comfort that Hardy (though I must confess he spoke first) said he agreed entirely with my conclusion, and only doubted whether there were not a greater number of practical reasons as well. (I don't know if you've read my lectures sufficiently to see the full difference between means and ends, and so know that "practical" always involves the former. I felt handicapped then by the fact that Fry and Smyth hadn't: for I can't repeat it all, and without it nobody can understand.) Mayor voted with us two (chiefly because he understood the issue better), though his speech was mostly against me. I just think of the question and the vote: isn't it really astonishing? I wonder what the elder brothers will think, if they see the book at the Dinner.'[8]

The dinner for 1899 took place on 14 June at a London hotel and was well-attended. Moore and most of his friends were there, but the star attractions were Vernon Lushington, now an important sixty-seven-year-old judge, who had become an Apostle in 1854, and, even more impressive, the Rev. Francis J. Holland, who had been born in 1828 and elected to the Apostles in 1846.

Moore filled the long vacation of 1899 with visits and travels. In June he went to Wedgwood at Hartlepool, and while there encountered the Russells at Barnard Castle – he had been avoiding their company throughout the Lent term. He then stayed with the MacCarthys in London at 8 Cheyne Gardens – in April they had consulted Moore about their new furnishings – and in July he returned to Cambridge. Changing rooms, he moved into the cloisters, where MacCarthy joined him for ten days at the end of the month, and Moore read him his poems – which no longer exist. In August he was off to Bayreuth to hear Wagner with Crompton Llewelyn Davies, Dakyns and Mayor. Then with Theodore and Crompton Llewelyn Davies and Sanger, he walked in the Tirol. After that the party went to Venice, and then they appear to have walked a considerable distance through the Alps starting at the Rhône glacier. In Sepember Moore went to his parents at Cheriton, then on with Bob Trevelyan to visit the Whiteheads; and, finally, he paid another visit to Wedgwood at Hartlepool.

The Apostles met on 14 October 1899 to choose subjects, and a week later Smyth read 'Are men more amiable than women?' This led to quite a funny vote: Smyth and the homosexual Dickinson voted for Men. MacCarthy, Hardy, Mayor, Theodore Llewelyn Davies and Sanger were Neutral; so was Moore, save that he added, 'Perhaps not less amiable'. Only the staunchly heterosexual George Trevelyan voted for Women.

Acting on Moore's nomination, the Apostles elected to membership in November 1899, Alfred Richard Ainsworth (1879–1959), and for the next ten years or so, Ainsworth was to be the most important person in Moore's life. One of a family of ten children, his father was an Inspector of Schools for Southeast Suffolk, so young 'Fred' was educated at Ipswich Grammar School, until, after four years there, his father was moved to London and he was sent to Dulwich College, Moore's old school. Ainsworth went up to King's as a scholar in October 1898, just one year before his election to the Apostles. Moore had been cultivating Ainsworth's acquaintance for some time; perhaps Moore was alerted to Ainsworth's promise by someone at Dulwich – in June 1899 Moore had gone to Oxford for an old Alleynian dinner and renewed his ties with Dulwich. At Cambridge Ainsworth's achievement was even greater than his mentor's: Moore had failed to get a first in part II of the classics tripos; but Ainsworth got a first in classics part I in 1900, and in moral sciences part II in *and* classics part II 1902. He then went directly to Manchester University where he lectured in Latin in 1902–3 and then to Edinburgh University where he taught Greek from 1903 to 1907. In 1904, on the expiry of his Trinity Fellowship, Moore went to Edinburgh to live with Ainsworth. They remained there until 1908 when Ainsworth became an Inspector at the Board of Education and married Moore's youngest sister, Sarah.

Everything after this was tragedy. Ainsworth's father had died in 1906, and he assumed responsibility for the education of five younger children; this may have necessitated the move to London and a better-paid job. Whatever relations between Ainsworth and Moore had been earlier, Moore was delighted at the prospect of having Ainsworth for a brother-in-law. The birth of Alfred and Sarah Ainsworth's first child was a difficult one, but the baby was handsome, with the Moore family's looks, and was christened George Herbert, after Moore and his brother Bertie. When six months old, the baby showed signs of illness, and serious epilepsy was diagnosed. Sarah devoted all her time to the care of 'Georgy', so much so that her mother-in-law prophesied that, should anything happen to Sarah, the child would certainly die. When a second, normal son, John, was born, Ainsworth was disturbed by his wife's obsession with her first child; he wanted George placed in a specialized home for brain-damaged children, as he thought it was not good for John to grow up so close to his brother. Sarah of course vetoed every institution they inspected. This was probably what weakened the marriage so seriously that it ended in divorce. (George, incidentally, was a handsome young man of twenty when Sarah died, but, as predicted, he died in a home three months later.)

Ainsworth married again in 1929, and his second wife was Ethel Morgan, a clerk at the Board of Education. Ainsworth's family did not greatly care for her, but made the best they could of a bad situation. (In 1967 or 1968 – the body was found too late to determine the date of death – Ethel committed suicide by taking an overdose of pills, with her will open on the table beside her : she left everything to Ainsworth's astonished youngest sister.) Meanwhile the second son, John, had grown up, gone to university, and got married just before war broke out and he was called up. On his first leave, while cycling to meet his wife, he was killed by a car driven by a drunk. Ainsworth had by then become Deputy-Secretary at the Board of Education and had been made a Companion of the Bath. The death of his second son set off a physical and mental decline : he retired in 1940 and spent the next nineteen years moving house at irregular but very frequent intervals until Christmas Day 1959, when he collapsed and died while his sisters were at church.[9]

E. M. Forster sketched a famous portrait of the undergraduate Ainsworth as Ansell in *The Longest Journey*. According to Forster's biographer,[10] the truth of the opening scene, where Ansell is flicking matches on to Rickie's carpet, is confirmed by Sir Charles Tennyson's disguised description of Ainsworth as 'a philosopher from King's' in his *Cambridge from Within*. At a meeting of a Cambridge society discussion is growing heated when interruptions

'are forestalled by a philosopher from King's, who makes a dash for the fireplace, climbs on the curb, puts his back against the mantelpiece, and launches into a long harangue. First of all he tells the reader exactly what *he* has said, then he explains the metaphysician's meaning to *him* with equal certainty and detail, and finally launches into his own views. Unhappily he is less lucid in this exposition than in the preceding one. He has a singularly involved style of gesture and exegesis. He writhes against the overmantel, shrugging and twisting his shoulders, like an intellectual Atlas upbearing a world of argument. He is incessantly climbing on and off the curb, twisting his forelock between his forefinger and thumb, taking his pipe out of his mouth and stroking his forehead, chin, or the bridge of his nose with the stem of it. Meanwhile his periods get more and more involved, his manner more and more provocative. Before long he has completely abandoned the subject of the paper and passed to a minute analysis of the motives of human action in all ages. . . . There seems no reason why he should ever stop, when, in the midst of a more than usually tortuous parenthesis, he bites through the stem of his pipe, which drops with a crash into the hearth (he has almost turned his back on the room in the crisis of expression) scattering a cascade of ashes on the carpet.'[11]

We have seen that up to this year, 1899, Moore was without sexual experience and had had few emotional attachments outside his family and his best friend, Desmond MacCarthy; apart from these, the greatest feature of his sentimental life was his growing dislike for Russell (Moore records a 'quarrel with Russell at the beginning of Lent Term'), and it was this relationship that came closest to engaging his passions. Of girls, Moore had very little experience, even less than could be expected of a twenty-six-year-old fellow of a Cambridge college. The reasons for this are that he chose to spend the tenure of his fellowship in residence at Trinity, which meant that his acquaintances remained largely confined to his already established social circle, the Apostles. He did no teaching yet at Cambridge, so he had not even the opportunity of meeting girls from Newnham and Girton. From the viewpoint of sex, Moore's undergraduate and postgraduate career as well was merely an extension of school, with the exception that at school he had been a day boy; now he was the equivalent of a boarder. From the Apostles he had learnt the existence of homosexuality, and following the fashion, he had got the knack of using homosexual jargon to spice his papers in the manner approved by the Society. But from an older generation – from Lowes Dickinson and McTaggart – he had learnt of the existence and nature of genuine homosexual desire, as opposed to the spurious, verbal mannerisms that were *de rigueur* for his own, mainly heterosexual generation of the Apostles.

It seems unlikely from Moore's frank comments on sex in his Apostles' papers and letters that he was highly sexed. Nonetheless he had a passionate character. Everyone who ever heard him sing *Lieder* to his own piano accompaniment was struck and touched by the passion he openly displayed in his performances; and the same aspect of his character was remarked by all who heard him discuss philosophy in his youth. His passionate nature was a large part of his attraction for his disciples. But in 1899 Moore was a young man with great warmth of affection and no object upon whom to bestow it. Thus it was – and not because he was genuinely homosexual – that he became infatuated with Ainsworth.

Ainsworth was aged twenty when Moore first took Hardy to call on him to vet him for the Apostles in May term. A photograph of him, which may date from that time, shows a boyish face surmounted by fair hair: an attractive enough young man, without being either handsome or pretty. Moore's need may simply have been for an intimate friend; MacCarthy had gone down before the end of May term the previous year; in any case, Moore was attracted to Ainsworth. Here is Moore's own, terse chronicle of his relations with Ainsworth in 1899–1900: 'Ainsworth. Elected Michaelmas Term. Comes to see me, when I am in bed with influenza at beginning of Lent Term. Walk to Ely with Crompton, Dakyns and him in May Term: hold his hand.'[12] It can be said with confidence that this last sentence details the full extent of Moore's and Ainsworth's physical relations.*

The story continues in Moore's record of 1900–01: 'Ainsworth. Begin to see less of Hardy . . . *Lent Term*. Speak out to Ainsworth';[14] and then in Lent term, 1903: 'Come up January 3 to meet A.: he stays two nights: very affectionate: important Sunday night.'[15] Moore's relationship with Ainsworth was begun under no influence other than the examples of some older Apostles; but it developed and was encouraged – certainly by 1903 – by the example and precept of a younger Apostle, Lytton Strachey, who revelled in the idea of his hero and mentor being homosexual, and he, and later Maynard Keynes, did everything they could to encourage Moore and Ainsworth to think of themselves as lovers. Ainsworth's letters to Strachey have survived. From the time of Ainsworth's departure for Manchester in the autumn of 1903 they are

* This is confirmed by Leonard Woolf who was interested in their relationship.[13]

romantic and silly. On 23 November 1903 Ainsworth writes in a mood of languid torpor: 'I feel hollow and echo-less. But – if I were with you I could not do it – I should like to reach three hundred miles and kiss you. Shall I just whisper that you are neither absurd nor exaggerated? Won't you believe me?'¹⁶ Those who know Strachey's correspondence for this period can easily reconstruct the mood, if not the content, of the letter that prompted this reply; the style of Ainsworth's letter is itself pure Strachey. Strachey saw a great deal of Moore when they were both at Cambridge and Ainsworth was first at Manchester and then at Edinburgh; he did his best to convince Moore that he was in love with Ainsworth. From 1903 Strachey conducted a postal campaign to convince Ainsworth that he was equally in love with Moore. When the two actually began to live together in Edinburgh in 1904, they rapidly discovered that they were only good friends, and Strachey changed his mind: from late 1905 to early 1906, he attempted to persuade Ainsworth that he was really in love with J. T. Sheppard, Lytton's contemporary in the Society. But as Ainsworth was no more homosexual than Moore, that effort too was a failure. What remains likely, however, is that in 1899–1900 Moore *thought* he was in love with Alfred Ainsworth.

Russell, it must be pointed out, thought the relationship had had bad consequences for Moore. Twenty years later he told Virginia Woolf, and she recorded it in her diary entry for Saturday, 23 February 1924, that Moore

> ' "When he first came up to Cambridge, . . . was the most wonderful creature in the whole world. His smile was the most beautiful thing I have ever seen. We believed in Berkeley" (perhaps). "Suddenly, something went wrong with him; something happened to him and his work. *Principia Ethica* was nothing like so good as his Essay on Judgment. He was very fond of Ainsworth. I don't know what happened – it ruined him. He took to putting out his tongue after that. You" (I, that is) "said he had no complexes. But he's full of them. Watch him putting his tongue round his mouth." '¹⁷

On 4 November 1899 Ainsworth attended his first Apostles' meeting to hear Moore read a paper on 'Is anything as good as persons?' It is extremely unfortunate, but this essay, with its clear connection to *Principia Ethica*, is lost. Hardy, R. C. Trevelyan and Ainsworth voted that there were other things as good as persons, whereas MacCarthy, Fred Pollock, G. M. Trevelyan, Mayor, Dickinson, Sanger, Smyth, and

McTaggart agreed with Moore on the proposition that was the ancestor of the principal teachings of *Principia*.

Eight days later Moore read a long paper on 'Religious belief' to the Sunday Essay Society. This paper is interesting because Moore not only distinguishes between the sort of reasons that can be given for religious and moral beliefs, but argues that the only thing to be said in favour of religious belief is that it makes people behave better : that the only sound reasons for religious belief are moral ones. But intelligent people, Moore says, ought to be 'able to believe that things are right, whether God said them or not'. In short, Moore argues that there is no need for religious belief; and as for Pascal's argument that, 'in our state of doubt, we should decide for that belief which promises the greater reward, I have nothing to say of it except that it seems to me absolutely wicked.'

In *Principia Ethica* there is an important theory called the principle of organic unity, which, put simply, says that it is not possible to tell in isolation whether a thing is good or bad, for something thought bad in isolation might come to be seen as making up *part* of a whole which is itself good, and conversely. This theory developed, at least in part, as a response to the problem raised by the paper Moore read to the Apostles on 24 February 1900, 'Should things be real ?' The problem of the value of existence is that it seems that imaginary goods are less good than goods that exist, and that therefore existence is itself a good; but it also seems that imaginary evils are better than real ones, so, paradoxically, existence is also an evil.

Moore sees no way out of this dilemma, and simply leaves the problem as he has put it; he goes on to ask whether it would be worse to be universally and systematically deceived (as by Descartes' Evil Demon, though Moore does not refer explicitly to Descartes) or to have the same experience and beliefs veridically. Moore says he cannot see *why* it would be worse, but he realizes that there is a tendency to feel it would be. The only justification Moore can find for this tendency is something like the original belief that existence is a good :

'The only escape from this paradox would seem to be by way of saying that only existent things can be called good or evil; that there is no good at all in an imaginary world. But, if we take this way, we seem to be landed in another paradox that is just as bad. For if nothing is good except what exists, then at once this is the best possible world. We can never say that works of art give us a glimpse into a better world : for any world, except what does exist, cannot even be good, far less better than this. There will be absolutely no meaning in an ideal.'

The Society divided on the question, 'Should things be real?' Ainsworth, G. M. Trevelyan and Moore voted Yes; Hardy voted No, and Smyth voted both ways. At the conclusion of this inconclusive vote, the Apostles accepted Hardy's nomination of Ralph Hawtrey (1879–1975) as the 235th brother.

Hawtrey came from a family long associated with Eton, where he was educated himself, before coming up to Trinity in 1898. In 1901 he was 19th Wrangler; in 1903 he briefly entered the Admiralty, before going to the Treasury, where he found his vocation as an economist and remained for forty-one years. He was a very faithful Apostle, attending every annual dinner until 1954, when he was prevented from going by ill health. He was devoted to Moore, whose impassioned singing of *Die Beiden Grenadiere* made him realize how horrible war was for the soldiers who actually did the fighting: this constituted an epiphany for Hawtrey, and reinforced his life-long Liberalism. Moore was so much the most important influence on the life and career of Sir Ralph Hawtrey that he spent his last years working on a systematic philosophical treatise (inspired also by Robin Mayor), which was to have been a *summa* of his twenty-odd books and the hundreds of letters he published in *The Times*. He was married to the famous pianist Titi d'Aranyi.[18]

Ralph Hawtrey attended his first meeting in 1900, and by May had suggested that Hugh Owen Meredith be elected. Meredith (or HOM, as he was always known, at least in writing, to his friends) played a crucial part in this story – he is the missing piece in the *Principia Ethica* jig-saw puzzle. For it was Meredith who was the friend in conversation with whom Moore formed 'the whole plan of the last chapter of *Principia*'.[19] The date of this history-making conversation was a Sunday in Lent term 1903, when Moore recorded: 'Meredith to tea, talks of intrinsic goods'.[20] (The implications of this date are several and surprising. As *Principia* was published in October 1903, it is probable, even allowing for the fact that publishers worked quickly at that long-ago time, that the rest of the book was already with the printers by then. Further, it would seem that, though the gestation period of the first five chapters was five or six years, the last chapter was written in a startlingly small number of weeks.)

There is a beautifully drawn portrait of Meredith in P. N. Furbank's *E. M. Forster: A Life*:

'Meredith was one of the eight children of an Irish legal shorthand writer, living in Wimbledon. The father was a talented and thwarted man, largely self-educated, and the family, though badly off, was socially ambitious, so Hugh was sent to a good prep school; . . . He had gone on to Shrewsbury, where he had won every sort of prize for work and athletics. All the same, his had been a troubled boyhood; he quarrelled bitterly with his father and tended to conceive of himself as a friendless outsider. Some time in his middle teens, he had announced that he had become an atheist, and this had led to a violent flurry in the family, various clerical friends being called in, in vain, to shepherd him back to orthodoxy.'[21]

As so many other unhappy but intellectual boys before him had done, Meredith found that Cambridge was his idea of paradise. His subject was classics, but his métier was conversation, and he spent a good deal of time at King's, where he came up in 1897, wandering from one set of rooms to another, dropping in on, and taking part in, discussions on anything – but he particularly enjoyed abstract argument. Thus, unlike Forster, Meredith was attracted to the circle around Moore. If Moore's lieutenant was Ainsworth, his troops were MacCarthy, Hawtrey, Hardy and Smyth; and Meredith was made welcome by them, for his 'intellectually impressive . . . quiet-voiced manner', for his 'tall, good looking, altogether rather noble . . . appearance', and for his restlessness and high spirits, under which 'ran a vein of cynicism, a shrugging conviction that nothing in the world was much good'. Furbank reports that Forster felt that Meredith had infected 'all his friends with his pessimism', and that though there were many who thought Meredith the cleverest of his group of friends, Oscar Browning once told him, 'You are very brilliant, but you will never do anything.'[22]

Browning was both right and wrong. Meredith did great enough things at Cambridge: he was a scholar and prizeman of King's, got a first in classics part I and history part II, and was elected a fellow of his college from 1903 to 1908. During this latter period he became an economist and lectured at Manchester in economic history from 1905 to 1908, when he got a university appointment at Cambridge. He stayed there until 1911, when he went to Belfast as professor. At thirty-three, Meredith was young to be professor; but his career at Belfast was interrupted by his war work from 1916 to 1918 at the Ministry of Munitions (for which he received the OBE) and at the Ministry of Labour in 1918 and 1919. Yet Browning's prophecy was true in that Meredith squandered his brilliance by not concentrating it on any one subject or project, a point that is illustrated by the titles of only three of his books: *Four Dramas of Euripides, Outlines of English Economic History*, and *Weekday Poems*. Meredith was a renaissance man and poet in a specialized and prosaic world.

Meredith, who was 'born' into the Society by Hawtrey, attended his first meeting on 26 May to hear Moore read 'Is conversion possible?' This essay, strikingly unlike anything else written by Moore, gives a glimpse of an ideal very different from that of Chapter VI of *Principia Ethica*. The ideal here presented is not dependent on beauty or affection, but is self-contained; it is an almost mystical vision of life as a succession of conversions, a permanent state of what Tolstoy called New Birth. Using what he calls the 'literary method', allusion and description rather than analysis, Moore in this paper achieves an uncustomary eloquence, as he tries to capture for his audience the feeling of an elusive experience – but an experience that he thinks he has had himself, and once, perhaps, even shared with MacCarthy. In short, in this paper Moore is canvassing a third candidate for being an intrinsically good state of mind; he also thinks it good as a means: it occurs frequently among children, with increasing rarity after the age of twenty, and its absence is one of the marks of middle age; it is New Birth that keeps us young, that keeps the spirit agile, but never out of harmony with Reason. Can we will ourselves to have the experience of New Birth? Matthew Arnold, says Moore, denies the possibility in the poem all too aptly called 'Morality':

> *We cannot kindle when we will*
> *The fire which in the heart resides;*
> *The spirit bloweth and is still,*
> *In mystery our soul abides.*
> *But tasks in hours of insight willed*
> *Can be through hours of gloom fulfilled.*

Paradoxically, Wordsworth holds out the possibility of continuing conversion in his 'Ode to Duty': 'Serene will be our days and bright/ And happy will our nature be,/When love is an unerring light/And joy its own security.' 'This is a description of the New Life,' says Moore,

'and the poet goes on to say that he desires the help of Duty, . . . It might be thought that this Duty is the Duty of Morality – the pis-aller of Mr Matthew Arnold. Yet even if the whole spirit of the poem did not make it plain that this was not so, it is positively proved by a stanza which he suppressed, when he grew old

Yet not the less would I throughout
Still act according to the voice
Of my own wish; and feel past doubt
That my submissiveness was choice.
Not seeking in the school of pride
For 'precepts over dignified,'
Denial and restraint I prize
No farther than they breed
A second Will more wise.

It must be remembered that this is 1900, and that Moore had now for some time dismissed Lowes Dickinson's Absolute as a chimaera and brought McTaggart's heaven down to earth. Yet in this paper it is Moore who is the visionary and seer, and what he here envisages is an *alternative* to *Principia Ethica's* chapter on the Ideal. The most remarkable feature of this alternative is that it is slightly mystical. In the whole of his adult life this must have been the only time when Moore responded at all to the allure of mysticism, a tendency of intellect and emotion that his whole being – ordinarily – found not only unattractive but repulsive. But here is the mystical vision of G. E. Moore, and at the heart of the experience is its most thrilling aspect, the thought of which ravished Moore's mind and exhilarated his spirit – enhanced rationality :

'Is it possible that this state of mind, with all its professions of clear and true sight and its promise of power against every temptation, merely deludes us ? I feel the doubt uncomfortable and certainly I have never possessed it long enough to try. I feel it possible that the states of those, religious enthusiasts for example, whom I cannot suppose to see nothing but the truth, may be psychologically indistinguishable from mine. And, if psychologically indistinguishable, then the chief hope of my panacea vanishes. It is still possible certainly that my states may really be ones in which I see nothing but the truth. And in defence of this possibility I may point out that they do not overlook the existence of evil. Further, even if they are in error, I think it may be fairly urged in favour of their enormous practical importance, that they contain no beliefs contradictory of what I should ever by any means be capable of conceiving. This certainly cannot be said of Moral Laws : the life of "chance-desires" may reveal truths, which the precepts of Morality would blind you to forever. But its practical importance depends not only, on this value in themselves which I think may really belong to these states, but on the possibility of discovering the principle which might render them permanent. . . . Finally I have only to ask the Society, whether it is not possible that any one of us might discover, tonight or any moment, this true philosopher's stone, the true Wisdom of the Stoics, a discovery which might permanently remove for him who made it, and perhaps for others, by far the most obstructive part of the difficulties and evils with which we have to contend.'

Following this stunning piece, which one can imagine Moore delivering in a breathless, eye-bulging frenzy of excitement, the question put to the vote was 'Can we turn Monday mornings into Saturday nights?', i.e. can one live every moment as though one is participating in a meeting of the Society? After the soaring flights of Moore's paper, the sophomoric wit of the question brings one thudding down to *terra firma*. But at least some connection can be seen between it and the subject of Moore's paper. Whitehead was present to hear this paper; perhaps it had some effect on his later writing – he voted Yes, along with Smyth, Meredith and Moore, who added the sadly deflating afterthought, 'Personally I am particularly incapable of doing so.' Those who thought permanent conversion impossible, and voted No, were MacCarthy, Hardy, Ainsworth, Hawtrey, Dickinson, Mayor and Sanger. McTaggart seems to have been present, but no vote is recorded for him. The new brother, Meredith, was infamous in his own college for his arrogance; it is not difficult to see how after Moore's performance at this first meeting of the Apostles, even Meredith could find in himself sufficient humility to become a follower of Moore.

The annual dinner for 1900 was very well attended. It took place on 13 June at the Royal Palace Hotel. Perhaps the large turnout was in celebration of the new century; in any case the list of those present was headed by the Society's most eminent living member, the seventy-three-year-old Sir William Harcourt. Others present were Montagu Butler, Bowen, Fletcher Moulton, Jebb, McTaggart, Fry, the Trevelyan brothers, Lowes Dickinson, Walford Green, Ainsworth, Russell, Mayor, A. H. Smith, MacNaghten, Whitehead, A. J. Butler, Vincent Stanton, the Llewelyn Davies brothers, Moore, Meredith, M. R. Pryor, S. E. Spring, Rice, Walter Leaf, Jackson, Yates Thompson, Sanger, Smyth, Hardy, Hawtrey, Babington Smith, Clough, Walter Raleigh, Arthur Strachey, MacCarthy, Marsh, Duncan Tovey, B. H. Holland, Parker Smith and Pollock.

July and August of the long vacation Moore spent at Cambridge, where hardly any of his friends save Hardy was up; though Amos appears to have been living near Parker's Piece. He now had his first female pupil, a Miss Iles whom he was engaged to coach. At the end of August Moore went to Hallsteads, to the Vaughan Williamses, and in September he had his holiday: 'Walk in Vosges with Crompton and Maurice Davies; meet MacCarthy. Then to Munich. Then to Salzburg. Tirol with Crompton and Harry Davies. Then to Vienna and Dresden.'[23]

On 10 November 1900 Moore delivered the last paper he was to write especially for the Apostles (he re-read his old papers from time to time after this, some more than once). This paper, called 'Is it a duty to hate?', was a milestone on the road to *Principia Ethica*, for in it Moore develops the position that came to be called Ideal Utilitarianism* – as distinguished from the Hedonistic Utilitarianism of Bentham and the Eudaimonistic Utilitarianism of Mill, both of which Moore, by implication, dismisses in the beginning of this paper. It starts with a consideration of what is meant by the Christian injunction to love your neighbour, and continues in the good-humoured vein of blasphemy that Moore seemed to save up for his Apostles' papers (as he could hardly give vent to it in his pieces for the Sunday Essay Society):

'What a muddle this Christian doctrine is, it is easy enough to see. In the first place . . . it assumes that because love is a duty, 'tis a duty to love *all* men, and that since this is so, it can't be also a duty to hate any of them. And in the second place it assumes "loving" to mean the same as "doing good to" and "hating" the same as "doing evil to": as when Mr Christ says "Love your enemies, do good to them that hate you." Again it commonly supposes that to give a man pain is to do him harm: whereas when they of old time took an eye for an eye or a tooth for a tooth, it is probable they often did much good to one another. And finally it fails to recognize that it may be our duty to do anything, however revolting, to one individual, if by that means the sum of good is increased. For good is not a private thing, like pleasure and pain, of which you can say "So much belongs to each man." Even if pleasure were the sole good, and pain the sole evil, as Christians like other folk too commonly assume, 'twould still be true that it might be good for a man – to his best interests, to his real advantage – to suffer nothing but pain all through his life, if by that means the general balance of pleasure over pain were made greater. Thus it may quite well happen that to put your enemy to the most excruciating tortures, ending in death, even though he is

---

* 'Ideal' is here used in the sense of the last chapter of *Principia Ethica*, that is, in its ordinary language sense of perfection, not in the technical philosophical sense in which Idealism is opposed to Realism.

perfectly innocent, and without any chance of a future life, may be to do him the greatest possible good. And, since pleasure and pain are *not* the sole good and evil, 'tis much less plain that any cruelty on our part may not be a blessing to him. 'Tis, indeed, true that we can discriminate to some extent between what a man is in himself and what his effects are on the world at large: it may be said that to make him worse a man in himself is not to do him good. Yet certainly it may be for his advantage that he should be made worse: since no man has any true interest but that as much good as possible should exist, whether in him or elsewhere.

'I find nothing in the Christian teaching, then, to which I can assent as a universal rule, except that we ought always to go good to all men, understood in the wide sense that we ought always to do what will make the sum of good, present and future, as great as possible. And this, plainly, does not justify the assertion that it is always wrong to hate and always our duty to love all men.'

Moore never says explicitly in this paper what he means by 'good'; but that question, after all, has been settled in the case of ultimate goods – at least so far as the Apostles are concerned. As we saw when Moore read his paper in February 1899, and Russell responded a week later, the Apostles accepted that nothing was intrinsically good or evil except states of mind. So the good that one has a duty to maximize on Moore's utilitarian calculus is good states of mind – exactly the conclusion of *Principia Ethica*. In fact, Moore wants to argue for a very extreme position:

'I seem bound to admit then, what I have been strenuous in denying in most cases, that there are ethical judgments the objects of which defy analysis; that there is a meaning in harmony, in organic unity, and what not. But it is this very principle which may be pleaded in support of the [poet and novelist, George] Meredith-view that nothing is really bad. If it is possible that two bad things put together may make a good one, certainly, it may alter our views as to whether the world is good on the whole. For it must be possible that the good proceeding from the junction of two evil things, may be greater than the evil there is in both put together. We must, indeed, distinguish here. The world can never be absolutely perfect on this view, since the evil things, even in their junction, remain evil. But what we must admit, and what is certainly surprising, is that the world containing them may be a better world than any that is, not merely possible, but even conceivable without them. Here is a very different justification of evil from that which merely consists in shewing it may be a means to good.'

The reason for Moore's having been 'strenuous in denying' that the principle of organic unity is meaningful is stated simply in *Principia Ethica*: 'Philosophers, especially those who profess to have derived great benefit from the writings of Hegel, have latterly made much use of the terms "organic whole", "organic unity", "organic relation".'[24] In that book Moore states the paradox of the organic whole thus: 'the value of such a whole bears no regular proportion to the sum of the values of its parts,'[25] and the principle of organic unity, he formulates as: 'The value of a whole must not be assumed to be the same as the sum of the values of its parts.'[26] The later formulation is, of course, more precise, but Moore was clear about the essentials of the principle in his 1900 Apostles' paper. The brothers present divided on 'Should God hate the Devil?' Hawtrey and MacCarthy voted Yes, along with Moore, who added: 'Certainly, if there is one.' Meredith, Ainsworth and Hardy voted No. Dickinson heard the paper but no vote is recorded for him.

On 17 November Moore re-read one of his old papers, though which one it was does not emerge from the question, which seems to have been 'Shall we loaf and invite our souls?' The Cambridge contingent of Moore, Ainsworth, Hardy, Hawtrey and Meredith was augmented by MacCarthy, Sanger and R. C. Trevelyan. But the next week, on 24 November, only Moore, Ainsworth, and Meredith were there to hear Hawtrey read a paper that bore importantly on Moore's theories. 'Are all moral judgments judgments about our present state of mind?'

In December 1900 a very exceptional thing happened. On the 1st Mac-Carthy read a paper called 'Is this an awkward age?' and on the 8th Moore re-read the paper (which remains in the Moore Papers). This might have come about because the paper was unpolished and required revision to make MacCarthy's meaning plain; but, in fact, the version Moore read, with revisions in his hand, is still not entirely coherent. A more likely reason for re-reading the paper was that those who heard it the first time thought the subject so important and the argument so difficult to make out, that they wished to hear and discuss it again. MacCarthy was claiming that there was a difference in attitude between the present Apostles and those of thirty or so years earlier, and that this difference was reflected in the world outside the Society – in politics, art, letters and manners. What MacCarthy was trying to describe is of enormous interest, because the changes he thinks have taken place are those for which Moore is often given the credit for bringing about.

MacCarthy thinks it evident that 'this is a self-conscious analytical age. Intellectual speculation is commoner . . . between friends than it was.' The age is an awkward one, though, as is shown by 'a few, obvious disquieting, often-pondered facts in our life up here'. He lists some of them at random:

'The barrenness of the Society [its inability to choose new members], the smallness and aloofness of college sets, the uneasiness of a good deal of intercourse among people between whom there yet exists a really close and affectionate understanding, the quantity and appreciation of subjective novels, the boredom of general gatherings, the absence of high-spirited and brilliant talk. This sounds a depressing list; but it will recall a good many experiences, which it is necessary to pass in review in order to refute me.'

Some of the changes between his generation and an older one that MacCarthy finds cause for complaint are changes that others would find cause for congratulation – the lifting of Victorian taboos and the breakdown of Victorian certainties represented by the works and actions of Darwin and men like Sidgwick and Leslie Stephen. Those are phenomena of society at large, but some of the burden of MacCarthy's plaint is specific to the Society, and refers to changes that Moore might be thought to have at least encouraged or justified, if not actually caused. Impressionistically, but impressively, MacCarthy launches into his argument:

'It seems that we take everything much more *personally* than our predecessors. It is much more difficult for *us* to feel things in various capacities, from citizenship or membership of the University to membership of the Society, and the fact that they did so naturally gave them a superior versatility and definiteness of interest. They saw life more dramatically. We may have more intuitive and psychological insight; but at the cost of a comparative weakness of the imagination. We see the relations of men to each other and to their aims on the whole less broadly. This is no doubt primarily due to all institutions, the family, state, laws of honour, etc., which have a claim on the individual having been asked to produce their warrants, and having failed to produce convincing proofs of their authority.'

Part of what McCarthy thinks is better about earlier Apostles might be connected with the influence of Moore's refusal to tolerate imprecision among the present Apostles, for he goes on :

'The last generation were much less sceptical. They were therefore gayer and more generally interested and every topic of conversation offered more opportunities of saying something which anyhow *seemed* to the point.

'But this difference that there are fewer ideas about which we are enthusiastic is not the one which I wish to emphasize in this paper. It is this.

'I do not think they noticed the circumambient atmosphere so much. They were not so liable to be stifled by the dusty particles which float so thickly in the ordinary social atmosphere. And for this reason, that in proportion to their other aims in life, the state of personal relations *at any particular time* was not so important to them as it is to us. There were no doubt nearly as many motes in the sun beams; but they had their keen interests and therefore their attention was fixed on other things. They did not think less *of* their friends; but they thought less about them, not less of friendship, but less of intimacy.'

This was certainly not offered as criticism of Moore, and it would not have been taken as such. In any case, no one would have mistaken a tradition of the Apostles for an innovation by Moore. And no one would have blamed him for placing too much emphasis on friends, or for worrying about 'intimacy'. After the publication of *Principia Ethica* Moore was to be praised for having brought about the positive side of each of these things; though, of course, all he did in that book was to provide the theoretical justification for established practices – but practices to which he was given himself. We have seen in Moore's letter to Marsh of 17 April 1896 [p. 188] that he was used to resort to introspection to discover the exact nature of his feelings about his friends, and that he would take great pains to communicate them with precision. While there seemed nothing morbid or unhealthy about Moore's habits of analysis of his relations with his fellows, MacCarthy was inclined to think the practice just that when indulged in by the whole group :

'I do not mean that [the last generation of Apostles] were necessarily much less self-conscious or that they did not, sitting around, think, in the gaps of conversation, each other's thoughts; but I believe they did not ruminate upon or talk over these thoughts afterwards. I think they would have probably been rather shocked by a kind of gossip and intimate speculation, which is now common enough – at any rate at its commonness. I think they would have been probably bored by the topic of this paper.'

Here MacCarthy has inadvertently scored a bull's-eye, as his contemporaries were so far from bored by the topic of the paper that they took the unprecedented step of having it read a second time the next week ! He continues his conservative indictment of the Society :

'But there is another characteristic, which is the result of a shaken belief in rules of thumb and the usual aims of life, which also contributes directly to the greater interest taken in personal relations.

'They did *not* trust their immediate judgments as completely as we do, which simplified for them the social as well as all the other relations in life. They had more rules which they trusted to instead. If for instance we could believe a rule that the presence of certain qualities in a person made him fit to be elected, the business of propagation would be much easier. It is much easier to convince yourself that you have gauged a man's intellect than that you have estimated rightly his worth; unless you trust your personal feelings towards him.

'The Society has always been a collection of affinities; but in its early days it was rather an affinity of interests and capabilities than of nature. Hence an apparent paradox, that though they did not analyse so much, they trusted their eyes less and we who analyse more also trust our eyes more.

'Our judgments are simpler, though we are more self-conscious and our lives are not so simple. I am certain the interest of general conversation used to be more detached from personal relations in the days when the Society discussed the execution of Charles I. And it is the increased importance of persons as opposed to their opinions and qualities which is the influence which I think I find everywhere at the present time in the world.'

When this paper was read for the first time Hawtrey, Moore, Meredith, Ainsworth and G. M. Trevelyan heard it; a week later, Moore reread it to the same group, plus Crompton Llewelyn Davies, Hardy and Dickinson. It was Moore's last duty as secretary, for that evening he formally resigned his membership in the Society. Hardy took his place as secretary.

Moore, who had patched up his quarrel with Russell sufficiently to meet him once a week to discuss philosophy, now visited the Russells at Friday's Hill, where an onlooker could have seen the two great philosophers playing football. Then he spent Christmas in the now traditional way, at Cheriton with his family. In January he visited Wedgwood at York, before returning to Cambridge on 19 January 1901, when the Society met in his rooms to choose topics for the term. Moore was present at every meeting that Lent term, and so participated in the election of E. M. Forster on 9 February.

Moore's reading party for 1901 took place at Birdlip in March and April. At first there were only Moore, MacCarthy, Ainsworth and Donald Robertson (a classical scholar of Trinity, of Ainsworth's age and a family friend of MacCarthy's, who, as has been mentioned, was one of only two Apostles ever to go on one of Moore's reading parties – he was probably regarded as an 'embryo'); they were joined by Smyth, the Llewelyn Davies brothers, Bob Trevelyan and Sanger. They found themselves at first a little disappointed with the Cotswold scenery and with the weather, but Moore got some work done on his articles for Baldwin's *Dictionary*.[27] Later in the month the holiday improved, as they discovered the Stroud valley and the sun shone; Painswick in particular appealed to Moore: 'the loveliest grey-stone built town, with hilly streets, that I have ever seen – better than Kirkby Lonsdale.'[28] The whole party left MacCarthy alone for a few days at the end, to see 'whether solitude would give him ideas for his novel'.[29] The dinner for 1901 was on 12 June. After it, Moore was accompanied to Cheriton by Ainsworth. Then with his sister Nellie he had his summer holiday at Lucerne and Locarno, returning home by coach over Gotthard and Grimsel to Interlaken.

Though he had taken wings, Moore continued to attend the Society's meetings with his customary regularity. Then he spent a part of the Christmas vacation with Ainsworth, before going to his parents in Devon. In the new year, on 25 January 1902, Ainsworth read a paper which culminated in a vote on the question, 'Ought we to be ashamed of being sentimental?' Moore voted on both sides of the division, saying Yes with Hawtrey and Ainsworth, and No with McTaggart.

After the election of Moore himself, eight years earlier, the Society had only once elected more than one new member a year. As MacCarthy pointed out in his paper of December 1900, the Society had been infertile for some time. Now all that was to change. On 8 February 1902 the Apostles gave 'birth' to twins – it was felt that they could help each other if they were elected together, and would be less affected by the inward-looking aspect of the present membership. John Tressider

Sheppard signed the book first, but Giles Lytton Strachey's was the more significant election. Strachey altered the character of the Society almost immediately, transmuting its naughty verbal mannerisms and Walt Whitmanesque feelings of comradeship into overt full-blooded – almost aggressive – homosexuality. The distinction of having nominated Strachey was Hawtrey's, but in fact Lytton's cousin Arthur was now in touch with the Apostles again via the Annual Dinners and Lytton's family was connected with Walter Raleigh. Lytton had been Raleigh's pupil at Liverpool, and Raleigh had been instrumental in sending him to Trinity; it was almost certainly he who called the Apostles' attention to his gifted student. Sheppard's connection with the Apostles is not known, but, like Ainsworth, he came to King's via Dulwich. At their first meeting, Sheppard and Strachey heard Meredith read a paper. Moore was present then, and on 22 February he re-read his dazzling paper on conversion. From that moment Strachey was Moore's disciple for life.

Though the ideas that were to coalesce into *Principia Ethica* had, in Moore's own view, been in the air for years, the book itself had sudden and modest beginnings. On 18 March 1902 Moore wrote to his mother:

'You will be glad to hear that the University Press have just agreed to publish my Lectures on Ethics. They will make a small book – about 200 8vo. pages. I don't yet know anything about the conditions; and I shall have to alter them a great deal, which may take some time and will not, I'm afraid, make a very good job, after all. Still they do say most of the things I want to say somehow or other; and I only hope they may convince some people; that the Press should be willing to publish them is some guarantee that they are interesting. I expect they will be out some time next October.'

The period of 24 March to 19 April was chosen for the 1902 reading party, held at the Black Gang Chine Hotel, near Ventnor, on the southwest side of the Isle of Wight. The large party included Ainsworth, MacCarthy, Sanger, Mayor, Bob Trevelyan, Dickinson and three surprising members: Strachey and Sheppard, who were very junior to have entered the 'inner circle', and Roger Fry, who it has been usually supposed had little to do with Moore.

When the party returned to Cambridge, almost the first thing they did was to listen to Sheppard's first Apostles' paper, which he delivered on 26 April 1902, quite soon after his election, on 'Shall we crusade?' The question Sheppard asked himself in the paper was whether Apostles ought to do missionary work among Christians, to help convert them from their false beliefs to a more correct view of things, which by now in the Society, implicitly meant Moore's views on ethics, and, to a lesser extent, idealism. Sheppard lamely concludes that there is some connection between beliefs held and actions done, even if the connection is not a causal one, and that it would be a pity to prevent Christian old ladies making marmalade to raise money for hospitals by convincing them that their Christianity is all a mistake.

On 10 May Strachey read for the first time; after Sheppard's dim début, a star was born. Strachey called his paper 'Ought the Father to grow a beard?' It was an astonishingly mature first effort, and it did not, as did many of his later offerings to the Society, bear too heavily the impress of Moore's *style*. In substance, though, it owed something to Moore, for it dealt with a question in aesthetics – art as representation – that greatly exercised Moore. The classical – or more accurately from the point of view of its parentage, neo-classical – theory that all art was representational, imitative or mimetic was normally coupled with the use of 'beauty' as the chief or only quality of works of art. Moore could see, even from his then limited acquaintance with modern works of art, which was confined to the theatre, the novel and music, almost to the exclusion of the visual arts, that 'beautiful' simply was not always the most appropriate term of praise for works of art that were successful. And the representational theory of art could not, it seemed obvious to him, account for what we find beautiful or take pleasure from in nature, and was not so obviously suited to the aesthetic analysis of the art form he knew best and loved most, music. Moore had read a paper to the Sunday Essay Society in May 1901, in which he attempted to discuss aesthetics in the conventional terms of 'beauty' and 'representation', but his essay made it apparent that he was aware of their conceptual deficiencies.

Lytton Strachey's first Apostles' paper is about the limits of art – in the sense of what it is legitimate for the artist to take as his subject-matter. He, too, conducts the discussion in terms of representation and the beautiful, but he ends, more explicitly than Moore, in challenging their conceptual supremacy – and in a paper in which the writing has more brilliance and a tougher surface than anything the Apostles had heard since Walter Raleigh was an active member.

The paper begins with an epigraph from Shakespeare, where Cleopatra says she will find the limit of Antony's love: 'I'll set a bourn how far to be beloved.' And Antony replies: 'Then must thou needs find out new heaven, new earth.' Strachey imagines Cleopatra watching down the ages as successive generations of artists use in their art aspects of life that the previous generation has considered taboo.

'And Cleopatra smiles, because she knows, after all, that Antony is right. That new heaven, that new earth which he thinks so impossible to be discovered, is, precisely, what *is* found out by his successor. The old order changes, perishes, gives place to the new. The glory of Apollo fades before the face of the pale Galilean, who in his turn vanishes beneath the glance of some subtle and sterile Dolores, some obscure Venus of the hollow hill. As in the mystic rite which was once performed under the shadow of the golden bough, the old king is slain by the new king, the new king by the newer still; . . .

'But although it is clear that the parts of Life with which Art chooses to deal are continually changing from age to age, the question remains as to whether there may not be *some* parts of life with which art should never deal. . . . Can we say to Antony, "you may enjoy the limbs and the head and the breasts of Cleopatra as much as you like, but there are some parts of her which you shall never enjoy; for with these you have nothing whatever to do"?

'Since the institution of Christianity and figleaves, there has been a remarkable unanimity as to which these parts precisely are. With an outer limit at the extreme top of the stomach on the one hand and at about the middle of the thighs on the other, the forbidden zone gradually deepens in intensity, enclosing within its boundaries the whole region of the bowels and most of the essential parts of the human economy, until it reaches the culminating and central point of the sexual organs.'

Suppose, Strachey went on, that the statue of the Prince Consort in the Albert Memorial one morning rose from its seated position, and was no longer robed, but totally nude, depicted as Roman emperors 'thought fit to appear before the millions of their subjects': 'Imagine the indignant rush up those sacred steps, the blind finger tearing, overturning, destroying . . . [in original] but to contemplate our late beloved Prince in such a situation is too painful; – I draw a shuddering veil.' What, Strachey asked, could be the reason for such a violent reaction to seeing so commonplace a sight?

' – Dear madam, why do you turn your eyes away from what, if you come to think of it, is merely a more or less exact image of one entire half of the human race? – Sir, why do you wave your umbrella so frantically at the sight of what is, after all, not very much more than a rough representation of your own appearance as you step into your morning bath?'

Probably, Strachey thought, there was no *reason* for this hypothetical but probable behaviour, only a 'confused mass of prejudices and stupidities and vulgarities'. But there could logically be two objections against 'the artistic treatment of any subject whatever' – 'objections on the score of morals, and objections on the score of art'.

Of course, Strachey continued, the two kinds of objection were 'constantly confused in practice', as witness the application of the word 'nasty', which is 'so often applied to certain kinds of books, which may either imply that they are morally vicious, or artistically bad'. If it could be shown conclusively, Strachey said, that the treatment of certain subjects in a work of art caused immorality, then society *might* be justified in forbidding it. But such immorality might very well be temporary, and might be ameliorated by education.

Strachey then presented a head-on challenge to the aesthetic hegemony of 'beauty':

'What interests me more is the question whether there is *any* subject which is *per se* incapable of artistic treatment? Is the presence in anything of ugliness, or dirt, or any disgusting quality, or any quality at all, a sufficient reason for its exclusion from artistic presentation? Can Baudelaire be artistic when he describes with minute detail the processes of animal corruption? Or Wagner when he makes sensuality audible? Or Hogarth when he depicts the sordid and disgusting phenomena of the dissecting room?'

There is no difficulty about the artistic depiction of what is agreed to be beautiful or good, Strachey argued; the difficulty only arises with ugliness or evil. But of course art can deal with evil; to anyone who says it cannot there is the counter-example of tragedy. And to the person who says that in tragedy evil is transmuted into beauty, Strachey offered the examples of Hogarth and Flaubert as artists – their works are undoubtedly art – in whose pictures and tales 'instances of evil and ugliness treated artistically separately or in combination abound'.

Strachey treated his topic in a very modern way, and arrived at a thoroughly modernist conclusion, one that would satisfy the avant-garde of the late twentieth century, and would have been strong meat for practising artists of 1902:

'I am, in fact, forced to the conclusion that *anything* is capable of artistic treatment; that the function of Art is to treat of *everything* whatever its qualities may be.

'I now venture to hazard a suggestion as to the meaning of Art. Personally I have always found it impossible ever to consider any one thing apart from everything else – apart, as it were, from its content. It appears to me that the relations borne by anything to other things are nothing more than a part of itself; and reality is thus not only made up of everything in existence, but of the relations between all these things and each other. What I consider that Art does is to put everything it treats of into its proper position as regards reality; and what that position is it is for the Artist alone to discover – the Artist who works not by rules but by genius and an invisible flame within him.'

'It is for the artist alone to discover'! This would do very well as a slogan for much of the artistic activity of the 1970s – similar sentiments can be heard ringing down the corridors of art schools and conservatories. And Strachey went on to give an illustration that would have shocked even his emancipated audience. How, he asked, is it possible to treat a subject such as defecation artistically?

'There is only one way – by finding out what relations it bears to reality. When you have done this you can treat it artistically, but only then. For me at least that mysterious and intimate operation has always exercised an extraordinary charm. I seem to see in it one of the few last relics of our animal ancestry – a strange reminiscence of the earth from which we have sprung. The thought of every member of the human race – the race which has produced Shakespeare and weighed the stars – retiring every day to give silent and incontestible proof of his matinal mould is to me fraught with an unutterable significance. There, in truth, is the one touch of Nature which makes the whole world kin! There is enough to give the idealist perpetual cause! There – in that mystic unburdening of our bodies – that unanswerable reminder of mortality!'

Strachey scored several firsts that Saturday night – not least the destruction, in this last paragraph, of the Apostles' only remaining taboo. The brethren, even the most liberated among them, were bludgeoned into confusion by Strachey's charming assault upon their sensibilities. There could be no question of outrage, so their response to the shock they had sustained had to be reflected in the confusion of the vote. But the discussion had to wait a moment anyway; there was one more convention to flout. Strachey had so far made not even a gesture in the direction of his assigned subject. So he tacked on a coda, a virtuoso verbal embroidery upon the title of his paper, which probably had no more to do with his ostensible subject than the body of the paper :

'And the Father ? . . . [in original]
'Michelet has a wonderful passage in his introduction to the history of the Renaissance on the position of God the Father in the Middle Age. He was deserted, he says, . . . forgotten. No altar was raised to Him, no shrine; the vows and prayers of men were turned towards the Son, the Saints, and the Virgin Mary. What is more the Father had no beard. Unlike the Ormuz of the Persians, the Jehovah of the Jews, the Zeus of the Greeks, the soft and melancholy God of the Middle Ages was "imberbe", was hardly a man, was unendowed with the generative force. With the Renaissance, indeed, – for so we may continue the allegory – the beard of God sprouted for a moment into a magnificent growth; and so we see it in the Sistine Chapel depicted by the hand of Michael Angelo. But today? What can we say today of the Father's beard, the generative force of the World? It is gone, it is vanished, it is shaved! And that rounded chin, that soft repletion of flesh and fat, is it not more hateful than ever was the bristling and curling hair? more base, more vile, more loathsome, more incomparably lewd?'

The question asked was 'When is an artist not an artist?' and no one seemed to know what the question meant; the vote is recorded with such elaborate commentary that it is not possible to tell who was present and voting. Ainsworth seems to have been one of those who was most annoyed by Strachey's performance: 'Never,' he thundered, 'the question is Strachey's and an indication of his illogicality.' 'Sometimes', voted the rest, who seem to have included Sheppard, Meredith and Hawtrey. Moore was not present, as he was visiting Wedgwood that week. But one can be certain that Moore received detailed reports of Strachey's first paper – a paper that produced stronger effects in the audience and that had greater consequences for the future of the Society than any since Moore's own first appearance eight years earlier. It was not merely the literary quality of Strachey's essay that was impressive – it was easily the most polished paper read to the Society in years – and that the argument of it *did* touch on important, even profound points; the great thing about this paper was that, in its cocking a snook at the taboos of society and the conventions of the Society, its effect was *calculated*. It was a take-over bid for the leadership of the Apostles, and it succeeded. Moore remained 'pope', but only in matters spiritual; the temporal power passed rapidly to Strachey. No *lèse majesté* was intended: Moore was still, and continued to be until the war, the group's guru and inspiration; but henceforth Strachey and his friends and allies would choose the new Apostles, fashion their subjects and determine the style of talk and behaviour.

Moore was not in the least perturbed about this (and Ainsworth's defences soon fell to Strachey's onslaught); he liked Strachey, found him not just amusing, but funny; and though Moore could not have brought himself to use defecation as an illustration of a point in an argument, he welcomed the destruction of outworn conventions which were barriers to free conversation.

In any case, Moore was now a little less concerned about how the Apostles conducted their affairs. He had something more pressing to think about. On 23 May 1902 he began writing *Principia Ethica*. By 18 March 1903 the manuscript was at the Cambridge University Press and by 15 June the proofs had been read. The conversation with Meredith that resulted in *Principia's* last chapter probably took place between the latter two dates; and so the last chapter was written rapidly. It was printed by the end of August, for publication in October 1903. As a whole, the book was written in a relatively short time; but years had gone into the preparation of the lectures that formed the basis of *Principia Ethica*, and, as we have seen, most of it had been discussed by the Apostles and benefited from their criticisms and, indeed, from their own papers that dealt with its matter.

The book, whose dark brown binding became so familiar that Virginia Woolf expected readers of *The Voyage Out* (1915) to recognize the book from its cover, carried the dedication

> *Doctoribus Amicisque Cantabrigiensibus*
> *Discipulus Amicus Cantabrigiensis*
> *Primitias*
> *D.D.D.*
> *Auctor.**

* To his teachers and friends of Cambridge, their Cambridge disciple and friend, the author, dedicates his first works.

9
Principia Ethica *and the* '*Manifesto*'

Lytton Strachey's reaction to reading *Principia* in its entirety for the first time was not untypical – except for Strachey's slight hysteria – of the reception the book received from the Apostles. On 11 October 1903 Strachey wrote to Moore from 69 Lancaster Gate:

'I have read your book, and want to say how much I am excited and impressed. I'm afraid I must be mainly classed among "writers of Dictionaries, and other persons interested in literature", so I feel a sort of essential vanity hovering about all my "judgments of fact". But on this occasion I am carried away. I think your book has not only wrecked and shattered all writers on Ethics from Aristotle and Christ to Herbert Spencer and Mr Bradley, it has not only laid the true foundations of Ethics, it has not only left all modern philosophy bafouée – these seem to me small achievements compared to the establishment of that Method which shines like a sword between the lines. It is the scientific method, deliberately applied, for the first time, to Reasoning. Is that true? You perhaps shake your head, but henceforward who will be able to tell lies one thousand times as easily as before? The truth, there can be no doubt, is really now upon the march. I date from Oct. 1903 the beginning of the Age of Reason.

'The last chapters interested me most, as they were newer to me than the rest. Your grand conclusion made me gasp – it was so violently definite. Lord! I can't yet altogether agree. I think with some horror of a Universe deprived for ever of real slaughters and tortures and lusts. Isn't it possible that the real Ideal may be an organic unity so large and of such a nature that it is, precisely, the Universe itself? In which case Dr Pangloss was right after all.

'. . . Dear Moore, I hope and pray that you realize how much you mean to us. It was very pleasant to be able to feel that one came into the Dedication. But expression is so difficult, so very difficult, and there are so many cold material obstructions, that the best of Life seems to be an act of faith.

'*This* is a confession of faith from

your brother
Lytton Strachey.'[1]

Lower-keyed, and possibly more welcome praise came from Russell, writing from Chelsea on 10 October:

'Many thanks for your book, which I have now read. It strikes me as a triumph of lucidity – except unavoidably in regard to Metaphysical Ethics, the whole seems to me intelligible to any attentive and candid reader.

'The only matters in regard to which I disagree with you are a few immediate judgments of value, and some of your maxims in Practical Ethics, which seem to me unduly Conservative and anti-reforming. But I should be willing to agree if you merely said that a rational opinion on such points it attainable.

'Your motto strikes me as admirable;* and I think the book all through is a model of exposition. I am to review it in the "Independent", so I shall be reading it again more carefully.

Yours ever,
B. Russell.'[2]

The response of professional philosophers may be illustrated by G. F. Stout's letter to Moore from St Andrew's on 1 November, in which Stout consulted Moore about finding a suitable reviewer for the book in *Mind*. To find a reviewer who 'might be trusted to see the value and importance of the book', Stout suggested the names of the most eminent philosophers of the time from all over the world! Bosanquet had offered himself, but Stout doubted that Moore would welcome him, just as Stout was aware that Moore might prefer a reviewer other than McTaggart. C. S. Pierce was a possibility, but his being across the Atlantic would prevent a review from appearing in the next issue; Meinong and Brentano seemed of sufficient stature to Stout, but he doubted their ability to write a review in English. From his own cursory reading, Stout said, 'it meets my very high expectations.'[3] In the end it was Bosanquet who wrote the review in the number dated April 1904.

---

* The motto appeared on the title page: 'Everything is what it is, and not another thing. Bishop Butler.' Ainsworth wrote to Lytton Strachey about it from Edinburgh on 17 October: 'The quotation makes me feel very much the force of Russell's criticism, that the only merit of this philosophy is its truth.'

Between 1902 and 1903 the Apostles, rejuvenated by Strachey's zeal and enthusiasm, had elected four new members within the space of a year – a record for the modern Society. The first, elected on 25 October 1902, was Saxon Arnoll Sydney-Turner (1880–1962), the son of a Sussex surgeon, who went from Westminster to Trinity in 1899. He received firsts in both parts of the classics tripos; the scrap of a remark in one of Moore's diaries sums up what many people felt about Sydney-Turner: 'S.–T. till 2 at night. Sometimes a little bored.'⁴ A clerk in the Estate Duty Office from 1904 to 1912, Sydney-Turner went to the Treasury in 1913. He was the silent man of Bloomsbury. Slightly less taciturn was Leonard Sidney Woolf (1880–1969), elected to the Apostles the same day. Woolf regarded himself as a member of Moore's 'inner circle', and he was in fact asked on the next reading party, held at the Lizard in Cornwall at Easter 1903. In November 1903 the Society elected a Kingsman from New Zealand, Leonard Hugh Graham Greenwood (1880–1965). Forster's biographer says of him that he 'became a Fellow and Director of Studies in classics at Emmanuel College. His *Aspects of Euripidean Tragedy*, published in 1953, is written in an exact reproduction of Moore's prose-style.'⁵ Then in February 1903 the brethren added to their number John Maynard Keynes. Sheppard brought him to tea with Moore early in the Lent term; Moore approved of Keynes, and his election was accomplished on 28 February. All four of these new Apostles were devoted to Moore; indeed, they hero-worshipped him, and, as Keynes said in 'My Early Beliefs', treated *Principia* as the scripture of a new religion.

Yet, as Keynes made abundantly clear, they did not get out of *Principia Ethica* what Moore had put into it. Skilled as some of them, especially Keynes, Woolf and Meredith, were at philosophical argument, the younger Apostles seemed almost to have neglected to read the book's first four or five chapters. These men, who became the male nucleus of the Bloomsbury Group, scarcely noticed the features of the book that made it a philosophical classic, the positions taken by Moore in the book that cause it to remain even today required reading for philosophy students. The characterization of 'good' as a simple, indefinable quality, the 'naturalistic fallacy', Moore's Intuitionism and his Ideal Utilitarianism were almost ignored by those whom we must suppose to have valued the book most.

Between the extremes of the dry enthusiasm of Stout, the professional philosopher, and the gush of the young Apostles, there was another sort of greeting for *Principia Ethica*. Oliver Strachey (1874–1960), one of Lytton's elder brothers (he worked on the East Indian

Railway and was an ace cryptographer in *both* world wars), paid Moore the tribute of writing a sixteen-page critical appreciation of the book. Moore took a great deal of trouble answering the letter Oliver Strachey wrote to him on 14 October 1903, and thus began a life-long series of philosophy tutorials conducted by post. Oliver Strachey, unlike Lytton, saw in *Principia* some of the problems that interested philosophers. So did Sir Frederick Pollock, who at fifty-eight was just retiring as the Corpus Professor of Jurisprudence at Oxford. He wrote on 30–31 December 1903:

'I have just finished your *Principia Ethica* just in time to send it the blessing of an ancient angel for the New Year. Truly, the speculative wings are stiff at my age, but it is good to see the young angels at play. Indeed it seems to me quite the most original and vital theory I have seen for a long time: and I think it largely convincing, though that matters much less. For a long time I have felt – and in a timid way said now and again – that Ethics *ought* to be independent of metaphysical systems: also that asking for an explanation of the moral sense, as present in the conscious judgment or impression –

This is $\left.{\text{good}\atop\text{bad}}\right\}$ – is like asking why red is perceived as red and violet as violet, or why different wave-lengths should correspond to specifically different colours at all.'[6]

And so on – all very much to the philosophical point. Old Apostles and amateur philosophers were capable of following Moore's dialectic in the way he patently intended: why not these clever young men, Strachey and Keynes? And why were they not corrected by their immediate and philosophically able predecessors, Ainsworth and Meredith? The answer is, it must be, that each of them put *Principia Ethica* to his own use; and if Moore was not oblivious to this, then at least he showed no aversion to it.

Russell, though, minded terribly. In his autobiography he fulminated:

'The generation of Keynes and Lytton ... aimed ... at a life of retirement among fine shades and nice feelings, and conceived of the good as consisting in the passionate mutual admirations of a clique of the élite. This doctrine, quite unfairly, they fathered upon G. E. Moore, whose disciples they professed to be. Keynes, in his memoir *Early Beliefs*, has told of their admiration for Moore's doctrine. Moore gave due weight to morals and by his doctrine of organic unities avoided the view that the good consists of a series of isolated passionate moments, but those who considered themselves his disciples ignored this aspect of his teaching and degraded his ethics into advocacy of a stuffy girls'-school sentimentalizing.'[7]

As always, Russell has chosen his words with care. In this passage he manages to convey to the reader that that generation of Apostles was homosexual ('the *passionate* mutual admirations') and his disapproval; but he has not chosen his words carefully enough to conceal his displeasure at that generation of Apostles professing themselves disciples of Moore – when they could have chosen Russell.

There is, of course, something in Russell's strictures; but they perhaps apply most strongly to Lytton Strachey. Michael Holroyd says, 'Lytton, in paying particular attention to the final chapter of *Principia Ethica* with its elevating accent upon the merits and virtues of human intercourse, turned his back upon ethics in relation to conduct. The impact which Moore had on him was pre-eminently not one of morals but of morale.'[8] In short, Lytton saw in *Principia Ethica* a justification for homosexuality. A few years later in April 1906, Lytton wrote to Maynard Keynes: 'We can't be content with telling the truth – we must tell the whole truth; and the whole truth is the Devil. Voltaire abolished Christianity by believing in god. It's madness of us to dream of making dowagers understand that feelings are good, when we say in the same breath that the best ones are sodomitical.'

Moore was a close friend of Strachey and saw him often during the writing of the book and for a year after its publication. If he objected to the construction Lytton placed upon its doctrines, why did he not say so? He could hardly have failed to notice Lytton trumpeting his view of good states of mind all around Cambridge and to Ainsworth in Edinburgh. We must infer from what we have seen about Moore's own feelings in these years that he was not inclined to correct Strachey. Moore intended *Principia* as an original contribution to ethics; he did not intend it to be used as homosexual propaganda, and that is not what Meredith had in mind when he suggested the plan of its last chapter to Moore. But the explanation of Moore's silence at this time – and much later, when he read Keynes's 'My Early Beliefs' – is that he did not then object to this use being made of his work, and had no very strong inclination to discourage it.

(It may be that it is in this context that Russell's laconic remark on homosexuality in the Apostles should be read: 'After my time the Society changed in one respect. There was a long-drawn-out battle between George Trevelyan and Lytton Strachey, . . . in which Lytton Strachey was on the whole victorious. Since his time homosexual relations among the members were for a time common, but in my day they were unknown.'⁹ The *causus belli* is not known. It could have been the election, in mid-February, 1905 of (Sir) Arthur Lee Hobhouse,* a nineteen-year-old Trinity undergraduate whose yellow hair was the brightest thing about him. Strachey and Keynes conspired to get him elected in his first year, and had to persuade Jackson and Moore to agree to bending the unwritten rule designed to prevent just that.)

In *Principia*, then, Strachey found precepts for what he wanted to believe was Moore's example. Leonard Woolf found life-long inspiration there, but chiefly from what he felt was Moore's commonsensical approach to difficult and perennial problems of philosophy. Woolf did not overlook Moore's chapter on 'Ethics in Relation to Conduct' (nor, really, did Strachey, who wrote to Woolf at the time of publication, 'The last *two* chapters – glory alleluiah!' [italics not in original]). Indeed Michael Holroyd maintains that Woolf 'later adapted and applied Moore's method of defining duty to an historical and political purpose, believing that the historian, by investigating the communal psychology of the past, might attain an understanding which would enable him to forecast the results of future policies.'¹⁰ E. M. Forster told his biographer a story with which Woolf had impressed him. Woolf

> 'had been riding with a man he disliked, and their horses had bolted, making for a gap in the hedge only wide enough for one man. It was clearly a problem in ethics; one of them had to die, and it was up to him to choose which. "I'm more worth keeping alive than he," had been Woolf's conclusion, and, quite calmly, he had prepared to murder his companion by charging at him. As it turned out, the other man, in panic, had fallen off his horse, so no murder was committed. And thereupon – the most characteristic touch, thought Forster – Woolf had proceeded to tell the man exacly what his reasoning had been. He wished, he told Forster, that the incident could happen again, this time with someone worth sacrificing himself to.'

And P. N. Furbank comments on the episode: 'A good instance of the influence of G. E. Moore's ethical theories.'¹¹

It is more difficult to describe, and to understand, the effect of the book on Keynes. In one way it was straightforward. The role played

* Born in 1886, he is disguised as 'Edgar Duckworth' in Holroyd's life of Strachey.

by the concept of probability in Moore's theory of right conduct was a *cause* of Keynes's writing *A Treatise on Probability* (published in 1921, though Keynes had worked on it from 1904 until 1911).[12] Richard Braithwaite, who as a much younger Apostle and as a philosopher knew both Moore and Keynes and their work, points out that part of one chapter of Keynes's work is given over to working out the details of Moore's theory.[13] Professor Braithwaite wrote a brief obituary on Keynes in *Mind* in 1946, in which he said that Keynes's ethical position was 'essentially that of *Principia Ethica*' and that Keynes had been 'a most "humane Utilitarian" '.

Braithwaite was therefore very surprised when Keynes's memoir, 'My Early Beliefs', appeared posthumously in 1949, in which Keynes gave the impression of repudiating at least parts of *Principia Ethica*. Keynes intended, when he read his paper originally to the Memoir Club, to tease the younger members of his audience, said Quentin Bell, who was one of them.[14] To this end, Keynes exaggerated the unworldliness of the younger Apostles' interpretation of *Principia Ethica*, so much so that there are passages in his memoir that seem to parody the doctrines of *Principia*. One has to remember this fact even when reading the memoir, and, as it were, listen for the teasing tone of voice that means 'what I am now saying is not to be taken entirely seriously'. However, Keynes means exactly what he says here of his own generation of Apostles:

> 'It was only for us, those who were active in 1903, that Moore completely ousted McTaggart, Dickinson, Russell. The influence was not only overwhelming; but it was the extreme opposite of what Strachey used to call *funeste*; it was exciting, exhilarating, the beginning of a renaissance, the opening of a new heaven on a new earth, we were the forerunners of a new dispensation, we were not afraid of anything.'

But in the very next sentence he is teasing Quentin Bell and Janie Bussy, the second generation members of Bloomsbury who were present to hear the paper: 'Perhaps it was because we were so brought up that even at our gloomiest and worst we have never lost a certain resilience which the younger generation seem never to have had. They have enjoyed, at most, only a pale reflection of something, not altogether superseded, but faded and without illusions.'[15]

Why did Keynes wish to annoy his younger hearers? Chiefly because they were Left-wing (Janie Bussy was a Trotskyite and Quentin Bell considered himself a 'fellow-traveller') and Keynes knew that they thought he had become reactionary. Keynes wanted to disparage their youthful Marxism by opposing to it his own youthful Mooreism. He succeeded in his teasing and also caused much subsequent confusion.[16] For one thing he hung what Quentin Bell called his 'lay sermon' on the wrong text: the memoir opens with some reflections on D. H. Lawrence's intense dislike of the 'young men', Keynes's generation of Apostles, whom Lawrence met and hated in 1915 – most of them were, of course, thirty-five when that meeting at Cambridge took place: hardly boys. Russell, who figures in the story, and Moore, who sat next to Lawrence in hall at Trinity that night, were in their mid-forties. Keynes was playing a sort of confidence-trick here, claiming that the men who so annoyed Lawrence were young men, drunk on the heady wine of *Principia Ethica*; but the unpleasant evening referred to in fact took place thirteen years later.*

More serious is the confusion Keynes caused by connecting 'Benthamism' to both Marxism and Mooreism. On the one hand he spoke of 'the final *reductio ad absurdum* of Benthamism known as Marxism' and on the other, he said that

> 'what we got from Moore was by no means entirely what he offered us. He had one foot on the threshold of the new heaven, but the other foot in Sidgwick and the Benthamite calculus and the general rules of correct behaviour. There was one chapter in the *Principia* of which we took not the slightest notice. We accepted Moore's religion, so to speak, and discarded his morals.'[18]

Keynes speaks in one sense of 'Benthamism' as a pernicious ideology, and, in another of it as a component of *Principia Ethica* which he, as a younger man, ignored. He does not, in the memoir, use the word 'utilitarianism', and fails to notice what Moore had retained of the thought of Bentham, James and John Stuart Mill, and what he had abjured.

Richard Braithwaite characterizes Moore's arguments in such a way as to make clear Keynes's own position, by identifying three strands of thought in *Principia Ethica*. The first is Moore's argument that goodness

---

* He deceived the late Dr Leavis who, in *The Common Pursuit* (1952), 'attacks Keynes when that author is dealing with the beliefs of young men at King's and Trinity around 1904 by quoting Lawrence's remarks about a completely different set of people whom he met ten years later.'[17] When Leavis spluttered the words 'incontinently flippant talk', 'shiny complacency' and 'triviality', he was actually depositing a bit more egg on his own face.

as an end – intrinsic goodness – is a simple concept which *ipso facto* cannot be analysed, so that when the word 'good' is used in this sense it cannot be defined. Braithwaite points out that it is 'this thesis in the logic of ethics' that continues to engage the attention of academic philosophers.[19]

'Moore's ethical pluralism is the second strand of his thought. Instead of the one thing – pleasure – which the Utilitarians had allowed to be good in itself, Moore postulated a plurality of such things, of which "by far the most valuable" are states of mind involving either "the pleasures of human intercourse" or "the enjoyment of beautiful objects." This thesis pointed to "the life of passionate contemplation and communion" as the "Ideal" for Keynes and his friends. Moore's third strand of thought, expounded in the penultimate chapter "Ethics in relation to conduct", argued for the classical Utilitarian doctrine that the rightness of an action derives from the character of its consequences – in Moore's language, an action is "good as a means". It is because the doctrine (which I shall for convenience call "consequentialism") is common to Moore and the Utilitarians that the ethics of *Principia Ethica* has been called "Ideal Utilitarianism" as contrasted with the "Hedonistic Utilitarianism" of Bentham, the Mills and Sidgwick.

'Of this "consequentialist" chapter of Moore's book Keynes says that "we took not the slightest notice".'[20]

Braithwaite's explanation of this is simply that the consequentialism of Moore held no novelty or excitement for Keynes or his friends. They had all (with the exception, Braithwaite thinks, of Leonard Woolf, who had a Jewish family background – and who flatly contradicted Keynes about accepting 'Moore's religion' and discarding 'his morals') been brought up in the tradition of classical utilitarianism, which they absorbed in childhood. Sidgwick was a Keynes family friend; Keynes may very well have found his personality unattractive, as Moore did, but he was steeped in his hedonistic utilitarianism. 'Moore's influence' on Keynes, Braithwaite says, 'made him spew out the hedonism, but left the consequentialism intact.' In other words, while Keynes rejected the hedonism of 'Benthamism', his rejection did not extend to the consequentialist aspect of utilitarianism, which was the feature retained by Moore. So Keynes did not jettison Moore's morals at all – they were an unconscious part of the way he had been brought up from childhood to look at the world. Keynes and his friends, Braithwaite maintains were like 'Christians, who, when they lose their faith, declare that they have rejected the whole of Christianity when in fact they have discarded Christian beliefs while retaining Christian principles of conduct.'[21]

What Braithwaite calls his 'de-rhetoricizing' of 'My Early Beliefs' has succeeded in clearing up some of the confusion Keynes caused by his too facile talk of discarded morals, but there is left a puzzle about what Keynes thought of as Moore's 'religion'. Why did he think 'that this religion of ours was a very good one to grow up under'? And if he thought that 'it remains nearer the truth than any other that I know, with less irrelevant extraneous matter and nothing to be ashamed of',[22] why did he think it responsible for there 'having been just a grain of truth when Lawrence said in 1914 that we were "done for" '?[23]

Keynes's version of his Mooreist religion had elements of puerile parody. He began by again teasing the younger people in his audience:

'Even if the new members of the Club know what the religion was (do they?), it will not do any of us any harm to try and recall the crude outlines. Nothing mattered except states of mind, our own and other people's of course, but chiefly our own. These states of mind were not associated with action or achievement or with consequence. They consisted in timeless, passionate states of contemplation and communion, largely unattached to "before" and "after". Their value depended, in accordance with the principle of organic unity, on the state of affairs as a whole which could not be usefully analysed into parts. For example, the value of the state of mind of being in love did not depend merely on the nature of one's own emotions, but also on the worth of their object and on the reciprocity and nature of the object's emotions; but it did not depend, if I remember rightly, or did not depend very much, on what happened, or how one felt about it, a year later, though I myself was always an advocate of a principle of organic unity through time, which still seems to me only sensible. The appropriate subjects of passionate contemplation and communion were a beloved person, beauty and truth, and one's prime objects in life were love, the creation and enjoyment of aesthetic experience and the pursuit of knowledge. Of these love came a long way first. But in the early days under Moore's influence the public treatment of this and its associated acts was, on the whole, austere and Platonic. Some of us might argue that physical enjoyment could spoil and detract from the state of mind as a whole.'[24]

The paragraph concluded with a remark about Strachey's 'edict that certain Latin technical terms of sex were the correct terms to use, that to avoid them was a grave error, and even in mixed company, a weakness'. Keynes doubts whether this had occurred by 1903.[25] The reader may take this as a cryptic reference to the homosexual love affairs mentioned by Russell and documented in Holroyd's *Lytton Strachey*, Furbank's *E. M. Forster*, and the present writer's essay on Keynes and 'The Bloomsbury Group'.[26]

Mooreism, Keynes continued, had in common with English puritanism, that 'being chiefly concerned with the salvation of our own souls. . . . there was not a very intimate connection between "being good" and "doing good"; and we had a feeling that there was some risk that in practice the latter might interfere with the former. . . . our religion was thoroughly unworldly – with wealth, power, popularity or success it had no concern whatever, they were thoroughly despised.'[27]

What though, Keynes asked, happened when there were conflicting intuitions about what was good? Either the parties were not talking about precisely the same thing, or one of the parties had better judgment than the other. The latter explanation usually prevailed:

'In practice, victory was with those who could speak with the greatest appearance of clear, undoubting conviction and could best use the accents of infallibility. Moore at this time was a master of this method – greeting one's remarks with a gasp of incredulity – *Do* you *really* think *that*, an expression of face as if to hear such a thing said reduced him to a state of wonder verging on imbecility, with his mouth wide open and wagging his head in the negative so violently that his hair shook. *Oh!* he would say, goggling at you as if either you or he must be mad; and no reply was possible.'[28]

No one has ever thought or suggested that Moore's mannerisms carried any overtones of arrogance, but arrogance is precisely what their critics charge Moore's disciples with. In place of Moore's stare of disbelief at what he was hearing, Strachey instituted 'grim silence', Woolf was adept at making his opponent feel the futility of arguing with him, Dickinson mastered the art of shrugging his shoulders in 'unconvinced' retreat, and Sheppard and Keynes himself 'could only turn like worms, but worms who could eventually be goaded into voluble claims that worms have at least the *right* to turn'.[29]

D. H. Lawrence's thirty-five-year-old antagonists *were* arrogant. They were also dons and writers, pampered and privileged products of the upper-middle-class culture of Cambridge. They were, in fact, several of the things that Lawrence was not. But worst of all for Lawrence must have been their invulnerability. They were mostly homosexual and mostly opposed to a war that had already begun; this ought to have put them outside the mainstream of life, even at Cambridge. But these men who refused military service were warriors, and the Mooreism of their youth was their armour; they were sure of their rightness – Lytton Strachey, in 1916, could face almost with equanimity the prospect of going to jail for his conscientious objection to conscription. Whatever society at large would have despised them for, they spoke of and even boasted of openly among themselves. They gave the impression that they could not be harmed, that they were not vulnerable to the very forces Lawrence feared, which hounded him and finally broke him. This was the carapace that caused Lawrence to write to Lady Ottoline Morrell and to David Garnett on 19 April 1915 of Keynes, the Stracheys and Duncan Grant as 'beetles'.[30]

Keynes did not endorse the *grounds* of Lawrence's hysterical outburst; but as an elderly man he did think that Lawrence had spotted one truth about himself when younger; and this was something to do with his Mooreism: 'I have called this faith a religion, and some sort of relation of neo-platonism it surely was. But we should have been angry at the time with such a suggestion. We regarded all this as entirely rational and scientific in character.'[31]

From this passage we can see what Richard Braithwaite called 'the genuine volte-face reported in the memoir',[32] a change not in Keynes's ethical beliefs, but a much more fundamental change in his psychological beliefs: 'the abandonment of the belief that "human nature is reasonable".'[33] 'This pseudo-rational view of human nature', Keynes had come to think, 'led to a thinness, a superficiality, not only of judgment, but also of feeling.' Moore's last chapter, he thought, left 'whole categories of valuable emotions' out of account[34] – an unfair criticism of Moore's list of good states of mind, which was never presented as exhaustive. 'We were not aware', said Keynes in the sentence that has become famous, 'that civilisation was a thin and precarious crust erected by the personality and the will of a very few, and only maintained by rules and conventions skilfully put across and guilefully preserved.' 'We had no respect', Keynes continued in what was perhaps the real point he was making to the young people, 'for traditional wisdom or the restraints of custom. We lacked reverence, as Lawrence observed and as Ludwig [Wittgenstein] with justice also used to say – for everything and everyone.'[35]

In Keynes's essay there is much praise of Moore and of *Principia Ethica*. He even quotes two very lengthy paragraphs from the chapter on the 'Ideal' because they are 'sweet and lovely ... so sincere and passionate and careful',[36] and says that, compared with that chapter, 'the New Testament is a handbook for politicians'. He says there is nothing like that chapter in all literature since Plato; but

> 'it is better than Plato because it is quite free from *fancy*. It conveys the beauty of the literalness of Moore's mind, and the pure and passionate intensity of his vision, *un*fanciful and *un*dressed-up. Moore had a nightmare once in which he could not distinguish propositions from tables. But even when he was awake, he could not distinguish love and beauty and truth from the furniture. They took on the same definition of outline, the same stable, solid, objective qualities and common-sense reality.'[37]

Nonetheless, what they made of Moore and his book – a scripture for youthful believers before the First World War – was deficient as a faith for adults on the brink of the second war. Thus Keynes can now see a little of the point of Lawrence's strictures against them :

> 'If, therefore, I altogether ignore our merits – our charm, our intelligence, our unworldliness, our affection – I can see us as water-spiders, gracefully skimming, as light and reasonable as air, the surface of the stream without any contact at all with the eddies and currents underneath. And if I imagine us as coming under the observation of Lawrence's ignorant, jealous, irritable, hostile eyes, what a combination of qualities we offered to arouse his passionate distaste; this thin rationalism skipping on the crust of the lava, ignoring both the reality and the value of the vulgar passions, joined to libertinism and comprehensive irreverence, too clever by half ... seducing with ... intellectual *chic* ... All this was very unfair to poor, silly, well meaning us. But that is why I say that there may have been just a grain of truth when Lawrence said in 1914 that we were "done for".'[38]*

---

* In 1914 many of those present in 1938 had been conscientious objectors, which was then a rational position to adopt. Keynes never did give up what was essential to the Mooreism of his youth – if it were possible to retain that structure while giving up the foundations of human rationality upon which it had been erected. In 'My Early Beliefs' Keynes, after all, repudiated nothing; but had he been present when Keynes delivered it on 9 September 1938, Moore himself would have agreed that it was necessary to make some concessions to Hitler and Mussolini, and even to D. H. Lawrence.

An example of the effect of *Principia Ethica* on an Apostle older than Moore is the unhappy and confused history of Lowes Dickinson's *The Meaning of Good*, which first appeared in 1901. In 1900 Lowes Dickinson, always the Platonist, decided to attempt a philosophical dialogue. Part of it was written while staying with Roger Fry in Surrey, but the idea had come to him earlier at Mistra, above Sparta, during his first tour of Greece. In his autobiography, he wrote:

'While I was writing it G. E. Moore's book *Principia Ethica* appeared and made a kind of furore among my Cambridge friends. "The age of reason has come", Lytton Strachey said. I remember that it appeared to me, on reading that book, that I had been guilty, in my own dialogue, of what Moore called the "naturalistic fallacy", a phrase which always amuses me, for it suggests some kind of unnatural vice. I tried to dodge this error in my book at the last moment, but I expect it is there, and also that it doesn't much matter. Moore has probably long ago altered his position, on this as on other points.'[39]

Forster tells the same story, but adds that 'Moore's *Principia Ethica* came out while *The Meaning of Good* was in proof'. In fact *Principia Ethica* did not appear until 1903, two years after *The Meaning of Good*. Either Lowes Dickinson had learned of Moore's views on the naturalistic fallacy at meetings of the Society in 1900 and 1901, or he only attempted to extirpate his 'error' in preparing the third or fourth editions (which were published in 1907) of *The Meaning of Good*. In any case, Noël Annan is closer to the truth when he says:

'A year or so later he wryly watched his junior, Moore, sweep aside his offering and in the same devastating manner refute the metaphysics of his friend McTaggart which up to that time had captivated Cambridge. The new philosophical climate was too bracing and vigorous for him, and he turned more to the study of history and politics which were then still concerned with people.'[40]

Temperamentally closer to poets than to philosophers, Lowes Dickinson learned from Moore that, as Forster put it, 'more care had evidently to be taken as to what one said and how one said it, and intuition seemed less than ever enough'.[41] Temperament would certainly have driven Lowes Dickinson from the ranks of philosophers eventually, though no doubt contact with Moore hastened his departure. Yet Noël Annan is surely right to hear echoes in *Principia Ethica* (and in Mc-

Taggart's philosophy) of the conclusion of *The Meaning of Good*, Lowes Dickinson's own strictly philosophical work :

> 'Whatever Reality may ultimately be, it is in the life of the affections, with all its confused tangle of loves and hates, attractions, repulsions, and, worst of all, indifferences, it is in this intricate commerce of souls that we may come nearest to apprehending what perhaps we shall never wholly apprehend, but the quest of which alone, as I believe, gives any significance to life, and makes it a thing which a wise and brave man will be able to persuade himself it is right to endure.'[42]

In the same month, October 1903, that *Principia Ethica* appeared, Moore published in *Mind* 'The Refutation of Idealism'. These two events seemed to mark a final break with the philosophy of the recent past. As the book continues to figure in every discussion of the Bloomsbury Group, so the article continues its life among philosophers. Writing critically of it in 1942, C. J. Ducasse said it was 'still one of the most famous articles written in philosophy since the turn of the century'.[43] In it, many philosophers felt, Moore showed that the Berkeleian proposition *esse* is *percipi* – to be is to be perceived – is false, and so put paid to the phenomenalist basis of all idealist philosophies. Moore nevertheless listened to McTaggart's lectures that year as he had done before.

Russell often called on Moore in his rooms that year, and they talked of their books. Russell's *Principles of Mathematics* had also been published in 1903, and in the preface Russell had said :

> 'On fundamental questions of philosophy, my position, in all its chief features, is derived from Mr G. E. Moore. I have accepted from him the non-existential nature of propositions (except such as happen to assert existence) and their independence of any knowing mind; also that pluralism which regards the world, both that of existents and that of entities, as composed of an infinite number of mutually independent entities, with relations which are ultimate, and not reducible to adjectives of their terms or of the whole which these compose. Before learning these views from him, I found myself completely unable to construct any philosophy of arithmetic, whereas their acceptance brought about an immediate liberation from a large number of difficulties which I believe to be otherwise insuperable.'[44]

Moore's and Russell's mutual influence is a vexed question, made more confusing by Moore's comments on the above passage, and by Moore's quite naturally not wishing to say anything public about their strained personal relations. As we have seen, Moore did influence his elder colleague more than Russell did Moore, but Moore with all too characteristic modesty, flatly denied this in his autobiography:

'Russell left Cambridge in June 1894, at the end of my second year. But, though he had left Cambridge, I used, for some six or eight years after that date, to see him frequently and discuss philosophical questions with him. These discussions took place either when I visited him at his house in the country or when he visited Cambridge. For several years in succession he and his wife took a house in Cambridge for the whole of the Lent term, and I had much discussion with him during these visits. In these discussions there was, of course, mutual influence. It is to ideas which he thought he owed to me as a result of them that Russell was referring in the Preface of his *Principles*; and we both of us subsequently discovered that these ideas were largely mistaken. I do not know that Russell has ever owed to me anything [positive (Moore's correction)] except mistakes; whereas I have owed to his published works ideas which were certainly not mistakes and which I think very important. After about 1901 we met but rarely for a period of about ten years, until, from 1911 to 1915, we were both of us lecturing in Cambridge, and both had rooms in Trinity; . . . I certainly owe much to all this personal contact with Russell; but I think I owe even more to his published works. I have certainly spent more time in studying what he has written than in studying the works of any other single philosopher.'[45]

Moore was nearly seventy when he wrote this passage; he did not want to open up old wounds or give pain to an equally elderly man, and the last two sentences are Moore's attempt to be candid without distorting the truth. The whole truth is conveyed better in this long passage from Moore's diary for 1909:

'Aug. 30–Sept. 2. Go to Russells' at Bagley Wood. Amos there. Talk a little about seeing and hearing first night. Go with Mrs R. to Logan's Tues. morning: Chinese poems with Logan; . . . see Miss M[arjorie] Strachey, Ray Costelloe, Miss Worthington. Keynes to lunch: probability. Karin Costelloe and two other ladies to tea. Walk with Russell after tea: try to explain to him about objects seeming bigger and smaller, and am annoyed because he seems to wish to drop subject. . . . After Mrs R. goes to bed, very hot dispute, before Amos as to means of "knowing": whether I can "know" Amos's tooth-ache; I get angry, and think R. bad at seeing point, apt to defend himself by bringing in irrelevant points, and too arrogant. Talk with him all next morning of knowledge of propositions and self-evidence, after reading him in Edinburgh on Pragmatism. Santayana, Miss M. Strachey and Ray to lunch: Santayana talks much and seems nicely frank; . . . Walk with R. after tea and discuss my lectures. We explain about probability to Amos: again I think R. misses points and is too confident of insufficient explanations as to meaning of words.'

On 5 July 1910 Moore recorded that 'Russell bores me', and on the 15th of that month, he noted his relief that Russell did not, as threatened, turn up after dinner at Sanger's. In March 1911 Moore was again staying with the Russells. On the 25th he recorded: 'Russell asks me about Free Will and behaves badly, *I think.*' The next week, on the 31st, Moore called on MacCarthy 'about reading party and tell him about Russell'. Russell was *not* invited to accompany them with Sanger, Lytton Strachey, Ainsworth, Hawtrey, Mayor and Bob Trevelyan at Lulworth from the 13–20 April. This was the pattern for the rest of Moore's life. His relations with Russell were cool; though not overtly hostile, he avoided certain kinds of social contact with Russell. Moore gave no hint of his feelings about Russell in public; and he supported Russell against those who wanted to strip him of his Trinity lectureship. Part of the reason for Moore's coolness was Russell's treatment of Alys after his famous bicycle ride in the autumn of 1901, when in cold blood he decided he no longer loved her.[46] But a more important part was played by Russell's intellectual deportment, about which he was able to deceive even himself, as when he wrote of his time at Cambridge that 'that one habit of thought of real virtue I acquired there was intellectual honesty'.[47]

Moore, in his autobiography, gave a very concise account of his movements following the publication of *Principia Ethica*, and his words captured something of the way his mind and feelings were engaged during his exile from Cambridge, which lasted from 1904 to 1911.

'My Fellowship elapsed at the end of September 1904. I had applied for its continuation in the form of a Research Fellowship; but election to a Research Fellowship was (and still is) a very rare and exceptional thing at Trinity, and I was not surprised that my application was refused. Nor was I, I think, at all sorry; I think I was glad to have the prospect of a change from Cambridge life. My mother and father had both very recently died; and, owing to the facts that two of my mother's maternal uncles, both of them childless, had been rich men, and that my mother, being the only child of her mother and having been left an orphan very early, had been almost in the place of a daughter to them, I and my brothers and sisters had now sufficient private means to enable us to live in moderate comfort without needing to earn anything. I was therefore in a position to go on working at philosophy, which was what I wanted to do, without a Fellowship and without needing to try to obtain any paid employment. The only question was where I should live. Having ceased to be a Fellow, and having no official post in the University, I should not be able any longer to live in College; and I did not like the idea of living at Cambridge in lodgings after having spent so many years in College.'

It was the necessity of Ainsworth's having a job that provided the solution to Moore's problem of where to live:

'A close friend of mine had recently been appointed to a post on the teaching staff of Edinburgh University; I was anxious to be near him, and also Edinburgh had a romantic attraction for me, chiefly owing to its association with Scott and his novels, which I loved and was in the habit of reading again and again. We decided that I should move to Edinburgh, and that we should take an apartment there together. We found one which suited us admirably, at the bottom of a huge forbidding building of dark grey stone on the south side of Buccleuch Place just opposite to George Square where Scott's father had lived at the time when Scott was a boy. At the back our house looked clear out towards the Meadows, with no houses intervening. We lived there for three years and a half, and I was not at all disappointed with Edinburgh: it still seemed to me very romantic, and I became very fond of it.'[48]

Before Moore left Cambridge he had struck up an important new friendship with an interesting and colourful man who contributed a good deal to the legend that grew up around Moore in the years of his absence from Cambridge. This was (Sir) Sydney Philip Waterlow (1878–1944). Waterlow was an Eton and Trinity man; for some reason he, like Clive Bell, his junior by three years, was not elected to the Apostles, and, like Bell, he was wounded and bitter all his life about his exclusion from this circle to which nearly all his friends belonged. (In both cases the fault was remedied in the next generation, by the election to the

Apostles of Bell's son, Julian, and Waterlow's son, John.) Waterlow was a life-long amateur of philosophy, and always more interested in the life of the mind than in the problems of the Foreign Office. Nonetheless, after a false start he served in that branch of the government. He was in the Diplomatic Service at Washington from 1901, but because his father was in financial difficulties[49] he resigned in 1905. After being employed at the Paris Peace Conference in 1919 he was re-appointed to the Foreign Office and made CBE in 1920; Waterlow was then British Minister successively in Bangkok, Addis Ababa, Sofia and Athens. In his professional as in his personal life he might have been a great man, except that he was a little bit ridiculous. Waterlow was friendly with Bloomsbury – at one time the Woolfs saw him nearly every day – and with anti-Bloomsbury, for he had a more than casual acquaintance with D. H. and Frieda Lawrence. He was also a great friend and admirer of Henry James, whose morale he helped to keep up when his sales figures stood lower than his reputation.[50] In a footnote in his autobiography, where Leonard Woolf said 'Sydney's life was in some ways stranger than fiction',[51] he was referring to the circumstances of the break-up of the first marriage of this 'infant prodigy at Eton and . . . brilliant classical scholar at Trinity': [52] Waterlow had married in 1902, Alice, sister of Sir Frederick Pollock Bt. (Apostle Number 160), and he had the grimly funny experience (which he never tired of telling both Woolf and Moore) of having his first marriage annulled for non-consummation in the same court in which he was cited a few weeks later as co-respondent in a divorce case.[53]

Moore first encountered Waterlow in the long vacation of 1898, when the younger man, in his first year at Cambridge, was living in McTaggart's old rooms; they continued to meet fairly often until Waterlow went down at the end of May term 1900. By 1903 they were corresponding on philosophical questions, and Waterlow, who had received advance notice of the publication of *Principia Ethica* from Moore, was nourishing an interest in becoming something more than an amateur philosopher. He had submitted an article on aesthetics to the *Independent Review*; it was not accepted, but, as he wrote to Moore, the problem seemed to him to have been solved in *Principia Ethica*. The *Independent Review* was a monthly magazine, launched in October 1903 by a group of people led by George Trevelyan, who assured a sceptical Lytton Strachey that 'there was a majority of Apostles on the editorial committee'.[54] This committee included not only Trevelyan, but Lowes Dickinson and Wedd, and the *Independent*'s first number had a cover designed by Roger Fry. Russell was a contributor, as was

Forster; and the magazine was, for a few years, an important and influential Liberal journal.

It was about this time that several of those involved with the *Independent Review* formed the idea of jointly producing in book form a sort of radical manifesto, with Moore as their acknowledged inspiration.* This idea gradually took shape in 1904 and on 12 December of that year Waterlow wrote to Russell:

'Moore is ready to do an article on the objectivity of truth, and can have it finished by June, but not before.

'But he doesn't see how the book, as sketched out, can have any homogeneity at all; and after a long discussion I agree with him as to that. It does seem pretty clear that what the rest of us are likely to say on our various special subjects can't be in any way hitched on to what Moore will say; or, if there is an apparent connection in *some* cases, in no case will there be a real connection; because all the other subjects are special subjects, very different from one another and from Moore's, and also the individual handling is certain to be

* The first mention of the project appears in a curious letter from George Trevelyan to Waterlow, written from Florence on 22 April 1904. The letter is a profound apology for an earlier letter in which Trevelyan vituperatively attacked Waterlow for his views on the marriage of Waterlow's brother-in-law, Jack Pollock. Pollock wished to marry Gladys Holman Hunt, but the couple refused on principle to be married in church, which angered his mother, Lady Pollock. Trevelyan was outraged that Waterlow did not appear concerned at what he called Lady Pollock's persecution of Jack and Gladys. In fact Trevelyan had suffered a nervous breakdown during the first few weeks of his marriage to Janet Ward, after they had encountered the same problem with her formidable mother, Mrs Humphrey Ward. But there was a stronger and better reason for having been so cross with Waterlow:

'Not having seen you for so long, I had not previously realized that you had altered your "manifesto" views, and the fact of this change came to me with such a shock, that I mixed it up with your not having the courage to put them into practice. This was of course wrong. But you will see that it was a little natural to feel aggravated that Jack and I should not have been backed up by the writer of the "manifesto" when we tried to put its principles in practice. An earlier knowledge that you had theoretically abandoned those principles, would have prevented me giving vent to my aggravation in passionate language, and imputing motives.'[55]

This first impassioned reference to a 'manifesto' by a bad-tempered George Trevelyan is the only trace of the project for several months, and does not at first sight seem to have any particular connection with Moore; indeed, given Trevelyan's preoccupation in 1904, it was almost certainly meant to be a manifesto for the *Independent*.

different to some extent. It's true that most of the writers hold philosophical views inspired by or similar to those of Moore. But what he questions is whether this fact will stand out, as it should do, from *his* treatment of truth side by side with, e.g. someone else's treatment of international morality: whether the underlying philosophical agreement will be shewn at all. It can't be brought out (where it exists) without long and intricate philosophical discussion, such as is out of the question. And it isn't as if it even existed in all cases. Indeed *you* are perhaps the only case of clear and definite philosophic agreement: Hawtrey is a case of clear philosophic disagreement.*

'Of course, there is a general agreement of tone between us and Moore as against the rest of the world. But we can't rely on that to make a good book. Moore's article will be purely philosophical and he can't undertake to make it less stiff than his writing usually is. So that whatever harmony of tone there might really be, would scarcely be perceptive.

'However, as I say, he's willing to do it on these terms; partly because he doesn't feel certain that a fairly good result mightn't be produced after all; and partly because he doesn't like not to do what we all want him to do. I said you would let him know if this was satisfactory. Perhaps before doing this you would like to talk it over with me, especially as he said several other interesting things, which I haven't time to write.'[56]

Then, in a letter to Moore, dated 17 December 1904, Russell refers negatively to the 'proposed book' as a 'manifesto':

'Waterlow has written me a short account of his conversation with you on the subject of the proposed book. I agree entirely with what you said as to the difficulty of getting any sort of unity. At the same time, I think what is most necessary is a certain unity of point of view, which probably would be possible. Waterlow says you could not undertake to make the article on Truth any easier than your

---

* Hawtrey had forgotten about his own participation in the group. When interviewed on 22 March 1969, he remembered nothing about the manifesto group at all, but thought it likely that the others were 'smitten' with Moore's views and wanted to popularize them. When Hawtrey first encountered Moore, his own views were more like Herbert Spencer's — a view of morals and conscience as instincts that evolved by natural selection. Moore's clarity about the difference between means and ends, said Hawtrey, made him see that his own view was untenable.

usual writing. Now the scope and purpose of the book is popular, and it is rather important that the first chapter should not be too difficult. Would it be equally agreeable to you to do God and immortality, if I did the introductory chapter on Truth? I fancy what is said on God will be what people will chiefly notice, and it is therefore very important it should be well done. But I think your existing paper on God, rather expanded, would do. The idea had been that Waterlow should do God, but he could probably do Ethics better, as your book would be a help to him.

'I do not conceive the book as a Manifesto, but merely as a careful endeavour to say exactly what we think: something in the same tone as Sidgwick's "Practical Ethics". Are you coming South for Xmas? If so, please give me an opportunity of talking to you. Will you be able to come to George Trevy's to dinner on January 6, when all the other proposed contributors will be there? . . .

'I am very glad indeed that you are not unwilling to co-operate. I am myself in favour of going slowly, and considering the plan for a good while before deciding on it. I am sure you could do God in a way at once generally intelligible and cogent.'[57]

The comic possibilities of Moore 'doing' either God or Truth in a popular book seemed to have escaped the other members of the manifesto group – Russell's denial that he sees the book as a 'manifesto' is a clear indication that it was, in fact, intended by some as a manifesto. (Nonetheless, the identities of the participants, as they emerge, make it clear that political liberalism was one of the ties that bound them together.) Waterlow was the only non-Apostle in the group, the leadership of which he appeared to share with George Trevelyan; for Russell wrote again to Moore on 27 December:

'Waterlow and George Trevy have reported to me what you feel on the subject of collaborating in the book which they propose. I am very anxious (as we all are) to get you to do as much as you will of the philosophical part; but it is quite essential that everything should be intelligible to ordinary educated people, and not only to those who have philosophic capacity. I should like to talk over the matter with you, to see what prospect there is of our being able to achieve this, and also to hear what you say about the plan of the book. I think the want of unity which you spoke of to Waterlow is almost if not quite unavoidable. My own belief is that it may turn out to be better for us all to keep separate; but I should like to have meetings for papers

and discussions, so as to find out our agreements and disagreements.
. . .

'I heard very interesting scraps of your present views from Waterlow, e.g. that you think Idealism may be true. I am very anxious to
find out how you have got there; also whether it is true that you
think you can prove that there is such a thing as causality.'⁵⁸

There was something wonderful, as well as funny, about the competition of the two great minds to be the plain man's philosopher. The
comedy is compounded by the poor quality of Waterlow's report to
Russell on the Party Line. Here is Moore's reply to Russell, written on
28 December:

'I'm sorry I didn't answer your first letter. George Trevy had said he
would tell you about the arrangements for our meeting in London,
and I forgot that you had asked me another question, about whether
I would do God instead of Truth.

. . . . .

'I have more fancy for doing the article on Truth than that on
God, and I don't see any reason why I shouldn't be able to make it
equally intelligible. Besides I think Waterlow would probably do
God better than the Ethics.

'I don't think I've changed my views in any interesting manner:
I don't see any argument in favour of Idealism, and am not the least
disposed to believe in it. I have only got a little clearer about the
nature of a proposition, and about what it is that is the case when a
proposition is true.'⁵⁹

Russell replied the next day:

'By all means let it be Truth. I don't know whether you would feel
the same as I should, but if I had to do a more or less popular article
on such a topic, I should first write an ordinary technical article,
and then boil it down; so that in the second revision I should not be
thinking what was true, but only how to express things clearly. –
I will tell Waterlow about God.

. . . . .

'I gather Waterlow had rather misunderstood your views. But I
should like to know what is the case when a proposition is true.'

Willingly as Russell acknowledged his discipleship to Moore in most
areas of philosophical concern, there was still one that was a preserve
of his own – symbolic logic. Waterlow's reports of Moore's views were

so unreliable that he might almost have been a journalist; this time, he not only claimed that Moore had something to say about Russell's special corner of philosophy, he even misreported to the extent of making it appear that Moore claimed to have solved the problem of the contradiction (e.g. the paradox of the Cretan who says all Cretans are liars) which had bedevilled Russell's work for a very long time. It was essential to Russell's dignity that he put Moore in his (philosophical) place:

'Waterlow tells me you thought you had got round my contradiction. I have ways of getting round it; but I think if you don't know Symbolic Logic you can hardly judge of solutions, because the objection to most of them is that, in some remote and roundabout way, they involve the falsehood of obvious truths, such as $2+2=4$. This applies to the view which Waterlow said you favoured, that there is not a class of *all* entities.'[60]

Russell got his way about persuading the group to meet to read and discuss papers on the topics to be dealt with in the manifesto.

Trevelyan's dinner meeting came off as planned on 6 January 1905. Russell's next letter to Moore was dated 19 March:

'We have a meeting of the people concerned with Waterlow's proposed book here [Russell's house in Chelsea] on March 25, dining first at 8. Is there any chance of your coming? It is vacation, so you might be in the South. Hawtrey is reading on the reasons for believing in Causality. He read an excellent paper a week ago on what we mean by Causality.'[61]

Russell was now the only person who communicated with Moore about the project. On 2 May he wrote:

'We are going to have a meeting of the people concerned in Waterlow's project of a book on Saturday in Dickinson's rooms at 9 p.m. If you are in Cambridge, as I hear you may be, I hope you will come, though I shall be rather alarmed, as I am reading on Ethics, and the paper I have written is merely your [book] boiled down, popularized, and with almost all the exactitude omitted. I have gone on the plan of not discussing points which everyone except a trained philosopher would regard as trivial or logic-chopping.

'I wonder whether you and Hawtrey got to any result about secondary qualities.'[62]

It seems likely that Russell was right to be apprehensive: Moore did come to that meeting (he was in Cambridge, and noted in his diary that he had had conversation with Russell) and he did not think much of Russell's effort. Later that month Russell wrote to say that it had been 'arranged to continue the discussion of Ethics' at Dickinson's London address. 'I suppose there is no chance of your being there? It would be a great help, and very nice, if you were.'[63] As late as 23 October 1905 Moore was writing to Russell with corrections to his ms on Ethics. Moore commented: 'After insisting that "right conduct" depends so much on good results, I think it would be absurd not to try to indicate what results are good: let alone the fact that I think it both important and easy to combat convincingly both your "moralist's fallacy" and Hedonism.' And Moore continued:

> 'I think your Section is unsatisfactory, not because any such section must be too dogmatic, but because you have laid too little emphasis on what are undoubtedly great goods and great evils, as compared with comparatively disputable points. E.g. I don't think there is the least need to mention the questions whether pleasure or knowledge are at all good per se, except simply to emphasize the point that pleasure per se is certainly not a great good; nor do I see any need to mention the question whether true and false beliefs affect the value of good or bad wholes.
>
> 'I don't know what Keynes's view about goods and organic unities is. But it seems to me plain that, in the form you mention it, it must be wrong.'[64]

And so on, laying down the law quite firmly about ethical matters – but expressing with decided humility great interest in Russell's theory of 'knowledge by acquaintance'.

This entire episode would be merely a diverting footnote to the intellectual history of the early years of the century were it not for the distinction of most of the men and the depth of their allegiance to Moore. Four philosophers (or would-be philosophers) and a very Liberal historian earnestly set about the thankless task of preaching to the unconverted not a simple gospel, but a philosophical outlook so complicated that the cleverest of the philosophers sometimes got it wrong. There are no more documents that bear upon the group's project; but we can be confident that it foundered, as it was bound to do, on the shoals of disagreement and the reefs of Moore's insistence on precision. One could hardly choose a more unpromising prophet or invent a more unlikely inspiration than G. E. Moore.

After Lytton Strachey's effusion and the homage of his peers, Moore was probably used to being a philosophical lion. But how could this genuinely modest man tolerate the mixture of flattery and wheedling to which Waterlow and Russell had to resort to capture Moore's interest and hold his attention in an undertaking he must have found at least partly repugnant? The answer can only be that Moore felt so keenly that the 'manifesto' views were true ones that he could not object to them on grounds that he had inspired them. Perhaps Moore, in the face of so much adulation, made, in his own mind, a distinction between true and false modesty, and discarded the latter in the interests of truth.

Whatever psychological accommodations were necessary for Moore to take part in this droll attempt to reform civilization through his philosophy, he did do it, and he acknowledged his role as guru to the band of seekers after truth. It is unlikely that the dry humour of the situation altogether escaped his attention; though he was only just over thirty years old at the time the proceedings to deify him were afoot, he managed to avoid succumbing to the temptation to let his whiskers grow and his manner become pompous.

How are we to assess the significance of the gesture of these men, one senior to Moore, two junior, and two his contemporaries, clubbing together for the purpose of making his views known to the world at large? It is not uncommon, when an academic has reached his seventieth or eightieth birthday for his colleagues and students to present him with a *Festschrift* of pieces inspired by or touching on his own interests. But this must have been the first, and perhaps only time in history, when an academic was honoured by a group of people seeking to transform his views – those of a man in his early thirties – into a manifesto. It was a gesture without precedent or sequel.

10

From 1904 to the War Years

Moore remained with Ainsworth in Edinburgh until the spring of 1908, when Ainsworth took up his post at the Board of Education in London. Ainsworth and Sarah Moore were married that year, and Moore and his remaining single sisters, Hettie and Nellie, had all to be rehoused. They decided to live together.

'After house hunting in a good many different directions in the neighbourhood of London, we found a house on The Green, at Richmond, Surrey, which we thought would suit us. The Green has a good deal of charm, with the row of red-brick Georgian houses called "Maids of Honour" Row, along one side of it, and the still older red-brick palace in which Elizabeth died in its far corner. Our house moreover looked out behind over the Old Deer Park. I lived at Richmond, as I had at Edinburgh, for three years and a half, and I became very fond of Richmond also.'[1]

Living first in Edinburgh and then in Richmond did not prevent Moore from keeping up with Cambridge and the Apostles, and in particular he continued his annual reading parties. In 1905 the party was held at Middlesmoor in Nidderdale, Yorkshire. Moore, Lytton Strachey and Ainsworth were by themselves for the first fortnight, and then were joined by MacCarthy, Crompton Llewelyn Davies, Sanger, Bob Trevy, Dakyns and Dodgson. Tragedy struck that summer. All the Apostles, most particularly Moore and Russell, were grief-stricken when they learned that on 25 July Theodore Llewelyn Davies, perhaps the best-loved of their number, had drowned accidentally while bathing near his home at Kirkby Lonsdale. He was aged thirty-four. Crompton was almost crazed by his loss. Theodore had been deeply in love with Margaret Booth, daughter of Charles Booth, who had refused his proposal of marriage. Crompton tried to carry out his brother's intentions by proposing to her himself in the autumn of 1905, but she turned him down as well.

No reading party was held in 1906, but with Moore's approval two new Apostles had been elected on 17 February: James Beaumont Strachey and Henry Tertius James Norton (Apostles Number 245 and 246). James Strachey (1887–1967) was Lytton's younger brother, and twenty-seven years younger than the eldest of the ten Strachey children; several of James Strachey's nieces and nephews were older than he, and they called him 'Uncle Baby'. James Strachey began his Cambridge career reading classics, but he did so badly in his first examination that he changed to moral sciences. He did no better, though, in his triposes and he only took an ordinary degree. In middle life James Strachey decided to begin a new career, and, after a few unrewarding weeks as a medical student, went to Vienna to begin training in a new field: he was psychoanalysed, along with his wife, Alix, by Sigmund Freud. In old age Strachey was the editor of the monumental standard edition of the works of Freud. He was also an eminent musicologist and wrote the programme notes for the Glyndebourne productions of Mozart's operas. The other new Apostle was Harry Norton (1887–1936). Norton, whose name often figures in works on the Bloomsbury Group, was a mathematician who did pioneering work in the mathematical theory of genetics.[2] His brilliance was generally recognized, but his work on the Cantorian theory of numbers was unfinished when he died. Moore was fond of both Norton and the younger Strachey, and found that both of them displayed an aptitude for philosophical discussion. He invited Norton on the 1907 reading party at North Molton, along with Ainsworth, Lytton Strachey, and Bob Trevelyan.

Like everyone else, Moore was captivated by the good looks and easy charm of the next new Apostle, Rupert Chawnor Brooke (1887–1915) who was elected on 25 January 1908. James Strachey had been at prep-school with Brooke, and they had corresponded while Strachey was at St Paul's and Brooke at Rugby; by 1908 James Strachey was helplessly and hopelessly in love with Brooke, who alternately returned and spurned his affections. James Strachey and Norton enjoyed the chaffing of Lytton and Keynes on the subject of the Higher Sodomy, and the spectacle of the elder two chasing the boys who had replaced Hobhouse in their affections in pursuit of the Lower. But Brooke was not so easy-going. He registered his disapproval in a passage of an Apostles' paper, 'Why not try the other leg?' which he read on 13 May 1909. Brooke spoke of the Apostles of his own time, adopting a vantage point far in the future: 'The subjects they discussed must have been of the utter-most variety. It has been suggested that they almost confined themselves to one or two little personal emotions and to the subject of copulation. Ridiculous!'

Moore liked the golden-haired young poet enough to ask him on the 1908 reading party just a few months after his election. The rest of the party at Market Lavington was Hawtrey, Keynes, Sanger, Bob Trevelyan and both Strachey brothers. The 1909 reading party was again at the Lizard. Norton, James Strachey, Brooke, Sanger, MacCarthy and Crompton Llewelyn Davies made up Moore's party, along with the new brother, Gerald Frank Shove (1887–1947). Shove was a classicist at the time of his election in January 1909; but he took the new economics part II tripos in 1911 and got a first. He stayed at King's as fellow, lecturer and then reader in economics. Like every Apostle of this vintage except Rupert Brooke, Shove was a conscientious objector in the war. He married the poet, Fredegond Maitland, daughter of F. W. Maitland.

In 1910 there was no reading party, but there was one election, that of Cecil Francis Taylor, in November. Taylor, who was the special friend of Sheppard, was up at Emmanuel.* The election of Taylor was difficult and was complicated by his 'stable but very odd' relations with Sheppard.³ Taylor was finally elected in November, after a débâcle in October, which Keynes described to Duncan Grant in a letter of 18 October 1910: 'Last Saturday at the Society, the horrible embryo question was discussed, – as it always is on the first Saturday of the October term. Of course Sheppard desperately proposed Cecil, and was *very* much depressed by our firmness. I *hated* the whole business.' Moore was present at Taylor's first meeting, at which Taylor 'behaved', wrote Keynes on 15 November, 'as if he had been there every week since he first came up'. Keynes took wings at the same meeting: 'I have been in the Society nearly eight years and have read twenty papers to it. What a stretch of time it seems.'

Moore shared with all Bloomsbury the sense that the most important event of 1910 was the Grafton Galleries exhibition of 'Manet and the Post-Impressionists'. Moore first went to see the pictures on 13 December with James Strachey and was spotted by Desmond MacCarthy, the exhibition secretary, who persuaded him to stay on to hear a lecture by Sickert.

During the years at Richmond, 1908 to 1911, Moore was doing many of the same things as the people who were just beginning to think of

* After leaving Cambridge he became a much loved schoolmaster at Clifton.

themselves as the Bloomsbury Group, and he also met several of the younger people, the Cornfords, Raverats, and the Olivier girls, whom Keynes had dubbed the 'neo-pagans'. Visiting Cambridge in October 1910, he saw them and met, for the first time, David Garnett. With Duncan Grant, whom Moore knew of and had probably met through Keynes, Garnett was one of the few non-Cambridge men in the Bloomsbury set. Moore did not go to Virginia Stephen's Thursday evening *soirées*, but his work was one of the chief topics of conversation at them. The other Miss Stephen, Vanessa, had married Clive Bell, who was intoxicated by *Principia Ethica*, in 1906. Moore's social life in 1910 overlapped with Bloomsbury's, as he saw Desmond MacCarthy continuously and helped him out by taking over from him for some months the editorship of the *New Quarterly*; he was also constantly in the company of Lytton Strachey, and he saw a great deal of James Strachey, much of Oliver and sometimes Marjorie. Norton, Shove and Rupert Brooke figure frequently in his diaries for these years, and he also saw Waterlow, Marsh, Sheppard, Hardy, Hawtrey, Fry, McTaggart and Dickinson. Ainsworth and the friends who were his own age he saw as often as he was able. He and his brother Tom, the poet T. Sturge Moore, had many friends in common, and Moore saw, if anything, more of Tom and his wife Marie than he had done in earlier years.

Keynes was now leading a movement to bring Moore back to Cambridge. On 3 March 1911 he wrote to Duncan Grant: 'We're beginning to intrigue with the object of making Moore a fellow of King's! Wouldn't it be splendid? But I expect nothing will come of it. (This had better be kept private.)' And it was Keynes who first sounded out Moore as to whether he would be interested in a university lectureship. By an extraordinary coincidence, a lectureship had become vacant owing to the election of Keynes's father, J. N. Keynes, the author of *Formal Logic*, as the University Registrar. Moore was so eager to return to Cambridge that he agreed to take up this undesirable post. It was not an endowed lectureship, it did not carry with it a college fellowship, and it paid only about £40 per year, plus students' fees, which could hardly be expected to yield more than another £100. But to Moore, the financial question was unimportant – he had sufficient private means to require no salary, and he yearned to go back to Cambridge in an official capacity. So he celebrated on 3 May 1911, when McTaggart telegraphed that he had been elected to a lectureship.

There was, of course, a drawback. The lecturer had either to replace the elder Keynes, which Moore, being uninterested in the Moods and Figures of the Syllogism was not inclined to do; or he had to lecture on psychology. In the end, Moore felt that what was required for the psychology part I of the moral science tripos was not 'an empirical science at all but a part of philosophy – something which might fairly be said to belong to the Philosophy of Mind.'[4]

Moore had held a reading party that spring, again at Lulworth in Dorset. Sanger, MacCarthy, Ainsworth, Hawtrey, Bob Trevelyan and Mayor joined Lytton Strachey and Moore, who were working on their books commissioned for the Home University Library, Lytton on his *Landmarks in French Literature* and Moore on his little book, *Ethics*. Moore said 'This book I myself like better than *Principia Ethica*, because it seems to be much clearer and far less full of confused and invalid arguments.'[5] Nonetheless, at the end of the smaller book, the reader who requires to see the argument set out and developed fully is referred to *Principia Ethica*.

Now that he was back at Cambridge – as a courtesy to a past fellow he was allowed rooms in Trinity – Moore attended Apostles' meetings regularly. As he was now about fifteen years older than the current members he was not inclined to take too active a part in their choice of new members; but he was usually consulted, and his approval sought, before an election took place. Greenwood introduced one of his students at Emmanuel, Gordon Hannington Luce, to the Apostles, and in his last year Luce became the 250th member in January 1912; on the same occasion the Apostles elected Ferenc István Dénes Gyula Békássy (1893–1915), a Hungarian aristocrat, educated at Bedales and King's. Both men were poets. Keynes wrote to Grant on 23 February 1912: 'As you've probably heard we elected Luce and Békássy on Saturday. The birth was wonderfully easy but Sunday as usual rather unpleasant. The Hun sucked it all down like jujubes, but Lucy turned very much enraged and has left Cambridge for the Holy Land. However I'll say no more and won't drag you into the horrors of our beastly Society.' Luce was a devout follower of Moore; his first letter to Keynes (undated) is an apology for inadvertently carrying off Keynes's own copy of *Principia*. Luce had a first in classics part I, and then read for the English section of the modern languages tripos, in which he got a second. After Cambridge he went to Burma to teach English at the University of Rangoon; he wrote to Keynes in 1912 about the charms of 'Burman' boys, but in 1913 married a Burmese girl. Keynes arranged for Macmillan to publish a small volume of Luce's verse in 1920. In 1939, his son John Marlowe Luce was elected to the Apostles.

The slim volume of verse *Adriatica* published by the Woolfs' Hogarth Press in 1925, a memorial tablet at King's, and a slight article in the

New Hungarian Quarterly for 1971 is all that remains to recall Békássy. After Keynes had lent him the money for his return fare to Hungary, he was killed while fighting in the Hungarian army in Bukovina on the Eastern Front in June 1915. In the preface to the poems, F. L. Lucas, who became an Apostle in January 1914, just before Békássy's departure for Hungary, said:

> 'The unique and fascinating thing about him ... was his gift for being outside and inside himself almost at the same time. He lived in the moment, intensely; but he was bigger than the moment, and saw at once beyond it, how it fitted into the exciting pattern of life, and what part of the past it would hereafter become. The intellectual east wind of Cambridge sharpened him, but never enslaved. He seemed to play his part in life so intelligently – without muddle, seeing through things, yet not casting them aside as therefore worthless.'[6]

Békássy's family lived in splendour at Rum, near Budapest, where Keynes visited him in September 1912. His parents believed strongly in the virtues of English education, and 'Feri' Békássy was very English. But he retained some of his prejudices, and these showed in his voting against the election to the Apostles of a fellow Austro-Hungarian against whom he had 'inherited prejudice'[7]: Ludwig Wittgenstein (1889–1951).

Wittgenstein had been at Manchester University during 1911, when Gottlob Frege advised him to go to Cambridge to study with Russell. Moore first met him in 1912. Later that year, as he wrote to Wittgenstein's cousin, F. A. Hayek:

> 'at the beginning of the October term 1912, he came again to some of my psychology lectures; but he was very displeased with them, because I was spending a great deal of time in discussing Ward's view that psychology did not differ from the Natural Sciences in subject-matter but only in point of view. He told me these lectures were very bad – that what I ought to do was to say what *I* thought, not to discuss what other people had thought; and he came no more to my lectures. But this did not prevent him from seeing a great deal of me. He was very anxious at the beginning of this year to improve the discussion of our philosophical society, which is called the Moral Science Club; and he actually persuaded the Club, with the help of the Secretary and me, to adopt a new set of rules and to appoint me as Chairman. He himself took a great part in these discussions.

'In this year both he and I were still attending Russell's Lectures on the Foundations of Mathematics; but Wittgenstein used also to go for hours to Russell's rooms in the evening to discuss Logic with him.'[8]

Wittgenstein was elected to the Apostles on 16 November 1912, along with Francis Kennard Bliss, a Kingsman from Rugby who got a first in classics part I in 1914. Bliss was killed in action at Thiepval in September 1916, having joined up as a private in the Artists' Rifles; when killed he held that most vulnerable rank in the First World War – 2nd Lieutenant.

Enormous confusion attended the election of Wittgenstein to the Apostles. The election was supported and finally effected by Keynes, against the opposition of Russell, whose motives many Apostles found suspect. Russell, who went to the Society's meeting the week before the election to warn them against electing Wittgenstein, wrote to his mistress Lady Ottoline Morrell on 10 November, 'but they elected him and a man called Bliss.' Russell went on, 'They say W. and Bliss hate each other, but I know nothing of that. I *feel* it will lead to some disaster, but I cannot see any reason for feeling that.'[9] Russell wrote the next day to Keynes, complaining that:

'All the difficulties I anticipated have arisen with Wittgenstein. I persuaded him at last to come to the first meeting and see how he could stand it. Obviously from his point of view the Society is a mere waste of time. But perhaps from a philosophical point of view he might be made to feel it worth going on with. I feel, on reflection, very doubtful whether I did well to persuade him to come next Saturday, as I feel sure he will retire in disgust. But I feel it is the business of the active brethren to settle this before next Saturday. If he is going to retire, it would be better it should be before election.'[10]

Russell's attitude was widely interpreted as jealousy, and a desire to keep his discovery of Wittgenstein to himself. To Sydney-Turner, Lytton Strachey wrote of Russell on 20 November that:

'The poor man is in a sad state. He looks about 96 – with long snow-white hair and an infinitely haggard countenance. The election of Wittgenstein has been a great blow to him. He dearly hoped to keep him all to himself, and indeed succeeded wonderfully, until Keynes at last insisted on meeting him, and saw at once that he was a genius and that it was essential to elect him. The other people (after a slight wobble from Békássy) also became violently in favour. Their decision was suddenly announced to Bertie, who nearly swooned. Of course he could produce no reason against the election – except the remarkable one that the Society was so degraded that his Austrian would certainly refuse to belong to it. He worked himself up into such a frenzy over this that no doubt he got himself into a state of believing it: – but it wasn't any good. Wittgenstein shows no signs of objecting to the Society, though he detests Bliss, who in turn loathes him. I think on the whole the prospects are of the brightest. Békássy is such a pleasant fellow that while he is in love with Bliss, he yet manages to love Wittgenstein. The three of them ought to manage very well, I think. Bertie is really a tragic figure, and I am very sorry for him; but he is most deluded too. Moore is an amazing contrast – fat, rubicund, youthful, and optimistic. He read an old paper – on Conversion – very good and characteristic.'[11]

MacCarthy had received a less dramatic version of the story from Strachey, which he told Moore in a letter from Bayonne, dated 4 December :

'I saw Lytton Strachey in London about a fortnight ago – no three weeks. We dined together and had a long talk. Much of the time we discussed the Society and he succeeded in making me rather less positive in my criticisms. We both hoped Wittgenstein would be elected. He has been; and now you say he may resign! Lytton had heard that the brothers were most indignant with Russell for having (I could not gather what had passed) talked to W. in a way likely to dissuade him from accepting election. You must write and tell me what is going on, if I do not see you soon. Lytton thought the Society limp; but he thought that their lassitude in discussion was due to the fact that they were less naive and more mature than the previous generation, that they just felt that such and such views were absurd, without having much to say about them, and such and such questions too complicated to discuss adequately. He thought that since your advent and Russell's, that philosophy had grown much more a subject for specialists and therefore that there was some excuse for the attitude of the brothers towards such questions. I felt rather doubtful about these explanations, but was glad when I heard Wittgenstein was elected for he *is* I suppose as eager to find reasons and definitions as you were, and he struck me as a passionate arguer.'[12]

Strachey wrote to Moore the same day, saying that Turner had told him that Wittgenstein was still thinking of resigning. If there was an 'imminent crisis', Strachey wrote, perhaps he ought himself to come to the next Apostles' meeting and talk to Wittgenstein: 'I might possibly be able to give the fellow a more correct and sensible notion of the Society than, so far as I can see, he at present has. On the other hand it might be only an added disturbance.' Moore had a high opinion of Strachey's diplomatic skills, for he replied by return of post (in a letter beginning, unusually, 'Dear Lytton'; for Strachey had so signed himself in his letter of the 4th):

'All that I know about the matter is this. I had a long talk with Wittgenstein, more than a fortnight ago, in which it appeared quite plainly that he was doubtful whether he wouldn't resign: his reason being that he couldn't see that it was worthwhile for him to spend the time discussing with Békássy and Bliss. I saw Gerald [Shove] last Saturday, who had also found out exactly the same thing: Wittgenstein had begged him to come to the Society, so that he mightn't be alone with Békássy and Bliss; and Gerald thought he might resign at any moment. And of course Wittgenstein practically told Turner the same thing on Saturday evening.

'I haven't heard anything at all since Sunday. I tried to find Keynes today, but he was out. So I don't know whether anything may have happened since, to make it likely that he will resign at all, or that he will resign *soon*. You see all I have reason to suppose is that he might make up his mind to resign *at any time*. That he's likely to resign soon, I haven't any reason to suppose; as that I don't know that any crisis is *imminent*.

'But unless something has happened since to make him decide to stay on, I think it would be a very useful thing if you could make him understand the point of the Society. I expect you could do it: and he certainly didn't understand last Saturday. I tried to argue with him about it, but I expect I did more harm than good. I wish you could explain to me, at the same time, what the real point is: but perhaps you can't do that.

'. . . I don't see how you could possibly do any harm; and if you can make him see the point, I think you'd better come, as otherwise he may resign before you get the chance.'[13]

Strachey replied the next day, 6 December, that 'though to be sure it sounds pretty grim', he would come on the Monday. Too late, Moore told him when he wrote back on the 8th, 'The crisis has already come;

he has resigned some time this week. But I hope it is not too late for you to have a chance of making him change his mind.' Moore's intuition was correct – Strachey was the one person who could mollify Wittgenstein. Strachey came to Cambridge as scheduled, and persuaded Wittgenstein not to resign; though he does not appear to have had any success in convincing Wittgenstein to take an active part in the Society's proceedings, and Wittgenstein's name simply drops out of sight in further correspondence about the Apostles of this time.

What was the fuss really all about? In a letter to Michael Holroyd dated 14 September 1966, Russell denied that he had been upset about Wittgenstein and the Apostles in language as vigorous as that in which Strachey had accused him of being worried about it:

'I knew nothing at the time about Wittgenstein's relations with the Society, nor had I any strong views as to whether he should be elected or not. I was interested in his intellectual potentialities, but I should have been glad of any outside influences that distracted him from the long monologues, lasting sometimes through the night, well into morning, during which he examined his own mind and motives. I do not think that I ever "worked myself into a frenzy" or "got quite ill" with any private worry, and, though I had anxieties at that time which were severe, they had nothing to do with the Society. I cannot imagine how the people whom you cite got these impressions of me, unless they thought the affairs of the Society were more important than I did at that time. I never felt any "mortification" at Wittgenstein being elected, nor can I think why I should have felt any such emotion.'[14]

It was untrue when Russell said that he 'had no strong views as to whether he should be elected or not', for he had, as he wrote to Lady Ottoline, attended the Society's meeting on 9 November 'to warn them of the dangers about Wittgenstein'.[15] Old men forget, but one cannot help feeling that Russell was concealing something – perhaps exactly what he stood accused of by Strachey. Equally likely, and a better explanation of Russell's nonagenarian fib, was that Russell wished to keep Wittgenstein out of the rival orbit of Moore's influence.

Wittgenstein's own behaviour is, in some respects, much easier to understand. A member of a cultivated Viennese industrial family, Wittgenstein had a particular dislike for Békássy, a scion of the landed Hungarian aristocracy. This was pure prejudice, and it was reciprocated. Bliss seems not to have had any great aptitude for philosophical discussion; and sometimes they would have been the only members present on a Saturday night, as James Strachey, Taylor and Luce had gone down, Rupert Brooke was having emotional difficulties and only made sporadic appearances, Norton and Shove were not regular in their attendance, and Moore, Russell, Keynes and the other angels at Cambridge did not attend as frequently as they had done in the past.

But there was another reason. Wittgenstein was this autumn 'on the verge of a nervous breakdown, not far removed from suicide, feeling himself a miserable creature, full of sin', so Russell wrote to Lady Ottoline on 31 October 1912. 'I hate seeing his misery – it is so real, and I know it all so well, I can see it is almost beyond what any human being can be expected to bear. I don't know whether any outside misfortune has contributed to it or not. I had him to meet Keynes yesterday, but it was a failure. W. was too ill to argue properly.'[16]

Wittgenstein was in no mood just then for silliness, and this was a particularly unpropitious time to introduce him to the Society, for it *was* 'degraded'. As Strachey said, Bliss and Békássy did have a close attachment; this would not have bothered Wittgenstein, had they not been so frivolous about their own relationship and sex in general. Wittgenstein was homosexual himself, but he could not abide the schoolgirlish part of the attitude that is summed up in the expression the Higher Sodomy. Though Russell may have had his own reasons for warning the Society against Wittgenstein, he was perfectly correct about what Wittgenstein's reaction to the Society would be. Wittgenstein simply could not have a tolerable discussion with the younger Apostles; the equally flamboyant homosexuality of Keynes and Strachey did not disturb him, for he could speak to them as easily as he could to their elders, Russell and Moore.

(Wittgenstein did formally resign from the Apostles many years later. After the war and his capture and imprisonment by the Allies, Wittgenstein did not return to Cambridge until 1929. He then re-joined the Apostles. On 19 January he was elected an honorary member at a supper meeting given by Keynes to Sheppard, Shove, W. J. H. (Sebastian) Sprott, Richard Braithwaite, Frank Ramsay, George (Dadie) Rylands, G. D. Thompson, D. W. Lucas, Dennis Robertson, Alister Watson, Anthony Blunt and Julian Bell. Wittgenstein attended the subsequent meetings and on 20 April was 'declared to have been absolved from his excommunication at the appropriate time'.)

Moore had again taken his reading party to the Lizard in 1912: this year he had MacCarthy, Bob Trevelyan, Ainsworth, Sheppard and the latter's friend (Strachey and Keynes cattily called him 'Madam') Taylor, who was about to go down after the next term. In 1913 the last reading party was held at Becky House on Dartmoor. It was sadly depleted, and consisted only of MacCarthy and Moore himself.

But it was Wittgenstein whose personality impressed itself upon everyone and everything in these few years before the war. The Apostles were so un-nerved by their scrape with him that they only managed to elect two new members until after the war was over : Frank Lawrence (Peter) Lucas in January 1914 and the pianist, Maurice Oswald Marshall, in the following November. Russell, for better or worse, was completely bound up intellectually with his pupil; Moore was not so involved as that with Wittgenstein, but their relationship was also stormy. Wittgenstein was so emotionally volatile that an intellectual disagreement or an imagined social slight was quite enough to make him attempt to break off all relations.[17]

During the Easter vacation of 1914 Moore accepted Wittgenstein's invitation to visit him in Norway :

'I arrived late on March 26th, 1914, and found W. there to meet me. We spent two nights at Bergen, and then went on by train, sledge, steamer and motor boat to Skolden where Wittgenstein was staying, spending one night on the way at Flaam, at a hotel which was mostly shut up, because it was out of season; W. had arranged beforehand that we should be able to sleep there, but we were the only guests. I was with him at Skolden only 15 days. He dictated to me there some notes on logic, which I still have and which I let von Wright see recently.[18] He also took me to a site where he proposed to build a house; but the house which he afterwards actually built near Skolden was on a different site. At the end of 15 days he accompanied me back to Bergen, and we again spent one night together at Flaam, and one night at Bergen. It was during this visit that I first learnt that W. suffered from a rupture and had to wear a special kind of belt : he bought a belt of the right kind at Bergen.'[19]

Thus Moore got to know Wittgenstein well, and summed up his intellectual relationship with Wittgenstein in his autobiography :

'When I did get to know him, I soon came to feel that he was much cleverer at philosophy than I was, and not only cleverer, but also much more profound, and with a much better insight into the sort of inquiry which was really important and best worth pursuing, and into the best method of pursuing such inquiries. I did not see him again after 1914, until he returned to Cambridge in 1929; but when his *Tractatus Logico-Philosophicus* came out, I read it again and again, trying to learn from it. It is a book which I admired and do admire extremely. There is, of course, a great deal in it which I was not able to understand; but many things I thought I did understand, and found them very enlightening. When he came back to Cambridge in 1929 I attended his lectures for several years in succession, always with admiration. How far he has influenced positively anything that I have written, I cannot tell; but he certainly has had the effect of making me very distrustful about many things which, but for him, I should have been inclined to assert positively. He has made me think that what is required for the solution of philosophical problems which baffle me, is a method quite different from any which I have ever used – a method which he himself uses successfully, but which I have never been able to understand clearly enough to use it myself.'[20]

Emotionally the relationship of Moore and Wittgenstein was seldom on an even keel. Their correspondence is full of quarrels and apologies for having them, and more than once, Wittgenstein attempted to break off relations altogether. Wittgenstein's relations were like this with nearly everybody, but Moore was not used to such capricious displays of temperament, and bewilderment was very often his first response to Wittgenstein's show of temper. Still, Moore several times records in his diary that he has lost his own temper with Wittgenstein, and once, on 31 April 1914 at lunch in Norway with Wittgenstein, that he nearly cried. Their relationship did have its rewards, even apart from philosophy. For example, their musical tastes and talents were alike, and there are several people who can recall the occasions marked by Moore in his diary, when Wittgenstein would *whistle* the violin's part of a concerto while Moore took the entire orchestra's part at the piano.

Moore and Wittgenstein did have one serious breach, entirely owing to a misunderstanding on Wittgenstein's part, which resulted in their having no contact with each other from 1914 until Wittgenstein's return to Cambridge in 1929. Wittgenstein had probably submitted an essay in 1914 for the degree of BA, so that he could work at Cambridge as an Advanced Student. He seems to have infringed some petty regulation, and wished Moore to intercede on his behalf with the Trinity College authorities, which Moore probably did do. Wittgenstein seems to have thought that it was Moore himself who was unwilling to make an exception of his case, but this was untrue. Moore was too downcast by Wittgenstein's hostile letter of 7 May 1914[21] to bring himself to answer the friendlier one of 3 July.[22] Moore noted receipt of the letter in his diary entry for 13 July: 'Think I won't answer it, because I really don't want to see him again!'

Ten days later, when Russell talked to Moore about his own quarrel with Wittgenstein, it made Moore 'doubt again whether I oughtn't to write to Wittgenstein'. He did not write, but was reminded of Wittgenstein again in the summer, when on 27 August he lost the copy of Frege lent him by Wittgenstein, and made desperate but unsuccessful efforts to find it. The next diary entry concerning Wittgenstein is not until 18 October, when Russell told Moore that Wittgenstein had joined the Austrian army as an artillery soldier and had been sent to Cracow. Moore now stopped avoiding Russell in hall, and even brought himself to shake hands with him – an attempt at reconciliation over their *contretemps* concerning Wittgenstein's Notes on Logic; but it failed, and on the 20th and again on the 23rd Moore shunned Russell's company.

On 18 January 1915 Moore told MacCarthy 'all about Wittgenstein', which presaged more bad feeling between Moore and Russell. Wittgenstein and Russell had both been in the habit of putting their complaints about Moore in writing, since Wittgenstein's first letter to Russell of June 1912,[23] when he told Russell how much he disliked *Principia Ethica*. Now on 20 January 1915 Russell showed Moore a letter from Wittgenstein, in which he said 'I find it inconceivable that Moore wasn't able to explain my ideas to you.' (Wittgenstein was referring to the ideas of the 'Notes Dictated to G. E. Moore in Norway'. These notes on logic he dictated to Moore at Skolden in spring of 1914.) Moore was furious: 'Russell must have told him I couldn't [explain Wittgenstein's ideas]: but he had no right to say this, because he had never tried to get me to explain them.' Then on 10 February Moore noted that he disliked Russell's conversation in hall: 'Russell asks to see my notes of Wittgenstein.' And this made Moore reflect on his relations with Wittgenstein: 'Think what ought to do about Wittgenstein and what is right generally.'

On 14 February Russell gave Moore a letter Keynes had received from Wittgenstein. It was Russell's way of firing the next shot in his battle with Moore, for its last sentence was: 'I wonder if Russell has been able to make anything out from the notes I gave to Moore last Easter?'[24] By 29 April Moore had relented a bit; he had shown Russell Wittgenstein's dictated notes, but Russell still could not make out Wittgenstein's views; Moore was pleased to learn from Russell in hall that night that he had heard from Wittgenstein's mother, and that

Wittgenstein was in a 'safe place'. Moore noted on 17 May, ten days after he learned of the sinking of the *Lusitania*, that it occurred to him at tea to write a 'Diary about what I feel about Wittgenstein'.

Wittgenstein's name doesn't recur in Moore's existing diary until 7 August 1915, when Moore was visiting the Wedgwoods and was asked by their great friend Richard Curle (who edited Julia Wedgwood's letters and was also a friend of Joseph Conrad), to talk about his quarrel with Wittgenstein. It was then that Curle and Iris Wedgwood bluntly asked Moore 'about [Wittgenstein's] being normal (about women) which I don't like'.

Moore's last reference to Wittgenstein, until their accidental reunion in 1929 when they found themselves on the same train, is poignant. It was 12 October 1915, and Moore wrote: 'Dream of Wittgenstein, he looks at me as if to ask if it is all right, and I can't help smiling as if it was, though I know it isn't; then he is swimming in the sea; finally he is trying to escape arrest as an enemy alien.' Part of the dream was prophecy: Wittgenstein was not arrested as an enemy alien, but he was captured as an enemy soldier and imprisoned in southern Italy in November 1918.

Another celebrated person figures in Moore's life in these years. Virginia Stephen had cultivated an interest in Moore's writings and doings several years before her marriage to Leonard Woolf. It was at the urging of her brother-in-law, Clive Bell, that she began reading *Principia Ethica* in 1908, and it was to him that she wrote the first of a profusion of letters describing the saga of her struggle with the book. From Wells on 3 August she said: 'I am climbing Moore like some industrious insect, who is determined to build a nest on top of a cathedral spire. One sentence, a string of "desires" makes my head spin with the infinite meaning of words unadorned; otherwise I have gone happily.' And a week later she wrote to Saxon Sydney-Turner of her 'nightly 10 pages of Moore', and soon after that another letter to him about the difficulties she was having with the book. Then again to Clive Bell on the 19th: 'I split my head over Moore every night, feeling ideas travelling to the remotest part of my brain, and setting up a feeble disturbance, hardly to be called thought.' Finally, she wrote from Pembrokeshire to her sister Vanessa on the 29th: 'I finished Moore last night; he has a fine flair of arrogance at the end – and no wonder. I am not so dumb foundered as I was; but the more I understand, the more I admire. He is so humane in spite of his desire to know the truth; and I believe I can disagree with him, over one matter.'[25]

In late June 1914 Moore spent three nights at Asheham House as the guest of the Woolfs. Moore and Virginia Woolf may have met before, possibly at the Sangers in London. But his stay with them from 27–30 June is the first meeting that can be documented; and Moore's diary entry provided a different view of his relationship with the great novelist than the one presented by Leonard Woolf in *Beginning Again*. There the latter says that Virginia Woolf was

> 'deeply affected by the astringent influence of Moore and the purification of that divinely cathartic question which echoed through the Cambridge Courts of my youth as it had 2300 years before echoed through the streets of Socratic Athens: "What do you mean by that?" Artistically the purification can, I think, be traced in the clarity, light, absence of humbug in Virginia's literary style.'[26]

Woolf maintained strongly that Moore was the only philosopher who had any influence upon his wife's work – meaning specifically to exclude Bergson – and thought that Moore was the only modern philosophy Virginia Woolf ever read.[27] But he never commented on what happened at Moore's and Virginia Woolf's infrequent meetings. Here are Moore's diary jottings for the Asheham visit – written in a style very like the book he was then reading:

> '27, Sat. to Charles Baker's and Marie's for music. Lunch at Mac-Carthy's: Sydney-Turner there. Walk with Woolf to top of Downs after tea. Sing in evening. On Sun. walk with Woolf to Tilscombe Cliff, meet Virginia and MacCarthy on way back. Read "Diary of a Nobody" in evening, but don't find amusing. On M. walk with Woolf to Seaford and bathe.'

If Moore and Mrs Woolf had a great deal to talk about it seems not to have struck Moore as noteworthy enough to record, and though Virginia Woolf did not begin to keep her own, more famous diary until the next year, she did re-work the visit in her letters. She had originally invited Lytton Strachey to be Moore's fellow guest, but in the event it was Lytton's sister Pernel who shared Moore's stay – and the combination was a success. Virginia wrote to Vanessa Bell on 25 August 1916 that 'Moore sang to us every night. He is quite easy and much more human than his followers; but one can see how they've copied him, but he has much more vigour than they have. Perhaps they no longer exist though.' And to Sydney-Turner she wrote on 30 September a letter that shows that Moore had retained the enthusiasms he had remarked on in his own letters to his family in his early undergraduate days:

> 'We had Moore to stay with us at Asheham. He . . . came with a box like lead, and it was full of music books, which he meant to sing to us, but we had no piano, so he sang without one – some very nice old German and English songs. Do you know one about the "foggy foggy dew", and another about "lost in the Lowland seas"? He is a very great man, I think, so solid and direct: and not the least hard to talk to. He knows all the wild flowers and butterflies. He spent his time writing a review, and when he went he had scratched it all out and begun a new one.'[28]

Snapshots of Moore taken in the course of that visit show that he had acquired the paunch of middle-age, though he was not yet forty-one.

The visit to Asheham resulted in Moore's having a kind of immortality conferred upon him. When dining in hall at Trinity on 12 April 1915, the Rev. F. A. Simpson (the historian of the Second Empire) asked Moore if he had seen the reference to himself in the new novel. 'Which novel?' Moore wondered in his diary entry for that day. It was, of course, *The Voyage Out*, Virginia Woolf's first novel, which he discussed with a friend at Newnham on 7 May and called 'Virginia's book'. In those of Moore's diaries that survive, only one other woman of his acquaintance – Iris (Mrs Ralph, later Lady) Wedgwood is referred to by Christian name (Iris Wedgwood's letters to Moore begin 'Dear Dormouse'; she and Moore were very fond of each other). Moore and Virginia Woolf were in fact on more intimate terms than one would guess from the paucity of the mentions of each in the other's diaries. For example, Moore and Desmond MacCarthy called casually on the Woolfs at Hogarth House, Richmond, the day after an Apostles' dinner,[29] and when Nicholas Moore was born, the Moores felt close enough to the Woolfs to see that they were informed of the birth the very same day though Virginia Woolf and Dorothy Moore did not meet until 1923.[30]

The First World War took some time to make an impression on Moore. At the end of July 1914 he spent several days with the Oliver Stracheys at Clark's End, near Pangbourne. Ray Strachey's sister Karin Costelloe (she had not yet married Adrian Stephen) and Keynes were the other house guests; Moore lost the considerable sum of 16s 6d to Keynes at Auction Bridge. Keynes was an inveterate gambler, and perhaps this was why Moore noted that 'Keynes somehow leaves bad taste in my mouth'. On Tuesday, 4 August, Moore did not seem to be aware that war had begun, but the next day he began a habit he would continue through most of the war, of going to the union for the news – sometimes several times a day. By the 11th, Moore noted in his diary, he was packing clothes for the Red Cross. But in spite of keeping almost constant company at Trinity with Harry Norton and G. H. Hardy, who were both anti-war, it took Moore a very long time to reach his own conclusions on the issue.

The Apostles were badly divided over the war, with some older men like Jackson, Ward, McTaggart and Whitehead being ferociously in favour of killing Germans, and the youngest, Bliss and Lucas, enlisting, as their immediate predecessors, Békássy and Wittgenstein did on the other side. The intermediate generations of Apostles, the Strachey brothers, Keynes, Sydney-Turner, Woolf, Norton and Shove, were, with the exception of Rupert Brooke, vehemently opposed to the war. Dickinson, Sanger and Russell too were anti-war. Pro-Germanism, especially when it took the mild form of admiration for German culture, was widespread among the war's opponents.

By mid-August, Russell was beginning to give expression to his anti-war opinions in hall. Moore was not very well disposed to Russell just then: he disliked being in his company and subjected anything Russell said to more careful scrutiny than usual. Moore was not easily to be convinced by Russell's arguments against the war. Russell's position and that of the Bloomsbury Apostles has often, even by themselves, been described as pacifist. This usage is unfortunate, because it erodes the useful distinction between those who opposed this war in particular for political or moral reasons, and those who thought *all* war wrong. The positions became clearer in 1916, when conscription was introduced, and most of those who were of service age were conscientious objectors; the grounds of their objections then showed whether or not they were total pacifists. The total pacifist position was easier to maintain before the tribunals that heard the cases against conscientious objectors, at least in part because its resemblance to a religious conviction made it more palatable to the local government officials (often ex-servicemen) who so often ran the Appeals Tribunals. Lytton Strachey, for example, risked jail when he explicitly disavowed the total pacifist position in his heroic and historic hearing before the Hampstead Tribunal on 7 March 1916:

'I have a conscientious objection to assisting, by any deliberate action of mine, in carrying on the war. This objection is not based on religious belief, but upon moral considerations, at which I arrived after long and careful thought. I do not wish to assert the extremely general proposition that I should never in any circumstances, be justified in taking part in any conceivable war; to dogmatize so absolutely upon a point so abstract would appear to me to be un-reasonable. At the same time, my feeling is directed not simply against the present war: I am convinced that the whole system by which it is sought to settle international disputes by force is pro-foundly evil; and that, so far as I am concerned, I should be doing wrong to take any active part in it.

'These conclusions have crystallized in my mind since the out-break of war. . . . My convictions as to my duty with regard to the war have not been formed either rashly or lightly; and I shall not act against those convictions, whatever the consequences may be.'[31]

G. E. Moore's influence is present not only in the language, but in the sentiments of that statement.

One of the great lacunae in Moore's autobiography, and in every book or article ever written that mentions Bloomsbury and the war, is the absence of any account of Moore's own attitude to the war. Not only Strachey, but other opponents of the war like Norton, Shove, Sydney-Turner, James Strachey, Clive Bell, Leonard Woolf, Lowes Dickinson and even Russell himself, were so used to taking their lead from Moore in matters of this sort that it is inconceivable that none of them should have tried to learn Moore's opinion on the war, and un-likely that any of them should have become so militant in their opposi-tion to the prosecution of the war without Moore's at least tacit bless-ing. But there is not a word about Moore's feelings about the war in Keynes's memoir or in the autobiographies of Russell or Woolf. Neither Leonard Woolf nor Ralph Hawtrey could even remember what Moore had thought or said about the war.[32]

Moore's position was unmemorable because he took so long to arrive at it – and even then he never shared Strachey's or Russell's certainty in the rightness of their own positions. He was first challenged to say what he thought of the war on 16 August, when Ward brought an officer to dine in hall at Trinity : 'Ward asks if I am going to fight; I say "Not, unless I have to;" he says it's fortunate others don't say the same.' Moore's candour probably upset Ward no more than the sight of soldiers everywhere in Cambridge distressed Moore. In late August there were soldiers at Moore's favourite bathing-place, on all his favourite walks, and on the 20th, a general and his entire staff dined at

Trinity. By 29 August Moore found it remarkable that there were *no* officers in hall that night. The next day Moore met Rupert Brooke at the union, and was told of his application for a commission (which he eventually got through the offices – good or evil – of Eddie Marsh), and a few days later, on 5 September, the eminent mathematician J. E. Littlewood told Moore that he 'means to join Regular Army as private'. The war was the principal topic of conversation in hall and in the Combination Room, which was in one way a blessing to Moore: now, in spite of his extreme shyness and the difficulty in making small talk that had formerly paralysed his tongue at the High Table, he always had something to talk about that was guaranteed to be of interest to everyone – the latest war news. Hardy returned to Cambridge (after the long vacation) on 25 September, and immediately took up a distinctive position on the war: 'Hardy just back, thinks we ought to make peace as soon as France and Belgium are safe.' Hardy soon became one of the people whose opinions on the war most interested Moore; from autumn, 1914 until Moore's diaries break off in 1916 (the later diaries were destroyed), Hardy's views on all aspects of the war are recorded. Those who themselves had an influence on Moore were mostly anti-war. For example, on 9 October Dora Sanger came to lunch: 'she is very miserable about war, and thinks we are much to blame.'

About this time Moore's attention was diverted from the war by Norbert Wiener, the twenty-year-old American prodigy who was attending Moore's lectures, and began by reducing Moore to despair by making criticisms that both he and Moore knew the other listeners could not possibly understand. This put Moore's spirits alternately down and up: on the 22nd Wiener made him feel 'it's no use for me to lecture'; but the next day Moore was comforted because Wiener didn't 'disprove me'.

From the viewpoint of Moore's emotional life, this was merely a distraction from the question that was growing more pressing: what should he do about the war? Lucas came to Moore on 24 October to ask Moore to call on him that night, when he broke the news that he had applied for a commission. Keynes came along later and said, 'war has destroyed his opinions of Germans; he didn't think they would seriously believe and act on such absurd principles, as war had shown they do.' This statement by Keynes nicely captures the pro-German background against which such points were argued. The next day Moore visited Johnson, where he showed an interest in a very different aspect of the war: 'Belgian and his wife there till after 6; stay on because they begin asking questions about war and different types of ships.'

Thereafter, during the next month, though he discussed little but the wrongness of the war with Hardy, and talked to Mary Fletcher of Newnham of the 'horrors of war', his conversation with Hardy on 6 November about the latest estimates of German casualties was more representative of what interested Moore about the war. Although he was reading Bernard Shaw and Norman Angell on the war that month, he had to confess that he did not yet share their feelings. He wrote to Desmond MacCarthy on 15 November, in a letter that demonstrates again his remarkable candour:

'I don't understand people being really *miserable* about the war; though I rather admire people who are, and feel rather ashamed that I can't be. I believe, really and truly, it gives me much more pleasure than pain, simply because I am so interested in it; and though I do truly believe that war is horrible, and though, if I could, I would arrange that there should never be any, I can't really *feel* miserable about it, though no doubt I should if I saw the horrible things. But, so far as I can gather, Russell does really *feel* miserable, and so does Sanger, and a few others. But I think most people are much more like me.'[33]

Admirable though Moore felt Russell's sentiments to be, he still couldn't bring himself to face the man who held them: on 27 November he was so desperate to avoid sitting next to Russell in hall that he had to arrange for another place to be laid next to Simpson. But two days later he was within earshot of Russell, whom he heard say 'that in 1887 when we were friends with Germany we approved of her plan of marching through Belgium'. Moore was not swayed by anti-German propaganda; he wrote of a lecture that he heard on 30 November that it was 'horrible – all suspicious of German intentions'.

At this time he was seeing a very great deal of Mary Fletcher, and in early January, his sister Nellie said 'she hoped I would marry Miss F.' So did Mary Fletcher. But Moore was not ready to make up his mind. In early December, he had had tea, discussed philosophy and played duets with Miss Fletcher nearly every day; but on the 4th he had met Margaret Darwin and noted in his diary: 'she *is* nice.' Just before Christmas Moore moved to new rooms, as troops had been billeted in his court, and he decided on reflection that it would be wiser to remove himself.

Saxon Sydney-Turner surprised Moore on 3 January 1915, by being vehemently anti-German. And on the 9th Rouse Ball, a Trinity don, astonished him by saying in Combination Room that Kitchener expected an invasion. The whole of the afternoon of the 19th Moore spent discussing the war with MacCarthy. He was making up his mind, and by that evening, when Hardy came to inquire, he had made his decision. The next day he came out against the war and became a founder member of the Cambridge branch of the Union of Democratic Control.

Russell claimed that he had organized the Cambridge branch of the UDC and found willing recruits especially among the dons at Trinity[34]; it is not impossible that this is the truth, but the founding meeting was held in Lowes Dickinson's rooms at King's on 20 January 1915. Russell was one of the founding fathers of the national UDC:

> 'A few pacifist M.P.'s, together with two or three sympathizers, began to have meetings at the Morrells' house in Bedford Square. I used to attend these meetings, which gave rise to the Union of Democratic Control. I was interested to observe that many of the pacifist politicians were more concerned with the question which of them should lead the anti-war movement than with the actual work against the War. Nevertheless, they were all there was to work with, and I did my best to think well of them.'[35]

The Union of Democratic Control was not a pacifist organization. It had three main aims: first, to see that parliament had actual control over foreign policy, so that secret treaties like those entered into by Sir Edward Grey and presented to the country as *faits accomplis* would no longer be possible; second, to establish links with genuinely democratic continental political *parties*, with whom open negotiations could be conducted after the war, instead of dealing with governments; and third, to reach agreement on peace terms that would not 'through the humiliation of the defeated nation or an artificial re-arrangement of frontiers merely become the starting point for new national antagonisms and future wars'.[36] Some of the founders were total pacifists – Lord Ponsonby and the Quaker Joseph Rowntree certainly were but Trevelyan's position was not so clear cut* and Ramsay MacDonald,

---

* Sir Charles Trevelyan, 3rd Bt, (1870–1958) provided the main impetus for founding the UDC. He had, for some years before the war, been an opponent of Grey's policies, and resigned his position as Private Secretary at the Board of Education when war was declared. His views were somewhere between those of his brothers. George Trevelyan had favoured British neutrality but became the commandant of the first British Ambulance Unit for Italy from 1915 to 1918; in 1918 Robert Trevelyan applied for recognition as a non-religious conscientious objector on total pacifist principles.

despite efforts to make him out a pro-German pacifist, was neither of those things. 'There were men', wrote Russell, 'in the Union of Democratic Control, who, without having definite opinions about wars in general, thought that our pre-war diplomacy had been at fault, and that the belief in the sole guilt of Germany was a dangerous falsehood.'[37]

In 1914 the UDC was a fairly respectable group, high-minded and catholic enough to appeal to most people of the Left, liberals as well as socialists, except that it was quite openly and unabashedly against the war. This position was merely unpopular – at Cambridge as everywhere – until the sinking of the *Lusitania* in May 1915 hardened hearts and opinion. So when Moore joined, the disapproval of McTaggart, Jackson, Whitehead, Ward and the other war-like dons of Trinity was the fiercest opposition he had to face – and Russell's more radical position drew most of their wrath away from Moore. Moore was over forty, and there was as yet no conscription, so no suspicion of evading one's military responsibilities could then attach to a step like joining the UDC. After the *Lusitania* things were different. The geriatric warriors of Trinity then sniped at Norton and even Moore from what, Russell pointed out, was a position of complete safety from the call-up. Moore stuck with the UDC (which itself survived even the Second World War) through the whole of the war, having occasional flirtations, after the introduction of conscription in 1916, with the more radical organization, the No Conscription Fellowship, which attracted Russell and much of Bloomsbury to its ranks.

Moore's main service to the younger Bloomsbury men was, in a way, philosophical, as when, for example, on 19 July 1915 he discussed conscientious objection with Hardy and C. D. Broad, and was congratulated after hall by Norton for his explanation of the meaning of the phrase 'conscientious objection'. As the war went on and general conscription was introduced, this became crucial to those who had an objection to taking part in the war, whether as soldiers or also in any form of war work ('absolutism'), for the only men with ready-made arguments against serving were Quakers and members of a very few other religious sects. Lytton Strachey's statement, and those of his brother James, Norton, Duncan Grant, Adrian Stephen, David Garnett, Bob Trevelyan and many others owed a great deal to Moore's clarifications of the various grounds for having a conscientious objection to serving. Moore read and assimilated the arguments of everyone against the war: E. D. Morel, Norman Angell, Clive Bell, Russell, and the pacifist Independent Labour Party.

After the sinking of the *Lusitania*, which Moore seemed to agree with Norton was 'more inexcusable than anything else the Germans have done', Moore's attitude to his own stance on the war became ambivalent. On the one hand he felt keenly the pressure of ordinary opinion about men of military age not being in uniform, and was worried that summer when he visited Fred and Sally Ainsworth in London, that people would think he was 'a slacker' when they saw him pushing his nephew in his pram. On the other hand he was worried that active support for the UDC fell short of the fullest possible commitment to anti-war work; the diary entry for 25 May reads: 'Troubled in conscience with idea I ought to be working to get the war over.' Was this statement ambiguous? Could it have meant that he thought he ought to enlist or do war work instead of remaining a don? This interpretation is unlikely, but Moore had been relieved to learn earlier that month from Lytton Strachey that Desmond MacCarthy was no longer under fire driving an ambulance in France, but was employed in the War Office under Oliver Strachey.

Things got worse as the summer of 1915 went on. On 20 July Norton informed Moore that Békássy had been killed. Moore spent 13–16 August with Lytton and his sister Pippa Strachey at Lockeridge; they talked of little but the war. The question of conscription hung heavy in the air. There were reports that the cabinet was divided on the issue, but on 5 October Lord Derby began his infamous recruiting scheme designed to induce men who had not enlisted to do so on the condition that they would not be forced to serve before other men who had less strong claims to exemption. This was meant to be a voluntary plan: men were to 'attest', to agree to enlist whenever called upon to do so, but the obligation was to be moral, not legal. In fact the Derby Scheme led only to coercion and blackmail, whether by elderly employers (James Strachey was so treated by his cousin and editor on the *Spectator*, St Loe Strachey) or by hawkish, greybeard Trinity dons. Worse, the scheme helped make conscription acceptable to moderate opinion, which had heretofore regarded it as the supreme encroachment on the liberty that supporters of the war claimed they were fighting to defend. By Christmas the Derby Scheme had failed to produce the needed manpower, and the government proposed to conscript all unmarried men under forty-five who were physically fit and not exempt on grounds that they did work of national importance or had exceptional domestic responsibilities. That measure too was insufficient, and by May 1916 there was general conscription.

In November 1915 the UDC became involved in a battle with the council of Trinity College, the governing body of the college which was composed only of permanent fellows, and had, therefore, a large majority of Trinity's aged fierce patriots. (This was the same body that eight months later deprived Russell of his college lectureship.) A meeting had been scheduled for Thursday, 18 November, in Littlewood's rooms in Trinity, where C. R. Buxton was going to address a private meeting of the UDC on the subject of the Balkans. The college authorities forbade the meeting to take place within the walls of Trinity, and when the committee of the UDC learned that they had been banned, they engaged a room at the Liberal Club, only to be informed on the day before the meeting by the chairman of the club that he had taken it upon himself to forbid the UDC the use of their premises. The resulting furore was terrific, and much of the noise was made by Moore.

A good deal of the *Cambridge Magazine* for 27 November was taken up with comments, statements and a letter from Moore on the banning of the UDC. A statement was issued by the committee of the Cambridge Branch of the UDC* which stated the aims of the organization and remarked:

'The Chairman of the Committee of the Liberal Club gave as his reason the existence of a feeling that the holding of the meeting would be contrary to the national welfare. In what sense the giving of an address on the Balkans by Mr Buxton to a private meeting of a society existing for the purpose stated can be regarded as contrary to the national welfare, we are at a loss to understand.

'The members of the Cambridge Branch of the Union of Democratic Control claim to be as good citizens and patriots as their opponents. Many of its members hold commissions in the Army and are fighting in the trenches. The principles for which they stand have been endorsed in whole or in part by the Prime Minister and other members of His Majesty's Government. And the members conceive that they have a right to advocate them publicly within the limits allowed by the law.'[38]

And the editorial of the *Cambridge Magazine* said:

'We are delighted to have secured a contribution from the author of *Principia Ethica* on the subject of the Council of Trinity College. . . . With regard to the general problem raised we do not wish to say more at present, save to voice the almost universal feeling of the University that the Council have been guilty of an indiscretion which will not readily be forgotten.'[39]

* J. Baker, E. Cunningham, G. Lowes Dickinson, G. H. Hardy, B. A. Howard, L. E. Matthaei, E. Power and R. R. Sedgwick.

The issue, the editors pointed out, had now become one of freedom of speech, and the UDC had gained sympathizers who, like the *Magazine* itself, did not care about the problem of the Balkans or the aims of the UDC. Moore habitually saw both sides of a question; though he was a member of it, he could see that there was a case against the UDC's position, but there was no case for refusing to let the UDC carry on its discussions. Native reticence made Moore reluctant to advertise his feelings about the war, and he was worried and anxious about the reaction of his peers and the fellows of Trinity to his association with the UDC. But he could not keep silent about this denial of elementary rights, and on Saturday, 27 November, he was 'really afraid and in a fever' about the long and bitter satirical letter printed under the headline 'Suggestions for the Council of Trinity College'.

'Dear Sir,
'The spirited action, on the part of the Council of Trinity College, which you had the privilege of announcing on your first page last week, must have given great encouragement to all true patriots. It gives ground for a confident hope that the Council of this great College may be relied on to adopt at once any further measures on the same lines, of which the need may be pointed out to them. Two such measures have occurred to me. Both, it will be seen, are fully in harmony with the spirit in which they have already acted; we may, therefore, rest assured that the rare qualities of heart and head, which must have prompted the admirable decision of last week, will cause them to embrace with enthusiasm these two further opportunities for beneficient activity, when once they see how unanswerable are the arguments which (as I flatter myself) I have been able to adduce in their favour.
'The two measures which I wish to suggest, as plainly enjoined by their duty to their Country and their College in this trying time, are as follows : –
'1. That they should at once make the following orders –
' "That no meeting of the Cambridge University Moral Science Club is to be held within the precincts of the College."
'The urgency of this measure will be evident from the fact that, as I write, a meeting of the Club in question is actually announced to be held in the rooms of a *Fellow* of the College on Friday next, November 26. And anybody who is acquainted with the objects both of the Moral Science Club and of the Union of Democratic Control, will see at once that the same dangerous consequences are to be

apprehended from a meeting of either body. The Council is, perhaps, not so well-informed with regard to the Club as it *evidently* is with regard to the Union, and may not, therefore, have realised how dangerous to the patriotism of young men the meetings of this Club may be, and what a serious effect they may have upon recruiting. But it is, in sober earnest, possible that young English men should, at one of its meetings, be urged to believe a proposition as that *the greatest good of humanity as a whole ought, in cases of conflict, to be preferred to that of their own countrymen!* Now it is, I know, arguable that, in times of peace, an enlightened College should, in the interests of freedom of thought, allow such a proposition to be discussed within its precincts, *even* at a private meeting; but the risk to patriotism is obvious, and, in times of war, it is surely evident that such a dangerous liberty must be utterly abolished. The experience of the Council may, perhaps, lead them to think that nothing that is said at any meeting connected with a subject for examination, can possibly be taken seriously by any undergraduate. But I can assure them, from personal knowledge, that this rule does not hold quite invariably. It is actually the case, incredible as it may seem, that the practical views of undergraduates have, in some cases, been seriously influenced by the study of Moral Science, in spite of the fact that it is an examination subject. Action, therefore, against the Moral Science Club is just as necessary as was action against the Union of Democratic Control. And the usefulness of such action would undoubtedly be greatly enhanced, if the Council would again take care to communicate their decision to the Press, even before announcing it to the Fellow concerned. Such a vigorous and prompt proceeding, following upon the similar action which they took last week, will unquestionably raise to a still higher pitch the reputation they have already earned for patriotism, liberality of mind, and courtesy; and they may expect to see the increased confidence of the public reflected in the increased number of parents who will be anxious to send their sons to a College so wisely governed.

'2. The other measure, which I wish to suggest, is on exactly the same lines, and I need not elaborate the arguments in its favour. It is that the Council should forthwith suspend all services in the College Chapel until the conclusion of the war. The absolute necessity for this measure, in the interests of recruiting and of national unity, is obvious. It is necessary, because at services of the Christian churches young men are liable to have brought to their notice maxims quite as dangerous to patriotism as any which they will hear at a meeting of the Union of Democratic Control or of the Moral Science Club. I need only give one single instance. The maxim *"Love your enemies; do good to them that hate you,"* actually occurs in one of the books habitually read in Churches. Here, again, it may, of course, be argued that nobody ever takes seriously what they hear in Church. But I can again assure the Council, from personal knowledge, that this is not absolutely *always* so. There really is *some* risk that an under-graduate may (however illogically) draw practical conclusions, un-favourable to the patriotic action which the times require, from such a maxim as that which I have quoted. In view of the action which the Council have already taken, we may, I think, feel a quiet confidence, that they will at once take the further steps necessary to secure that no undergraduate shall, within the walls of the College, run the very *smallest* risk of being perverted by such principles.

Yours faithfully,

G. E. MOORE

Trinity College.
November 23'.

This whole episode underlined the moderation of the UDC. It was not even necessary to be an opponent of the war to be in favour of the UDC's plans for the peace. But Moore, though it was some time before he felt 'miserable' about the war, was quite definitely against it. The action of the council of Trinity made him feel even more alienated from those who supported the war and impotent. Worst of all, as a prize fellow he had no vote in the proceedings in council and so was unable to support Russell.

In 1916 McTaggart and Henry Jackson led the fight to expel Russell from his lectureship. As would be expected, McTaggart was a vocifer-ous supporter of Britain's role in the war, and a staunch antagonist of its opponents. McTaggart justified his part in this shameful episode in a letter to Wedd of 12 November 1916 by saying that Russell was sacked because of his conviction in the courts, and not for his opinions. This, McTaggart claimed, was demanded by the college statutes relating to fellows who have been convicted of a crime. McTaggart acknow-ledged that the statutes merely gave the college council the power to expel any fellow convicted of a crime and did not call for the automatic expulsion of such a fellow. But he felt that Russell's offence – 'making statements likely to prejudice the recruiting and discipline of HM Forces' – was so serious that the council was bound to sack him. He added, 'I do not blame Russell morally. I think he acted honourably. . . . But I do think that, after such a conviction, he ought not to be a lecturer of Trinity.' He claimed to Wedd (who did not condemn McTaggart for the way he had voted) that he had deliberated for a long time and that the decision he reached gave him much pain. As G. H. Hardy makes it clear in his account of the matter in *Bertrand Russell and Trinity*, McTaggart's decision was almost certainly vindictive: he thought Russell ought to be punished by the college, in spite of his having been punished already by the authorities. G. H. Hardy wrote of McTaggart, 'He was voting against the reinstatement of conscientious objectors in their scholarships long after such an attitude had ceased to be in any sense "popular".'*

Dickinson and many other Apostles fell out with McTaggart over the Russell affair, and for a long time he ceased to communicate with many old friends. There was, of course, a serious split in the Apostles over the war in any case, with such admirers of the military as Jackson, Raleigh† and McTaggart ranged against many Apostles of the older vintage and nearly all the younger ones, but the disgraceful dismissal of Russell greatly exacerbated the breach. McTaggart never gave the reasoned defence of the council's action that he sometimes seemed to promise, and he opposed Russell's reinstatement when the war ended.[41]

Eventually – probably after the introduction of conscription – Moore grew so militant in his opposition to the war that he handed out anti-war literature to passers-by at the Cambridge railway station.[42] In the last resort it was conscription that caused anyone who was not whole-heartedly in favour of the war to examine his position carefully. Temporary exemptions were the best that could be hoped for by those who opposed the war, but did not feel they could conscientiously object. In 1916 there was a lot of undignified scrambling to get exemptions: in January a Trinity don, Sydney Chapman, told Moore that 'he and Norton are going to apply for exemption, that Hardy is uncertain – thinks if [Adam] Sidgwick takes Commission, he will too.' And on 7 February Norton reported that Hardy had attested – much too late for it to do any good. An acquaintance called Bartlett, Hardy told Moore in late February, had got an exemption for one month only. Moore decided to ask Bartlett how one went about applying for exemption. In mid-March Sydney Chapman decided to declare himself a con-

---

* 'There is no justification for the statement on p. 117 of Lowes Dickinson's *McTaggart* that McTaggart "in the difficult years after the war always played the part of a reconciler at Trinity".'[40]

† Raleigh became a propagandist for the war and in 1918 the official historian of the Royal Air Force.

scientious objector. He was helped a good deal by Moore with arguments for use before the tribunal, as was Norton, and Lytton Strachey earlier in the month. The trouble was that some intelligent, humane and sympathetic people thought there was an inconsistency in claiming one had a conscientious objection to taking part in the war and not being able to say that one was opposed to war as such; i.e. many people felt that total pacifism was the only possible grounds for conscientious objection. It was Moore's crucial role to make a case for conscientious objection that did not rest on an absolute objection to war or to killing in general (– some tribunals would only accept these as grounds for objection if they stemmed from the standard beliefs of some widely accepted religion). This he did by clarifying the nature of the grounds on which the objection really rested; these were usually moral or political, as in Lytton Strachey's statement quoted above. But while Moore accepted virtually the whole of Strachey's case, he did not apply the arguments in it to his own position.

On 26 March Moore, now aged forty-three, quoted in his diary that he had 'been afraid lately that they may raise age for compulsion to 45: can't help thinking a good deal of what would happen to me ... depressed'. His spirits had been low for some time; he had been dissatisfied with his lectures, and the month before, he noted on 14 February that, 'on walk feel as if I can hardly bear it – should go mad: but easier when I allow myself to go on thinking.' Once, even earlier, on 7 December 1915, Moore had noted with unconscious humour: 'Feel very incapable of thinking, so read *Mind*.' By late March 1916 then, Moore was justifiably worried about being conscripted, and had to confess to himself that he was also afraid; on the 26th he felt 'rather afraid of Zeppelins: altogether depressed and worried' and on the 31st, he was distressed by the partial blackout in hall at nine o'clock, which he took as a sign of the approach of Zeppelins, for which he waited about, 'listening in my rooms'. Then there was the discomfort of having to mix with officers at dinner in hall, where champagne was always served when some of their number left Trinity for their new assignments.

This was the most painful and difficult time Moore had in his whole life. Finally the man who had counselled so many younger men about conscientious objection decided that he himself was not a conscientious objector, and this gave him relief. On 19 April 1916 Moore recorded in his diary: 'Have reconciled myself to idea of military service, and feel much happier.' He was, in fact, never called up.

Epilogue

Moore's misery was intensified in 1915 and 1916, because something else was going wrong for him. He saw Mary Fletcher very often in this time, but they had not come to an understanding, and on 22 October 1915 there was a 'letter from Miss F. in which she says, "As to meeting I think not, at present." This hurts me and makes me angry: I want to see her because she's the only person up here I can talk freely to: *why* won't she meet me?' The rift mended soon enough, but in November there were new troubles, and when in December the two of them went to visit Bob and Bessie Trevelyan at their house, The Shiffolds, they were 'told Russell is coming on Saturday: and Miss F. tells me it will spoil her comfort'. In late January he had a talk with Mary Fletcher about the 'unmarried losing opportunities which married have had', but this did not lead to their own engagement, or to a final breach. This last was fast approaching, however, for Moore had been seeing someone else since October term 1915.

Dorothy Mildred Ely (1892–1977) was twenty years younger than Moore, and an exceedingly handsome young woman. Her father, George Herbert Ely, lived in Croydon; he was one half of the team who wrote adventure stories for boys under the nom de plume of 'Herbert Strang'. Miss Ely, who was up at Newnham reading classics, had an independent spirit and a quick and flexible intelligence. She demonstrated these by attending the lectures of both Moore and Russell and taking notes on them in parallel columns – this she hoped would solve the question of which one had the more influence over the other. A few days after her first meeting with Moore in October 1915, his diary entry for the 30th stated, 'Miss Ely catches up with me and asks to tea: says she's afraid I'll be bored, that she was shy when she came to me, and thinks I was too, and she doesn't usually talk such nonsense.'

Moore told MacCarthy the history of his courtship in a letter of 15 November 1916:

'I didn't know Dorothy at all till just over a year ago, when she began coming to my lectures, and I asked her to tea. And I didn't begin to like her at all particularly till about the middle of the Lent Term. And the idea that I might possibly like to marry her didn't occur to me till nearly the end of the May Term. It did occur to me then, and I was very fond of her and very anxious to see her as often as possible; but I felt very doubtful about it. I did begin telling you about it after the dinner in June; only what I said didn't catch your attention and you changed the subject. What made all the difference was that she was up here all July; and we used to see one another 3 or 4 times a week, and constantly go for long walks together. I spent so much time thinking whether I would ask her to marry me or not; sometimes thinking I didn't like her well enough, and being afraid of other things too, but generally wanting to. But I couldn't finally make up my mind, till the day came when she was going down. We went for a long walk that morning, hardly talking at all, partly because I was thinking whether I should ask her; and it was only at the end, when she said Good-bye and that she supposed that she would never see me again, that I asked her. She was utterly taken by surprise; and of course we had to meet again and discuss it all. We were both very doubtful, if it would be wise, and I put all the objections as fairly as I could. I thought she did behave beautifully. One reason she was doubtful was that she had quite made up her mind before that she would never marry, and disliked the idea of marriage altogether. She hated the idea of being dependent on any one.

'. . . I went and stayed [at her home] for ten days towards the end of September, and I don't think I've ever been so happy.

Yours very affectionately,
G. E. Moore

P.S. She is rather silent, as a general rule, in the same sort of circumstances and for the same sort of reasons as I am : I think perhaps she is *as* silent as I am.'[1]

This altogether Moore-ish courtship resulted (in 1916) in the happiest of marriages. Moore had a positive vocation for marriage and fatherhood, so strong that even the occupation of a don could only conceal it temporarily. When convention allowed G. E. Moore and Dorothy Ely to address each other by Christian name, she did him the great favour of ridding him of the hated 'George'. 'If he had to have a plain name,' she told me, 'let it at least be an honest one' : from then on she, and then their children, always called him 'Bill,' though she sometimes referred to him as 'Moore'.

Their first child, Nicholas, was born in November 1918, only a few days after the armistice, so that Moore had great joy at the conclusion of his greatest sorrow – though he was too immersed in married life for the last two years of the war to notice it or to mind it as much as he had done. Nicholas Moore was famous as a poet in the 1940s and 1950s, being associated with Tambimuttu and the poets around *Poetry London*. Another son, Timothy, was born in February 1922; he gained a scholarship to Trinity and a first in moral sciences part I, but his career was interrupted by service in the Second World War. He also inherited his father's musical gifts, and became a composer and music master at Dartington Hall, the progressive school in Devon. For many people still at Cambridge their most typical memory of G. E. Moore is the astonishing sight of him wheeling one of the boys in his pram at breakneck speed along the Backs.

Moore was forty-three when he married and nearly fifty when his second son was born. He became Professor of Philosophy at Cambridge University in 1925 when he was well over fifty. The university had had the three greatest living philosophers – Moore, Russell and Wittgenstein – as members at various times since the advent of Wittgenstein in 1912, and Moore's appointment in 1925 was belated recognition of part of its good fortune. Moore had, after all, been a Fellow of the British Academy and had the Honorary Degree of Doctor of Laws from St Andrews since 1918.

Having made such an extraordinary impact at the age of thirty with *Principia Ethica*, and having played mentor to his elders from an earlier age than that, Moore stayed young in some remarkable way – which perhaps explains a little why he did everything else so late in life. In saying this one does not intend to imply that Moore's feelings were in general immature or undeveloped, but that specific needs and desires came late to him. For example, when on the brink of middle-age he experienced the wish to marry, Moore was having, in his forties, the feelings many men have in their thirties. He felt the *need* of marriage rather later in life than is usual. In the same way he had exprienced with Ainsworth what amounted to a schoolboy crush in his late twenties.

And things seemed to *happen* to Moore later than they might have done, as when he returned to Cambridge only in 1911, to resume the academic career that had been temporarily abandoned in 1904: through no fault of his own, Moore had had to give up his academic career at the crest of the *Principia Ethica* wave. Similarly, his university had only offered him a chair in 1925, four years after his pre-eminence had been recognized by making him editor of *Mind* and three years after the publication of *Philosophical Studies*, which was not a book-length work of philosophy like *Principia*, but a collection of articles, the oldest dating from 1903 and the newest from 1921. Many of these articles are of lasting importance, but they were written and delivered or published in fairly regular progression over the eighteen-year period. Moore's fame did not increase so greatly after 1903; in spite of his youth, it would not have been outrageous if he had been offered a professorship at that time, instead of being allowed to depart from Cambridge because there was no post for him there.

Perhaps the fact of important things happening later in life than is usual has some connection with the character trait of Moore most noticed by those who have written about him – the trait that is variously called innocence, purity or even childishness. It was what Leonard Woolf was indicating when he said Moore

'resembled Socrates in possessing a profound simplicity, a simplicity which Tolstoy and some other Russian writers consider to produce the finest human beings. These human beings are "simples" or even "sillies"; they are absurd in ordinary life and by the standards of sensible and practical men. . . . In many ways Moore was one of these divine "sillies". It showed itself perhaps in such simple, unrestrained, passionate gestures as when, if told something particularly astonishing or confronted by some absurd statement at the crisis of an argument, his eyes would open wide, his eyebrows shoot up, and his tongue shoot out of his mouth.'[2]

This trait was what Russell wished to highlight when he said of Wittgenstein that 'he had a kind of purity which I have never known equalled except by G. E. Moore'.[3] And it was this trait that Wittgenstein commented on in his reply to Norman Malcolm's letter about Moore's lack of 'professional vanity':

'Now as to Moore – I don't really understand Moore, and, therefore, what I'll say may be quite wrong. But this is what I'm inclined to say : – That Moore is in some sense extraordinarily childlike is obvious, and the remark you quoted (about vanity) is certainly an example of that childlikeness. There is also a *certain* innocence about Moore; he is, e.g., completely unvain. As to its being to his *"credit"* to be childlike, – I can't understand that; unless it's also to a child's credit. For you aren't talking of the innocence a man has fought for, but of an innocence which comes from a natural absence of a temptation, – I believe that all you wanted to say was that you *liked*, or even *loved*, Moore's childlikeness. And that I can understand. – I think that our discrepancy here is not so much one of thoughts as of feelings. I *like* and greatly respect Moore; but that's all. He doesn't warm my heart (or very little), because what warms my heart most is human kindness, and Moore – *just like a child* – is not kind. He is kindly and he can be charming and nice to those he likes and he has great *depth*. – That's how it seems to me. If I'm wrong, I'm wrong.'[4]

Running throughout the pages of all the books and memoirs in which Moore figures there is a single, magnificent theme: to understand the Cambridge Apostles, to understand the Bloomsbury Group, to understand the development of modern philosophy, it is vital to understand and appreciate the character of G. E. Moore. Thus in G. J. Warnock's *English Philosophy Since 1900*:

'Among the immediately operative factors contributing to the decay of Absolute Idealism, special notice should be paid to the *character* of Moore. The word may [seem], perhaps, curiously chosen; but it was chosen deliberately. For it was not solely by reason of his intellectual gifts that Moore differed so greatly from his immediate predecessors, or influenced so powerfully his own contemporaries. He was not, and never had the least idea that he was, a much cleverer man than McTaggart, for example, or Bradley. It was in point of character that he was different, and importantly so. He seems to have been, in the first place, entirely without any of the motives that tend to make a metaphysician. He was neither discontented with nor puzzled by the ordinary beliefs of plain scientists. He had no leanings whatever towards paradox and peculiarity of opinion. He had no particular religious or other cosmic anxieties; and he seems to have felt that in aesthetics and morality (not, of course, in moral or aesthetic *philosophy*) all was as well, at least, as could reasonably be expected. He thus did not hanker for any system on his own account. But secondly, he had the great force of character that was necessary to resist the temptation to conform himself with his environment. He soon overcame, if he ever had, the desire so natural in any clever young man, to excel in the same line of business as his admired elders. He did not borrow a modish metaphysical idiom to make up for, or to conceal, his own real lack of relish for any such thing. And thirdly, he seems never to have had the slightest difficulty in causing his views to be taken seriously. It was always clear that his opinions, however unorthodox or naïve they may have been or seemed, were not those of one who could safely be disregarded.'[5]

In this passage it is made admirably clear that there is nothing paradoxical about seeing Moore's philosophy as an aspect of his character, a character so remarkable that when people like Lytton Strachey, John Maynard Keynes, Leonard Woolf and Virginia Woolf[6] sought for comparisons they mentioned – without conscious hyperbole – Prince Myshkin, Socrates and Jesus Christ.

It is not extravagant to claim that Moore's philosophy mirrored his character, but the reflection of Moore's philosophy in the Bloomsbury Group gave rise to lyrical conceits – as in this passage of Leonard Woolf's autobiography where he seems to compare Moore's influence to that of nature herself:

'There have often been groups of people, writers and artists, who were not only friends, but were consciously united by a common doctrine and object, or purpose artistic or social. The utilitarians, the Lake poets, the French impressionists, the English Pre-Raphaelites were groups of this kind. Our group was quite different. Its basis was friendship, which in some cases developed into love and marriage. The colour of our minds and thought had been given to us by the climate of Cambridge and Moore's philosophy, much as the climate of England gives one colour to the face of an Englishman while the climate of India gives quite a different colour to the face of a Tamil.'[7]

Seldom have such things been said about the influence of one person over other men, or have such claims been made about the example of a teacher whose character was as potent a force as his doctrines – the other outstanding case was the leader of a very different set of Apostles. It is not a question of whether, but of *how* exaggerated were the claims the Bloomsbury Group made for its own prophet. Yet the large kernel of truth in these statements remains and resists even the attention of would-be debunkers. Because of the coincidence of a man with his character appearing at the historical moment when the worn-out morality of the Victorians gave its death kick to civilization in the war, Moore's influence can be compared to the funnel of an hour-glass through which the long tradition of the British intellectual aristocracy and the Cambridge Apostles filtered into Bloomsbury.

Noël Annan thought Moore was behind a change that came about in the 1920s – not so much a change in the lives of ordinary people, or in the life of the country as a whole, but a change in 'the intellectual configuration of the times', a change in the mood of 'that tiny minority who change opinion'. 'True', Annan said in his BBC broadcast,

> 'the new mood was expressed in ideas propagated by the Bloomsbury circle and Freud, and in art-forms from the Continent which were all anterior to the twenties. What had been revolutionary between 1900 and 1920 was now to become orthodox. The ethical revolution which had previously been on paper was now put into practice: and produced that violent change in the code of behaviour which severed the twenties from the *Ancien Régime*.'

The bankruptcy of Victorian morality, the usefulness of Benthamist utilitarianism, had been felt strongly for some time and was familiar enough before the 1920s. But, Noël Annan went on,

> 'this to the twenties now seemed to be proved by the great event which preceded the decade and appeared to sever it from the past; the event which to people of that generation is still called the Great War. The profound emotional impact of the horror and slaughter convinced many that the values which had held good before the war must now, by definition, be wrong – if indeed they were not responsible for causing the war. A society which permitted such a catastrophe to occur must be destroyed, because the presuppositions of that comfortable pre-war England were manifestly false. Searching for a new way in which to regard conduct, the twenties came to see it through the eyes either of Mrs Webb or of Mrs Woolf.
>
> 'With Mrs Webb the difficulty of relating the individual to society was achieved by eliminating him. Conduct was depersonalised through Fabian blueprints and such concepts as "the poor" or "other people" were transformed into "poverty" and "community"....
>
> 'The other new way of looking at conduct symbolised by Mrs Woolf was the more important. And behind Mrs Woolf and Bloomsbury stands G. E. Moore.'

In Annan's view, what Virginia Woolf symbolized, what she and Bloomsbury derived from Moore was an emphasis upon 'the growth of the private virtues – that is, of personal relations and the creative instincts'. 'People delighted in those who were bright, amusing, intellectually outrageous, who could turn the world upside down for its own good. The new virtues,' which people in the 1920s derived from Moore, said Annan, 'were humility towards the intellect, hostility towards worldly success, personal affection, liberation of the emotions, admiration of sensibility, hatred of philistinism and compromise and, above all, ruthless honesty about oneself. Human beings had to be judged according to their own merits and for no other reason.'[8] The familiarity of this litany of the virtues and vices *chez* Moore does not make any less just this assessment of his influence by an historian of Bloomsbury. The claims are smaller and less stridently put than those made on Moore's behalf by those who experienced his influence themselves, but they are still large claims.

It is natural to make inflated claims when praising one's own hero – or the subject of one's own book. So let us hear some words that appear to prick the balloon. Here is a contrary view of Moore's character as seen by Wittgenstein – not Wittgenstein's final or most considered pronouncement on the subject; but one that contradicts much that has been said in this book. The sense of a passage written by Wittgenstein in 1939 or 1940 is that Moore has conscience, but lacks heart. Probably, thought Wittgenstein, the truth is that Moore's likes and dislikes are immature. He went on to say that Moore's heart was like a bud, which has not withered, but which has never opened fully, and concluded that Moore was not capable of stimulating anyone.[9]

And to that we ought to join the comments Leonard and Virginia Woolf made about Moore's influence on their youthful selves from the retrospective vantage of middle age. In 1920 when Moore was just over fifty, Virginia Woolf reflected:

> 'He has grown grey, sunken, toothless perhaps. His eyes small, watchful, but perhaps not so piercing as of old. A lack of mass somewhere.... I don't see altogether why he was the dominator and dictator of youth. Perhaps Cambridge is too much of a cave. Yet (I don't attempt to balance this properly) of course there's his entire innocency and shrewdness: not the vestige of falsehood obscuring him anywhere.'[10]

Moore visited the Woolfs on the weekend of 18 May 1940 in the company of Desmond MacCarthy. It was to be the last time they would meet, for Moore was soon to leave England and Mrs Woolf was less than a year away from her suicide in the River Ouse. She enjoyed that weekend enormously, taking a great deal of pleasure in the events of the present. But once again doubts about the past presented themselves to her mind. Moore was now old. She wondered how she and her friends could have *revered* this old man when they were all younger. Once again she was struck, even more powerfully than she had been twenty years earlier, by Moore's lack of what she could only call *mass*. In 1940 she could no longer recapture the sense of Moore's *force*.

Quentin Bell has told us how the party went over to Charleston one afternoon that weekend, and 'there they discussed Moore's famous taciturnity: he was accused of silencing a generation. "I didn't want to be silent", he replied. "I couldn't think of anything to say." '[11]

Leonard Woolf was more fortunate. He could recollect the feelings of the past. 'There we sat in May 1940, Moore, Desmond, Virginia, and I in the house and under a hot sun and brilliant sky in the garden, in a cocoon of friendship and nostalgic memories.'[12] 'Desmond and Moore together, the one talking, talking, the other silent in the armchair, were inextricably a part of my youth, of the entrancing excitement of feeling life open out in one and before one. I could shut my eyes', Woolf continued,

> 'and *feel* myself back in 1903, in Moore's room in the Cloisters of Trinity or the reading parties at the Lizard or Hunters Inn. With the eyes open we were older. I myself either have never grown up or was born old, for I have always had the greatest difficulty in feeling older. . . .
>
> 'Moore was older. The extraordinary purity and beauty of character and of mind were still there, the strange mixture of innocence and wisdom. The purity, moral and mental, was the most remarkable of Moore's qualities; I have never known anything like it in any other human being.'[13]

Moore's work published in his lifetime besides *Principia Ethica* included *Ethics* (1912), for the Home University Library, *Philosophical Studies* (1922), and *Some Main Problems of Philosophy* (1953), which actually consisted of the lectures he had given at Morley College in 1910–11. At some time after he became professor it was rumoured that Moore was offered, but refused, a knighthood. But there were honours he did accept: in addition to the degree of Doctor of Letters which he earned from his own university in 1913, there was the previously mentioned honorary degree from St Andrews and his fellowship of the British Academy; and in 1951 he consented to be appointed to the greatest fraternity of all, the Order of Merit.

During the Second World War his friends and students joined together to convince Moore, who was nearing the age of seventy and was not in good health, that he would be – not safer – but of more use to philosophy and thus to the civilization being fought for, by removing himself from the home in Cambridge that he so hated to leave. And so from 1940–44 he and Dorothy Moore went to America, where he was visiting professor at several colleges and universities.

In 1948 the Society gave a dinner in Cambridge to celebrate Moore's seventy-fifth, and E. M. Forster's seventieth, birthday. He and Russell and Wittgenstein were the most important living philosophers in the world; but apart from a few Bloomsbury survivors like Leonard Woolf and James Strachey, who read every journal article Moore ever wrote, Moore's influence was by now confined to philosophical circles. He was read and his work discussed almost exclusively by other philosophers. Thus this book effectively closes with the end of the 1914 war, by which time there had been a change in the nature of Moore's philosophical work. He had become a true professional – a philosopher's philosopher.

G. E. Moore died in Cambridge on 24 October 1958. He is buried in St Giles's churchyard, next to Desmond MacCarthy and a few steps from the grave of Ludwig Wittgenstein.

Appendix: The Apostles' Elections up to the First World War

	No. of Election	Died	Elected	Resigned	Degree, Date
TOMLINSON George	1	1863	Founder	May 1822	BA 1823, DD 1842
BRICE Edward Cowell	2	1881	Founder	Feb. 1821	BA 1821
THOMPSON Henry	3	1878	Founder	April 1822	BA 1822
HARFORD Henry Charles	4	1879	Founder	April 1823	BA 1824
PUNNETT John	5	1863	Founder	Dec. 1823	BA 1823
AINGER Thomas	6	1863	Founder	Dec. 1820	BA 1821
HENDERSON Robert	7	1875	Founder	Feb. 1822	BA 1822
SHAW George (or SHAW Halsnod)	8	1888	Founder	Nov. 1820	MB 1824
	8	1844			
WISEMAN Charles	9	1823	Founder	Dec. 1820	BA 1821
BATTERSBY Richard	10	1866	Founder	Dec. 1820	BA 1822
FURNIVAL James	11	1878	Founder	April 1822	BA 1822
SIMPSON John	12		Founder	Nov. 1820	BA 1821
GUEST Benjamin	13	1869	Nov. 1820	Dec. 1821	BA 1822
BROWNE Thomas Witmore Wylde	14		Dec. 1820	May 1821	
BRICE Henry Crane	15	1867	Feb. 1821	March 1823	BA 1825
FESTING George Charles Ruddock	16	1857	Feb. 1821	March 1821	BA 1822
FENNELL Samuel	17	1843	Feb. 1821	April 1821	11th Wrangler 1821
POWER Joseph	18	1868	April 1821	Feb. 1824	10th Wrangler 1821
VEAS(E)Y Alfred	19	1834	March 1821	May 1821	BA 1821, DD 1831

No. of Election	Name	Died	Elected	Resigned	Degree, Date
20	ROBERTS John		Nov. 1821	Nov. 1825	BA 1825
21	JUDGE Edward Conduitt	1875	Nov. 1821	Nov. 1823	BA 1824
22	STOCK John Shapland	1867	Dec. 1821	Feb. 1826	BA 1826
23	SIMPSON George	1866	Feb. 1822	Feb. 1824	17th Wrangler
24	PARKE John		March 1822	Dec. 1823	BA 1823
25	OUTRAM Thomas Powys	1853	April 1822	May 1824	BA 1825
26	TAYLOR Alfred	1823	Nov. 1822		died before taking degree
27	BURDON William Wharton		Dec. 1822	Nov. 1823	LLB 1824
28	MARRIOTT (Sir) William Marriott Smith (Bt)	1864	March 1823	Oct. 1824	BA 1825
29	DARWIN Erasmus Alvey	1881	May 1823	Nov. 1823	MB 1828
30	MAURICE John Frederick Denison	1872	Nov. 1823	March 1827	Civil Law Classes 1826-7
31	PATTON George (Lord Glenalmond)	1869	Dec. 1823	April 1826	BA 1826
32	WHITMORE Charles Shapland	1877	Dec. 1823	Nov. 1826	BA 1827
33	BOYLAN Richard Dillon		Feb. 1824	March 1826	
34	CARTER (Sir) James	1878	March 1824	Nov. 1824	
35	HARRISON Thomas Wayne	1871	April 1824	Nov. 1824	BA 1827
36	ROMILLY Edward	1870	Nov. 1824	Oct. 1827	Civil Law Classes 1st Class 1826-7
37	BACON Francis	1840	Nov. 1824	Nov. 1825	BA 1826
38	O'BRIEN William Smith	1864	Nov. 1824		BA 1826
39	GEDGE Sydney	1883	Dec. 1824	Nov. 1825	14th Wrangler, 7th Classic 1824
40	KENNEDY Benjamin Hall	1889	Dec. 1824	Feb. 1826	Senior Classic 1827
41	WILSON George St Vincent	1852	Feb. 1825	Dec. 1826	
42	FARISH James	1853	March 1825	Nov. 1826	BA 1825, MB 1828
43	RICHARDSON William	1855	(?) 1825	Nov. 1826	BA 1827

	No. of Election	Died	Elected	Resigned	Degree, Date
STERLING John	44	1844	Nov. 1825	Dec. 1827	BA 1834
BAINES Edward	45	1882	Nov. 1825	Nov. 1826	4th Classic 1824
POWER (Sir) Alfred	46	1888	Nov. 1825	Nov. 1826	2nd Classic 1826
MALKIN Frederick	47	1830	March 1826	Oct. 1827	Senior Classic 1824
ROMILLY Henry	48	1884	March 1826	Feb. 1828	BA 1828
SMITH Theyre Townsend	49	1852	April 1826	Dec. 1826	BA 1827
(or SMITH Edward Herbert)	49	1887			BA 1827
WALPOLE Spencer Horatio	50	1898	Nov. 1826		BA 1828
HALL Richard	51	1857	Nov. 1826		BA 1828
KEMBLE John Mitchell	52	1857	Nov. 1826	Dec. 1828	BA 1830
SUNDERLAND Thomas	53	1867	Dec. 1826	Feb. 1830	BA 1830
BULLER Charles	54	1848	Dec. 1826		BA 1828
TALBOT The Hon. James (Baron Talbot de Malahide)	55	1883	March 1827	May 1827	10th Classic 1827
DONNE William Bodham	56	1882	March 1827	Feb. 1828	did not take degree
WRANGHAM George Walter	57	1855	May 1827	Feb. 1828	BA 1828
TRENCH Richard Chevenix	58	1886	May 1827	Dec. 1828	BA 1829
MARTINEAU Arthur	59	1872	Nov. 1827	Feb. 1829	3rd Classic 1829
BLAKESLEY Joseph Williams	60	1885	Nov. 1827	Nov. 1831	21st Wrangler, 3rd Classic 1831
BULLER (Sir) Arthur William	61	1869	Feb. 1828	March 1830	BA 1830
BARNES Richard Nelson	62	1889	Feb. 1828	March 1830	BA 1830
O'BRIEN Edward	63	1840	March 1828	Dec. 1828	BA 1829
HORSMAN Edward	64	1876	May 1828	May 1838	did not take degree
COOKESLEY William Gifford	65	1880	Nov. 1828		BA 1826
TENNANT Robert John	66	1842	Nov. 1828	Feb. 1831	BA 1831
SPEDDING James	67	1881	Nov. 1828		BA 1831

Name	No. of Election	Died	Elected	Resigned	Degree, Date
HALLAM Arthur Henry	68	1833	May 1829	Dec. 1831	BA 1832
MORRISON Alexander James William	69	1865	May 1829		BA 1832
TENNYSON Alfred (Lord)	70	1892	Oct. 1829	Feb. 1830	
MILNES Richard Monckton (Lord Houghton)	71	1885	Oct. 1829	March 1830	MA 1831
PICKERING Percival Andree	72	1876	Nov. 1829	Dec. 1831	BA 1832
MONTEITH Robert Joseph Ignatius	73	1884	March 1830	Nov. 1835	BA 1834
GARDEN Francis	74	1884	March 1830	Nov. 1833	BA 1833
ALFORD Henry	75	1871	Oct. 1830	May 1833	34th Wrangler, 8th Classic 1832
FARISH George	76	1836	Oct. 1830	Feb. 1833	BA 1832
THOMPSON William Hepworth	77	1886	Nov. 1830	Oct. 1835	BA 1832
HEATH Douglas Denon	78	1897	Feb. 1831	May 1835	Senior Wrangler, 1st Class Classic 1832
MACAULAY Kenneth	79	1867	Dec. 1831		BA 1835
VENABLES George Stovin	80	1888	March 1832	Nov. 1832	5th Classic 1832
MERIVALE Charles	81	1893	March 1832	March 1834	4th Classic 1830
MORTON Savile	82	1852	March 1832		22nd Wrangler 1834
SPRING RICE Stephen Edmund	83	1865	Feb. 1833	May 1835	6th Classic 1834
LUSHINGTON Henry	84	1855	May 1833		31st Wrangler
HELPS (Sir) Arthur	85	1875	Nov. 1833	Oct. 1835	27th Wrangler 1830
HEATH John Moore	86	1882	Feb. 1834	May 1835	Senior Classic 1832
LUSHINGTON Edmund Law	87	1893	March 1834	May 1835	
WILKIER William Clarke	88	b.1814	Nov. 1834		
POLLOCK (Sir) William Frederick (Bt)	89	1888	Nov. 1834		BA 1836
HARDCASTLE Joseph Alfred	90	1899	April 1835		11th Classic 1838

	No. of Election	Died	Elected	Resigned	Degree, Date
HEATH Dunbar Isidore	91	1888	Oct. 1835		5th Wrangler 1838
LAWRENCE Effingham John	92	1888	Nov. 1835		29th Wrangler 1839
VAUGHAN Edward Thomas	93	1900	Dec. 1835		29th Wrangler, 7th Classic 1834
CHRISTIE William Dougal	94	1874	April 1836	March 1839	BA 1838
HOLWORTHY Wentworth Samuel	95	1867	Nov. 1836	Dec. 1842	BA 1844
LAW Edmund	96	1885	Nov. 1836		BA 1840
OLDFIELD Edmund	97		Dec. 1836		
SPRING RICE Thomas Charles William	98	1870	Nov. 1837	Dec. 1839	MA 1840
FORTESCUE The Hon. Hugh (Viscount Ebrington; 3rd Earl Fortescue)	99	1905	Nov. 1837		
BARKER Peter Williams	100	b. 1818?	Feb. 1838		BA 1841
STOKES Charles Samuel	101	1895	March 1838		BA 1841
ROBINSON Thomas	102	1863	Nov. 1838		7th Wrangler, 3rd Classic 1839
MAITLAND John Gorham	103	1880	Nov. 1839		5th Classic 1840
TAYLOR Tom	104	1841	Feb. 1840	March 1844	1st Classic 1840
GOODEN Alexander Chisholm	105	1887	Nov. 1840		BA 1842
MANSFIELD Horatio	106	1898	Nov. 1841		BA 1843
GIBBS Frederick Waymouth	107	1900	March 1842	March 1844	BA 1843
JOHNSON Henry Robert Vaughan	108	1901	March 1842	May 1847	Senior Classic 1846
LUSHINGTON (Sir) Franklin	109	1850	Nov. 1842	May 1847	1st Class Classical Tripos 1846
HALLAM Henry Fitzmaurice	110	1888	Nov. 1842	Nov. 1847	Senior Classic 1844
MAINE (Sir) Henry James Sumner	111	1892	Nov. 1843	Nov. 1845	BA 1846
JOHNSON William (post Cory)	112	1909	March 1844	March 1845	5th Wrangler 1845
BLACKBURN Hugh	113		May 1844		

	No. of Election	Died	Elected	Resigned	Degree, Date
EVANS Charles	114	1904	April 1845	Nov. 1847	(1st in 1st Class Classical Tripos) 1847
HOLLAND Francis James	115	1907	Dec. 1846	May 1850	BA 1850
HARCOURT (Sir) William George Granville Venables Vernon	116	1904	May 1847	March 1851	1st Class Classical Tripos 1851
STANLEY The Hon. Edward Henry (Lord Stanley; 15th Earl of Derby)	117	1893	Oct. 1847	? 1848	10th Classic 1848
STEPHEN (Sir) James Fitzjames	118	1894	Nov. 1847	May 1851	BA 1852
WATSON Henry William	119	1903	May 1848	Oct. 1853	2nd Wrangler 1850
FANE The Hon. Julian Henry Charles	120	1870	Nov. 1848	May 1850	MA 1850
YOOL George Valentine	121	1907	Dec. 1848	Oct. 1854	3rd Wrangler 1851
WILLIAMS John Daniel	122	1904	May 1849	Feb. 1854	6th Classic 1851
JAMES Henry Alfred	123	1898	Nov. 1849	June 1861	BA 1851
LOCOCK (Sir) Charles Brodie (Bt)	124	1890	Dec. 1849	Oct. 1852	BA 1850
HAWKINS Francis Vaughan	125	1908	March 1851	Dec. 1854	41st Wrangler, Senior Classic 1854
HORT Fenton John Anthony	126	1892	June 1851	March 1857	BA 1850
ELPHINSTONE (Sir) Howard Warburton (Bt)	127	1917	Nov. 1851	June 1857	17th Wrangler 1854
MAXWELL James Clerk	128	1879	Nov. 1852	June 1860	2nd Wrangler 1854
FARRAR Frederick William	129	1903	Nov. 1852	Feb. 1854	4th Classic 1854
BUTLER Henry Montagu	130	1918	Nov. 1853	Nov. 1859	Senior Classic 1855, DD 1865
MONRO Cecil James	131	1882	Feb. 1854	Feb. 1856	38th Wrangler, 8th Classic 1855
LUSHINGTON Vernon	132	1912	Feb. 1854	Dec. 1854	Civil Law Classes 1854-5 (1st Class) LLB 1859

	No. of Election	Died	Elected	Resigned	Degree, Date
POMEROY Robert Henry	133	1922	Oct. 1854		BA 1862
ROBY Henry John	134	1915	Feb. 1855	Resigned and cursed 1855	Senior Classic 1853
PULLER Charles	135	1892	March 1855	June 1860	15th Wrangler 1857
FISHER Edmund Henry	136	1879	Feb. 1856	Dec. 1859	20th Wrangler 1858
BRANDRETH Henry	137	1904	March 1856	Dec. 1860	11th Wrangler 1857
SIDGWICK Henry	138	1900	Nov. 1856	Nov. 1865	33rd Wrangler, Senior Classic 1859
BOWEN Edward Ernest	139	1901	March 1857	Dec. 1858	4th Classic 1858
NOEL The Hon. Roden	140	1894	March 1857	Jan. 1861	MA 1858
TAWNEY Charles Henry	141	1922	May 1858		Senior Classic 1860
BROWNING Oscar	142	1923	Dec. 1858	Oct. 1864	4th Classic 1860
COWELL John Jermyn	143	1867	March 1859		BA 1860
TREVELYAN (Sir) George Otto (Bt, OM)	144	1928	Oct. 1859	Nov. 1862	2nd Classic 1862
JEBB (Sir) Richard Claverhouse (OM)	145	1905	Nov. 1859	Feb. 1868	Senior Classic 1862
YOUNG Edward Mallett	146	1900	May 1860		7th Classic 1863
THOMPSON Henry Yates	147	1828	Nov. 1860		1st Class Classics Tripos 1861
WARRE CORNISH Francis	148	1916	Nov. 1860		3rd Classic 1861
SIDGWICK Arthur	149	1920	Feb. 1861	Feb. 1865	2nd Classic 1862
CURREY William Edmund	150	1908	May 1861	Oct. 1870	5th Classic 1863
HEATHCOTE Charles Gilbert	151	1913	May 1861	April 1865	9th Classic 1863
STANNING John	152	1904	Nov. 1861		BA 1864
EVERETT William	153	1910	March 1862	May 1863	BA 1863
LEE-WARNER Henry	154	1925	Nov. 1862		1st Class Classics Tripos 1864
PAYNE John Burwell	155	1869	April 1863	Nov. 1864	1st Class Moral Science 1864

	No. of Election	Died	Elected	Resigned	Degree, Date
LYTTELTON The Hon. Charles George (8th Viscount Cobham)	156	1922	April 1863	Dec. 1864	1st Class Law Tripos
JACKSON Henry (OM)	157	1921	May 1863	Oct. 1870	3rd Classic 1862
HOWARD George James (9th Earl of Carlisle)	158	1911	May 1864		
TOVEY Duncan Crookes	159	1912	Feb. 1865		BA 1865
POLLOCK (Sir) Frederick (Bt)	160	1937	March 1865	May 1869	BA 1865
CROMPTON Albert	161	1908	June 1865		2nd Classic 1867
STUART James	162	1913	Nov. 1865	Nov. 1872	3rd Wrangler 1866
CONYBEARE John William Edward	163	1931	Nov. 1865	Nov. 1868	BA 1866
BUTLER Arthur John	164	1910	Dec. 1865		8th Classic 1867
CLIFFORD William Kingdon	165	1879	Nov. 1866		2nd Wrangler 1867
MOULTON John Fletcher (Lord Moulton of Bank)	166	1921	June 1867	March 1869	Senior Wrangler 1868
ANDERSON Frank Eustace	167	b. 1844	Nov. 1867		BA 1869
BLAKESLEY George Holmes	168	1922	Feb. 1868	March 1872	1st Class Classics Tripos 1868
COLBECK Charles	169	1903	Oct. 1868	March 1872	5th Classic 1869
PRYOR Marlborough Robert	170	1920	Nov. 1869		BA 1870
HOPKINSON John	171	1898	Oct. 1870		Senior Wrangler 1871
SYMES John Elliotson	172	1921	Nov. 1870		BA 1871
RIVES George Lockhart	173	b. 1849	Feb. 1871	Feb. 1873	5th Wrangler 1872
VERRALL Arthur Woolgar	174	1912	Feb. 1871	Feb. 1877	2nd Classic 1873
PRATT John Henry	175	1878	Nov. 1871		Senior Classic 1872 (?)
BUTCHER Samuel Henry	176	1910	Nov. 1871	June 1876	Senior Classic 1873
LITTLE Thomas Shepherd	177	1910	Feb. 1872		1st Class Law and History Tripos 1872, BA 1873

	No. of Election	Died	Elected	Resigned	Degree, Date
HARDING Thomas Olver	178	1896	May 1872	May 1876	Senior Wrangler 1873
MYERS Arthur Thomas	179	1894	June 1872	Feb. 1876	12th Classic 1873
STANTON Vincent Henry	180	1924	Nov. 1872		20th Wrangler 1870
BALFOUR Gerald William (2nd Earl of Balfour)	181	1945	Nov. 1872	Feb. 1877	5th Classic 1875
MAITLAND Frederic William	182	1906	May 1873	May 1877	1st Class Moral Science Tripos
BUTCHER John George (Lord Danesfort)	183	1935	Oct. 1873	May 1878	8th Wrangler and Classic 1874
LEAF Walter	184	1917	Feb. 1874	Nov. 1877	Senior Classic 1874
WELLDON James Edward Cowell	185	1937	Feb. 1875	Oct. 1878	Senior Classic 1877
BALFOUR Francis Maitland	186	1882	May 1875	Feb. 1877	1st Class Natural Science Tripos 1873
SPRING RICE Stephen Edward	187	1902	Feb. 1876	Nov. 1879	18th Wrangler, 14th Classic 1878
SMITH James Parker	188	1929	March 1876	Nov. 1880	4th Wrangler
WARD James	189	1925	March 1876	Dec. 1879	1st Class Moral Science 1874
MACAULAY William Herrick	190	1936	May 1876	May 1884	6th Wrangler 1878
M(A)CALISTER (Sir) Donald (Bt)	191	1934	Oct. 1876	March 1882	Senior Wrangler 1877
ROWE Richard Charles	192	1884	Nov. 1877	Nov. 1880	3rd Wrangler 1877
LYTTELTON The Hon. Alfred	193	1913	Feb. 1878		BA 1879
HOLLAND Bernard Henry	194	1926	March 1878	Oct. 1883	1st Class History Tripos 1878
MORTON Edward John Chalmers	195	1902	Nov. 1878		BA 1880
STRACHEY (Sir) Arthur	196	1901	April 1879	June 1883	BA and LLB 1881
STEPHEN James Kenneth	197	1892	May 1879	June 1882	1st Class History Tripos 1881
GOODHART Henry Chester	198	1895	Jan. 1880	Oct. 1883	2nd Classic 1881
WYSE William	199	1929	May 1880	March 1884	4th Classic 1882
TURNER Herbert Hall	200	1930	May 1880	Feb. 1884	2nd Wrangler 1882

	No. of Election	Died	Elected	Resigned	Degree, Date
BECK Theodore	201	1899	Feb. 1881	June 1885	BA 1883
WILSON (Sir) Henry Francis	202	1937	Dec. 1881	Feb. 1885	6th Classic 1882
SMITH Arthur Hamilton	203	1941	March 1882	Oct. 1886	BA 1884
RALEIGH (Sir) Walter Alexander	204	1922	Oct. 1882	Oct. 1887	BA 1885
CLOUGH Arthur Hugh	205	1943	Jan. 1883		BA 1884
CUST Henry John Cokayne	206	1917	May 1883		BA 1884
DUFF James Duff	207	1940	Feb. 1884	Oct. 1886	1st Class Classics Tripos I 1882
WHITEHEAD Alfred North (OM)	208	1947	May 1884	Feb. 1887	4th Wrangler 1883
DICKINSON Goldsworthy Lowes	209	1932	Feb. 1885	June 1888	1st Class Classics Tripos I
SMITH (Sir) Henry Babington	210	1923	May 1885	Dec. 1887	1st Class Classics Tripos I and II
TATHAM Herbert Francis William	211	1909	Nov. 1885		1st Class Classics Tripos I and II
McTAGGART John McTaggart Ellis	212	1925	May 1886	May 1891	1st Class Moral Science Tripos 1888
CANE Arthur Beresford	213	1939	Nov. 1886		1st Class History Tripos 1886
FRY Roger Eliot	214	1934	May 1887	Nov. 1891	BA 1888
WEDD Nathaniel	215	1906	Feb. 1888	Feb. 1892	1st Class Classics Tripos I 1885, II 1887
McLEAN Norman	216	1947	Oct. 1888	Feb. 1892	1st Class Classics Tripos I 1888
MAYOR Robin John Grote	217	1947	March 1889	Nov. 1894	Senior Classic 1890
DAVIES Crompton Llewelyn	218	1935	Nov. 1889	June 1895	1st Class Classics Tripos I 1889, II 1891
DAVIES Theodore Llewelyn	219	1905	Nov. 1889	May 1894	1st Class Classics Tripos I 1891, II 1892
DODGSON Walter	220	b. 1866	Nov. 1890		BA 1890
FURNESS John Monteith	221	b. 1869	Feb. 1891	Jan. 1895	1st Class Classics Tripos I 1891
MACNAGHTEN The Hon. (Sir) Malcolm Martin	222	1955	June 1891		1st Class History Tripos I 1891

Name	No. of Election	Died	Elected	Resigned	Degree, Date
SANGER Charles Percy	223	1930	Feb. 1892	Feb. 1897	2nd Wrangler 1893
RUSSELL The Hon. Bertrand Arthur William (3rd Earl Russell) (OM)	224	1971	Feb. 1892	Feb. 1897	7th Wrangler 1893
GREEN Walford Davies	225	1941	Feb. 1892		BA 1891
TREVELYAN Robert Calversley	226	1951	Feb. 1893	April 1900	BA 1894
WEDGWOOD (Sir) Ralph Lewis (Bt)	227	1956	Oct. 1893		1st Class Moral Science Tripos I and II
MARSH (Sir) Edward Howard	228	1953	Jan. 1894	March 1899	1st Class Classics Tripos I and II
MOORE George Edward (OM)	229	1958	Feb. 1894	Jan. 1901	1st Class Classics Tripos I and Moral Science Tripos II 1896
TREVELYAN George Macaulay (OM)	230	1962	March 1895	April 1900	1st Class History Tripos 1896
MacCARTHY (Sir) Charles Otto Desmond	231	1952	May 1896	May 1901	BA 1897
SMYTH Austin Edward Arthur Watt	232	1949	Nov. 1897	March 1903	1st Class Classics Tripos I 1898, II 1899
HARDY Godfrey Harold	233	1947	Feb. 1898	Dec. 1901	BA 1899
AINSWORTH Alfred Richard	234	1959	Nov. 1899	Nov. 1911	1st Class Classics Tripos I 1900, II 1902, and Moral Science 1902
HAWTREY (Sir) Ralph George	235	1975	March 1900	May 1906	19th Wrangler 1901
MEREDITH Hugh Owen	236	1964	May 1900	Oct. 1904	1st Class Classics Tripos I, History II 1901
FORSTER Edward Morgan (OM)	237	1970	Feb. 1901	Oct. 1905	BA 1900
SHEPPARD (Sir) John Tressider	238	1968	Feb. 1902	June 1908	1st Class Classics Tripos I 1902
STRACHEY Giles Lytton	239	1932	Feb. 1902	May 1912	BA 1903
TURNER Saxon Arnoll Sydney	240	1962	Oct. 1902	Jan. 1914	1st Class Classics Tripos I 1902, II 1903

	No. of Election	Died	Elected	Resigned	Degree, Date
WOOLF Leonard Sidney	241	1969	Oct. 1902	Oct. 1904	1st Class Classics Tripos 1902
GREENWOOD Leonard Hugh Graham	242	1965	Nov. 1902	Jan. 1909	1st Class Classics Tripos I 1902, II 1903
KEYNES John Maynard (Baron Keynes of Tilton) (OM)	243	1946	Feb. 1903	Nov. 1910	1st Class Maths Tripos 1905
HOBHOUSE (Sir) Arthur Lee	244	1965	Feb. 1905		BA 1907
STRACHEY James Beaumont	245	1967	Feb. 1906	Dec. 1919	
NORTON Henry Tertius James	246	1936	Feb. 1906	May 1913	
BROOKE Rupert Chawnor	247	1915	Jan. 1908		BA 1909
SHOVE Gerald Frank	248	1948	Jan. 1909	March 1919	1st Class Economics Tripos II 1911, BA 1910
TAYLOR Cecil Francis	249		Nov. 1910	Nov. 1919	
LUCE Gordon Hannington	250		Jan. 1912	Dec. 1921	
BÉKÁSSY Ferenc István Dénes Gyula	251	1915	Jan. 1912		BA 1914
WITTGENSTEIN Ludwig	252	1951	Nov. 1912	Jan. 1929	PH.D. 1929
BLISS Francis Kennard	253	1916	Nov. 1912		BA 1914
LUCAS Frank Lawrence	254	1967	Jan. 1914	Nov. 1923	1st Class Classics Tripos 1920
MARSHALL Maurice Oswald	255		Nov. 1914		BA 1916

Notes

Unpublished material:

Quotations in the text for which no citation or location is given are from the Moore papers or from papers in the collection of the Strachey Trust that were in the author's possession at the time of writing. Wherever possible catalogue numbers are given for letters in the Moore papers.

McMaster University – The Bertrand Russell Archives, McMaster University, Hamilton, Ontario.

Berg – The Henry W. and Albert A. Berg Collection of English and American Literature in the New York Public Library (Astor, Lenox and Tilden Foundations).

The Keynes-Grant correspondence is at The British Library. Other unpublished Keynes material is at King's College, Cambridge. The R. C. Trevelyan papers are at Trinity College, Cambridge. The Wedd papers are at King's College, Cambridge.

Introduction

1. Leonard Woolf, *Sowing* (New York 1960), p. 131.
2. Ibid., p. 142.
3. *Sunday Times*, 2 July 1978.
4. A. R. Jones, *The Life and Opinions of Thomas Ernest Hulme* (London 1960), p. 57.
5. John Paul Russo, *I. A. Richards* (London, forthcoming), chapter 4.
6. Norman Mackenzie (ed.), *The Letters of Sidney and Beatrice Webb* (Cambridge and London 1978) vol. II.
7. J. B. Priestley, *The Edwardians* (London 1970), p. 81.
8. Richard Braithwaite, 'Keynes as a Philosopher', in *Essays on John Maynard Keynes*, ed. Milo Keynes (London 1975), p. 243.
9. Bertrand Russell, *Autobiography* (Boston 1967), I, p. 95.
10. P. N. Furbank, *E. M. Forster, A Life* (London 1977), I, p. 77.
11. R. F. Harrod, *The Life of John Maynard Keynes* (London 1951), p. 76.
12. Norman Malcolm, 'George Edward Moore', in *G. E. Moore: Essays in Retrospect*, ed. Alice Ambrose and Morris Lazerowitz (London and New York 1970), p. 34.
13. Ibid., p. 36.
14. A. J. Ayer, *Part of My Life* (London 1977), p. 54.
15. Ibid., p. 125.
16. Ibid., pp. 149–50.
17. Woolf, *Sowing*, p. 137.

1 The 'Intellectual Aristocracy'

1. Noël Annan, 'The Intellectual Aristocracy', in *Studies in Social*

History, ed. J. H. Plumb (London
1955), p. 244.
2. Ibid., p. 245.
3. Ibid., p. 250.
4. Ibid., p. 284.

2 Moore's Ancestry, Childhood and Schooldays

1. A. H. Gilkes, *A Day at Dulwich* (London 1905), p. 3.
2. Compton Mackenzie, *Sinister Street* (Penguin edition), pp. 88–90.
3. G. E. Moore, 'An Autobiography', in *The Philosophy of G. E. Moore*, ed. P. A. Schilpp (Evanston and Chicago 1942), pp. 10–11.
4. Ibid.
5. Ibid., p. 11.
6. Ibid., p. 6.
7. Ibid.
8. Ibid., p. 8.
9. Ibid.
10. Ibid., p. 9.
11. Ibid.
12. Ibid., p. 10.
13. Ibid.
14. Ibid., p. 12.

3 Moore at Cambridge: the First Two Years

1. Schilpp, op. cit., p. 11.
2. Ibid., pp. 12–13, in G. E. Moore's corrected copy.
3. Bertrand Russell, *Portraits from Memory* (London 1956), p. 69.
4. Edward Marsh, *A Number of People: A Book of Reminiscences* (London 1939), p. 48.
5. Goldsworthy Lowes Dickinson, *A Modern Symposium* (London 1903), p. 119.
6. Robert Gathorne-Hardy (ed.), *Ottoline: The Early Memoirs of Lady Ottoline Morrell* (London 1963), p. 134.

7. Bertrand Russell, *Autobiography* I, p. 75.
8. Ibid., p. 76.
9. Ibid., p. 77.
10. Ibid.
11. Gathorne-Hardy (ed.), *Ottoline*.
12. Phyllis Grosskurth, *John Addington Symonds* (London 1964), p. 77.
13. Schilpp, op. cit., p. 12.
14. Ibid., p. 13.
15. Ibid., p. 16.
16. Ibid., p. 17.
17. Ibid.
18. Ibid., p. 18.
19. Ibid.
20. Ibid.
21. Ibid., p. 19.
22. Ibid., p. 20.

4 The Apostles

1. Frederick Maurice, *The Life of Frederick Denison Maurice* (London 1884), I, p. 165.
2. Ibid., quoted p. 110.
3. Ibid., p. 70.
4. Ibid., II, p. 530.
5. F. M. Brookfield, *The Cambridge Apostles* (London 1906), p. 301.
6. Ibid., p. 305.
7. Christopher Ricks, *Tennyson* (London and New York 1972), p. 215.
8. Ibid.
9. Ibid.
10. Brian Reade, *Sexual Heretics: Male Homosexuality in English Literature from 1850 to 1900* (London 1970), p. 9.
11. Ricks, *Tennyson*, p. 219.
12. Quoted, ibid.
13. The MS fragment is at Harvard University and the prologue is printed in Hallam, Lord Tennyson, *Alfred Lord Tennyson: A Memoir by His Son* (London 1897), I, p. 497.
14. Ibid., p. 44, n. 1.

15. Arthur Sidgwick and Mrs E. M. Sidgwick, *Henry Sidgwick: A Memoir* (London 1906), p. 34.

16. Ibid., pp. 34–5.

17. Ibid.

18. Oscar Browning, *Memories of 60 Years* (London and New York 1910), p. 39.

19. Ibid., p. 30.

20. E. F. Benson, *As We Were* (London and New York 1930), p. 129.

21. Ibid., p. 134.

22. G. M. Trevelyan, *Sir George Otto Trevelyan* (London and New York 1932), pp. 58–9.

23. G. M. Trevelyan, *English Social History* (Pelican edition, London 1967), p. 564.

24. *Cambridge University Reporter*, 7 December, 1900, quoted in H. A. L. Fisher, *F. W. Maitland* (Cambridge 1910), p. 17.

25. M. A. Bayfield, 'Memoir', in A. W. Verrall, *Collected Literary Essays* (Cambridge 1913), pp. xv–xvi.

26. Ibid., p. xl.

27. Ibid.

28. James Strachey, 'Autobiography of a Hebephrenic'. Unpublished paper, Oral History Research Office, Columbia University, 1965.

29. Samuel Hynes, *The Edwardian Turn of Mind* (London 1968), pp. 140–1.

30. Ibid.

31. Ibid., pp. 143–7.

32. G. M. Trevelyan, *British History in the Nineteenth Century and After, 1782–1919* (Pelican edition, London 1971), p. 345.

33. Charlotte M. Leaf, *Walter Leaf: Containing a Fragment of Autobiography* (London 1932), pp. 90–1.

34. Trevelyan, *British History*, pp. 345–6.

35. James Ward, 'Mechanism and Morals', in *Hibbert Journal* (1905), quoted in John Passmore, *A Hundred Years of Philosophy* (Penguin edition, London 1968), p. 83.

36. Passmore, ibid., pp. 83–4.

37. Ibid., p. 82.

38. Schilpp, op. cit., p. 17.

39. W. A. Raleigh, *Laughter from a Cloud* (London 1923), p. 1.

40. Ibid., p. 3.

41. Ibid., p. 8.

42. Ibid., p. 10.

43. Ibid., p. 15.

44. Ibid.

45. Ibid., pp. 15–16.

46. Enid Bagnold, *Autobiography* (London 1969), p. 152.

47. Ronald Storrs, *Orientations* (London 1937), p. 32.

48. Russell, *Autobiography*, I, p. 189.

49. Ibid., pp. 190–1.

50. Schilpp, op. cit., p. 35.

51. Russell, *Autobiography*, I, p. 226.

52. Ibid., p. 227.

53. G. Lowes Dickinson, *McTaggart* (Cambridge 1931), pp. 34–5.

54. Trevelyan, *English Social History*, pp. 565–6.

55. Dennis Proctor (ed.), *The Autobiography of G. Lowes Dickinson* (London 1973), p. xiv.

56. Ibid., p. 90.

57. Dickinson, *McTaggart*, p. 6.

58. Ibid., p. 10.

59. Ibid.

60. Ibid., p. 11.

61. Ibid., p. 12.

62. Fry to Lady Fry, 18 October 1885 (letter no. 6) in Denys Sutton (ed.), *Letters of Roger Fry* (London 1972), I, p. 108.

63. Dickinson, *McTaggart*, pp. 12–13.

64. Ibid.

65. Ibid., p. 24.

66. Ibid., pp. 22–3.

67. Ibid.

68. Ibid., p. 47.
69. Ibid., p. 82.
70. Ibid., pp. 82–3.
71. C. D. Broad, *Examination of McTaggart's Philosophy* (Cambridge 1933), I, p. li.
72. Schilpp, op. cit., p. 21.
73. Ibid., pp. 18–19.
74. Ibid., p. 22.
75. Virginia Woolf, *Roger Fry* (London 1940), pp. 38–9.
76. Ibid., p. 23.
77. Ibid., p. 35.
78. Ibid., p. 40.
79. Ibid., p. 46.
80. Ibid., p. 47.
81. Ibid., p. 49.
82. Sutton (ed.), *Letters of Roger Fry*, I, p. 114.
83. Woolf, *Roger Fry*, p. 50.
84. Ibid., p. 51.
85. Ibid.
86. Ibid.
87. Ibid., p. 57.
88. Ibid.
89. Ibid., p. 73.
90. Fry to Basil Williams, May 1891 (letter no. 42), in Sutton (ed.), *Letters of Roger Fry*, I, p. 147. Elision in text.
91. Clive Bell, *Old Friends* (London 1956), p. 133.
92. J. K. Johnstone, *The Bloomsbury Group* (New York 1963), p. 45.
93. Ibid., p. 46.
94. Michael Holroyd, *Lytton Strachey*, (London 1967, New York 1968), I, p. 419. Mr Holroyd thinks this information may have come from Gerald Brenan.
95. Sutton (ed.), *Letters of Roger Fry*, p. 75.
96. E. M. Forster, *Goldsworthy Lowes Dickinson* (London 1934), pp. 73–4.
97. Wilfred Stone, *The Cave and the Mountain: A Study of E. M. Forster* (Stanford and London 1966), pp. 67–8.
98. Quoted in Forster, *Dickinson*, p. 74
99. Ibid., pp. 66–7.

5 Moore as an Apostle

1. Schilpp, op. cit., pp. 13–14.
2. Russell to Alys Pearsall Smith, 18 Feb. 1894. Barbara Strachey Halpern collection.
3. Idem, 21 Feb. 1891. Russell and Alys always addressed each other with the 'thee' of Quaker plain speech.
4. Idem, 25 Feb. 1894.
5. Ibid.
6. Ibid.
7. Ibid.
8. Idem, 28 Feb. 1894, loc. cit.
9. Idem, 4 March 1894, loc. cit.
10. Schilpp, op. cit., p. 13.
11. Russell, *Autobiography* I, p. 99.
12. Russell to Alys Pearsall Smith, 25 Feb. 1894, loc. cit.
13. The later formulation, cited by Broad, infra, is in H. Sidgwick, *Methods of Ethics*, 6th edition, III, Chapter xiii, p. 382. The first edition was published in 1874.
14. C. D. Broad, in Schilpp, op. cit., p. 45.
15. Ibid., p. 57.
16. Sanger to Russell, 27 May 1894. McMaster University.
17. Russell to Alys Pearsall Smith, 16 May 1894, loc. cit.
18. Idem, 20 May 1894, loc. cit.
19. Russell, *Autobiography*, I, p. 85.
20. Verrall to Moore, 18 June 1894. Moore papers (Verrall O3).
21. Wedgwood to Moore, 22 June 1894. Moore papers (Wedgwood O3).
22. Sanger to Russell, 22 Oct. 1894. McMaster.
23. G. E. Moore, *Principia Ethica* (Cambridge 1903), p. 189.

24. Sidgwick, *Methods of Ethics* (London 1874), p. 103.
25. Moore, *Principia Ethica*, p. 184.
26. Sanger to Russell, 11 Nov. 1894. McMaster.
27. Sanger to Russell, 27 Nov. 1894, loc. cit.
28. Marsh to Russell, 28 Jan. 1895. McMaster.
29. Sanger to Russell, 13 Feb. 1895. McMaster.
30. Ibid.
31. Quoted in Russell, *Autobiography*, I, p. 168.
32. Ursula Vaughan Williams, *Ralph Vaughan Williams* (Oxford 1964), p. 38.
33. G. M. Trevelyan to Vaughan Williams, n.d. Ursula Vaughan Williams. Collection.
34. G. M. Trevelyan to R. C. Trevelyan, 5 April 1895. R. C. Trevelyan papers, Trinity College, Cambridge.
35. Moore to Henrietta Moore, 1 April 1895. Moore papers.
36. Moore to Henrietta Moore, 15 June 1895, loc. cit.
37. Information about the Pearsall Smith family supplied to the author by Mrs Barbara Halpern, 19 October 1976.
38. Moore to Henrietta Moore, 5 July 1895. Moore papers.
39. Moore to Henrietta Moore, 10 July 1895, loc. cit.
40. Schilpp, op. cit., p. 20.

6 Moore's Philosophical Apprenticeship

1. Teddy Brunius, *G. E. Moore's Analyses of Beauty* (Uppsala 1964).
2. Ibid., p. 69.
3. Moore to Wedgwood, 14 Dec. 1895. Moore papers (G.E.M. 121).
4. Moore to Wedgwood, 1 Jan. 1896, loc. cit. (G.E.M. 122).
5. R. L. Wedgwood to G. E. Moore, 7 Jan. 1896, loc. cit. (Wedgwood 06).
6. Moore to Wedgwood, 8 Jan. 1896, loc. cit. (G.E.M. 120). The letter is wrongly dated by Moore as 1895.
7. Dostoevsky, *The Idiot*, translated by David Magarshack (Penguin Classics, London), pp. 501–2.
8. C. Llewelyn Davies to G. E. Moore, 18 Feb. 1896. Moore papers (C.Ll.D. 02).
9. Moore to Marsh, 12 April 1896. Berg Collection.
10. Moore to Marsh, 17 April 1896, loc. cit.

7 Working For A Fellowship

1. Schilpp, op. cit., pp. 20–1.
2. Ibid., pp. 21–2.
3. G. H. Hardy, *A Mathematician's Apology* (Cambridge and New York 1967), p. 9. The first edition was 1940.
4. Leonard Woolf: interview with the author, 14 December 1968, at Monk's House, Rodmell, Sussex.
5. Schilpp, op. cit., p. 22.
6. Forster, *Dickinson*, pp. 113–14.
7. G. L. Dickinson to Moore, 17 Dec. 1897. Moore papers (G. L. Dickinson 01).
8. Dickinson to R. C. Trevelyan, 20 Aug. 1898. R. C. Trevelyan papers.

8 A Fellow of Trinity: 1898–1904

1. Schilpp, op. cit., p. 23.
2. Bertrand Russell, *My Philosophical Development* (London 1959), p. 54.
3. Schilpp, op. cit., p. 24.
4. Ibid., pp. 24–5.
5. Ibid.

6. 'Was the world good before the 6th day?' Russell papers, McMaster University.
7. Holroyd, *Strachey*, I, p. 128.
8. Moore to MacCarthy, 30 May 1899. Moore papers (G.E.M. 10).
9. Letters to the author from Edith Ainsworth, 27 June and 4 August 1974.
10. Furbank, *E. M. Forster*, I, p. 262.
11. Sir Charles Tennyson, *Cambridge from Within* (London 1913), pp. 142–3.
12. The list Moore called 'People I See'. Moore papers.
13. Leonard Woolf: interview.
14. 'People I See'. Moore papers.
15. Moore's list, 'Chronological Table of my Life'. Moore papers.
16. Ainsworth to Lytton Strachey, 23 Nov. 1903. Strachey papers. British Library.
17. Anne Olivier Bell (ed.), *The Diary of Virginia Woolf* (London 1978), II, pp. 293–4.
18. Sir Ralph Hawtrey: interview with the author on 22 March 1969 at 29 Argyll Road, London W.8.
19. Schilpp, p. 25.
20. 'Chronological Table'. Moore papers.
21. Furbank, *E. M. Forster*, I, p. 60.
22. Ibid., p. 61.
23. 'Chronological Table'. Moore papers.
24. Moore, *Principia Ethica*, p. 30.
25. Ibid., p. 27.
26. Ibid., p. 28.
27. Moore to his parents, 21 March 1901. Moore papers.
28. Moore to Henrietta Moore, 3 June 1901, loc. cit.
29. Ibid.

9 Principia Ethica *and the* 'Manifesto'

1. Strachey to Moore, 11 Oct. 1903. Moore papers (G. L. Strachey 01).
2. Russell to Moore, 10 Oct. 1903 Moore papers (B.R. 25).
3. Stout to Moore, 1 Nov. 1903. Moore papers (Stout 05).
4. 'Chronological Table'. Moore papers.
5. Furbank, *E. M. Forster*, I, p. 77n.
6. Pollock to Moore, 30–1 Dec. 1903. Moore papers (Sir F. Pollock 02).
7. Russell, *Autobiography*, I, p. 95.
8. Holroyd, *Strachey*, I, p. 184.
9. Russell, *Autobiography*, I, p. 99.
10. Loc. cit.
11. Furbank, *E. M. Forster*, I, p. 217 and n.
12. J. M. Keynes, 'My Early Beliefs', in *Two Memoirs* (London 1949), p. 95.
13. Braithwaite, in *Essays on John Maynard Keynes*, p. 242.
14. Ibid., and Quentin Bell's conversation with the author.
15. Keynes, in *Two Memoirs*, pp. 81–2.
16. Quentin Bell, *Bloomsbury* (London 1968), p. 74.
17. Ibid., p. 77.
18. Keynes, in *Two Memoirs*, p. 82.
19. Braithwaite, in *Essays on John Maynard Keynes*, p. 243.
20. Ibid.
21. Ibid., p. 244.
22. Keynes, in *Two Memoirs*, p. 92.
23. Ibid., p. 103.
24. Ibid., pp. 83–4.
25. Ibid.
26. Paul Levy, 'The Bloomsbury Group', in *Essays on John Maynard Keynes*, p. 60–72.
27. Keynes, in *Two Memoirs*, p. 84
28. Ibid., p. 85.
29. Ibid., pp. 85–6.
30. Ibid., pp. 76–7.
31. Ibid., p. 86.
32. Braithwaite, in *Essays on John Maynard Keynes*, p. 245.
33. Ibid.
34. Keynes, in *Two Memoirs*, p. 101.
35. Ibid., p. 99.

36. Ibid., p. 92.
37. Ibid., p. 94.
38. Ibid., p. 103.
39. Proctor (ed.), *Dickinson*, p. 164.
40. Ibid., p. XIII.
41. Forster, *Dickinson*, p. 110.
42. G. Lowes Dickinson, *The Meaning of Good* (Glasgow 1901), p. 231.
43. Schilpp, op. cit., p. 225.
44. Bertrand Russell, *Principles of Mathematics* (Second edition, New York and London 1948), p. xviii.
45. Schilpp, op. cit., p. 15.
46. Russell, *Autobiography*, I, p. 222.
47. Ibid., p. 100.
48. Schilpp, op. cit., p. 26.
49. Waterlow to Moore, 22 July 1904. Moore papers (S. Waterlow 07).
50. Woolf, *Sowing*, p. 108.
51. Ibid., p. 107n.
52. Ibid.
53. Woolf : interview. Moore diaries, passim.
54. Furbank, *E. M. Forster*, I, p. 108.
55. G. O. Trevelyan to Waterlow, 22 April 1904. Collection Dr John Waterlow.
56. Waterlow to Russell, 12 Dec. 1904. Russell papers. McMaster.
57. Russell to Moore, 17 Dec. 1904. Moore papers (B.R. 26).
58. Russell to Moore, 27 Dec. 1904. loc. cit. (B.R. 27).
59. Moore to Russell, 28 Dec. 1904. Russell papers. McMaster.
60. Russell to Moore, 29 Dec. 1904. Moore papers (B.R. 28).
61. Russell to Moore, 19 March 1905, loc. cit. (B.R. 29).
62. Russell to Moore, 2 May 1905, loc. cit. (B.R. 30).
63. Russell to Moore, May 1905, loc. cit (B.R. 31).
64. Moore to Russell, 23 Oct. 1905. Russell papers. McMaster.

10 *From 1904 to the War Years*

1. Schilpp, op. cit., p. 26.
2. Harrod, *Keynes*, p. 188.
3. Keynes to Duncan Grant, 13 August 1910. British Library.
4. Schilpp, op. cit., p. 29.
5. Ibid., p. 27.
6. F. I. D. G. Békássy, *Adriatica* (London 1925), pp. v–vi.
7. The opinion of Wittgenstein's biographer, Brian McGuiness.
8. Moore to F. A. Hayek, in 'Unfinished Draft of a Sketch of a Biography of Ludwig Wittgenstein written in 1953 for private circulation by F. A. Hayek with Some Later Corrections and Insertions', p. 14; enclosed with letter to Russell dated 7 November 1959. McMaster.
9. Russell to Lady Ottoline Morrell, 10 Nov. 1912, quoted in Ronald W. Clark, *The Life of Bertrand Russell* (London and New York 1975), p. 193.
10. Russell to Keynes, 11 Nov. 1912. Keynes papers, King's College, Cambridge.
11. Strachey to Sydney-Turner, 20 Nov. 1912, quoted in Holroyd, *Strachey*, II, p. 71–2.
12. MacCarthy to Moore, 4 Dec. 1912. Moore papers (D. MacCarthy 26).
13. Moore to Strachey, 5 Dec. 1912. Strachey papers. British Library.
14. Holroyd, *Strachey*, II, p. 71 and n.
15. Quoted in Clark, *Russell*, p. 193.
16. Ibid., p. 192.
17. Vide : *Wittgenstein*, G. H. von Wright (ed.), *Letters to Russell, Keynes and Moore* (Oxford 1974).
18. Published as an appendix, 'Notes Dictated to G. E. Moore in Norway', to Wittgenstein's *Notebooks, 1914–16* (Oxford 1961).
19. Letter to Hayek, op. cit., p. 26.
20. Schilpp, op. cit., p. 33.

21. Von Wright, *Wittgenstein*, M8 p. 150.
22. Ibid., M9 p. 151. The editor's conjecture about the dating of the letter is wrong : Moore received the letter on 13 July.
23. Ibid., R1 p. 9.
24. Ibid., K8 p. 111.
25. Nigel Nicolson (ed.), *The Letters of Virginia Woolf* (London and New York 1975), I : 1888–1912, *passim*.
26. Leonard Woolf, *Beginning Again* (London and New York 1963 and 1964), p. 25.
27. Woolf : interview.
28. Nicolson (ed.), *Letters* (1978), II, *passim*.
29. Ibid., p. 160.
30. Ibid., p. 297, and Virginia Woolf, *Diary*, II, p. 231.
31. Paul Levy (ed.), *Lytton Strachey: The Really Interesting Question* (London and New York 1972), pp. XIII and 3–39.
32. Interviews.
33. Moore to MacCarthy, 15 Nov. 1914. Moore papers (G.E.M. 43).
34. Russell, *Autobiography* (Boston 1968), II, p. 8.
35. Ibid., p. 6.
36. Circular letter signed by Ramsay MacDonald, Charles Trevelyan, E. D. Morel, August 1913. Quoted in Clark, *Russell*, p. 252.
37. Julian Bell (ed.), *We Did Not Fight* (London 1935), p. 351.
38. Ibid., p. 139.
39. Ibid., p. 138.
40. G. H. Hardy, *Bertrand Russell and Trinity* (Cambridge 1942), p. 55n.
41. Ibid., pp. 55–6.
42. Information from Timothy Moore to the author, 15 November 1977.

Epilogue

1. Moore to MacCarthy, 15 Nov. 1916. Moore papers (G.E.M. 45).
2. Woolf, *Sowing*, p. 137.
3. Russell, *Autobiography*, II, p. 136.
4. Norman Malcolm, *Ludwig Wittgenstein: A Memoir* (London and New York 1958), p. 80.
5. G. J. Warnock, *English Philosophy Since 1900* (Galaxy edition, New York 1966), p. 10.
6. Anne Olivier Bell (ed.), *The Diary of Virginia Woolf* (London and New York 1977), p. 155.
7. Leonard Woolf, *Beginning Again*, p. 25.
8. *The Listener*, 8 February 1951, p. 211.
9. Information from Professor G. H. von Wright.
10. Virginia Woolf, *Diary*, II, p. 49.
11. Quentin Bell, *Virginia Woolf: A Biography* (London 1972), II, p. 215.
12. Leonard Woolf, *The Journey not the Arrival Matters* (London 1969), p. 49.
13. Ibid., pp. 47–8.

Bibliography

Sources consulted, but not cited in the notes. Published in London unless otherwise indicated.

Amos, Sir Maurice, *Lectures on the American Constitution* (1938).

Annan, Noël, *Leslie Stephen* (1951).

Ayer, A. J., *Russell and Moore, the Analytical Heritage* (1971).

Balleine, G. R., *A History of the Evangelical Party* (1911).

Barnes, James Strachey, *Half A Life* (1933).

Bartley, William Warren III, *Wittgenstein* (1973).

BBC, Third Programme, *Ideas and Beliefs of the Victorians* (1949).

Beck, W., Wells, W. F., Chalkey, H. E. (eds.), *Biographical Catalogue, Being an Account of the Lives of Friends* (1888).

Bell, Clive, *Civilization* (1928).

Bloomfield, Paul, *Uncommon People: A Study of England's Elite* (1955).

Brinton, Crane, *The Society of Fellows* (Cambridge, Mass., 1959).

Bromley, John, *The Man of Ten Talents: A Portrait of Richard Chenevix Trench, 1807–1861* (1959).

Brown, A. W., *The Metaphysical Society: Victorian Minds in Crisis* (New York 1947).

Brown, Ford K., *Fathers of the Victorians* (Cambridge, 1961).

Cornford, F. M., *Microcosmographia Academica* (Cambridge, 1908).

Cox, C. B. and Dyson, A. E., *The Twentieth-Century Mind* (1972).

Darroch, Sandra Jobson, *Ottoline* (1976).

Forbes, Duncan, *The Liberal Anglican Ideal of History* (Cambridge, 1952).

Forrest, D. W., *Francis Galton: The Life and Work of a Victorian Genius* (1974).

Fox, Robin, 'Prolegomena to the Study of British Kinship', in Gould, J. (ed.), *The Penguin Survey of the Social Sciences* (1965).

Fox, Robin, *Kinship and Marriage* (1967).

Fry, Roger, *Transformations* (1926).

Fussell, Paul, *The Great War and Modern Memory* (1975).

Galton, Francis and Schuster, Edgar, *Noteworthy Families* (1906).

Garnett, David, *The Golden Echo* (1954).

Garnett, David, *The Flowers of the Forest* (1955).

Garnett, David, *The Familiar Faces* (1962).

Green, T. H., *Prolegomena to Ethics*, (ed.) A. C. Bradley (5th edition, Oxford 1906).

Grubb, Isabel, *Quakerism and Industry before 1800* (1930).

Hadwick, Elizabeth, *Seduction and Betrayal* (1974).

Harrison, Jane Ellen, *Reminiscences of a Student's Life* (1925).

Hassall, Christopher, *Edward Marsh* (1959).

Hassall, Christopher, *Rupert Brooke* (1964).

Hobhouse, S., *Joseph Sturge* (1919).

Hughes, W. R., *Sophia Sturge* (1940).

James, M. R., *Eton and King's* (1926).

Johnson, Catherine B., *William Bodham Donne and His Friends* (1905).

Keynes, Florence Ada, *Gathering up the Threads: A Study in Family Biography* (Cambridge 1950).

Keynes, Geoffrey, *Henry James in Cambridge* (Cambridge 1967).

Keynes, J. M., *Essays in Biography* (1933).

Klemke, E. D., *The Epistemology of G. E. Moore* (Evanston, Ill. 1969).

Luce, G. H., *Poems* (1920).

MacCarthy, Desmond, *Portraits* (1931).

MacCarthy, Desmond, *Experience* (1935).

MacCarthy, Desmond, *Memories* (1953).

MacCarthy, *Humanities* (1953).

MacDonnell, A. G., *England, Their England* (Reprinted) (1941).

Martin, Kingsley, *Father Figures* (1966).

Moore, G. E., *Commonplace Book 1919–1953*, (ed.) C. Lewy (1962).

Moore, G. E., *Lectures on Philosophy*, (ed.) C. Lewy (1966).

Moore, Nicholas, *The Cabaret, The Dancer, The Gentlemen: Poems* (N.d.).

Moore, Nicholas. *The Glass Tower: Poems 1936–43* (1944).

Moore, Nicholas, *Identity* (1969).

Moore, T. Sturge, *Art and Life* (1910).

Mortimer, Raymond, *Channel Packet* (1942).

Mortimer, Raymond, *Duncan Grant* (1944).

Parry, R. St. John, *Henry Jackson, O.M.* (Cambridge 1926).

Pears, David, *Wittgenstein* (1971).

Pitcher, George, *The Philosophy of Wittgenstein* (1964).

Pollock, F., *For My Grandson* (1933).

Pollock, J., *Time's Chariot* (1950).

Pollock, W. F., *Personal Remembrances*, 2 vols. (1887).

Pope-Hennessy, J., *Monckton Milnes*, 2 vols. (1949).

Raistrick, Arthur, *Quakers in Science and Industry* (Newton Abbot, Devon 1968).

Raleigh, Sir Walter, *Letters 1879–1922*, (ed.) Lady Raleigh, 2 vols. (1926).

Ramsey, F. P., *The Foundation of Mathematics*, preface by G. E. Moore (1931).

Reid, Sir Thomas Wemyss, *Life, Letters and Friendships of Richard Monckton Milnes*, 2 vols. (1890).

Richard, H., *Memoirs of Joseph Sturge* (1864).

Rosenbaum, S. P., (ed.), *The Bloomsbury Group* (1975).

Russell, G. W. E., *A Short History of the Evangelical Movement* (1915).

Sanders, C. R., *Coleridge and the Broad Church Movement* (Durham, North Carolina 1942).

Sanger, C. P., *The Place of Compensation* (1901).

Sanger, C. P., *The Structure of 'Wuthering Heights'*. Reprinted with Willis, I. C., *The Authorship of 'Wuthering Heights'* (1967).

Schneewind, J. B., *Sidgwick's Ethics and Victorian Moral Philosophy* (1977).

Shove, Fredegond, *Fredegond and Gerald Shove* (Cambridge, 1952).

Skeats, H. S. and Miall, C. S., *History of the Free Churches of England, 1888–1891* (1891).

Stephen, Adrian, *The 'Dreadnought' Hoax* (1936).

Stephen, J. K., *Quo Musa Tendis?* (Cambridge 1891).

Trench, M. M. F., *Letters and Memorials, Richard Chenevix Trench*, 2 vols. (1888).

Trevelyan, R. C., *Windfalls: Notes and Essays* (1944).

Turner, F. M., *Between Science and Religion* (New Haven, Conn. 1974).

White, Alan R., *G. E. Moore: A Critical Exposition* (Oxford 1958).

Winstanley, D. A., *Early Victorian Cambridge* (Cambridge 1940).

Index

Académie Julien, 114
Acton, Lord, 147n.
Ainger, Thomas, 300
Ainsworth, Alfred Richard,
283; friendship with
Moore, 184, 197, 216, 263;
becomes Apostle, 209, 310;
education, 209; Moore's
infatuation with, 209, 212–
13, 292; descriptions of,
210–11; at Apostles' meetings, 213, 215, 219, 222,
225–6, 232; reading
parties, 226, 227, 250, 260,
261, 264, 270; response to
Principia Ethica, 235n.,
237, 238; lives with Moore
in Edinburgh, 251, 260;
marriages, 209–10, 260;
death, 210
Ainsworth, Ethel, 210
Ainsworth, George Herbert,
210
Ainsworth, John, 210
Ainsworth, Sarah (Sarah
Moore), 29, 36, 209–10,
260, 283
Alford, Henry, 303
Alleyn, Edward, 36, 37
Amos, Maurice, 164, 179,
181, 219, 249–50; friend-
ship with Moore, 124, 167;
reading parties, 139, 186–
7; on Moore, 150–1;
Trinity Sunday Essay
Society, 153
Anderson, Frank Eustace,
307
Angell, Norman, 280, 282
Anglo-Indian College,
Aligarh, 137
Annan, Noël (Lord Annan),

14, 19–20, 21, 99, 247–8,
295–7
Anonymous Club, 70
Anti-Corn-Law League, 30
Apostles: 'angels', 65–6, 86;
1894 annual dinner, 137–8;
1895 annual dinner, 163;
1898 annual dinner, 198;
1900 annual dinner, 219;
Ark, 103; beliefs, 61–2, 69,
77; Oscar Browning and,
78–80; celebrates Moore's
seventy-fifth birthday, 299;
changing direction, 90–4;
Lowes Dickinson and, 99;
'embryos', 48–9, 57, 65;
'Eranos', 96; in First
World War, 277–8, 288;
Roger Fry joins, 112–13,
123–4; history of, 65–120;
homosexuality, 72–3, 98,
103, 140, 227, 238–9;
interest in education,
85–7; interest in para-
psychology, 77–8, 84;
interest in sex, 139–46;
MacCarthy's criticisms of,
222–5, 226; J. F. D.
Maurice and, 67–70; meet-
ings, 61, 65, 66–7; mem-
bers, 2, 52–3, 61, 66–7,
300–11; Moore elected to,
60, 124–7; Moore's friendships with members of,
52–8; Moore's influence
on, 2, 126, 294–5; Moore's
maiden essay, 129–34;
Moore's reading parties,
196–7; *Principia Ethica's*
influence on, 9; Henry
Sidgwick's influence on,
75–8, 82; rituals, 65–6;

secrecy, 65–6; John Sterl-
ing and, 70–1; Strachey's
influence on, 227, 231–3;
suppers, 203, 207; Verrall
and, 83–4; James Ward
and, 88; Wittgenstein's
membership, 265–70;
women members, 127–9
Appeals Tribunals, 277
Appia, Georges, 31, 32
Appia, Helen, 31, 32–4
Aristotelian Society, 184,
201
Aristotle, 60, 96, 149, 155,
168, 170, 173–6, 234
Arnold, Matthew, 81;
'Morality', 217–18
Ashbee, C. R., 111, 112
Asheham House, Sussex,
275–6
Asquith, H. H. (1st Earl of
Oxford and Asquith), 147
Astor, William Waldorf (1st
Viscount), 93
Athenaeum, 68, 70
Austen, Jane, 28, 187
Ayer, Sir Alfred (A.J.), 11–12

Bacon, Francis (d. 1840), 301
Bagnold, Enid (Lady Jones),
94
Baines, Edward, 302
Baker, Charles, 275
Baker, Marie, 275
Baldwin, *Dictionary of
Philosophy and Psychology*,
200, 226
Balfour, A. J. (1st Earl of
Balfour), 77, 147, 152
Balfour, Eleanor Mildred,
see Sidgwick, Eleanor
Mildred

323